CONSTITUTIONAL COURTS IN ASIA

The founding of a constitutional court is often an indication of a chosen path of constitutionalism and democracy. It is no coincidence that most of the constitutional courts in East and South East Asia were established at the same time as the transition of the countries concerned from authoritarianism to liberal constitutional democracy. This book is the first to provide systematic narratives and analysis of Asian experiences of constitutional courts and related developments, and to introduce comparative, historical and theoretical perspectives on these experiences, as well as debates on the relevant issues in countries that do not as yet have constitutional courts. This volume makes a significant contribution to the systematic and comparative study of constitutional courts, constitutional adjudication and constitutional developments in East and South East Asia and beyond.

ALBERT H. Y. CHEN is an LLB and LLM graduate of The University of Hong Kong (HKU) and Harvard University, respectively. He began his academic career in 1984 at HKU. He served as Head of the Department of Law (1993–1996) and Dean of the Faculty of Law (1996–2002) and is currently the Cheng Chan Lan Yue Professor in Constitutional Law at HKU. His areas of specialization include Hong Kong constitutional law, the study of Chinese law and Asian law from the comparative law perspective, and legal and political theory. He is the author of *An Introduction to the Legal System of the People's Republic of China* (2011) and co-editor of *Human Rights in Asia* (2006), *Administrative Law and Governance in Asia* (2009), *Legal Reforms in China and Vietnam* (2010) and *Public Law in East Asia* (2013). He is the editor of *Constitutionalism in Asia in the Early Twenty-First Century* (2014).

ANDREW HARDING works in the fields of Asian legal studies and comparative constitutional law. He commenced his academic career at the National University of Singapore (NUS) before moving to SOAS, University of London, where he became Head of the Law School and Director of the Centre for South East Asian Studies. In 2012, he moved from the University of Victoria, Canada, to join NUS as Director of the Centre for Asian Legal Studies and Director of the Asian Law Institute. He has worked extensively on constitutional law in Malaysia and Thailand, and more recently Myanmar, and has made extensive contributions to scholarship in Asian comparative law. He is co-founding editor of the book series *Constitutional Systems of the World*, a major resource for constitutional law in context, and has authored the books on Malaysia and Thailand in that series (2011, 2012). He has recently edited *Constitutionalism and Legal Change in Myanmar* (2017).

COMPARATIVE CONSTITUTIONAL LAW AND POLICY

Series Editors
Tom Ginsburg
University of Chicago
Zachary Elkins
University of Texas at Austin
Ran Hirschl
University of Toronto

Comparative constitutional law is an intellectually vibrant field that encompasses an increasingly broad array of approaches and methodologies. This series collects analytically innovative and empirically grounded work from scholars of comparative constitutionalism across academic disciplines. Books in the series include theoretically informed studies of single constitutional jurisdictions, comparative studies of constitutional law and institutions, and edited collections of original essays that respond to challenging theoretical and empirical questions in the field.

Books in the Series

The Politico-Legal Dynamics of Judicial Review: A Comparative Analysis Theunis Roux

The Invisible Constitution in Comparative Perspective edited by Rosalind Dixon and Adrienne Stone

Constituent Assemblies edited by Jon Elster, Roberto Gargarella, Vatsal Naresh and Bjorn Erik Rasch

Judicial Review in Norway Anine Kierulf

The DNA of Constitutional Justice in Latin America: Politics, Governance, and Judicial Design Daniel M. Brinks and Abby Blass

The Adventures of the Constituent Power: Beyond Revolutions? Andrew Arato

Constitutions, Religion and Politics in Asia: Indonesia, Malaysia and Sri Lanka Dian A. H. Shah

Canada in the World: Comparative Perspectives on the Canadian Constitution edited by Richard Albert and David R. Cameron

Courts and Democracies in Asia Po Jen Yap

Proportionality: New Frontiers, New Challenges edited by Vicki C. Jackson and Mark Tushnet

Constituents before Assembly: Participation, Deliberation, and Representation in the Crafting of New Constitutions Todd A. Eisenstadt, A. Carl LeVan, and Tofigh Maboudi

Assessing Constitutional Performance edited by Tom Ginsburg and Aziz Huq

Buddhism, Politics and the Limits of Law: The Pyrrhic Constitutionalism of Sri Lanka Benjamin Schonthal

Engaging with Social Rights: Procedure, Participation and Democracy in South Africa's Second Wave Brian Ray

Constitutional Courts as Mediators: Armed Conflict, Civil–Military Relations, and the Rule of Law in Latin America Julio Ríos-Figueroa

Perils of Judicial Self-Government in Transitional Societies David Kosař

Making We the People: Democratic Constitutional Founding in Postwar Japan and South Korea Chaihark Hahm and Sung Ho Kim

Radical Deprivation on Trial: The Impact of Judicial Activism on Socioeconomic Rights in the Global South César Rodríguez-Garavito and Diana Rodríguez-Franco

Unstable Constitutionalism: Law and Politics in South Asia edited by Mark Tushnet and Madhav Khosla

Magna Carta and Its Modern Legacy edited by Robert Hazell and James Melton

Constitutions and Religious Freedom Frank B. Cross

International Courts and the Performance of International Agreements: A General Theory with Evidence from the European Union Clifford J. Carrubba and Matthew J. Gabel

Reputation and Judicial Tactics: A Theory of National and International Courts Shai Dothan

Social Difference and Constitutionalism in Pan-Asia edited by Susan H. Williams

Constitutionalism in Asia in the Early Twenty-First Century edited by Albert H. Y. Chen

Constitutions in Authoritarian Regimes edited by Tom Ginsburg and Alberto Simpser

Presidential Legislation in India: The Law and Practice of Ordinances Shubhankar Dam

Social and Political Foundations of Constitutions edited by Denis J. Galligan and Mila Versteeg

Consequential Courts: Judicial Roles in Global Perspective edited by Diana Kapiszewski, Gordon Silverstein and Robert A. Kagan

Comparative Constitutional Design edited by Tom Ginsburg

CONSTITUTIONAL COURTS IN ASIA

A Comparative Perspective

Edited by

ALBERT H. Y. CHEN

The University of Hong Kong

ANDREW HARDING

National University of Singapore

CAMBRIDGE
UNIVERSITY PRESS

CAMBRIDGE
UNIVERSITY PRESS

University Printing House, Cambridge CB2 8BS, United Kingdom

One Liberty Plaza, 20th Floor, New York, NY 10006, USA

477 Williamstown Road, Port Melbourne, VIC 3207, Australia

314–321, 3rd Floor, Plot 3, Splendor Forum, Jasola District Centre, New Delhi – 110025, India

79 Anson Road, #06–04/06, Singapore 079906

Cambridge University Press is part of the University of Cambridge.

It furthers the University's mission by disseminating knowledge in the pursuit of education, learning, and research at the highest international levels of excellence.

www.cambridge.org
Information on this title: www.cambridge.org/9781107195080
DOI: 10.1017/9781108163903

First published 2018

Printed and bound in Great Britain by Clays Ltd, Elcograf S.p.A.

A catalogue record for this publication is available from the British Library.

Library of Congress Cataloging-in-Publication Data
Names: Chen, Hongyi, 1957-, editor. | Harding, Andrew, 1950-, editor.
Title: Constitutional courts in Asia : a comparative perspective / Edited by Albert H.Y. Chen, The University of Hong Kong, Andrew Harding, National University of Singapore.
Description: New York : Cambridge University Press, 2018.
Identifiers: LCCN 2018013798 | ISBN 9781107195080 (hardback) | ISBN 9781316646663 (pbk.)
Subjects: LCSH: Constitutional courts–Asia.
Classification: LCC KNC459 .C66 2018 | DDC 347.5/035–dc23
LC record available at https://lccn.loc.gov/2018013798

ISBN 978-1-107-19508-0 Hardback

CONTENTS

FIGURES

TABLES

CONTRIBUTORS

NGOC SON BUI is an Assistant Professor at the Chinese University of Hong Kong Faculty of Law. He holds a PhD in law from The University of Hong Kong. He writes on comparative constitutional law and theory from an interdisciplinary perspective. His works include the book *Confucian Constitutionalism in East Asia* (2016) and journal articles published by the *American Journal of Comparative Law*, *Law & Social Inquiry*, the *Illinois Law Review*, the *International Journal of Law in Context*, and the *Australian Journal of Legal Philosophy*, among others.

SIMON BUTT teaches Indonesian law and private international law at The University of Sydney. He has written widely on Indonesian law; his books include *The Constitutional Court and Democracy in Indonesia* (2015), *Corruption and Law in Indonesia* (2012) and *The Constitution of Indonesia: A Contextual Analysis* (with co-author Tim Lindsey, 2012). He has recently completed *Indonesian Law* (with co-author Tim Lindsey, 2018 forthcoming).

WEN-CHEN CHANG is Professor at the College of Law, National Taiwan University. She is a leading scholar of constitutional law in Taiwan and has published major scholarly works on comparative constitutional law, including *Asian Courts in Context*, with co-editor Jiunn-rong Yeh (Cambridge University Press, 2015) and *Constitutionalism in Asia: Cases and Materials*, with Kevin Y. L. Tan, Li-ann Thio and Jiunn-rong Yeh (2014). Her teaching and research interests lie in comparative constitutional law, international human rights, administrative law, and law and society. She serves on the editorial boards of a number of academic journals, including the *International Journal of Constitutional Law;* the *Cambridge Journal of Global Constitutionalism; Human Rights, Democracy and the Rule of Law;* the *Asian Journal of Comparative Law* and *National Taiwan University Law Review.*

ALBERT H. Y. CHEN is an LLB and LLM graduate of The University of Hong Kong and Harvard University, respectively. He began his academic career in 1984 at The University of Hong Kong. He served as Head of the Department of Law from 1993 to 1996, and Dean of the Faculty of Law from 1996 to 2002, and he is currently the Cheng Chan Lan Yue Professor in Constitutional Law at The University of Hong Kong. His areas of specialization include Hong Kong constitutional law, the study of Chinese law and Asian law from the comparative law perspective, and legal and political theory. He is the author of *An Introduction to the Legal System of the People's Republic of China* (4th edn., 2011) and co-editor of *Human Rights in Asia* (2006), *Administrative Law and Governance in Asia* (2009), *Legal Reforms in China and Vietnam* (2010), and *Public Law in East Asia* (2013). He is the editor of *Constitutionalism in Asia in the Early Twenty-First Century* (Cambridge University Press, 2014).

BJÖRN DRESSEL is an Associate Professor in the Crawford School of Public Policy at the Australian National University and holds an Australian Research Council Early Career Research Award (2013–2017). His research is concerned with issues of comparative constitutionalism, judicial politics, and government and public-sector reforms in Asia. He has published in a range of international journals, including the *Journal of Democracy*; *Governance*, *Administration & Society*; the *Journal of Contemporary Asia* and the *Pacific Review*. He is the editor of *The Judicialization of Politics in Asia* (2012) and co-editor of *Politics and Constitutions in Southeast Asia* (with Bünte, 2017).

CHIMID ENHBAATAR is Professor and Chair of the Legal Studies Department, the Academy of Management, Ulaanbaatar. He holds a doctorate from the Central European University and served as a member of the Mongolian Constitutional Court (Tsets) from 1994 to 2000.

TOM GINSBURG is the Leo Spitz Professor of International Law at the University of Chicago and a research professor at the American Bar Foundation. He holds BA, JD and PhD degrees from the University of California at Berkeley. He currently co-directs the Comparative Constitutions Project, a data set cataloguing the world's constitutions since 1789. His books include *The Endurance of National Constitutions* (with Zachary Elkins and James Melton, 2009), *Judicial Review in New Democracies* (2003) and *Judicial Reputation* (with Nuno Garoupa, 2015). He is a member of the American Academy of Arts and Sciences and serves as International IDEA's senior advisor on constitution building.

CHAIHARK HAHM is Professor of Law at Yonsei University School of Law in Seoul, Korea. He teaches and writes on constitutional theory, comparative constitutional law, Confucian political theory, Korean legal culture and history, citizenship education and human rights. He has held fellowships at the National Endowment for Democracy, the Netherlands Institute for Advanced Study and the Center for Advanced Study in the Behavioral Sciences. He has published in the *Journal of Democracy, American Journal of Comparative Law* and *I•CON: International Journal of Constitutional Law*, among others. He is co-author of *Making We the People: Democratic Constitutional Founding in Postwar Japan and South Korea* (Cambridge University Press, 2015) and an editorial board member of I•CON. He holds law degrees from Yale (LL.M.), Columbia (JD) and Harvard (SJD).

ANDREW HARDING works in the fields of Asian legal studies and comparative constitutional law. He commenced his academic career at the National University of Singapore (NUS) before moving to the School of Oriental and African Studies, University of London, where he became Head of the Law School and Director of the Centre for South East Asian Studies. In 2012, he moved from the University of Victoria, Canada, to join NUS as Director of the Centre for Asian Legal Studies and Director of the Asian Law Institute. Professor Harding has worked extensively on constitutional law in Malaysia and Thailand, and more recently Myanmar, and has made extensive contributions to scholarship in Asian comparative law. He is co-founding editor of Hart Publishing's book series *Constitutional Systems of the World*, a major resource for constitutional law in context, and has authored the books on Malaysia and Thailand in that series (2011, 2012). He has recently edited *Constitutionalism and Legal Change in Myanmar* (2017).

YASUO HASEBE teaches constitutional law at the School of Law, Waseda University in Tokyo. He taught constitutional law at the University of Tokyo for twenty-one years, until March 2014. He moved to Waseda University in April 2014. He was a visiting scholar at University College London from 1988 to 1990 and a visiting professor at New York University in 2004 and Columbia University in 2013. His publications in

English include 'Constitutional Borrowing and Political Theory', *International Journal of Constitutional Law* (2003); 'The Rule of Law and Its Predicament', *Ratio Juris* (2004); 'War Powers', in Michel Rosenfeld and András Sajó (eds.), *Oxford Handbook of Comparative Constitutional Law* (2012); 'Constitutions', in Mark Tushnet, Thomas Fleiner and Cheryl Saunders (eds.), *Routledge Handbook of Constitutional Law* (with Cesare Pinelli, 2013); and 'Privacy in the Age of Ubiquitous Computing', *Percorsi costituzionali* (2014).

TEILEE KUONG is Associate Professor at Nagoya University Center for Asian Legal Exchange. His research focuses on legal developments in South East Asian countries, particularly in the areas of constitution, property law and judicial institutions. He teaches subjects related to constitutional systems and legal and institutional development in South East Asia and the institutionalization of ASEAN at Nagoya University and the Graduate School of Policy Studies of Aichi Gakuin University. He used to work as a resource person for UN projects related to constitutional and legal reforms in Vietnam and Myanmar, and Japanese projects on evaluation of legal technical assistance programs in Vietnam and Cambodia.

CHERYL SAUNDERS is Laureate Professor Emeritus at the University of Melbourne and the founding director of the Centre for Comparative Constitutional Studies. Her research interests lie in the field of comparative constitutional law, including comparative method and constitutional design and change. She is a president emeritus of the International Association of Constitutional Law, a senior technical advisor to International IDEA and co-convenor of the Constitution Transformation Network.

JIUNN-RONG YEH is Chair Professor at the College of Law, National Taiwan University. He is known for his policy science approach to various law and policy issues, including constitutional change, regulatory theories and environmental sustainability and climate change. Professor Yeh's extensive publication record of books and articles in both English and Chinese covers topics such as constitutional law, environmental law and administrative law. His recent publications include *Constitutionalism in Asia: Cases and Materials* (with Wen-Chen Chang, Li-ann Thio and Kevin Y. L. Tan, 2014), *Asian Courts in Context* (co-edited with

Wen-Chen Chang, Cambridge University Press, 2015) and *The Constitution of Taiwan: A Contextual Analysis* (2016). Professor Yeh has held teaching positions in many major foreign institutions, including Columbia University (SIPA, 1999), Harvard (Law, 2003) and Melbourne (Law, 2012). He was named Distinguished Visiting Faculty 2000–2001 by the Faculty of Law, University of Toronto, where he taught Transformative Constitutionalism in East Asia. He was appointed as Professorial Fellow by Melbourne University in 2014. Professor Yeh has been actively involved in many constitutional, legislative and regulatory issues in Taiwan and in the region.

KHEMTHONG TONSAKULRUNGRUANG is a lecturer at the Faculty of Law, Chulalongkorn University. His research interests are constitutional development in Thailand, public accountability, administrative law and Buddhism and law. He is also a regular contributor to 'New Mandala' and other blogs with articles on Thailand's democratic process and Buddhist politics. He graduated from Chulalongkorn University before earning his LLM at Yale Law School. He is currently a PhD candidate at the University of Bristol Law School.

MAARTJE DE VISSER is Associate Professor of Law and Associate Dean (Postgraduate Teaching & Curriculum) at Singapore Management University. Prior to this, she held appointments at Maastricht University and Tilburg Law School in the Netherlands. Maartje holds law degrees from Maastricht (LLB), Oxford (MJur) and Tilburg University (PhD). Her main areas of interest are comparative constitutional law and regional integration. Between 2008 and 2013, she participated in a European Research Council-funded project researching the organisation and operation of constitutional review in eleven European countries and the European Union. The resulting monograph, *Constitutional Review in Europe – A Comparative Analysis*, was published by Hart in 2014. Her current research focuses on cross-border judicial networking in Asia and constitutional interpretation by state institutions other than courts.

QIANFAN ZHANG is a leading constitutional law scholar and public intellectual in China. He joined the Law Faculty of Peking University in 2003, where he is the Director of the Center for People's Congress and Parliamentary Studies and Deputy Director of the Constitutional and Administrative Law Center. He has been a Vice-President of the Chinese

Constitutional Law Association since 2004. He has published widely in areas of constitutional law and legal and political reform. His representative works (mainly in Chinese) include a two-volume treatise *The Constitutional Systems in the West* (2nd edn., 2004/2005), *From Constitution to Constitutionalism: A Comparative Study of Judicial Review* (first author, 2008), *Legalizing Central-Local Relations* (co-edited with Paul Gewirtz, 2009), *Principles of Constitutional Law* (2011), *The Constitution of China: A Contextual Analysis* (2012), *Introduction to the Study of Constitutional Law* (3rd edn., 2014) and *Human Dignity in Classical Chinese Philosophy: Confucianism, Mohism, and Daoism* (2016).

PREFACE

This volume consists of essays on constitutional courts and related judicial developments in Asia, that is to say, East and South East Asia. The purpose is to examine the experiences of these constitutional courts and developments and to introduce comparative, historical and analytical perspectives on such experiences as we near the end of the second decade of the twenty-first century. It is hoped that this volume can contribute to the comparative study of constitutional courts, constitutional adjudication and constitutional developments in Asia and beyond.

We seek to provide a systematic study of all seven constitutional courts that have been established (those of Taiwan, South Korea, Mongolia, Cambodia, Thailand, Indonesia and Myanmar) in East and South East Asia from the perspectives of comparative constitutional law and regional studies. Thus, this volume contains case studies of these seven constitutional courts, as well as, for appropriate comparison, constitutional adjudication or discourse concerning constitutional review in four other countries. Furthermore, the volume provides general theoretical and comparative reflections on Asian constitutional courts in a global context. Hence, the chapters in this volume fall into two categories.

The first category consists of 'country studies', each focusing on an individual country, introducing the historical and institutional background of the constitutional court (or constitutional council or tribunal), explaining the sociopolitical context in which it operates and analysing selected major (especially recent) cases decided by it. To provide a comparative perspective, some East Asian countries which do not have a constitutional court are also covered in this volume: Japan, the Philippines, China and Vietnam. In the cases of Japan and the Philippines, constitutional adjudication by their supreme courts are examined. In the cases of China and Vietnam, the relevant discourse and institutional developments relating to constitutional review are considered.

The second category of chapters consists of theoretical and comparative analysis of, and reflections on, the experience of Asian constitutional courts, their role in the political system and their performance in constitutional adjudication. These chapters also include a study of the reception in Asia of different Western models of constitutional judicial review, a study of the informal or personal relations dimension of constitutional politics in Asia and a study of regional judicial cooperation and dialogue in Asia in the domain of constitutional adjudication.

The drafts of most of the chapters in this volume were presented for discussion as conference papers at the Sixth Asian Constitutional Law Forum held at the National University of Singapore (NUS) in December 2015. We are grateful to the Centre for Asian Legal Studies at NUS Law Faculty for their generous support for this conference. We are also much indebted to the contributors to this volume for setting aside their precious time and energy to participate in this book project. Last but not least, we record our gratitude to Mr Joe Ng and his colleagues at Cambridge University Press for their encouragement and support, without which this book could not have been published.

Albert H. Y. Chen and Andrew Harding

1

Constitutional Courts in Asia

Western Origins and Asian Practice

ALBERT H. Y. CHEN*

Whereas law and courts, and to some extent, ideas of the rule of law, have existed in human history for millennia, written constitutions of states only have a history of approximately two centuries, and the earliest constitutional courts were established less than one century ago. The concept and institution of a constitutional court are, thus, relatively new inventions in the legal history of humankind. Yet, in the early twenty-first century, constitutional courts exist and operate in all corners of the world. They are a global phenomenon that deserves scholarly investigation from legal doctrinal, theoretical and comparative perspectives.

In this chapter, we will first trace the origins and evolution of constitutional courts in the Western world and examine the transplantation of this legal or judicial institution to other continents and cultures (Section I of this chapter). The nature, functions and operation of constitutional courts will then be discussed (Section II). Next, we will focus on constitutional courts in East Asia and consider the history, experience and performance of the seven constitutional courts in this part of the world (Section III). Comparative observations on various features of these courts will be made (Section IV). Finally (Section V), we conclude by reflecting on the lessons and implications of the existence and operation of Asian constitutional courts.

* I am grateful for my co-editor's comments on the draft of this chapter. All errors and omissions remain mine.

I The Origins, Evolution and Globalization of Constitutional Courts[1]

Since the practice of enacting a written constitution as the supreme and fundamental law of the state began to become popular after American Independence and the French Revolution of the late eighteenth century, thinkers on constitutionalism have grappled with a challenge of institutional design: what kind of political and legal structures should be put in place for the purpose of ensuring that the provisions of the constitution will actually be put into practice. Modern constitutional law has developed various means of 'controls of constitutionality' – means of supervising and guaranteeing the effective implementation of the constitution. A distinction may be drawn between political and judicial controls of constitutionality.[2] Political control of constitutionality is exercised by political or nonjudicial organs of the state, while judicial control is exercised by the judiciary. The principal means of judicial control of constitutionality is judicial review of the constitutionality of legislation enacted by the parliament, or constitutional judicial review.

Since the nineteenth century, two principal models of constitutional judicial review have been developed. They are (a) the American model of 'decentralized' review by ordinary courts,[3] or what Saunders calls 'diffuse review' in Chapter 2, and (b) the Continental European model of 'centralized' review by a specialized constitutional court, or what Saunders calls 'concentrated review'.[4] There also exist mixed or hybrid systems which contain features of both the American and European models. The American model of constitutional judicial review is usually traced back to the legendary decision of the US Supreme Court in *Marbury* v. *Madison*.[5] In his famous judgment in this case, Chief Justice Marshall pointed out that the power of the legislature is limited by the constitution that has been

[1] Sections I and II of this chapter draw upon the author's previous work: Albert H. Y. Chen and Miguel Poiares Maduro, 'The judiciary and constitutional review', in Mark Tushnet, Thomas Fleiner and Cheryl Saunders (eds.), *Routledge Handbook of Constitutional Law* (London: Routledge, 2013) 97–109.

[2] See Mauro Cappelletti, *Judicial Review in the Contemporary World* (Indianapolis, IN: Bobbs-Merrill, 1971).

[3] Juliane Kokott and Martin Kaspar, 'Ensuring constitutional efficacy', in Michel Rosenfeld and András Sajó (eds.), *Oxford Handbook of Comparative Constitutional Law* (Oxford: Oxford University Press, 2012) 795–815 at 813–815.

[4] Cappelletti (note 2 earlier). See Chapter 2 (by Saunders) of this volume for a comparative analysis of these two models and their transplantation to Asia.

[5] 1 Cranch 137 (1803).

established by the people; any law made by the legislature that is repugnant to the constitution is void, and it is the power and responsibility of the court to determine what is the applicable legal norm in a particular case where there is a conflict between a statute and the constitution. In the American system of constitutional judicial review that has evolved since *Marbury* v. *Madison*, every court has the power to review whether a statutory provision is unconstitutional and, therefore, void. Standing at the apex of the hierarchy of courts, the US Supreme Court is the final court of appeal in deciding whether any statutory provision is inconsistent with the federal constitution of the United States.

Britain does not have a written constitution, and there is, therefore, no practice of constitutional judicial review.[6] However, colonies in the British Empire had written constitutions which were enacted by the Crown or Parliament in Britain. Under British colonial law, colonial courts had the power to review whether any provision in an enactment of the colonial legislature was *ultra vires* the colonial constitution and, therefore, void.[7] This colonial tradition of constitutional judicial review was inherited by Commonwealth countries such as Canada and Australia. Constitutional judicial review by ordinary courts has also been practised to varying extents in newly independent countries which were formerly parts of the British Empire, such as India, Pakistan, Bangladesh, Sri Lanka and some other common-law countries in Asia and Africa, such as Malaysia and Kenya.

The European model of constitutional judicial review by a specialized constitutional court can be traced back to the Austrian Constitution of 1920, which, under the influence of Hans Kelsen's jurisprudence, established a constitutional court.[8] According to Kelsen's theory of the hierarchy of legal norms, the constitution stands at the foundational level, and the validity of all legal norms in a state is ultimately derived from the

[6] However, under the law of the European Communities (now the European Union), British courts and the European Court of Justice may review and invalidate UK law that is inconsistent with applicable European law. Under the European Convention on Human Rights, the European Court of Human Rights may review the compatibility of UK law with the Convention. Following the enactment by the British Parliament of the Human Rights Act 1998, UK courts may also review the compatibility of UK law with the Convention (as incorporated into the Act), though they may not invalidate such incompatible law.

[7] See generally Kenneth Roberts-Wray, *Commonwealth and Colonial Law* (London: Stevens, 1966).

[8] Cappelletti (note 2 earlier) 46–47, 71–72.

constitution. Kelsen proposed the creation of a constitutional court which (unlike ordinary courts) had jurisdiction to determine whether any legal norm was consistent with the constitution. In his view, the constitutional court was the complement to the legislature; it performed a political and legislative function – that of negative legislation, or nullification of an unconstitutional norm. In Kelsen's theory, such constitutional judicial review was limited to dealing with logical inconsistencies between, on the one hand, constitutional norms – particularly norms governing the division of power between various state organs – and, on the other hand, other lower-level legal norms; it was not concerned with the protection of individuals' human rights.[9]

The Austrian Constitutional Court (*Verfassungsgericht*) epitomized the 'archetypal form'[10] of the kind of constitutional judicial review that is (a) centralized, (as distinguished from the decentralized American model in which every court may exercise the power of constitutional review), (b) abstract (i.e., review of the constitutionality of a law but not in the context of the facts and circumstances of any concrete case that is litigated before an ordinary court) rather than concrete (as in the American system or the systems in former British colonies, under which the court reviews the constitutionality of a law only where the application of that law is relevant to a case litigated before the court), and (c) review *principaliter* (i.e., review in a legal action where the principal or only issue is the constitutionality of a law) rather than review *incidenter* (as in the American system or the systems in former British colonies, where the review is only incidental to the making of a judicial decision as to which party wins the litigated case).[11]

In the Austrian system that existed from 1920 to 1929, the constitutional court only conducted abstract review of the constitutionality of laws in actions initiated by other governmental organs for the purpose of such review. In particular, the federal executive could request review of laws of the Länder (constituent states of the federation); the governments of the Länder could request review of federal legislation.[12] Hence the purpose of the system was to police the constitutional division of

[9] See generally Hans Kelsen, 'Judicial review of legislation: A comparative study of the Austrian and the American constitution' (1942) 4 *Journal of Politics* 183; Hans Kelsen, *General Theory of Law and State*, Anders Wedberg (trans.) (New York: Russell, 1961).

[10] Cappelletti (note 2 earlier) 69.

[11] Ibid., 69.

[12] Ibid., 72.

power between the federation and its member states. The Austrian system was modified by the constitutional amendment of 1929, under which the supreme court and central administrative court acquired the right to refer the question of the constitutionality of a law to the constitutional court when such a question arose in cases being tried by them.[13] Thus, an element of concrete review or review *incidenter* was introduced into the Austrian system of centralized review by a constitutional court.

After World War II, major developments in constitutional judicial review occurred in Europe. These developments may be understood in the context of the post-war international movement to enhance the protection of human rights, including the adoption by the United Nations of the Universal Declaration of Human Rights in 1948 and the signature of the European Convention on Human Rights and Fundamental Freedoms in 1950 by member states of the Council of Europe. Both the Basic Law (1949) of West Germany and the new constitution (1947) of Italy provide for the establishment of constitutional courts, which started to operate in these countries in 1951 and 1956, respectively. In France, the constitution (1958) of the Fifth Republic provides for a constitutional council. Constitutional courts were established in Spain and Portugal in 1978 and 1982, respectively, after their transition to democracy. Poland also established a constitutional court, in 1985.[14] Another wave of founding of constitutional courts followed the collapse of communism in the former Soviet Union and Eastern Europe. Since the early 1990s, constitutional courts have been established in most of the new democracies in the former Soviet Union, Eastern Europe and Central Europe.[15] By the early twenty-first century, constitutional courts existed in eighteen of the twenty-seven member states of the European Union.[16]

[13] Ibid., 72–74.

[14] Lech Garlicki, 'Constitutional Court of Poland: 1982–2009', in Pasquale Pasquino and Francesca Billi (eds.), *The Political Origins of Constitutional Courts* (Rome: Fondazione Adriano Olivetti, 2009) 13–39.

[15] See generally Wojciech Sadurski (ed.), *Constitutional Justice, East and West: Democratic Legitimacy and Constitutional Courts in Post-Communist Europe in a Comparative Perspective* (The Hague: Kluwer Law International, 2002).

[16] Víctor Ferreres Comella, 'The rise of specialized constitutional courts', in Tom Ginsburg and Rosalind Dixon (eds.), *Comparative Constitutional Law* (Cheltenham: Edward Elgar, 2011) 265–277 at 265. See generally Maartje de Visser, *Constitutional Review in Europe: A Comparative Analysis* (Oxford: Hart, 2014).

In Latin America, the power of constitutional review is exercised by a specialized constitutional court in six countries.[17] Since the 1970s, constitutional courts, or 'constitutional guarantees tribunals', have been established in Chile, Ecuador and Peru.[18] There are no constitutional courts in Mexico, Argentina and Brazil, which have adopted the American system of constitutional review.[19] A hybrid system of constitutional judicial review, in which 'the ordinary courts may have power to refuse to apply an unconstitutional law, but only a single court has the power to declare a law invalid',[20] evolved in the course of the nineteenth century in some Latin American countries, including Venezuela and Columbia.[21] By the early twenty-first century, there were ten Latin American countries in which the supreme court has the power to declare a law unconstitutional and to annul it; in five of these ten countries, there exists a special constitutional chamber in the supreme court.[22]

From its European roots, the institution of constitutional review by a constitutional court has been transplanted to all parts of the world and is now clearly a global phenomenon.[23] In many countries, the founding of a constitutional court is an important indication that the country has chosen the path of constitutional democracy. Examples of countries outside the European and American continents which have established constitutional courts include Turkey, Egypt, Senegal, Ethiopia, South Africa, Zimbabwe, Taiwan (Republic of China), Mongolia, South Korea, Thailand and Indonesia. It is no coincidence that some of these courts were established in the 1980s (in South Korea), 1990s (in Mongolia, South Africa[24] and Thailand) or the first decade of the twenty-first

[17] They are Peru, Guatemala, Chile, Ecuador, Bolivia and Colombia: see Víctor Ferreres Comella, *Constitutional Courts and Democratic Values: A European Perspective* (New Haven, CT: Yale University Press, 2009) 5; Vicki C. Jackson and Mark Tushnet, *Comparative Constitutional Law*, 2nd edn. (New York: Foundation Press, 2006) 493.

[18] Allan-Randolph Brewer-Carías, *Judicial Review in Comparative Law* (Cambridge: Cambridge University Press, 1989) 190; Ferreres Comella (note 17 earlier) 5.

[19] Brewer-Carías (note 18 earlier) 128.

[20] Jackson and Tushnet (note 17 earlier) 466.

[21] Brewer-Carías (note 18 earlier) 128, 130.

[22] Jackson and Tushnet (note 17 earlier) 493; Ferreres Comella (note 17 earlier) 5.

[23] See generally Andrew Harding and Peter Leyland (eds.), *Constitutional Courts: A Comparative Study* (London: Wildy, Simmonds & Hill Publishing, 2009).

[24] Since its establishment in 1995, the South African Constitutional Court has played a remarkable role in the democratic transition in South Africa and quickly established its international reputation and importance in comparative constitutional law. See, e.g., James Fowkes, *Building the Constitution: The Practice of Constitutional Interpretation in Post-Apartheid South Africa* (Cambridge: Cambridge University Press, 2016).

century (in Indonesia), at the same time as the countries transitioned from authoritarianism to liberal constitutional democracy, which was also the case in European countries that have undergone such a transition.

II The Nature, Functions and Operation of Constitutional Courts

The core functions of constitutional courts as they originally evolved have been the review of the constitutionality of laws and the adjudication of jurisdictional disputes among different branches, organs and levels of government; the precise boundary between the jurisdiction of a constitutional court and that of ordinary courts in the same legal system is sometimes contested.[25] Contemporary constitutional courts are often given additional functions, such as supervising elections and referendums, determining the legality of political parties and impeaching or enforcing the law against political leaders or senior officials.[26] The nature, functions and operation of a modern constitutional court can be best illustrated by examining the first generation of post-War constitutional courts in Western Europe. We first consider the Federal Constitutional Court (*Bundesverfassungsgericht*, or BVerG), originally of West Germany and subsequently of the united Germany (after 1990).[27] This constitutional court is one of the first constitutional courts in the Western world and has served as a model for many countries which subsequently chose to establish constitutional courts, including several countries in East Asia.

The BVerG consists of sixteen judges divided into two chambers, or senates. Half of the judges are elected by the Bundestag (Federal Parliament), and the other half by the Bundesrat (Council of Constituent States).[28] The types of cases over which the court has jurisdiction include,

[25] See Saunders, Chapter 2 of this volume; Lech Garlicki, 'Constitutional courts versus supreme courts' (2007) 5 *International Journal of Constitutional Law* 44–68.

[26] Ferreres Comella (note 17 earlier) 6.

[27] See generally Donald P. Kommers, *The Constitutional Jurisprudence of the Federal Republic of Germany*, 2nd edn. (Durham, NC: Duke University Press, 1997); Werner Heun, *The Constitution of Germany: A Contextual Analysis* (Oxford: Hart, 2011) 159–189.

[28] See the Basic Law, Art. 94, which also provides that the court 'shall consist of federal judges and other members.' At least six of the sixteen judges of the court must have served as federal judges. In practice, law professors constitute the largest group of appointees to the court, which is also the case in the Italian and Spanish constitutional

among others, (a) abstract review (upon the request of certain governmental actors, such as the federal government, a state government or one-third of the members of the Bundestag); (b) concrete review, which means that other courts may, in the course of hearing cases, refer to the constitutional court a question regarding whether a statutory provision is unconstitutional; and (c) constitutional complaints (*Verfassungsbeschwerde*)[29] by persons who allege that their basic rights have been violated by governmental actions, including administrative actions and judicial decisions. In practice, most of the cases dealt with by the court arose from constitutional complaints, and most of such complaints were against decisions of other courts. It has been pointed out that the institution of constitutional complaints has contributed to the high standing of the constitutional court in the eyes of members of the public and to the 'rising constitutional consciousness among Germans generally'.[30] Apart from exercising the power of constitutional review of laws and governmental actions, the constitutional court also exercises other powers conferred upon it by the Basic Law and other laws, including the jurisdiction to adjudicate disputes between constitutional organs, between the federal government and a state (Länder) government or between state governments; to handle some electoral matters; to decide on the impeachment of the president of the Republic; and to decide whether a political party is unconstitutional.[31]

The constitutional courts in Italy and Spain are also widely known and influential. The Spanish Constitutional Court has been an exemplar for Latin America, while the mode of appointment to the Italian court has been replicated in several East Asian jurisdictions. The Italian court consists of fifteen judges; Parliament, the president and the judiciary

courts discussed below. See Alec Stone Sweet, *Governing with Judges: Constitutional Politics in Europe* (Oxford: Oxford University Press, 2000) 48.

29 This can also be translated as 'constitutional recourse' (Cappelletti, note 2 earlier) 22. Generally speaking (but subject to exceptions), this remedy can only be pursued when other judicial remedies have been exhausted. The jurisdiction to hear constitutional complaints was not provided in the original Basic Law of 1949 but was first introduced by statute in 1951 and then given constitutional status by the constitutional amendment of 1969.

30 Kommers (note 27 earlier) 28.

31 Louis Favoreu, 'Constitutional review in Europe', in Louis Henkin and Albert J. Rosenthal (eds.), *Constitutionalism and Rights: The Influence of the United States Constitution Abroad* (New York: Columbia University Press, 1990) 38–62 at 52; Justin Collings, *Democracy's Guardians: A History of the German Federal Constitutional Court 1951–2001* (Oxford: Oxford University Press, 2015) xxv.

each elect or appoint one-third of them. It has jurisdiction over the review of the constitutionality of laws (including concrete review upon reference by other courts); competence disputes between state organs, between the national and provincial governments and between provincial governments; certain criminal proceedings against the president and ministers; and the acceptance of abrogative referendums.[32] The Spanish Constitutional Court, which began to function in 1980, has twelve judges appointed by the king, four of whom are upon nomination by the congress, four by the senate, two by the government and two by the judiciary. Its jurisdiction includes the review of the constitutionality of laws (including abstract review, upon reference by the president, fifty members of the congress or of the senate, etc., and concrete review upon reference by a court in the course of litigation), the adjudication of conflicts between state organs, the review of the legality of treaties and dealing with individuals' petitions of *amparo* against administrative acts and judicial decisions that affect their fundamental rights.[33] The writ of *amparo* was first developed in Latin America and provides a channel of access to the constitutional court similar to the constitutional complaint in the German system.

One of the basic questions raised by the comparative study of constitutional adjudication is why many European states and new democracies in other parts of the world chose to establish specialized constitutional courts instead of adopting decentralized constitutional review by ordinary courts. In the case of the civil law jurisdictions in Continental Europe, factors which have favoured the option of having a constitutional court include the following:[34] (a) the traditional conception of separation of powers according to which the judiciary (of the ordinary courts) should not engage in the political function of invalidating Acts of Parliament; (b) the absence of a doctrine of *stare decisis* (binding precedents) in civil law countries, which means that if even one court rules that a statute is unconstitutional, the ruling does not bind other courts; (c) the structure (such as the plurality of courts specializing in different kinds of litigation), procedure and mentality and training of judges of ordinary courts are such that they may not be effective in performing the task of constitutional review.

[32] Favoreu (note 31 earlier) 52–53; G. Leroy Certoma, *The Italian Legal System* (London: Butterworths, 1985) 155–157.

[33] Favoreu (note 31 earlier) 54.

[34] Cappelletti (note 2 earlier) 54–66; Jackson and Tushnet (note 17 earlier) 467–468.

In the case of countries undergoing a transition from authoritarianism to democracy, the need to establish a new constitutional court rather than relying on existing ordinary courts to serve as guardians of the new democratic constitution can be particularly acute. Judges of existing courts have served the authoritarian regime in the past; they hardly have the training, skills and experience to meet the challenges of constitutional adjudication, nor can they be trusted to do so.[35] In these circumstances, it may be necessary and desirable to have a new system of constitutional adjudication centred on a new constitutional court that is separate and distinct from the existing judicial system. Furthermore, in a new democracy, the establishment of a new constitutional court can be an important symbol of political and legal progress and of the new era of constitutionalism, rule of law, democracy and human rights, with the new court entrusted with the guardianship, and serving as a focal point, of the new constitutional order.[36] The legitimacy of and public confidence in the new constitutional order will, thus, be enhanced.

Constitutional judicial review, whether by a constitutional court or by ordinary courts led by a supreme court, involves the invalidation of provisions in Acts of Parliament by a court on the grounds that the provisions are unconstitutional. Where this power of review of laws is exercised by a constitutional court rather than an ordinary court, there may even be a built-in tendency or structural pressure towards judicial activism in the exercise of this power.[37] Insofar as the court consists of unelected and elite judges, while Parliament consists of the elected representatives of the people, the institution of constitutional judicial review is apparently undemocratic or counter-majoritarian, and its legitimacy has thus been questioned from time to time.[38] Some jurists defend

[35] Jackson and Tushnet (note 17 earlier) 468; see also Saunders, Chapter 2.

[36] Alec Stone Sweet, 'Constitutional courts', in Michel Rosenfeld and András Sajó (eds.), *Oxford Handbook of Comparative Constitutional Law* (Oxford: Oxford University Press, 2012) 816–830 at 826–827.

[37] Ferreres Comella (note 16 earlier) 271–272: 'The decision by the constitutional framers to establish such special tribunals [constitutional courts] rests, to a significant extent, on their expectation that a sufficiently large number of statutory provisions will be constitutionally problematic in the future. Only under that assumption does it make sense to set up specific institutions in charge of striking down statutes on constitutional grounds.' Kokott and Kaspar (note 3 earlier) at 807 also suggest that '[i]t is safe to assume that the formal existence of a centralized constitutional court tends to at least increase the degree of judicial review.'

[38] Alexander M. Bickel, *The Least Dangerous Branch: The Supreme Court at the Bar of Politics*, 2nd edn. (New Haven, CT: Yale University Press, 1986).

it by explaining that it enables the values of natural law (as a higher law than positive law) that the constitution affirms to be realized in a legal system that is largely positivist;[39] thus, constitutional justice through constitutional judicial review contributes to the realization of justice, human dignity and human rights. Others point out that constitutional judicial review is necessary for the maintenance of the basic institutions, processes and conditions of a democratic polity;[40] democracy or majoritarian rule itself cannot guarantee such maintenance. Furthermore, the rights of minorities need to be safeguarded by constitutional justice, as majoritarian rule may result in such rights being threatened.[41]

Actually, in many countries in the contemporary world, the traditional conception of separation of three powers for the purpose of checks and balances has lost much of its efficacy because both the executive and legislature may, as a result of elections, fall under the control of the same political party or political force. In this scenario, the availability of the channel of constitutional judicial review and the existence of an independent and respected constitutional court that administers constitutional justice – as a check on the ruling power that dominates both the executive and legislature – becomes all the more important and valuable.[42]

Contemporary political scientists have pointed out that in designing a constitutional system and drafting a new constitution, particularly at a 'constitutional moment'[43] or 'axial moment'[44] when political forces with conflicting interests and ideologies negotiate the terms of a new social contract that is democratic, it is rational for actors to choose to confer authority on a constitutional court to engage in future enforcement of the terms of the constitutional bargain currently being negotiated[45] so that they, themselves, may go to the court for remedies should

[39] Cappelletti (note 2 earlier).

[40] See, e.g., John Hart Ely, *Democracy and Distrust: A Theory of Judicial Review* (Cambridge, MA: Harvard University Press, 1980).

[41] See, e.g., the famous footnote 4 of Justice Stone's opinion in *United States* v. *Carolene Products Co* (1938) 304 US 144.

[42] Tim Koopmans, *Courts and Political Institutions: A Comparative View* (Cambridge: Cambridge University Press, 2003) 247–251; Favoreu (note 31 earlier) 56.

[43] The concept of constitutional moment was first developed in Bruce Ackerman, *We the People: Foundations* (Cambridge, MA: Belknap Press, 1991).

[44] Andrew Harding, Peter Leyland and Tania Groppi, 'Constitutional courts: Forms, functions and practice in comparative perspective' (2008) 3 *Journal of Comparative Law* 1–21 at 4: 'The creation of a constitutional court may be the result of an axial moment such as . . .'

[45] Sweet Stone (note 36 earlier) 820–821: '[T]he availability of the CC [constitutional court] gives drafters the confidence to strike constitutional bargains *ex ante*, as well as a means

they lose in the new election and become a minority in, or even absent from, the executive and legislative institutions.[46] Hence 'independent judicial review serves a valuable insurance function for competitors in a stable democracy.'[47]

In a state undergoing a transition from authoritarianism to democracy, the constitutional court usually has an important role to play in the new democratic constitutional order by arbitrating disputes and resolving conflicts among political actors competing for power in the new order. Unlike an authoritarian system in which power is concentrated in the hands of a single strongman, a dominant political party or a ruling oligarchy, there is broad diffusion of political power in a democratic system and, hence, more disputes – including even disputes of a 'mega-political'[48] nature – that call for peaceful resolution in accordance with the principles and rules of constitutional law. This means that the constitutional court as the ultimate interpreter and enforcer of such principles and rules may be called upon to deal with questions of megapolitics by applying the constitutional law to politically controversial cases. If the court rises to the challenge and deals with such political issues wisely and effectively, it can contribute significantly to the democratic consolidation of the new constitutional order. Conversely, if the court proves to be ill-equipped and unable to manage the political crises that generate the megapolitical cases that come before it, the new democracy may falter or even collapse. Thus, the stakes can be very high for a constitutional court,[49] as the Asian experience discussed later will testify.

of guaranteeing the credibility of commitments made *ex post*. ... CCs help framers resolve a bundle of contracting problems.'

46 Tom Ginsburg, *Judicial Review in New Democracies: Constitutional Courts in Asian Cases* (Cambridge: Cambridge University Press, 2003).

47 Matthew C. Stephenson, '"When the devil turns ...": The political foundations of independent judicial review' (2003) 32 *Journal of Legal Studies* 59–89 at 85.

48 The term megapolitics was first used by Ran Hirschl, 'The judicialization of mega-politics and the rise of political courts' (2008) 11 *Annual Review of Political Science* 93–118. Hirschl (at 94) defines megapolitics to mean 'matters of outright and utmost political significance that often define and divide whole polities. These range from electoral outcomes and corroboration of regime change to matters of war and peace, foundational collective identity questions, and nation-building processes pertaining to the very nature and definition of the body politic.'

49 Ginsburg points out that courts have been 'called on to decide whether or not an elected political leader could take or continue to hold office. ... These types of decisions are critical junctures for the political and constitutional system; they are moments of choice when everything may be at stake, including whether the country will remain a democracy': Tom Ginsburg, 'The politics of courts in democratization: Four junctures in Asia',

III Constitutional Courts in East Asia

The earliest constitutional court in East Asia was that established by the 1946 constitution of the Republic of China, which is still largely in force in Taiwan today. This court started to operate in Taiwan in the 1950s and has played an active role since Taiwan's democratization in the 1980s. Democratization and the making of new constitutions have led to the establishment of new constitutional courts in South Korea (under the 1987 constitution), in Mongolia (under the 1991 constitution), in Thailand (under the 1997 constitution), and in Indonesia (under the constitutional amendment of 2001). A constitutional council was established in Cambodia in 1998 and a constitutional tribunal in Myanmar in 2011. We now review briefly the origins and development of these Asian constitutional courts according to the chronological order of their establishment.

Taiwan (Republic of China). The origins of Taiwan's Constitutional Court can be traced back to the constitution of the Republic of China adopted in 1946 by a constituent assembly led by the Kuomintang (Chinese Nationalist Party) government. In 1948, a nascent constitutional court known as the Council of Grand Justices of the Judicial Yuan was established under the 1946 constitution. After the communist takeover of the Chinese mainland in 1949 and the move of the Kuomintang government to Taiwan, the Council of Grand Justices began to operate in Taiwan, exercising both powers of issuing unifying interpretations of laws and of constitutional interpretation and review. As Yeh and Chang point out in Chapter 5, the first of these two functions constituted the bulk of the council's work in its first two decades. Some constitutional interpretations issued by the council gave the impression that it was more a legal adviser to the government or even a rubber stamp conferring legitimacy to the regime's decisions[50] rather than an independent guardian of the constitution. Yet, the low-profile and relatively technical legal work done by the council in its early decades did lay the institutional foundation for its becoming more assertive later as the political environment began to change.[51] In 1990, the Council's landmark Interpretation No. 261 mandated fresh elections to the parliamentary institutions whose

in Diana Kapiszewski, Gordon Silverstein and Robert A. Kagan (eds.), *Consequential Courts: Judicial Roles in Global Perspective* (Cambridge: Cambridge University Press, 2013) 45–66 at 46.

[50] See Chapter 5 of this volume.

[51] Albert H. Y. Chen, 'A tale of two islands: Comparative reflections on constitutionalism in Hong Kong and Taiwan' (2007) 37 *Hong Kong Law Journal* 647–688 at 676.

seats at that time were still largely occupied by deputies elected in mainland China in the late 1940s. As Taiwan entered its transition from authoritarianism to liberal constitutional democracy in the 1990s, the council played a crucial role in reforming the laws of the authoritarian era in areas such as criminal procedure, civil liberties and administrative law, as well as in adjudicating political conflicts generated by the democratizing political system. In 2000, it even asserted and exercised the power of review of constitutional amendments in Interpretation No. 499. During the era of 'divided government' in 2000–2008, when the executive and legislative branches were controlled by different political parties, the council settled many controversies successfully, generating adopting a pro-dialogue approach.[52] In the most recent decade, the council further developed its jurisprudence of human rights and due process, culminating in its interpretation in 2017 that legalizes same-sex marriage – the first Asian constitutional interpretation to do so.[53]

South Korea. South Korea began its transition from authoritarianism and military domination of the government to liberal democracy with the adoption of a new constitution in 1987. The 1987 constitution provides for the establishment of the first constitutional court in Korean history. The composition of the court follows the Italian model of one-third of its members appointed by each of the executive, legislative and judicial branches of government, respectively. It has powers of concrete review of laws, handling of individuals' complaints of constitutional violations, making decisions on the impeachment of the president and decisions on the legality of political parties, all of which have been exercised in the course of the last three decades. The court has contributed to law reform in many domains, including criminal, administrative and civil laws.[54] It has addressed issues of transitional justice. It has decided several cases with megapolitical dimensions, including two cases of presidential impeachment (one of which led to the removal from office of President Park Geun-hye in 2017), one case of outlawing a political party

[52] Jiunn-rong Yeh, 'Presidential politics and the judicial facilitation of dialogue between political actors in new Asian democracies: Comparing the South Korean and Taiwanese experiences' (2010) 8 *International Journal of Constitutional Law* 911–949; Jiunn-rong Yeh, *The Constitution of Taiwan: A Contextual Analysis* (Oxford: Hart Publishing, 2016), chap. 6.

[53] See Chapter 5 of this volume.

[54] See generally Tom Ginsburg, 'The Constitutional Court and judicialization of Korean politics', in Andrew Harding and Pip Nicholson (eds.), *New Courts in Asia* (London: Routledge, 2010) 145–157.

(which was a pro-communist party), and one case concerning the relocation of the capital (in which the court, relying on a customary or unwritten constitutional norm, held the proposed relocation to be unconstitutional). The heavy caseload of the court, particularly in dealing with individuals' complaints of constitutional violations, testifies to its popularity. As Hahm points out in Chapter 6, surveys on Koreans' 'perception of trustworthiness of various public and private organizations' have shown that '[a]mong the public organizations, the constitutional court has consistently ranked highest over a period of nine years.'[55]

Mongolia. As communism collapsed in Eastern Europe and the Soviet Union by the early 1990s, Mongolia also embarked upon political reform and adopted a new constitution in 1991. The constitution provided for a new constitutional court, which was duly established in 1992. The court consists of nominees by the parliament, the president and the supreme court, each nominating three of the members of the court. As discussed by Ginsburg and Enhbaatar in Chapter 7, the jurisdiction of the court lies mainly in abstract review of laws; the court has been inactive in concrete review of possible constitutional violations in cases concerning the rights of individuals and has not developed any significant jurisprudence on the protection of citizens' rights. The 1991 constitution provided for a 'two-stage, dialogic process' of constitutional review:[56] if a five-member bench of the constitutional court determines a legal provision to be unconstitutional, the parliament has the opportunity to consider the court's decision and decide whether to accept it. If the parliament rejects the court's decision, the full nine-member bench of the court will make the final decision, which will then be binding. The court has found violations of the constitution in a significant proportion of cases brought before it.[57] The most well-known cases decided by the court were a line of cases in the period 1996–2001, during which the court was in conflict with the parliament on the constitutional issue of whether members of the parliament could serve in the government without giving up their parliamentary seats. Because of the intensity and prolonged duration of this conflict, during the course of which the court struck down not only legislation but also constitutional amendments on the subject, and given

[55] See Chapter 6 of this volume. Ginsburg (note 54 earlier) at 145 writes that 'the Court has become the embodiment of the new democratic constitutional order of Korea'.

[56] See Chapter 7 of this volume.

[57] See Chapter 7 of this volume for detailed figures.

that the court has not developed a jurisprudence of individuals' rights, Ginsburg and Enhbaatar describe the case of the Mongolian Constitutional Court as 'an example of judicialization of politics without rights'.

Cambodia. Cambodia was in a state of civil war before international intervention led to a ceasefire under the Paris Peace Accord of 1991. The UN Transitional Authority in Cambodia oversaw the election of a new national assembly, which in 1993, adopted a new constitution based on the liberal democratic guidelines laid down by the Paris Accord.[58] The constitution provided for the establishment of a constitutional council of nine members, one-third of whom are appointed by each of the king, the national assembly and the Supreme Council of Magistracy. As Kuong points out in Chapter 10, the council was only established in 1998 in anticipation of a general election to be held that year, as there was a need to have an institution to adjudicate on electoral disputes, and the constitutional council could perform this role. Since it was established, the constitutional council has, indeed, decided a significant number of cases of electoral disputes. The council also has the power of review of laws, particularly before they are promulgated (i.e., *ex ante* review). In Chapter 10, Kuong demonstrates that the council has been cautious and restrained in exercising the power of constitutional review of laws. Although the council also has the power of concrete review of laws after they have been promulgated, the council points out that, in practice, the courts have not referred issues of constitutionality of laws to the council. Generally speaking, 'constitutional cases have so far revealed the vigorous political struggles in Cambodia, which have gradually been entrusted to the constitutional council instead of violence. . . . The rulings sometimes seem to have been a facilitating factor to promote the conclusion of political compromises.'[59]

Thailand. Unlike other Southeast Asian countries, Thailand has not been colonized by Western powers. Since Thailand became a constitutional monarchy in 1932, it has experienced frequent oscillations between military and civilian rule, with recurring cycles of constitution-making, general election, civilian government and military coup. A new constitution, sometimes known as the People's Constitution, was

[58] See Albert H. Y. Chen, 'The achievement of constitutionalism in Asia: Moving beyond "constitutions without constitutionalism"', in Albert H. Y. Chen (ed.), *Constitutionalism in Asia in the Early Twenty-First Century* (Cambridge: Cambridge University Press, 2014) 1–31 at 23.

[59] Kuong, Chapter 10.

adopted in 1997 after extensive public consultation with the aim of putting an end to the vicious cycles of the past.[60] The constitution provided for a constitutional court with broad powers of abstract and concrete review, which was duly established in 1998. The performance of the court in its first few years may be said to have been a mixed record. Tonsakulrungruang describes it in Chapter 8 as 'promising'; Harding points out that 'in practice the court did not exercise its jurisdiction vigorously during 1998–2001, and was in effect, during 2001–5 at least, converted into a weak institution' which 'failed ... to call to account in any meaningful way the authoritarian and manipulative government of 2001–6' led by the populist Prime Minister Thaksin Shinawatra.[61] However, since the court's landmark decision in 2006 to nullify the snap election called by Thaksin and won by his party amidst intensifying opposition to his rule, the Thai Constitutional Court has made dramatic interventions in megapolitics and has, in the eyes of many, become a highly politicized constitutional court. Tonsakulrungruang shows in Chapter 8 that in a series of highly controversial decisions, for which it is doubtful they can be well justified by relevant constitutional and statutory provisions, the constitutional court has dismissed three prime ministers, invalidated two general elections, disbanded two dominant political parties, stopped one attempt by the government to revise the constitution, and invalidated two constitutional amendments. Given the polarization of the Thai political community between the pro-Thaksin and anti-Thaksin camps, it is also noteworthy that all these major decisions of the constitutional court on matters of megapolitics were against the pro-Thaksin camp. This period of Thai constitutional history was also marked by two military coups, in 2006 and 2014. The first of these coups took place shortly after the constitutional court's decision to invalidate the general election won by Thaksin in 2006, and the second took place after the court invalidated another general election and dismissed Prime Minister Yingluck Shinawatra for misconduct.

Indonesia. Indonesia, the most populous state in Southeast Asia, underwent a remarkable transition from Soeharto's strongman rule to

[60] See Tom Ginsburg, 'Constitutional afterlife: The continuing impact of Thailand's post-political constitution', (2009) 7 *International Journal of Constitutional Law* 83–105.

[61] Andrew Harding, 'The constitutional court of Thailand, 1998–2006: A turbulent innovation', in Andrew Harding and Pip Nicholson (eds.), *New Courts in Asia* (London: Routledge, 2010) 121–144 at 136.

liberal democracy at the turn of the century. From the legal perspective, the transition was achieved by a series of constitutional amendments enacted by the national assembly in 1999–2002.[62] The constitutional amendment of 2001 provides for a constitutional court, which was duly established in 2003. The Korean model influenced the design of the composition and powers of the Indonesian Constitutional Court.[63] The court consists of nine members, one-third of whom are appointed by each of the president, the house of representatives and the supreme court. It has jurisdiction over constitutional complaints brought by citizens or state agencies to challenge laws, competence disputes between state organs, election disputes, dissolution of political parties and impeachment of the president. Indeed, the need to have a credible institution to deal with presidential impeachment was an important consideration in establishing the court,[64] as the impeachment of President Wahid by the national assembly in 2001 had been controversial. Since its establishment, the court has been fairly active in exercising the power of constitutional review of laws and has made good contributions to the development of political, economic and social rights. It has grappled with social policy and religious issues and defended its jurisdiction against attempted parliamentary encroachment.[65] The court has actively developed the remedies of declaring laws conditionally constitutional or conditionally unconstitutional.[66] As documented in Chapter 9 by Butt, the court has also played an important and useful role in adjudicating electoral disputes. Opinion polls have suggested that the court was well respected by members of the public,[67] although the prosecution and conviction for corruption in 2014 of Akil Mochtar – the third chief

[62] Chen (note 58 earlier) 28.

[63] Hendrianto, 'Institutional choice and the new Indonesian Constitutional Court', in Andrew Harding and Pip Nicholson (eds.), *New Courts in Asia* (London: Routledge, 2010) 158–177.

[64] Hendrianto, ibid., 162; Andrew Harding and Peter Leyland, 'The constitutional courts of Thailand and Indonesia: Two case studies from South East Asia' (2008) 3 *Journal of Comparative Law* 118–137 at 125; Butt, Chapter 9 in this volume, note 8.

[65] Bjoern Dressel, 'Courts and judicialization in Southeast Asia', in William Case (ed.), *Routledge Handbook of Southeast Asian Democratization* (London: Routledge, 2015) 268–281 at 273.

[66] See Butt, Chapter 9 in this volume.

[67] Björn Dressel, 'Courts and constitutional politics in Southeast Asia', in Marco Bünte and Björn Dressel (eds.), *Politics and Constitutions in Southeast Asia* (London: Routledge, 2017) 251–270 at 257–258.

justice of the court – has tarnished the court's reputation considerably.[68] As suggested by Dressel in Chapter 3, the potentially negative influence of informal personal networks on appointments to the court and the operation of the court is also a cause for concern.

Myanmar. Myanmar is the latest case of a transition from authoritarianism to democracy in Southeast Asia. In 2008, a new constitution was adopted by the military regime and approved in a referendum, providing for free elections to the parliament. Since then, two general elections have been held, in 2010 and 2015, with the latter election leading to the assumption of power by the National League for Democracy under the leadership of Aung San Suu Kyi. The 2008 constitution provides for a constitutional tribunal, which was established in 2011. The constitutional tribunal consists of nine members, of whom one-third are chosen by each of the president, the speaker of the upper house of Parliament and the speaker of the lower house of Parliament. The tribunal has powers to review laws and deal with competence disputes among state organs, but only upon the application of a court, a designated office holder or state institution; individual citizens have no right of access to the court.[69] As Harding recounts in Chapter 11, the tribunal has had a rough ride during its short history, mainly because of its decision in 2012 regarding the investigatory powers – or lack thereof – of parliamentary committees. The backlash was such that the entire membership of the tribunal was forced to resign as Parliament initiated proceedings to impeach them. Harding points out that the incident may be understood as a conflict between the military and the parliament, as when the tribunal was first formed in 2011, most members of the tribunal were, in effect, selected by the military. In 2013, the law on the constitutional tribunal was amended to strengthen the role of the parliament in appointments to the tribunal and to require members of the tribunal to report to the person or body nominating them.[70] So far, the tribunal has only decided a small number of cases; whether it will, in time, mature as a constitutional court remains to be seen.

[68] See Butt, Chapter 9 in this volume.

[69] Individual citizens may make a constitutional complaint against a law through members of parliament: see Wen-Chen Chang, Li-ann Thio, Kevin Tan and Jiunn-rong Yeh (eds.), *Constitutionalism in Asia: Cases and Materials* (Oxford: Hart, 2014) 330.

[70] See Harding, Chapter 11 in this volume.

IV Comparative Analysis

The Asian constitutional courts discussed earlier may be studied from a comparative perspective by comparing their origins and background, composition and mode of appointment, powers and functions, and performance and role in the respective political and legal systems. The following discussion is intended to be a point of departure for further and more detailed research on these issues.

Origins and background. Among the seven constitutional courts in Asia, five were created by constitutional provisions at a constitutional moment, which sees a new liberal democratic constitution being adopted largely by consensus among political forces in the nation for the purpose of inaugurating a new era of constitutional democracy. This was the case in South Korea (1987), Mongolia (1991), Cambodia (1993), Thailand (1997) and Indonesia (2001 constitutional amendment). In the case of the Republic of China (which moved to Taiwan in 1949), the 1946 constitution was also promulgated to herald a transition from one-party rule to liberal democracy, and it contained provisions for constitutional interpretation and review by the grand justices of the Judicial Yuan, who subsequently constituted Taiwan's Constitutional Court. When this constitutional court was established in 1948, it was the first constitutional court in Asia; its establishment even predated that of the German Federal Constitutional Court, which was established by the Basic Law of 1949 and started to operate in 1951. The last constitutional court established in East Asia to date is the constitutional tribunal in Myanmar, provided for in the constitution of 2010, adopted shortly before the military regime embarked upon liberalization and democratization.

Research into the history of constitutional drafting and the design of Asian constitutional courts has revealed that there has been learning and borrowing from foreign models. For example, the Korean Constitutional Court borrowed from the German model.[71] In turn, the Korean model had a significant impact on the design of the Indonesian Constitutional Court.[72] The French model of a constitutional council with a power of pre-promulgation review of laws was influential in the course of the design of the Cambodian Constitutional Council.[73] As may be seen

[71] Ginsburg (note 54 earlier) 146.
[72] See note 63 earlier.
[73] Chang et al. (note 69 earlier) 310.

below, the Italian model of how to organize a constitutional court was adopted by the majority of East Asian constitutional courts.

Composition and mode of appointment. There is a remarkable similarity between the majority of East Asian constitutional courts in terms of their composition and mode of appointment of members. Among the seven constitutional courts, six consist of nine members[74] and four have adopted the representation model[75] of appointment (which is the mode of appointment in the Italian Constitutional Court), whereby each of the three branches of government – executive, legislative and judiciary – appoints one-third of the members of the constitutional court.[76] The three cases that depart from this representative model are that of Myanmar, Taiwan and Thailand. In Myanmar, the president and the parliament are responsible for the appointment of three and six, respectively, of the nine members of the constitutional tribunal. Taiwan adopts the cooperation model[77] whereby all fifteen grand justices are appointed by the president with the consent of the Legislative Yuan (which is Taiwan's legislature). Thailand has a more complex mechanism of appointment in which five judges are chosen by the judiciary and four are chosen by a selection committee, with the appointment of all judges of the constitutional court being subject to the senate's confirmation.[78] It seems to be the norm that constitutional court judges do not have security of tenure. In some countries (such as Taiwan, Thailand and Cambodia), they are appointed for non-renewable terms, and in some (such as South Korea and Indonesia), the appointment is renewable.[79]

Powers and functions. The primary jurisdiction[80] of a typical constitutional court is to review the constitutionality of laws and to adjudicate

[74] The constitutional court in Taiwan consists of fifteen grand justices. When Thailand's Constitutional Court was first established under the 1997 constitution, it consisted of fifteen judges, but the number was reduced to nine under the 2007 constitution. The 2017 constitution maintains the number of nine.

[75] Chang et al. identify two models of appointment of judges to constitutional courts – the cooperation model and the representation model. Chang et al. (note 69 earlier) 369–371.

[76] This representation model has been adopted in South Korea, Mongolia, Cambodia and Indonesia. In the case of Cambodia (which, unlike the three other countries, is a monarchy), one-third of the nine members of the constitutional council are appointed by each of the king, the national assembly and the Supreme Council of the Magistracy.

[77] Chang et al. (note 69 earlier) 369–371.

[78] This is the position under the 2007 and 2017 constitutions. There was a similar mechanism under the 1997 constitution, with the total number of judges being fifteen.

[79] Chang et al. (note 69 earlier) 370.

[80] Chang et al. (note 69 earlier) 328–329. For the powers and functions of constitutional courts, see also, Harding, Leyland and Groppi (note 44 earlier); Kokott and Kaspar (note

disputes regarding the competence or jurisdiction of different state organs, and these powers are vested in all seven constitutional courts in East Asia. The systems of review of laws in different countries may be further studied and compared by examining who may bring proceedings before the constitutional court to initiate such a review.[81] In six of the seven constitutional courts (Korea being the exception among the seven), abstract review of the constitutionality of a law may be initiated by designated state organs, office holders or a number of members of the parliament. In Indonesia and Mongolia, individual citizens may also challenge the constitutionality of laws before the constitutional court. In Taiwan, South Korea and Thailand, individuals may bring a constitutional complaint to challenge a law affecting them after all other remedies have been exhausted. South Korea has a system of constitutional complaints by individuals with a broad scope, which deals with both (a) complaints against a court's decision in a litigated case to not refer a constitutional question to the constitutional court, and (b) complaints regarding constitutional violations in the exercise of governmental powers (other than a judicial decision). On the other hand, individual citizens in Cambodia and Myanmar have no access to the constitutional council or constitutional tribunal, respectively.[82]

As discussed earlier, the German system of concrete review (as distinguished from abstract review) refers to the constitutional court determining the constitutionality of a law upon reference by an ordinary court that encounters the constitutional question in the course of hearing a case litigated before it. Such concrete review exists in five of the seven East Asian constitutional courts.[83] The two countries that do not have such concrete review are Mongolia and Indonesia, but as mentioned earlier, in these two countries, individuals may directly challenge the constitutionality of laws before the constitutional court.

Apart from constitutional review of laws and adjudication of competence disputes between state organs – which are the functions of all seven

3 earlier); Tom Ginsburg, 'Constitutional courts in East Asia', in Rosalind Dixon and Tom Ginsburg (eds.), *Comparative Constitutional Law in Asia* (Cheltenham, UK: Edward Elgar, 2014) 47–79.

81 See, generally, Chang et al. (note 69 earlier) 328–335.

82 However, individuals in Cambodia can make a constitutional complaint against a law through members of parliament: see Chang et al. (note 69 earlier) 330.

83 In the case of Taiwan, concrete review was not expressly provided for by law but was established by a constitutional interpretation issued by the constitutional court in 1995. Chang et al. (note 69 earlier) 331–332.

East Asian constitutional courts, some of them exercise additional powers or 'ancillary jurisdiction',[84] which may be briefly described as follows.[85]

(1) Review of constitutional amendments. As discussed earlier, the potent power of the review and invalidation of constitutional amendments has, in fact, been exercised by the constitutional courts of Taiwan, Mongolia and Thailand. In Cambodia, the constitution provides for consultation with the constitutional council before a constitutional amendment is introduced. In Mongolia, the constitutional court has the power to propose a constitutional amendment itself.

(2) Adjudication of disputes relating to elections or referendums.[86] As discussed earlier, one of the most important functions of the constitutional court of Indonesia and the constitutional council of Cambodia has been to adjudicate disputes arising from elections. The Mongolian Constitutional Court has supervisory powers over the electoral authorities.[87] The constitutional court of Thailand does not adjudicate disputes relating to individual candidates in elections but has exercised the power to completely invalidate the results of two general elections and to disqualify politicians from participating in elections.

(3) Impeachment of the president or other high officials. The constitutions of South Korea, Mongolia, Indonesia[88] and Taiwan[89] expressly provide for impeachment powers of the constitutional court, and the South Korean court actually decided two cases of presidential impeachment. As discussed earlier, the Thai

[84] The term 'ancillary jurisdiction' is used in Chang et al. (note 69 earlier) 337. Ginsburg (note 80 earlier), at 66–67, uses the term 'ancillary powers'.

[85] See, generally, Chang et al. (note 69 earlier) 337–341.

[86] For a comparative study of how Asian courts (including constitutional courts and supreme courts) have handled issues of electoral laws and elections, see Po Jen Yap, *Courts and Democracies in Asia* (Cambridge: Cambridge University Press, 2017).

[87] Chang et al. (note 69 earlier) 341.

[88] The Indonesian Constitutional Court only investigates and determines whether the president or vice president is guilty of constitutional violations; it is up to the national assembly, i.e., the People's Consultative Assembly, to make the final decision on impeachment. See Chang et al. (note 69 earlier) 339.

[89] The constitutional amendment of 2005 in Taiwan confers on its constitutional court the power to decide on the impeachment of the president and vice president where such impeachment is initiated by the legislature.

Constitutional Court has exercised the power to disqualify or remove three prime ministers from office on the grounds of violations of law.

(4) Dissolution of political parties. The power to determine the constitutionality or legality of political parties has been vested in the constitutional courts of Korea, Taiwan,[90] Thailand and Indonesia. As discussed earlier, the constitutional courts of South Korea and Thailand have actually exercised such power and ordered the dissolution of political parties.

Performance and role. There are at least two criteria which may be used to evaluate the performance or role of a constitutional court: degree of judicial activism, and degree of success. It is well-known that some courts practise a greater degree of judicial restraint in exercising their powers and functions, while other courts engage in a greater degree of judicial activism. However, activism and success are two different criteria. An activist court is not necessarily a successful one.

A successful constitutional court is one which is well respected and trusted by citizens of the nation and its political actors as a guardian of the principles and values of the constitution. The jurisprudence the court develops in reviewing the constitutionality of laws contributes significantly to the improvement of the nation's laws. Its decisions also make a contribution to the peaceful resolution of political conflicts and constitutional controversies. Political actors, individual citizens and civil society groups bring cases to it with some degree of confidence that the court will adjudicate the case fairly and impartially. Ultimately, a successful constitutional court is one that enjoys legitimacy in the eyes of the public as an institution that applies legal reason to the resolution of constitutional disputes.[91]

[90] The constitutional amendment of 1992 in Taiwan confers this power on its constitutional court. See Chang et al. (note 69 earlier) 339.

[91] Some scholars use the criterion of effectiveness instead of success to evaluate a constitutional court's performance. According to Stone Sweet (note 36 earlier) at 825 (emphasis in original), 'Constitutional review can be said to be *effective* to the extent that the important constitutional disputes arising in the polity are brought to the CC on a regular basis, that the judges who resolve these disputes give reasons for their rulings, and that those who are governed by the constitutional law accept that the court's ruling have some precedential effect.' Harding, Leyland and Groppi (note 44 earlier) at 18 also employ the concept of effectiveness, which in their opinion, should be assessed 'by adopting a two-stage process which considers i) whether the court's interventions are consistent with the norms set out in the constitution, and whether these norms themselves are consistent with principles of "good governance" . . . and ii) whether the court's pronouncements are then actually embedded in practice, that is, whether they are followed.'

A third criterion for the performance of constitutional courts may also be introduced, which is the impact of the work of the constitutional court on the law, politics and society of the country concerned. Such impact includes the direct effect of the court's decisions in individual cases on the relevant law or the outcome of the litigation, as well as the general effect of the court's activities and jurisprudence on the legal and political culture of the country, such as people's rights consciousness or the values and behaviour of political elites. The concept of 'impact' used here is a neutral term from the perspective of evaluating the court's performance: its impact may be positively or negatively evaluated depending on 'its total effect on constitutional practice in light of widely supported principles of good governance'.[92] Impact depends on at least two factors: the scope of the powers or jurisdiction conferred upon the court by the constitution and the law and the degree of activism of the court. Where the scope of powers possessed by a court is narrow, then even if it is activist in exercising those powers, the impact of the court's decisions may be quite limited. Where the scope of a court's powers is great but the court practises judicial restraint, its impact may also be limited. The impact of the work of a constitutional court can be great when the scope of its powers is wider and it is activist in exercising those powers. There may also be situations where the court's activism seeks to expand the powers conferred upon it by the constitution and the laws so that the impact of the court's activities will also be considerable.

Taking into account the criteria mentioned earlier, the performance and role of the seven constitutional courts in East Asia – as documented in this volume and other scholarly writings – may be evaluated in the figures or diagrams below. In Figure 1.1, the horizontal axis at the bottom of the boxes indicates the scope of jurisdiction of the constitutional courts concerned, and the vertical axis on the left-hand side of the boxes indicates the degree of judicial activism of those constitutional courts. The Thai Constitutional Court occupies the upper right-hand side of the diagram, as it has very broad powers under the constitution and the law and has exercised them in the most activist manner in a series of controversial rulings since 2005, as noted in this volume. Being located at the upper right-hand side of the diagram would suggest a constitutional court with the greatest impact as just discussed. The Mongolian Constitutional Court – a court with fairly broad powers – was highly

[92] Harding, Leyland and Groppi (note 44 earlier) 19.

activist, at least in the period 1996–2001, in outlawing the system of parliamentary executive which the government wanted to introduce. Thus, the court occupies the upper middle box. The Myanmar Constitutional Tribunal and the Cambodian Constitutional Council are both institutions with relatively limited powers and no right of direct access by citizens, but the former engaged in a considerable degree of activism in nullifying the investigatory powers of parliamentary committees – a decision which backfired and led to the impeachment of the entire tribunal, hence the locations of the two courts on the lower and middle left boxes in the diagram. The bottom left of the diagram suggests a constitutional court with the least impact as just discussed. Finally, we have, in the middle box of the diagram, the 'trinity' of the constitutional courts of Taiwan, South Korea and Indonesia, as courts that have fairly broad jurisdiction that has been exercised with a moderate degree of judicial activism – a kind of middle path between extremes of judicial activism and restraint.

Figure 1.2 reproduces the four-tiered typology developed by Dressel in 2015[93] and applies it to the seven constitutional courts in East Asia. The horizontal axis indicates the degree of the constitutional court's involvement in megapolitics, while the vertical axis shows the degree of *de facto* judicial independence of the constitutional court. Whereas involvement in megapolitics is closely related to the breadth of the constitutional court's power and its degree of activism, as covered by Figure 1.1, the degree of judicial independence is a new dimension to be taken into account here. Although judicial independence is closely related to institutional design and the personal character and integrity of judges, whether *de facto* judicial independence exists for the purposes of Figure 1.2 is largely a matter of public perception as to the independence and political neutrality of judges. The high degree of involvement of the Thai Constitutional Court in megapolitics, coupled with doubts as to its *de facto* judicial independence, result in its being placed in the bottom right box, which is what Dressel calls 'politicization of the judiciary'. The Cambodian Constitutional Council occupies the bottom left box – that of 'judicial co-optation or muteness' – because it has low degrees of

[93] Dressel (note 65 earlier) 272. This typology was originally used to study courts in Southeast Asia (including the constitutional courts of Thailand, Cambodia and Indonesia, now shown in round brackets in Figure 1.2). I have added the constitutional courts of Taiwan, Korea, Mongolia and Myanmar (shown in square brackets) to Dressel's original chart.

[*activism: high degree*]		Mongolia (initial period)	Thailand (after 2005)
[*activism: moderate degree*]	Myanmar (initial period)	Taiwan Korea Indonesia	
[*activism: low degree*]	Cambodia		
	[*jurisdiction: narrow*]	[*jurisdiction: broad*]	[*jurisdiction: very broad*]

Figure 1.1 Asian constitutional courts: their jurisdiction and manner of exercise

[*high degree of de facto judicial independence*]	'Judicial restraint'	'Judicial activism' (Indonesia) [Taiwan, Korea, Mongolia, Myanmar]
[*low degree of de facto judicial independence*]	'Judicial co-optation/ muteness' (Cambodia)	'Politicization of the judiciary' (Thailand after 2005)
	[*low degree of judicial involvement in megapolitics*]	[*high degree of judicial involvement in megapolitics*]

Figure 1.2 Judicial independence and involvement in megapolitics
Source: Adapted from Bjoern Dressel, 'Courts and judicialization in Southeast Asia', in William Case (ed.), *Routledge Handbook of Southeast Asian Democratization* (London: Routledge, 2015) 268–281 at 272.

both involvement in megapolitics and *de facto* independence. The other Asian constitutional courts occupy the upper right box as cases of relatively high degrees of judicial involvement in megapolitics and of *de facto* judicial independence.

Figure 1.3 is based on a more recent typology developed by Dressel,[94] which introduces a dimension of demand for rule of law, which has not

[94] Dressel (note 67 earlier) 255. This typology was originally used to study six constitutional or supreme courts in East Asia (now shown in round brackets in Figure 1.3). I have added the constitutional courts of Mongolia, Cambodia, Taiwan, South Korea and Indonesia (shown in square brackets) to Dressel's original chart.

[*high demand for* (*thick*) *rule of law*]	'Reluctant constitutionalism' (pre-1987 Philippines, post-1945 Japan)	'Liberal-constitutional equilibrium' (Indonesia) [Taiwan, Korea]
[*low demand for rule of law*]	'Authoritarian constitutionalism' (Singapore, Malaysia)	'Juristocratic constitutionalism' (Thailand)
	[*low supply of judicialization*]	[*high supply of judicialization*]

Figure 1.3 Supply of judicialization and demand for rule of law
Source: Adapted from Björn Dressel, 'Courts and constitutional politics in Southeast Asia', in Marco Bünte and Björn Dressel (eds.), *Politics and Constitutions in Southeast Asia* (London: Routledge, 2017) 251–270 at 255.

[*high degree of public confidence and trust in court*]		Taiwan Korea Indonesia	
[*low degree of public confidence and trust in court*]	Cambodia (?)	Mongolia (?) Myanmar (?)	Thailand (after 2005)
	[*activism*: *low degree*]	[*activism*: *moderate degree*]	[*activism*: *high degree*]

Figure 1.4 Degree of judicial activism and degree of public confidence in the court

been previously covered. This refers to the demand in the community for 'more or less extensive notions of the rule of law'[95] such as its 'thin' and 'thick' versions.[96] Thus, in Figure 1.3, the vertical axis indicates such demand for the rule of law, while the horizontal axis shows what Dressel calls the 'supply of judicialization', which depends on the degree to which courts are empowered to meet the demand in political and civil society for the rule of law. The diagram, therefore, demonstrates the supply and demand for constitutional justice. The upper right box is particularly noteworthy as it seems to suggest a desirable liberal constitutional equilibrium, 'where empowerment of the courts is supported by popular

[95] Dressel, ibid., 253.
[96] Ibid., 255.

demand for deeper notions of the rule of law'.[97] The situation is stable and 'self-reinforcing insofar as actors seek to address contentious issues through constitutional means – within the parameters of the rule of law and principally through institutions like the courts.'[98] Dressel has put the Indonesian Constitutional Court into this box, and I have added to it the constitutional courts of Taiwan and South Korea, which were not included in Dressel's study.

The final figure to consider is Figure 1.4, which I have compiled on the basis of the information available from this volume and other scholarly works. In Figure 1.4, the horizontal axis indicates the degree of judicial activism of constitutional courts, which has already been included in Figure 1.1, while the vertical axis shows the degree of public confidence and trust in the constitutional court concerned. I have put the constitutional courts of Taiwan, South Korea and Indonesia in the upper middle box. The other constitutional courts are placed elsewhere, with a question mark behind some of them where there is a lack of information about the degree of public confidence in them.[99]

Taking into account the attributes or indicators of a successful constitutional court as discussed earlier, and considering the figures discussed earlier as a whole, it would appear that among the seven constitutional courts in East Asia, the trinity of the Taiwanese, South Korean and Indonesian constitutional courts are apparently the most successful constitutional courts. Figures 1.2–1.4 show that these three courts are perceived to have *de facto* judicial independence, they enjoy a high degree of public confidence and trust, and they contribute to the achievement of a liberal constitutional equilibrium, where there are high degrees of both supply and demand for constitutional justice. It is also noteworthy that, as suggested by Figure 1.1, these three courts enjoy a fairly broad jurisdiction conferred upon them by the constitution and the law, and they exercise their powers with a moderate degree of activism. This may be contrasted with the Thai situation, where the constitution and the law

97 Ibid., 256.

98 Ibid.

99 The existing literature in English on East Asian constitutional courts suggests that the constitutional courts of South Korea, Taiwan and Indonesia have enjoyed a fairly high degree of public confidence, though the reputation of the Indonesian Constitutional Court has been tarnished by the corruption case involving its third chief justice (as mentioned earlier). Public confidence in the Thai Constitutional Court is probably lower than the three courts above, given the former's politicization, as mentioned earlier.

confer upon the constitutional court extremely broad powers which the court has, since 2005, exercised in an extremely activist manner.

V Conclusion: Lessons and Implications

Even in the Western world, the concept and institution of a constitutional court specializing in the adjudication of the constitutionality of laws have a history of less than a century. Constitutional courts only began to flourish in the West after World War II, as legal and political systems were redesigned to safeguard liberal constitutional democracies. As more countries have democratized since the 1980s, more constitutional courts have been established all over the world. This chapter has reviewed both the Western origins and global spread of constitutional courts, particularly their transplantation to East Asia.

This chapter has briefly told the stories of the founding and evolution of the seven constitutional courts of East Asia and compared their various characteristics and aspects of operation. It can be seen that, whereas not all of these courts have been equally successful, and crises and setbacks have been experienced from time to time, there do exist cases of relatively successful constitutional courts that contribute significantly to law reform and peaceful resolution of political conflicts or electoral disputes, and further, these are cases where the courts are well respected by members of the public as faithful guardians of the democratic constitutional order. Just as the practice of constitutionalism may be said to be an achievement in the sense that there are just too many cases of constitutions without constitutionalism,[100] the establishment, operation and maintenance of a successful constitutional court must also be regarded as an achievement of no small magnitude.

This chapter and this volume celebrate the achievements of the constitutional courts of Taiwan, South Korea and Indonesia. There is much that countries with young and developing constitutional courts can learn and borrow from them. Regional judicial dialogue and cooperation, whether under the auspices of the Association of Asian Constitutional Courts and Equivalent Institutions or otherwise, is a welcome development.[101] The case of the Thai Constitutional Court deserves more in-depth study because it has been unusual both in terms of the very broad powers conferred upon it and the extremely activist manner in

[100] Chen (note 58 earlier).
[101] See de Visser, Chapter 4.

which it has exercised those powers. Have the breadth of its powers and its high degree of activism been negative factors in terms of its potential to become a successful constitutional court? Or was the Thai Constitutional Court destined to fail because of the extreme polarization in Thai politics and the intense civil strife between the pro-Thaksin and anti-Thaksin factions in the community? Given the deep division in a society torn by conflicting values, interests and political convictions, could the Thai Constitutional Court have done better so that history would have unfolded differently? These are questions to ponder.

As for Asian countries which do not yet have constitutional courts, the experience of their neighbours that have constitutional courts is also worth studying. For instance, the issue of whether a constitutional court should be established has been raised in Japan.[102] But the history, political culture and legal system of a country may be such that it is not receptive to the concept and institution of a specialized constitutional court. It is difficult to argue in the abstract that it is desirable to have such a court in every country. On the other hand, precisely because constitutional courts are highly specialized judicial institutions, it is possible that they may be better equipped than ordinary courts to perform the tasks that constitutional courts specialize in handling. Indeed, some of these tasks, including the core task of constitutional review of laws, may need to be effectively performed even in countries that are not liberal democratic, as the constitutional discourses in contemporary China and Vietnam reveal.[103] Insofar as the quest for constitutionalism and the rule of law is a universal aspiration of humankind in the contemporary world, the study of constitutional courts is and will remain important and relevant to the progress of our civilization.

[102] See Hasebe, Chapter 12.
[103] See Chapter 13 by Zhang (on China) and Chapter 14 by Bui (on Vietnam).

2

Constitutional Review in Asia

A Comparative Perspective

CHERYL SAUNDERS

I Introduction

Most, although by no means all, jurisdictions in Asia provide for constitutional review in the sense of judicial review of legislation by reference to the requirements of the national constitution. As with so much else in Asia, the institutions, principles and processes through which judicial review occurs are extraordinarily diverse.[1] The purpose of this chapter is to begin a process of mapping them so as to develop a deeper understanding of their similarities and differences, as well as insights into why they take their current form. The chapter thus offers a foundation for comparison of approaches to judicial review within Asia for the variety of purposes that comparison serves. It may also contribute to comparison between Asia and other regions of the world to the extent that regional generalization is plausible.[2] In any event, understanding the range of approaches to judicial review within Asia is integral to understanding the constitutional experience of the world as a whole.

Many points of differentiation might be used for this purpose. Most go to the contexts in which judicial review operates, which might be variously described in terms of the prevailing concept of constitutionalism[3]

[1] Cheryl Saunders, 'The impact of internationalisation on national constitutions' in Albert H. Y. Chen (ed.), *Constitutionalism in Asia in the Early Twenty-First Century* (Cambridge: Cambridge University Press, 2014) 391–415, 412–414.

[2] Ibid., 411.

[3] See, for an example, Li-ann Thio, '"We are feeling our way forward, step by step": The continuing Singapore experiment in the construction of communitarian constitutionalism in the twenty-first century's first decade', in Albert H. Y. Chen (ed.), *Constitutionalism in Asia in the Early Twenty-First Century* (Cambridge: Cambridge University Press, 2014) 270–294.

or the stage that constitutionalism has reached.[4] Factors of this kind have a bearing on any comparative project to a degree that depends on the goals that are being sought. The point of differentiation that is the particular focus of this chapter, however, concerns the distinction between diffuse and concentrated judicial review or, to put it more simply, the distinction between judicial review by ordinary and specialist constitutional courts.[5] Of course, the conclusions that are drawn must necessarily be tempered by the potential impact of other differentiating factors. The design of judicial review is sufficiently discrete, however, to suggest that the distinction between forms of review may be useful as a building block in any attempt at taxonomy as long as the claims for it are not overblown.

A focus on this distinction has other advantages for present purposes as well. It assists in tracing and explaining other differences in matters of important detail in the practice of judicial review in Asian jurisdictions insofar as the choice between diffuse or concentrated judicial review rests on assumptions about the demands of a separation of powers.[6] Moreover, this focus fits the wider theme of this volume. In addition, on the basis that, throughout Asia, judicial review of any kind is a transplant, this approach to the chapter provides an opportunity to investigate the dynamics of transplants in public law as well. Most obviously, it offers a case study on how institutions are modified, deliberately or inadvertently, when they are adopted by one jurisdiction from another. Given the nature of judicial review, it also has the potential to throw some light

[4] Albert H. Y. Chen canvasses several classifications and suggests one of his own in 'The achievement of constitutionalism in Asia: Moving beyond "constitutions without constitutionalism"', in Albert H. Y. Chen (ed.), *Constitutionalism in Asia in the Early Twenty-First Century* (Cambridge: Cambridge University Press, 2014) 1–31. For other formulations see, for example, Mark Tushnet and Madhav Khosla (eds.), *Unstable Constitutionalism* (Cambridge: Cambridge University Press, 2015) and Jiunn-rong Yeh and Wen-Chen Chang, 'The changing landscapes of modern constitutionalism: Transitional perspective' (2009) 4 *National Taiwan University Law Review* 145.

[5] For the distinction in using this terminology, see, for example, Lech Garlicki, 'Democracy and international influences' in Georg Nolte (ed.), *European and US Constitutionalism* (Cambridge: Cambridge University Press, 2005) 263–279, at 276–277. Other terminology is also in use, however, including decentralized and centralized, as in Albert H. Y. Chen and Miguel Polares Maduro, 'The judiciary and constitutional review', in Mark Tushnet, Thomas Fleiner and Cheryl Saunders (eds.), *Routledge Handbook of Constitutional Law* (Abingdon, UK: Routledge, 2013) 97.

[6] An argument to this effect is made, for example, in John Henry Merryman and Rogelio Pérez-Perdomo, *The Civil Law Tradition: An Introduction to the Legal Systems of Europe and Latin America*, 3rd edn. (Stanford, CA: Stanford University Press, 2007) 89–90.

on the question of what happens to underlying constitutional theories that have been developed to explain conditions in donor jurisdictions when the institution to which they relate is adopted for use elsewhere. These issues are not purely of theoretical interest. They have practical relevance for decisions about the form of judicial review that should be put in place in any one of the host of new constitutions that continue to be made across the world, including in the Asia-Pacific region.

This chapter begins, in Section II, by examining the distinction between diffuse and concentrated review in their origins and as they have evolved over time. In relation to each approach to review, the chapter considers the concept of judicial review that is in play, including its defining characteristics and underlying rationale; the structure of judicial review, including questions about the composition of courts and the terms and conditions of judges; key features of the process of judicial review as conducted under each approach; and the range of functions that courts perform in the course of judicial review or as an adjunct to it. Section III of the chapter moves to the design of judicial review in Asian jurisdictions in light of the conclusions from Section II, including the extent to which the dichotomy between these two broad approaches holds good and the nature of deviations from it. A final concluding section attempts an assessment of whether the distinction between diffuse and concentrated review remains relevant to judicial review in Asia and, if so, how.

II Diffuse and Concentrated Review

1 Dichotomy

The critical distinction between diffuse and concentrated judicial review is that in the former, generalist courts determine the constitutional validity of legislation while also dealing with the standard range of other legal questions, and in the latter, the authority to invalidate legislation is vested in a specialist body generally called a constitutional court.[7] In origin, each approach has a rationale of its own. The choice between the two also has implications for institutional design and for the process and function of judicial review. Neither approach is either monolithic or

[7] Useful sources on the properties of the two approaches include Chen and Maduro, note 5, and Lech Garlicki, 'Constitutional courts versus supreme courts' (2007) 5 *International Journal of Constitutional Law* 44–68.

static, however.[8] Core features aside, there are many variations within each type on matters of important detail.

As a generalization, diffuse review tends to be associated with common law legal systems and concentrated review with civil law systems, both empirically and conceptually. Empirically, with relatively few exceptions, constitutional courts across the world are typically embedded in civil law systems, while common law systems typically use diffuse review in some form.[9] To some extent, at least, differences between these two legal traditions seed the rationale for differences in the approach to judicial review. And the characteristics of each of the legal traditions in which the approaches to judicial review are embedded tend to differentiate them further in relation to, for example, the sources of law and the style of judicial reasoning.

As a further generalization, each of the legal systems tends to be associated with particular constitutional traditions, further augmenting the respective characteristics of diffuse and concentrated review. Thus, significantly for present purposes, differences in assumptions about the role of courts in resolving questions of public law in constitutional traditions historically influenced by France and the United Kingdom, respectively, affect the way in which judicial power is treated within a framework for a separation of powers and feeds into the choice between concentrated and diffuse review. In an example of a different kind, the gradual transition to constitutional monarchy in the British constitutional tradition seeded the practice that persists in many common law states whereby the executive branch appoints judges.[10]

Generalizations that link particular forms of judicial review to either legal systems or constitutional traditions necessarily offer only a starting point, however, which may be disproved or eroded by further inquiry. Legal families are not monolithic. Constitutional traditions are always in

[8] Merryman and Pérez-Perdomo, note 6, 147.

[9] The listing by the Venice Commission shows that around eighteen states, most of which are in Latin America or Scandinavia, depart from this rule of thumb. www.venice.coe.int/webforms/courts/.

[10] The practice is changing significantly as Commonwealth countries introduce judicial commissions or comparable bodies to play a role in judicial appointments in the interest of protecting judicial independence: J. van Zyl Smit, *The Appointment, Tenure and Removal of Judges under Commonwealth Principles: A Compendium and Analysis of Best Practice (Report of Research Undertaken by Bingham Centre for the Rule of Law)* (London: British Institute of International and Comparative Law, 2015) 16. The underlying practice of executive appointment, however, helps to explain both the powers of these bodies and the debates associated with them.

flux and highly context dependent. There are variations on matters of important detail between polities within each of the categories of diffuse and concentrated review. In addition, there are important exceptions to the equation of diffuse review with common law systems and concentrated review with civilian legal systems. The exceptions disturb both assumptions. Diffuse review is found in association with a significant number of civil law legal systems, particularly in Latin America and Scandinavia but also including, for example, Japan. Hybrid forms of review exist in both common law and civil law states, in which a generalist apex court has exclusive authority to determine the constitutional validity of legislation.[11] Specialist constitutional courts can be found in some states with common law or mixed legal systems. South Africa is a notable example, but there are signs that recourse to constitutional courts is increasing, drawing on the South African case and taking pragmatic advantage of the opportunity to create a new court in a country in transition.[12]

The range and significance of these exceptions suggest the need for analytical caution but do not negate the insights that can be derived from the putative links between approaches to judicial review and legal systems. It can be readily accepted, as Brewer-Carías has argued, that concentrated review is 'compatible with any legal system'.[13] Transplanting these approaches to judicial review across legal systemic lines nevertheless has consequences that tend to highlight the links of each approach with the legal system from which it derived. Thus, for example, the common law preference for resolving legal problems by reference to all applicable law, constitutional or not, finally prevailed in South Africa when the seventeenth amendment authorized the constitutional court to deal with non-constitutional matters.[14] In an example of another kind, the style of judicial reasoning in ordinary courts in civil law systems is not necessarily conducive to constitutional adjudication. This may be, at least in part, the explanation for the restrained approach to constitutional

[11] Chen and Maduro, note 5, 99–100.

[12] Thus, for example, in Zimbabwe, with a mixed legal system, the new constitution of 2013 provides for a constitutional court that 'decides only constitutional matters' (sec. 167(1)(b)).

[13] Allan-Randolph Brewer-Carías, *Judicial Review in Comparative Law (Cambridge Studies in International and Comparative Law)* (Cambridge: Cambridge University Press, 1989) 186.

[14] Constitution of South Africa, sec. 167(3).

review in Denmark, Sweden and Finland, where diffuse review applies.[15] It also assists in explaining Chile's decision, in 2005, to establish a discrete constitutional court.[16]

In what follows, I will sketch the principal characteristics of both of these approaches to review before examining their application in Asia. For the purposes of comparison, the characteristics of each case are organized around four broad categories: concept, structure, process and function. Concept identifies the key features of the approach and the rationales for it. Under the headings of structure and process, I deal, respectively, with the composition of the court or courts with authority to review the constitutional validity of legislation and the principal features of the procedures that are used for the purpose. The category of function comprises both the scope of the constitutional jurisdiction of the court and any other aspects of its responsibilities for adjudication.

2 *Diffuse Review*

Concept

The core characteristic of diffuse review is that, typically, generalist courts apply all sources of law to resolve all kinds of legal questions, including the constitutional validity of legislation, where it is constitutionally allowed. Constitutional questions, which also necessarily involve interpretation of the constitution, may be entertained by any court, although important questions are likely to be finally resolved on appeal by the highest court in a generalist court hierarchy. Once this occurs, in a common law setting, the decision binds all lower courts through a doctrine of precedent, reinforced by *stare decisis*.[17] The doctrine of precedent is, in turn, interdependent with a style of judicial reasoning that is inductive, builds solutions by analogy and may involve fine distinctions, drawing on facts.[18] Cases that appear to present a constitutional problem may be resolved instead by

[15] Victor Ferreres Comella, 'The European model of constitutional review of legislation: Toward decentralization?' (2004) 2 *International Journal of Constitutional Law* 461–491, 462.

[16] Javier Couso, Domingo Lovera Parmo, Matías Guiloff and Alberto Coddou, *Constitutional Law in Chile* (Alphen aan den Rijn, The Netherlands: Wolters Kluwer, 2011) 124–125.

[17] The former has been a characteristic of common law reasoning for centuries; the latter emerged in the nineteenth century, H. Patrick Glenn, *Legal Traditions of the World*, 3rd edn. (Oxford: Oxford University Press, 2007), 238, 246.

[18] Glenn, note 17, 238.

interpretation of the challenged statute or by recourse to other legislation or common law principles.

Diffuse review is the corollary of a commitment to a single system of generalist courts, applying the whole law in a manner that typifies the design of common law legal systems.[19] Generalist courts also deal with the lawfulness of executive action, placing a premium on the importance of judicial independence.[20] The authority of courts to determine the lawfulness of public action is regarded as consistent with, or even required by, the separation of powers.[21] The link made by A. V. Dicey between judicial review and the rule of law remains essential to an understanding of the latter.[22] There is no sharp distinction between public and private law in the common law legal tradition. A principle of parliamentary sovereignty derived from constitutional evolution in what became the United Kingdom inhibited judicial review of the constitutionality of legislation until the advent of written, entrenched constitutions. Once review of the validity of legislation became accepted as constitutionally possible, however, it was logical for the ordinary generalist courts to perform this function as well.

The justification often given for the extension of the authority of ordinary courts to encompass review of the validity of legislation draws on the reasoning of *Marbury* v. *Madison.*[23] In the face of conflict between statute and constitution, a court applies the latter as a higher source of law. In fact, however, the enforcement of higher law through judicial review by ordinary courts was familiar in any colony in which domestic law had been subject to the overriding authority of the British Parliament.[24] Constitutional review by ordinary courts typically does not raise questions of legitimacy per se, although criticism can be expected if a court is deemed to have overstepped the limits of the judicial role, the precise understanding of which varies between states.

[19] The generalist character of courts is subject, of course, to jurisdictional limits imposed by constitutions or statutes by which specialist courts may also be established for particular types of matters.

[20] On the historical reasons for the evolution of judicial independence in its common law form, see Glenn, note 17, 244. The point in the text is made in, for example, *Harris* v. *Caladine,* (1991) 172 CLR 84, 159, McHugh J.

[21] *Plaintiff S157/2002* v. *Commonwealth* (2003) 211 CLR 476 substantiates both points.

[22] Lord Bingham, 'The Rule of Law' (2007) 66 *Cambridge Law Journal* 67–85.

[23] 5 US 137 (1803).

[24] Cheryl Saunders, 'It seems . . . to be a leading case', in Elizabeth Zoller (ed.), *Marbury v Madison 1803–2003, A French-American Dialogue* (Paris: Dalloz, 2003) 97.

Treatment of the constitution as another source of law coupled with the doctrine of binding precedent gives decisions of unconstitutionality retrospective effect, at least as a default position.[25]

Structure

The detail of the structure of a system of diffuse review follows logically from this explanation of its rationale. Courts are staffed by judges deemed capable of dealing with the range of legal questions that come before them. The distinctive demands of constitutional review may be reflected in appointments to the highest court but even here are tempered by the need for judges to have generalist capability of a high order. Many, and in some cases all, judges are drawn from the legal profession after a lengthy and relatively distinguished career in practice, during which they have had ample time to develop lawyerly skills in forensic procedures and legal reasoning. The independence of the practicing Bar serves to reinforce the culture of judicial independence on which the common law places such store.[26]

Judicial independence also underlies the procedures for appointment to courts and judicial tenure and conditions. The classical trifecta is that judges are appointed by the head of state on advice of the elected government, hold office 'during good behaviour' and receive remuneration that cannot be diminished during their period of service. Appointment of judges by the executive alone now seems at odds with judicial independence, although it persists in some jurisdictions, including Australia, where it works reasonably well, underpinned by legal and political culture. Increasingly, however, appointment by a process that is mediated in some way by a more independent commission is becoming the norm.[27] The United States has always been atypical in this regard, with its requirement for Senate approval of presidential nominations to federal courts, including the Supreme Court.[28] In other respects, however, the terms and conditions under which judges hold office follow a broadly familiar pattern. Typically, they are appointed for life or until a relatively late retirement age. Removal is possible, for cause, through a procedure

[25] In Australia, for example, prospective overruling is precluded by the local understanding of judicial power, *Ha* v. *New South Wales* (1997) 189 CLR 465.

[26] Anthony Mason, 'The independence of the bench; the independence of the bar and the bar's role in the judicial system' (1993) 19 *Commonwealth Law Bulletin* 753–760.

[27] van Zyl Smit, note 10.

[28] Constitution of the United States, Art. 2, sec. 2.

that involves the legislature, is politically complex and, in most jurisdictions, is rarely used. The level of remuneration and, perhaps, associated terms and conditions are protected by the constitution, constitutional convention or both.[29]

Procedure

The procedures for a system of diffuse review also follow logically from its rationale. Constitutional questions typically arise in concrete cases brought by a plaintiff deemed by the applicable standing rules to have a sufficient interest in the matter. These characteristics reflect the interdependence of facts and law in common law judicial reasoning. Concrete review is the norm, and determination of abstract questions may be precluded on constitutional grounds as inconsistent with the role of a judge under the prevailing conception of separation of powers.[30] In these circumstances, judicial review cannot take place until legislation is promulgated and there is a competent plaintiff. There are some jurisdictions with diffuse review, of which Canada and India are examples, where constitutional questions can be raised before a court in an abstract form, without a factual setting, typically at the instance of the government.[31] However, what is often called an 'advisory opinion' is unlikely to have precedential effect as a matter of law, although in practise, it may be highly influential.[32]

Hearings for the purposes of diffuse review are typically oral and adversarial and open to the public. Where cases are determined by a bench of multiple judges, decisions may involve multiple opinions, both concurring and dissenting. Judicial reasons are often lengthy, discursive and fact dependent. The availability of an effective remedy is an important consideration that shapes the conception of judicial power and may preclude review in some cases.

[29] See, by way of example, Constitution of the Commonwealth of Australia, sec. 72.

[30] The claims of textual support for this doctrine in the United States and Australia – 'cases and controversies' in the former (Art. 3, sec. 2) and 'matter' in the latter (secs. 75, 76) – themselves rely on assumptions about the nature of adjudication. See, respectively, *Muskrat* v. *United States* 219 US 346 (1911) and *In re Judiciary and Navigation Acts* (1921) 29 CLR 257.

[31] Supreme Court Act RSC 1985 c. S-26, s.53 (Canada), upheld by *Reference re Reference Jurisdiction* 43 SCR 536 (1910); Constitution of India, Art. 143.

[32] James L. Huffman and MardiLyn Saathoff, 'Advisory opinions and Canadian constitutional development: The supreme court's reference jurisdiction' (1990) 74 *Minnesota Law Review* 1281–1283.

Function

Courts performing the function of judicial review in conditions of diffuse review apply all justiciable parts of a constitution against all actors bound by it, whether public or private. It follows that such courts may apply the constitution against the executive or the administration as well as the legislature. It also follows that constitutional questions may invoke structural provisions, including those dealing with separation of powers or devolution, in addition to those dealing with rights. There is no necessary procedural distinction between structural and rights-based constitutional questions as long as there is a justiciable issue. Nor is there any necessary distinction, procedural or otherwise, between the capacity of citizens and public authorities to mount a constitutional challenge as long as the requirements of standing are met.

Conversely, courts in a system of diffuse review in a common law setting typically do not perform functions other than the determination of questions of law (including constitutional law) in a concrete case. In a possible exception, attributable historically to the evolution of parliament, they may also resolve questions about disputed elections, sitting in reconstituted form as a court of disputed returns.[33] The standard remedies that a court may give typically derive from those that have been adapted over time for public law purposes: the prerogative remedies of prohibition, *certiorari*, mandamus and *habeas corpus*, and the equitable remedies of declaration and injunction. Judgments of a court are enforceable directly, and failure to comply may mean contempt of court.

3 *Concentrated Review*

Concept

The core characteristic of concentrated review is that a specialist constitutional court has exclusive authority to invalidate legislation on the basis of inconsistency with the constitution.[34] The constitutional court co-exists with a system of ordinary courts, often also organized along specialist lines that separate public from private law.[35] Typically, judges

[33] Graeme Orr, *Ritual and Rhythm in Electoral Systems: A Comparative Legal Account* (Farnham, UK: Ashgate Publishing, 2015) 174.
[34] Ferreres Comella, 'The European model', note 15, 465.
[35] Merryman and Pérez-Perdomo, note 6, 134–135.

of these courts are members of a career judiciary, reflecting the expectations of their role as technical rather than creative.[36]

This dualism[37] makes it necessary to identify the line that divides the jurisdiction of the constitutional court from that of other courts. Exactly where the line lies varies between states and over time.[38] Typically, however, at the very least, only the constitutional court can determine the constitutional validity of legislation *erga omnes*.[39] Familiar battlegrounds include the authority of a constitutional court to interpret statutes so as to comply with the constitution,[40] the extent of the authority of ordinary courts to determine the meaning of the constitution in the course of interpreting statutes[41] and the precedential weight of decisions of the constitutional court and the reasoning on which they are based.[42]

The rationale for concentrated review, as explained by its original theorist, Hans Kelsen, stemmed from the need for legal certainty in the interpretation and application of the constitution in the absence of a formal doctrine of precedent, the effect of which was compounded by multiple specialist court hierarchies.[43] In these conditions, if ordinary courts had jurisdiction to, for example, disapply what they considered to be an unconstitutional statutory provision, there would be no necessary consistency in the meaning attributed to the constitution.[44] The spread of specialist constitutional courts as the preferred vehicle for constitutional review in continental Europe in the latter part of the twentieth century was encouraged by an understanding of the separation of powers that placed formidable barriers in the way of conferring constitutional jurisdiction on ordinary courts particularly if, as the situation required, decisions had binding effect.[45] This conception of separation of powers

[36] Ibid., 36–37.

[37] The term is used by Victor Ferreres Comella, 'The consequences of centralizing constitutional review in a specialist court: Some thoughts on judicial activism' (2003–2004) 82 *Texas Law Review* 1705–1736 at 1706.

[38] Lech Garlicki, 'Constitutional Courts versus Supreme Courts', note 7, 44.

[39] Merryman and Pérez-Perdomo, note 6, 141.

[40] Ferreres Comella, 'The European model', note 15, 472–473.

[41] Garlicki, 'Constitutional Courts versus Supreme Courts', note 7, 58–59.

[42] Ibid., 59.

[43] Hans Kelsen, 'Judicial review of legislation: A comparative study of the Austrian and the American constitution' (1942) 4 *The Journal of Politics* 183–200; Ferreres Comella, 'Consequences', note 37, 1705.

[44] Comella, 'The European Model', note 15, 465.

[45] Sandrine Baume, *Hans Kelsen and the Case for Democracy*, John Zvesper (trans.) (Essex, UK: ECPR Press, 2012) 37.

was an amalgam of several elements: a relatively sharp division between public and private law; reluctance to accept a lawmaking role for judges, however vestigial; and respect for decisions of the legislature as the legitimate lawmaking institution. It was reinforced over time by judicial education and training, based on the same assumptions.[46]

The alternative was to create a specialist constitutional court outside the ordinary court hierarchies that could annul a statute that was found to contravene the constitution, thus performing a 'negative act of legislation'.[47] Such a holding would not necessarily be retrospective in its operation (except, perhaps, in an instant case) and might be prospective, to enable the legislature to replace the statute that had been annulled.[48] In recognition of the legislative character of the function of the court, judges would be elected by the parliament, using each house as an electoral college for half the appointments, in an endeavour both to enhance the democratic credentials of the court and to secure its independence.[49] This rationale for concentrated or centralized review broadly held true, with occasional misgivings, as the jurisdiction of constitutional courts expanded to encompass rights provisions,[50] the avenues of access to such courts increased[51] and the techniques of adjudication on constitutional questions took on the characteristics of positive legislation as well.[52]

Other rationales for the establishment of constitutional courts have been suggested more recently that are not necessarily connected to the conditions of civil law legal systems. Several are linked to the demands of transition from an authoritarian or totalitarian regime. In these circumstances, a constitutional court offers the opportunity to create a new court, with new judges who are not tainted by association with the previous regime, while leaving the existing court system more or less intact, consistent with the standards of judicial independence.[53] Provision for a constitutional court can also perform an expressivist function, symbolizing commitment to a new constitution and the rights that it

46 Chen and Maduro, note 5, 101; Merryman, note 6, 37.

47 Kelsen, note 43, 187.

48 Ibid.

49 Ibid., 188. The advantages from the standpoint of democracy are elaborated by Ferreres Comella, 'The European model', note 15, 468.

50 Chen and Maduro, note 5, 98.

51 Ibid., 99.

52 Garlicki, 'Democracy and international influences', note 5, 276.

53 Jan Komárek, 'National constitutional courts in the European constitutional democracy' (2014) 12 *International Journal of Constitutional Law* 525–544.

protects.[54] Establishment of a new court does not always serve the benign purpose that this justification suggests, however: it can also be used for authoritarian purposes to create a forum more likely to support the regime.[55]

Structure

Consistent with the original rationale for them, constitutional courts are organized in a way that gives them a degree of democratic legitimacy and that contrasts sharply with the procedures for the appointment of ordinary judges in civil law jurisdictions. Ferreres Comella describes the composition of such courts as 'political' rather than 'bureaucratic', appropriate for a body with a function of this kind.[56] Typically, the authority to make appointments to constitutional courts is shared by two or more organs of elected government that are deemed to have a stake in constitutional interpretation. Appointments generally are for a relatively long but non-renewable term and are staggered so as to ensure continuity of experience on the court. These features offer the potential for constitutional courts to comprise members with a variety of different skills, ranging from the technical expertise of serving judges, to the political savvy of former politicians, to the conceptual insights of constitutional scholars. Diversifying the appointment process also provides some protection for judicial independence from the elected branches while, at the same time, drawing a degree of legitimacy from them. Constitutional courts can be fragile, nevertheless. They lack the institutional longevity of ordinary courts. The difficulties of drawing clear jurisdictional boundaries around constitutional matters also increase the likelihood of ongoing tensions between the two.

Procedure

As originally conceived, a constitutional court would determine a question about the constitutionality of a statute in the abstract, at the instance of an organ of the state or a level of the government.[57] This procedure enhances the goal of legal certainty by decoupling decisions about validity from particular facts, and in that sense, it is closely linked to the very

[54] Ferreres Comella, 'Consequences', note 37, 1711.

[55] See, for example, the critique of the creation of a constitutional court by Mahmoud Abbas in Palestine in April 2016, www.abc.net.au/news/2016-04-11/palestinian-leader-establishes-constitutional-court/7318148 (accessed 3 July 2018).

[56] Ferreres Comella, 'Consequences', note 37, 1707; 'The European Model', note 15, 468.

[57] For a review of the range of organs entitled to file cases in constitutional courts in Europe, see Ferreres Comella, 'The Consequences', note 37, 1709, fn. 12.

concept of a court of this kind.[58] By removing private parties from the procedure, it is also consistent with the idea that a constitutional court, as negative legislator, acts in the public interest.[59] By definition, there is no necessary objection to *a priori* review under this model, drawn either from the absence of a factual setting or from a conception of the separation of powers.[60]

More usually now, however, there are also other ways to approach a constitutional court. The most common involves reference to the constitutional court of a constitutional question that arises in an ordinary court in the course of concrete proceedings,[61] thus requiring incidental review.[62] In these circumstances, the court suspends the proceedings until a decision on constitutional validity is made, enabling the case to be determined. In addition, in many, but not all, systems of concentrated review, an individual may file a constitutional complaint to claim that his or her fundamental rights have been violated or not vindicated by earlier judicial proceedings.[63] This procedure comes closest to those that apply in diffuse review, although by definition, it is available only in relation to parts of the constitution and typically requires other remedies to be exhausted first. Both of these additional procedures for approaching a constitutional court establish a more direct relationship with ordinary courts, potentially presenting tensions that are resolved in different ways in different jurisdictions.[64]

Consistent with its original rationale, procedures before a constitutional court may take place on the papers, without an oral or public hearing, although this is no longer necessarily the case. In a practice that derives from its association with the civil law tradition, it is not unusual for a constitutional court to deliver a single set of reasons without published dissent.[65] It has been suggested that continuation of the

58 Ferreres Comella, 'The European Model', note 15, 466.
59 Kelsen, note 43, 193, 195.
60 Maartje de Visser, *Constitutional Review in Europe* (Oxford: Hart Publishing, 2015) 96.
61 Comella, 'The Consequences', note 37, 1709.
62 Garlicki, 'Constitutional Courts versus Supreme Courts', note 7, 46. Garlicki notes that incidental review emerged within a decade of the establishment of the first constitutional court in Austria.
63 Comella, note 37, 1710.
64 For a detailed review of the position in Europe, see de Visser, note 60, 377–392.
65 Katalin Kelemen, 'Dissenting opinions in constitutional courts' (2013) 14 *German Law Journal* 1345–1371.

practice is useful for strengthening the fragile independence of constitutional courts.[66] Increasingly, however, publication of dissenting opinions is allowed as courts consolidate their authority or newly established courts adopt the practices of others.[67] In some states, acceptance of dissent in the constitutional court contrasts with the practice elsewhere in the judicial system, for reasons that may be attributable to the monopoly that the court enjoys over constitutional questions. In an interesting variation, in some jurisdictions, dissents are published not with the majority opinion but in other places and at other times.[68]

Functions

The core function of a constitutional court is to determine the constitutional validity of a statute. Such courts do not necessarily deal with all other constitutional questions, at least some of which may fall to the administrative jurisdiction or to other ordinary courts.[69] In any event, consistent with the rationale for this model of review, a constitutional court has no authority to resolve legal questions by reference to other legal standards.[70] While the effects of its constitutional decisions may, in fact, permeate the rest of the legal system, this is a manifestation of concentrated review in operation rather than a departure from it.[71]

Constitutional courts may also be given other particular functions relating to the proper functioning of the political process.[72] De Visser identifies four broad categories of these in the European context, encompassing electoral disputes, presidential impeachment, proscription of political parties and supervision of the regularity of referendums.[73] The list is not necessarily exhaustive. It is sufficiently wide-ranging, however, for the following observations to be made. All of these functions are critical to the proper functioning of the constitutional order, broadly conceived. Most involve the application of legal (although not necessarily

[66] Comella, 'The Consequences', note 37, 1729.

[67] Kelemen, note 65, 1350.

[68] Ibid., 1351, referring to Latvia, Slovenia and the Czech Republic.

[69] De Visser, note 60, 123.

[70] Christof Möllers, 'Scope and legitimacy of judicial review in German constitutional law – The court versus the political process', in Hermann Pünder and Christian Waldhoff (eds.), *Debates in German Public Law* (Oxford: Hart Publishing, 2014) 3–26, 8.

[71] Axel Tschentscher, 'Interpreting fundamental rights – Freedom versus optimization' in Hermann Pünder and Christian Waldhoff (eds.), *Debates in German Public Law* (Oxford: Hart Publishing, 2014) 43–56, 45.

[72] De Visser, note 60, 168–185.

[73] Ibid.

constitutional) standards to a contested issue, sometimes at the instance of individual complainants.[74] The standards in question may, however, involve the exercise of broad evaluative discretion by the court on matters of great political significance. The authority of the Conseil Constitutionnel of France to advise on a referendum question put to voters is an admittedly extreme example.[75] A constitutional court offers an obvious convenience for functions of this kind, as a body with specialist constitutional expertise, some democratic legitimacy, and institutional independence, which nevertheless, is distinct from the ordinary courts.

4 *Points of Contrast*

Of course, both of these approaches to constitutional review are in flux. Within each of the two broad categories, there are considerable variations, stemming from original design choices or from adaptations over time to deal with emerging needs. There has been significant cross-fertilization between the two, causing the boundaries to be blurred and justifying claims of convergence.[76] Thus, to take only a few examples, forms of abstract review can be identified on both sides of the divide, *de facto* if not *de jure*; procedures for individual complaint are common in both approaches to review, and the significance of apex courts in most systems of diffuse review creates at least some of the effects of specialization.

Even so, general points of contrast remain, which can assist with mutual understanding and comparative analysis.

Historically, each of these approaches was informed by different theoretical assumptions about the role that courts can and should play given the requirements of the separation of powers, as variously understood. Purely theoretical differences of this kind may be diminishing through cross-fertilization of ideas and the dynamics of transplants, although the extent to which this is so remains to be tested. Their effects, in any event, continue to be reinforced by ongoing differences in institutional realities, including the training and experience of judges, the formal arrangements for binding precedent, the range of sources of law, the conceptions of judicial power and the design of court systems.

In addition, each of these approaches must grapple with some problems that are non-existent or relatively unimportant in the other. By way

[74] Ferreres Commella, 'The Consequences', note 37, 1707.
[75] De Visser, note 60, 182.
[76] Merryman and Pérez-Perdomo, note 6, 38.

of example, a system of concentrated review must anticipate the problem of the relationship between the constitutional court and other courts, which is barely an issue at all in conditions of diffuse review. Conversely, however, courts in a diffuse system must decide how to manage the constraints typically associated with it, including requirements for a concrete case with its logical corollary of a competent plaintiff and the relative inflexibility of available remedies if judicial decisions are assumed to have retroactive effect.

Each of these approaches also brings a different set of perspectives to the question of legitimacy that is almost endemic to constitutional review. Concentrated review is deliberately designed to deal with this question conceptually and through institutional design. The issue is taken onboard only incidentally in diffuse review; however, where it is tackled through an assortment of mechanisms, the chief one being a limited conception of judicial power, the contours of and compliance with which are familiar fields for contestation, it may, in fact, be that the incentives for bold judicial review are different in the two approaches even if also sometimes internally contradictory. Thus, judicial review is always explicitly authorized in a system of concentrated review, whereas in diffuse review, it may simply be assumed as being incidental to the rule of law. The logic of concentrated review seems to favour less deferential review,[77] even if the institutions responsible for it are more vulnerable in practise than their diffuse review counterparts.[78]

III Mapping Constitutional Review in Asia

1 The Setting

Judicial review of the consistency of legislation with the constitution is now a global phenomenon. Approaches to review that, at least superficially, mirror diffuse or concentrated review can be found in all parts of the world. It cannot be assumed, however, that the patterns of similarity and difference that operate in one part of the world are replicated in others or, for that matter, that the types of review are the same in form or operation. For this purpose, it is useful to examine the experience of different regions more carefully, acknowledging at the same time the reality of differences within regions, between polities and over time.

[77] Ferreres Comella, 'The Consequences', note 37, 1713.
[78] Ibid., 1728.

This section explores the extent to which the distinction between diffuse and concentrated constitutional review performs a useful comparative function when mapped onto jurisdictions in Asia. The insights thus gained can assist with building a more truly global picture of constitutional review, while also enhancing understanding of constitutionalism in Asia.

Asia is one of the least cohesive regions of the world. It covers a vast territory, with indistinct boundaries that melt into Europe, the Middle East, the Pacific and Oceania. It is extraordinarily diverse in terms of culture, language, religion and governmental systems. There is no pan-Asian attempt at regional integration or human rights protection of the kinds that have encouraged convergence of constitutional arrangements elsewhere, although informal arrangements abound, fostering a sense of regional identity.[79] There is considerably greater cohesion within the subregions of which Asia is composed, although even here, diversity can be marked.[80] These considerations need to be borne in mind in a project that compares approaches to constitutional review in Asia, but they do not preclude such a comparison. On the contrary, the diversity of governing systems, stages of economic and political development and underlying cultures makes Asia a particularly interesting region from the standpoint of constitutional review. And there are commonalities in the Asian experience as well. While the region has been home to a series of ancient civilizations with deep historical roots, most of the contemporary constitutional systems are new, post-dating World War II. Constitutional review in any form is a transplant throughout the region, as are the legal systems with which it is associated and the concept of a written constitution itself.[81] The Asian experience thus offers the opportunity not only to trace the evolution of constitutional review but also to add to understandings of the complex but common global process whereby institutions migrate from one context to others that are different in most relevant respects.

This chapter considers constitutional review in twenty out of a possible thirty-three jurisdictions across four Asian subregions: East Asia,[82] South

[79] The Association of Asian Constitutional Courts and Equivalent Institutions is an example.

[80] The United Nations identifies these as Central Asia, Eastern Asia, Southern Asia, South Eastern Asia and Western Asia: UNdata, composition of macro geographical (continental) regions, geographical subregions and selected economic and other groupings, United Nations Statistics Division, https://unstats.un.org/unsd/methodology/m49/ (accessed 3 July 2018).

[81] Chen, note 4, 7–8.

[82] Hong Kong, Japan, South Korea, PRC, Taiwan, Mongolia, Vietnam.

East Asia,[83] South Asia[84] and Central Asia.[85] While not comprehensive, the sample is sufficiently extensive and varied to give a reliable indication of patterns of review across the areas of the region most commonly associated with Asia.[86] Anecdotally, it is unlikely that the experiences of the thirteen jurisdictions omitted would alter the impressions outlined below, although undoubtedly, they would enrich the detail.[87]

2 *Patterns*

Of the twenty polities covered here, two do not presently allow any form of judicial review of the constitutional validity of legislation: The People's Republic of China and Vietnam.[88] In addition, the position of two others requires qualification in this connection. The first, Sri Lanka, presently allows preview by the supreme court of the constitutionality of legislation, but on such restrictive terms that the option has been described as 'illusory'.[89] It seems at least possible, however, that the constitution-making process under way in Sri Lanka will provide for a more comprehensive form of constitutional review through a specialist constitutional court or a constitutional bench of the supreme court.[90] The second concerns Hong Kong, where judicial review is available but is not, in all cases, final. The Hong Kong Court of Final Appeal may, in some circumstances, be required to seek and

83 Malaysia, Singapore, Thailand, Philippines, Indonesia, Myanmar, Cambodia.

84 Bangladesh, Sri Lanka, India, Nepal, Pakistan.

85 Uzbekistan.

86 The eighteen states of Western Asia are more commonly treated as part of a region that also includes North Africa and/or the Mediterranean and are not covered here.

87 These are: Macao, North Korea, Brunei, Lao People's Democratic Republic, Timor-Leste, Afghanistan, Bhutan, Iran, Maldives, Kazakhstan, Kyrgyzstan, Tajikistan and Turkmenistan.

88 In both countries, the legislature itself reviews whether laws conform to the constitution, Wen-Chen Chang, Li-ann Thio, Kevin Y. L. Tan and Jiunn-rong Yeh, *Constitutionalism in Asia: Cases and Materials* (Oxford: Hart Publishing, 2014) 309.

89 Sec. 121 requires a petition to be filed within one week of a bill being placed on the order paper. For other restrictions and analyses, see International Crisis Group, *Sri Lanka's Judiciary: Politicised Courts, Compromised Rights* (2009) 172 *Crisis Group Asia Report* 5, also quoting a 1997 report of the International Commission of Jurists.

90 Asanga Welikala, 'Sri Lanka's search for constitutional consensus amid social and political divisions' (2016, July 19) *Constitutionnet*, www.constitutionnet.org/news/sri-lankas-search-constitutional-consensus-amid-social-and-political-divisions (accessed 3 July 2018); Tom Daly, 'A constitutional court for Sri Lanka? Perceptions, potential and pitfalls' (2017) 15 *Centre for Policy Alternatives CPA Working Papers on Constitutional Reform.*

act upon an interpretation of the Basic Law by the Standing Committee of the National People's Congress.[91]

The seventeen polities, now including Hong Kong, that recognize some form of constitutional review divide almost equally between models that might broadly be associated with diffuse review and concentrated review. Nine accept judicial review by at least the apex general court: Hong Kong, Japan, Malaysia, Singapore, the Philippines, Bangladesh, India, Nepal and Pakistan. Eight empower a constitutional court or constitutional tribunal to carry out judicial review: South Korea, Mongolia, Taiwan, Thailand, Indonesia, Myanmar, Cambodia and Uzbekistan. If Sri Lanka is added to the mix, the number of jurisdictions that rely on a form of diffuse review increases by one.

In very general terms, these two approaches to constitutional review in Asia possess the principal characteristics respectively associated with each of them elsewhere in the world in terms of concept, structure, procedure and function.[92] Collectively, they also display at least the standard range of variations encountered elsewhere in relation to, for example, methods of appointment of judges, the mix of abstract and concrete review, the additional functions that constitutional courts exercise and the format and style of judicial reasons.[93]

Three more specific observations about their constitution, structure and functions should be made, however, for comparative purposes.

First, in this sample of seventeen jurisdictions, there is currently remarkable consistency with the rule of thumb that situates diffuse and concentrated review in common law and civil law legal systems, respectively.[94] Changes that have occurred over time have further reinforced the connection.[95] There also are exceptions, however, which are instructive.

[91] Basic Law, Art. 158; Sir Anthony Mason, 'The Hong Kong court of final appeal' (2001) 2 *Melbourne Journal of International Law* 216.

[92] See, for example, the analysis of the rationale for centralized review in Chang et al., note 88, 308.

[93] Some of these are captured for some jurisdictions in Chang et al., note 88, chap. 5.

[94] There has been some movement over time. For example, constitutional review in South Korea was modelled on diffuse review between 1963 and 1972, Chang et al., note 88, 310. Sri Lanka, with a mixed jurisdiction, also had a (very weak) constitutional court from 1972 to 1978, International Crisis Group, note 89, 3.

[95] Thus, Sri Lanka moved its very weak form of constitutional review into the supreme court in 1978, and South Korea replaced hybrid review with a constitutional court in 1987, Chang et al., note 88, 331, 328.

Japan is a particularly interesting case in which the supreme court in an otherwise civilian legal system has powers of constitutional review.[96] Constitutional review is often claimed to be a conservative institution in Japan, judged at least by its record of invalidating statutes.[97] It is possible that this reflects the syndrome observed in other civil law systems in which constitutional review is carried out by ordinary judges through diffuse review: that a judiciary trained in the practice and procedure of the civil law does not readily adapt to the more creative challenges of interpretation and application of a constitution.[98] On this basis, while there are many cultural and institutional factors that can assist in explaining the passivity of constitutional review in Japan, it may be attributable as well to the competing influences inherent in this form of cross-systemic borrowing.[99] Yasuo Hasebe's Chapter 12 in this volume hints at a more nuanced explanation, however.[100] A judicial court such as the supreme court of Japan has a range of procedural and doctrinal means at its disposal to resolve constitutional challenges, which fall short of a finding of the invalidity of a law and which, typically, are not available to a constitutional court. Viewed from this perspective, it may be that the conservatism of the supreme court of Japan has been overstated to the extent that it depends on the number of laws invalidated, using constitutional courts as the relevant comparator.

Conversely, in essentially common law Myanmar,[101] the power of constitutional review is conferred on a constitutional tribunal under the constitution of 2008, broadly along lines that characterize a system of concentrated review.[102] Adoption of this approach followed a long period

[96] Arts. 76, 81. Art. 76(2) precludes establishment of any 'extraordinary tribunal'.

[97] For example, in David S. Law, 'Why has judicial review failed in Japan?' (2011) 88 *Washington University Law Review* 1426.

[98] For example, Ferreres Comella, 'The European model', note 15, 462.

[99] Tokiyasu Fujita, 'The supreme court of Japan: Commentary on the recent work of scholars in the United States' (2011) 88 *Washington University Law Review* 1508, 1517, 1525, noting the possibility that relatively brief opinions and avoidance of dissents are influenced by European civil law practice. Other relevant aspects of the context in which the supreme court of Japan works, including the Cabinet Legislation Bureau, are canvassed in this interesting piece.

[100] Yasuo Hasebe, Chapter 12 of this volume.

[101] This characterization refers to the formal, national legal system and is reinforced by, for example, the provision for traditional common law remedies in sec. 296 of the constitution. It does not overlook the many ways in which the legal system might also be described as pluralist.

[102] Sec. 293(c). Sec. 295 removes constitutional jurisdiction from the supreme court, which otherwise functions as an apex court.

of government of Myanmar as a Socialist Republic during which constitutional interpretation was the prerogative of the political branches.[103] Judicial review by a specialist body with tenure co-extensive with that of the legislature may have been seen as the logical next step.[104] The Tribunal has had a somewhat rocky history in the brief period since its establishment in 2011, and it remains to be seen whether it will be a continuing feature of constitutional arrangements in Myanmar or whether the constitutional jurisdiction will, over time, default to the supreme court.[105]

Constitutional review across Asia is the product of complex processes whereby institutions are adopted and adapted from one jurisdiction to another; various, sometimes competing, foreign influences are brought to bear, and local needs and preferences shape choices which, in turn, evolve over time. One consequence of these dynamics is a variety of shifts in the design of constitutional review in Asian jurisdictions that have the effect both of increasing convergence between the two approaches and further reducing the homogeneity of each. This can best be seen by examining diffuse review and concentrated review in turn.

The characteristics of diffuse review, as it originally evolved in a common law setting, are modified in particular Asian jurisdictions in a variety of ways. Most obviously, most confine constitutional questions to the superior courts, creating a form of hybrid review, although restriction of constitutional review to a single apex court is rarer.[106] The rationale presumably lies in assessment of the likely capacities of lower courts. Constraints of this kind, in any event, formalize what tends to happen in practise elsewhere. The constitutions of most systems of diffuse review in Asia now also authorize courts to deliver advisory opinions, usually at the instance of the head of state and on a variety of conditions that highlight the complications of this option for a precedential system. Thus, in Singapore, to take a particularly interesting case, a separate tribunal of three justices of the supreme court must give an advisory opinion on a reference from the president, which cannot thereafter be subject to

[103] Constitution of the Socialist Republic of the Union of Myanmar 1974, sec. 200, discussed in U Mya Theinn, Daw Hla Myo Nwe and U Myo Chit, 'Constitutional Tribunal of the Union, Myanmar', 2014, http://cale.law.nagoya-u.ac.jp/2013new_Topics/_userdata/Myanmar%20Constitutional%20Tribunal.pdf (accessed 3 July 2018).

[104] Constitution, sec. 335.

[105] Dominic J. Nardi, Jr., 'Is constitutional review moving to a new home in Myanmar?' (2014, June 11) *International Journal of Constitutional Law Blog*.

[106] Malaysia is an example, constitution, sec. 128.

question by any other court.[107] The same doctrine of precedent that oils the wheels of a system of diffuse review is weakened where an apex court has a huge caseload, as in India, leaving decisions to be made by panels of two to three justices of the court who lack the authority of a plenum. Recourse to a Constitution Bench of five or more justices to hear particularly important matters under section 145(3) of the constitution is only a partial solution in an overburdened court that has thirty-one justices when fully staffed.[108] Many Asian jurisdictions have overcome one classic problem of constitutional review in the common law tradition by adopting a practice of prospective overruling in appropriate cases, which a negative legislator is likely to take for granted.[109] And in an admittedly ambiguous example of another kind, some apex courts in Asian systems of diffuse review also play a role in resolving electoral disputes of various kinds, although typically by conferring the function on one or more members of the court rather than on the institution of the court itself.[110]

A similar shift can be observed in the characteristics of concentrated review in Asian jurisdictions. Some, although by no means all, constitutional courts can review administrative rules as well as primary legislation.[111] In many jurisdictions, constitutional courts deal with constitutional questions through concrete review, on individual complaint, or both.[112] Typically, these are add-ons to abstract review, although not in South Korea, where the constitutional court is authorized to conduct abstract review only in very limited circumstances.[113] In Taiwan, justices of the Constitutional Court are appointed in cooperation

[107] Constitution, sec. 100.

[108] Alok Prasanna Kumar, Faiza Rahman and Ameen Jauhar, 'The Supreme Court of India's burgeoning backlog problem and regional disparities in access to the Supreme Court', Vidhi Centre for Legal Policy Consultation Paper, October 2015, www.vidhilegalpolicy.ind. Proposals for a permanent constitution bench would ease the problem while eroding the diffuse character of the court, Ritwika Sharma, 'Bench structure and constitutional adjudication – the court at a crossroads' (2014, August 22) LiveLaw.in, www.livelaw.in/bench-structure-constitutional-adjudication-court-crossroads/ (accessed 3 July 2018).

[109] Chang et al., note 88, 448.

[110] For example, constitution of the Philippines, Art. 6, sec. 17 provides for an electoral tribunal for each house of congress, comprising three justices and six members of the house.

[111] Chang et al., note 88, 357–358, citing Taiwan as an example of a court with this jurisdiction and Indonesia and South Korea as examples of courts without it.

[112] Ibid., 329, 331–334, citing Taiwan and South Korea as examples that permit both.

[113] Art. 111; Chang et al., note 88, 330.

between the president and the legislature rather than by what Yeh describes as the 'representation' model, which is more typical of concentrated review and is in use elsewhere.[114] Dissenting reasons are common, but in some constitutional courts, a supermajority is required before a law is held invalid.[115]

It can be readily seen that at least some of these variations contribute to convergence of the two approaches to review. They are by no means uniform, however. All constitutional courts retain many of the features that distinguish this approach from constitutional review. In some cases, the variation is shaped in a way that reflects the concerns of the original model. The use of supermajorities is an example.

Most of the variations in constitutional review in Asia that contribute to the convergence of the two approaches and divergence within them are also familiar elsewhere in the world. Their trajectory in particular Asian jurisdictions depends in part on the dominant influences at work at the time review is initially put in place and as it continues over time. Thus, the Cambodian Constitutional Council was initially influenced by the Conseil Constitutionnel in France, which assists with explaining its *ex ante* jurisdiction.[116] In Taiwan, the Judicial Yuan has been shaped by experiences of judicial review in both Germany and the United States, accounting, perhaps, for the process of appointment of justices similar to that for the US Supreme Court.[117] The Constitutional Court of South Korea was an obvious model for the more recently established court in Indonesia with which it shares, for example, a jurisdiction confined to review of statutes and not administrative action.[118] The supreme court of the Philippines has authority to issue the writ of amparo in addition to common law remedies, reflecting continuing links with the Spanish tradition, filtered through developments in Latin America.[119]

[114] Chang et al., note 88, 369–370.
[115] Chang et al., note 88, 444, citing the courts of South Korea and Taiwan.
[116] Ibid., 310, 330.
[117] In Taiwan, justices are nominated by the president but require consent from the Legislative Yuan (Chang et al., note 88, 371); in the United States, justices are nominated by the president but require the consent of the Senate (Art. 2, sec. 2).
[118] Chang et al., note 88, 357–358; c.f., however, Jimly Asshiddique, 'Universality of democratic constitutionalism and the work of constitutional courts today' (2015) 1 *Constitutional Review* 19, noting that Indonesia learnt from the experience of constitutional review in seventy-eight states in designing its own review model.
[119] Chang et al., note 88, 348.

In addition, however, there are other variations in constitutional review in Asia that respond to distinctive local imperatives and insights, are relatively unusual and add new elements to world understanding of the phenomenon of constitutional review. The following examples illustrate the range: the impact of public interest litigation in South Asia;[120] the Mongolian requirement that a decision of unconstitutionality be returned to the legislature for a view on its acceptability before final judgment is made;[121] the formalized appointment of judges from other common law jurisdictions to the Hong Kong Court of Final Appeal;[122] the extent of judicial control over appointments to the judiciary in India, presently through the collegium system;[123] and the research capabilities available to the Constitutional Court of Korea, including, for the purposes of reference to foreign law, through the Constitutional Research Institute.[124]

IV A Distinction with How Much Difference?

Given the variations that have occurred over time in both the diffuse and concentrated approaches to constitutional review, there is a question whether the distinction remains useful for comparative purposes. The question might be asked in relation to any region of the world, including those from which these approaches to review originally derived. *A fortiori*, it is relevant in Asia, where modifications to both diffuse and concentrated review are at least as extensive as those that can be seen elsewhere.

The goal of this chapter was to map constitutional review in Asia with particular reference to the distinction between diffuse and concentrated review. It shows that, while the contours of the distinction have changed, it remains relevant for the usual gamut of comparative purposes: mutual understanding, evaluation of innovation and transplantation and

[120] Surya Deva, 'Public interest litigation in India: A critical review' (2009) 28 *Civil Justice Quarterly* 19–40.

[121] Constitution of Mongolia, Art. 66, sec. 2.

[122] The Basic Law of Hong Kong Special Administrative Region, Art. 82.

[123] The struggle between government and judges on this issue is recorded in, for example, Pradeep Thakuri, 'Collegium junks all major government proposals on judges' appointment', *Times of India* (2016, June 12), https://timesofindia.indiatimes.com/india/Collegium-junks-all-major-government-proposals-on-judges-appointment/articleshow/52708579.cms.

[124] Constitutional Court Act 1988, Art. 19.4.

theorizing constitutional review across Asia or its subregions. It has additional salience in choosing and designing systems of constitutional review for new constitutions if, as anecdotal evidence suggests, pragmatic considerations are driving a preference for constitutional courts, even in common law jurisdictions with no experience of concentrated review.[125] Cross-systemic considerations do not preclude provision for concentrated review if this is otherwise a good idea. They do, however, need to be borne in mind in scoping the jurisdiction of the constitutional court and crafting its relationship with and authority over other courts in the system.

Notwithstanding a degree of convergence, the distinction between diffuse and concentrated review is based on more than the superficial difference between a specialist constitutional court and an apex court applying both the constitution and other legal norms, often on appeal. By definition, these institutions have different functions that inform the understanding of their respective tasks and the ways in which they can and should be performed. These differences, in turn, feed into others about the sources of legitimacy of the practice of constitutional review and what is required to keep within acceptable boundaries.

The structure and function of diffuse and concentrated review explain their relative degree of comfort with, respectively, concrete and abstract review. Both are available in many jurisdictions on both sides of the line, but the modalities differ sufficiently to require explanation. Underlying distinctions between the two also explain differences in judicial procedures and decision rules. In addition, constitutional courts and apex courts with constitutional jurisdiction have and must manage different relationships with other courts in the legal system and face a range of different methodological challenges in dealing with the interface between constitutional and other legal norms. The judges in the two systems typically differ in the training, expertise and skills that they bring to the function of constitutional review. There may be differences also in the other tasks they are required to perform, which are sustained by different understandings of the scope of the functions appropriate for a court of the kind, consistent with the preservation of its independence.

[125] Andrew Harding, Peter Leyland and Tania Groppi, 'Constitutional courts: Forms, functions and practice in comparative perspective', in Andrew Harding and Peter Leyland (eds.), *Constitutional Courts: A Comparative Study* (London: Wildy, Simmonds & Hill Publishing, 2009) 1–30, at 1, 12–13.

Originally, diffuse and concentrated review grew of out particular historical experiences that subsequently were theorized by reference to concepts of separation of powers, judicial independence and the rule of law. The significance of historical experience inevitably dissipates over time and place, but its effects may be sustained by the theories used to explain it to the extent that these persist, or by the practices to which history and theory have given rise. It may be that, as institutions spread and diversify, the theories that underpin them also alter by weakening, changing or both. Nevertheless, the discourse that accompanies discussion of diffuse and concentrated review, including in Asia, suggests that there are continuing differences in the understanding of how separation of powers and the concepts associated with it shape the design and operation of constitutional review. To some extent, these are sustained by the practical differences that undoubtedly remain, in legal education, judicial training and habits of scholarly discourse.[126] An additional buffer is provided by intra-systemic networks of jurists and scholars more comfortable when comparing like with like.

The distinction between diffuse and concentrated review is not the only lens through which to examine constitutional review in Asia in order to compare Asian jurisdictions with each other or to compare Asia with the rest of the world. At least two other perspectives are relevant for these purposes. One takes into account the nature and stage of constitutional development for the processes and outcomes of constitutional review. To this end, Albert Chen, for example, has developed a flexible taxonomy with particular application to Asia involving what he refers to as 'constitutionalism in its classical sense ... communist/socialist constitutionalism ... and hybrid constitutionalism'.[127] There are some synergies here with the earlier tripartite classification of constitutionalism as traditional, transitional and transnational by Chang and Yeh, with which Chen takes issue in his own analysis.[128] Another perspective of a different kind focuses on the significance of what Dressel describes in this volume as a 'relational understanding' for the processes of constitutional review. This perspective draws attention to the potential implications of

[126] By way of example, the terminology of 'negative' and 'positive' legislator is found almost exclusively in scholarship on concentrated review.

[127] Chen, note 4, 14.

[128] Ibid., referring to Jiunn-rong Yeh and Wen-Chen Chang, 'The changing landscape of modern constitutionalism: Transitional perspective' (2009) 4 *National Taiwan University Law Review* 145.

the informal relationships that are a feature of cultures throughout the region for the performance of courts generally and in particular instances.[129]

It can readily be acknowledged that each of these perspectives adds to understanding of constitutional review in Asia. Neither has a monopoly on wisdom, however. On the contrary, each offers a different type of insight into the institution of constitutional review. Here, as in other comparative contexts, taxonomies may be cumulative, depending on the project at hand. Examination of constitutional review in any particular Asian jurisdiction that did not give regard to the nature of constitutionalism and the implications of underlying culture would be superficial, indeed. Equally, however, an analysis that has regard only for one or the other of those considerations and that does not, in addition, take into account the institutional arrangements for constitutional review and the rationales on which they are based risks failing to fully understand the subject matter of the study and deriving accurate insights from it.

129 Björn Dressel, Chapter 3 of this volume.

3

The Informal Dimension of Constitutional Politics in Asia

Insights from the Philippines and Indonesia

BJÖRN DRESSEL

I Introduction

High courts – both constitutional and supreme courts – have become central players in Asia's evolving constitutional landscape. But despite growing academic attention to this phenomenon,[1] there has long been considerable debate about how and when courts hold political authorities accountable and contribute to democratic consolidation in non-Western countries. Recently, excitement about courts as champions of liberty in developing democracies seems to have been replaced by more cautious, even sceptical, accounts, given how these judicial systems perform in relation to their formal duties.[2] A related question is how to explain why judges decide cases as they do, especially cases of major policy or political significance.

Developments in South East Asia illustrate the broader debates. For instance, while there is wide agreement that the region is seeing a trend

[1] Björn Dressel, 'Courts and Judicialization in Southeast Asia', in William Case (ed.), *Routledge Handbook of Southeast Asian Democratization* (Abingdon, UK: Routledge, 2015), 268–282; Andrew Harding and Pip Nicholson (eds.), *New Courts in Asia* (Oxford: Routledge, 2010), 122–140; Jiunn-rong Yeh and Wen-chen Chang (eds.), *Asian Courts in Context* (Cambridge: Cambridge University Press, 2015).

[2] Rachel Ellett, *Pathways to Judicial Power in Transitional States: Perspectives from African Courts* (Abingdon, UK: Routledge, 2013); Linn Hammergren, *Envisioning Reform: Conceptual and Practical Obstacles to Improving Judicial Performance in Latin America* (University Park, PA: Pennsylvania State University Press, 2007); Maria Popova, *Politicized Justice in Emerging Democracies: A Study of Courts in Russia and Ukraine* (Cambridge: Cambridge University Press, 2012); Alexei Trochev, *Judging Russia: The Role of the Constitutional Court in Russian Politics 1990–2006* (Cambridge: Cambridge University Press, 2008).

towards the judicialization of politics,[3] the unusual diversity its high courts exhibit in constitutional matters is perplexing to observers. Consider, for instance, how the Indonesian and Thai constitutional courts have diverged in electoral matters,[4] the uneven track record of the Malaysian Federal Court in religious and political cases[5] and the scandals related to high-profile political cases that have shaken the Philippines Supreme Court.[6]

The unusual degree of regime diversity in the region might partly explain these diverse patterns, but what is striking are the differences between states with very similar institutional and political environments. These raise real empirical challenges to the theories about judicial behaviour that have traditionally dominated the literature.

This chapter proposes a new theory that draws attention to some informal (more specifically, relational) aspects of judicial behaviour in South East Asia. According to a widely accepted definition, formal institutions are 'rules and procedures that are created, communicated, and enforced through channels that are widely accepted'; informal ones are 'socially shared rules, usually unwritten, that are created, communicated and enforced outside officially sanctioned channels'.[7] Since most countries in South East Asia are hybrid regimes in the sense that formal and informal rules are closely intertwined in day-to-day practice (e.g., clientelism, corruption), a concern with formal institutional roles and arrangements alone seems insufficient; it needs to be complemented by an understanding of how informal arrangements function. As highlighted by a growing number of studies of non-Western courts,[8] greater

[3] C. Neal Tate and Torbjörn Vallinder (eds.), *The Global Expansion of Judicial Power* (New York: New York University Press, 1995); Björn Dressel, *The Judicialization of Politics in Asia* (Abingdon, UK: Routledge, 2012).

[4] Björn Dressel and Marcus Mietzner, 'A tale of two courts: The judicialization of electoral politics in Asia' (2012) 25 *Governance* 391–414.

[5] Jaclyn L. Neo, 'What's in a name? Malaysia's "Allah" controversy and the judicial intertwining of Islam with ethnic identity' (2014) 12 *International Journal of Constitutional Law* 751–768; H. P. Lee, 'Constitutional developments in Malaysia in the first decade of the twenty-first century: A nation at the crossroads', in Albert H. Y. Chen (ed.), *Constitutionalism in Asia in the Early Twenty-First Century* (Cambridge: Cambridge University Press, 2014) 244–269.

[6] Marites D. Vitug, *Hour before Dawn. The Fall and Uncertain Rise of the Philippine Supreme Court* (Quezon City, Philippines: Cleverheads Publishing, 2012).

[7] Gretchen Helmke and Steven Levitsky, 'Informal institutions and comparative politics: A research agenda' (2012) 2 *Perspectives on Politics* 725–740.

[8] Gretchen Helmke, *Courts Under Constraints: Judges, Generals, and Presidents in Argentina* (Cambridge: Cambridge University Press, 2005); Jeffrey K. Staton, *Judicial Power and*

attention is needed to the role of peers, ideological communities, party alignments and the ideational, identity-based or clientelistic networks, all of which may affect how judges behave.[9]

Recognizing that the legal and judicial professions in the region are becoming ever more institutionalized and professionalized,[10] I argue here that justices in South East Asia, some at the highest echelons, must deal with a dynamic tension between relational ties of loyalty, friendship and clientelistic obligations and adherence to standards derived from the constraints of the law itself, as well as from the professional expectations generated by the domestic and international legal context. This dynamic tension, and the extent to which the highest courts are able to disentangle themselves from their ever-present relational ties, helps explain the unevenness of judicial performance, especially in high-profile constitutional cases.

This new approach is certainly long overdue. For instance, the region has often been analysed in terms of how patrimonialism, clientelism and personalized politics are expressed in such political institutions as parliaments, the executive or the state at large.[11] Yet, these approaches

Strategic Communication in Mexico (Cambridge: Cambridge University Press, 2010); Diana Kapiszewski, Gordon Silverstein and Robert A. Kagan, *Consequential Courts: Judicial Roles in Global Perspective* (Cambridge: Cambridge University Press, 2013).

[9] Alexei Trochev and Rachel Ellett, 'Judges and their allies: Rethinking judicial autonomy through the prism of off-bench resistance' (2014) 2 *Journal of Law and Courts* 67–91; Mariana Llanos, Cordula T. Weber, Charlotte Heyl and Alexander Stroh, 'Informal interference in the judiciary in new democracies: A comparison of six African and Latin American cases' (2016) 23 *Democratization* 1236–1253; Nuno Garoupa and Tom Ginsburg, *Judicial Reputation: A Comparative Theory* (Chicago: University of Chicago Press, 2015); Lawrence Baum, *Judges and Their Audiences: A Perspective on Judicial Behavior* (Princeton, NJ: Princeton University Press, 2006); Matthew C. Ingram, 'Crafting courts in new democracies: Ideology and judicial council reforms in three Mexican states' (2012) 44 *Comparative Politics* 439–458.

[10] Yves Dezalay and Bryant G. Garth, *Asian Legal Revivals: Lawyers in the Shadow of Empire* (Chicago: University of Chicago Press, 2010); Terence Halliday, Lucien Karpik and Malcolm Feeley, *Fighting for Political Freedom: Comparative Studies of the Legal Complex and Political Liberalism* (Oxford: Hart Publishing, 2007); Terence Halliday, Lucien Karpik and Malcolm M. Feeley (eds.), *Fates of Political Liberalism in the British Post-Colony: The Politics of the Legal Complex* (Cambridge: Cambridge University Press, 2012).

[11] Paul D. Hutchcroft, *Booty Capitalism: The Politics of Banking in the Philippines* (Ithaca, NY: Cornell University Press, 1998); Harold Crouch, 'Patrimonialism and military rule in Indonesia', in Atul Kohli (ed.), *The State and Development in the Third World* (Princeton, NJ: Princeton University Press, 1986) 242–258; Norman Jacobs, *Modernization without Development: Thailand as an Asian Case Study* (New York: Praeger, 1971).

have rarely been applied to the courts – even though some socio-anthropological accounts have illuminated very different legal and judicial dynamics within the region, such as the importance of relationship-based legal exchanges and customary notions of justice within courts and law enforcement agencies.[12]

Likewise, as will be seen later, empirical tests have not provided much support for current models of judicial behaviour,[13] perhaps because the models seem not to adapt well to rapid changes in the legal environment: a lack of ideological fault lines and institutions that are unable to deal with informal practices may generate much greater uncertainty (and, thus, less rational expectations and incentives) than current models would predict.[14]

Recognizing these difficulties, I first survey the literature in terms of the relational turn in recent studies in order to formulate a basic concept of the informality dimension that takes into account the types and nature of informal judicial networks, how and where they form and how they affect the workings of the courts. I then turn to the Philippines and Indonesia to identify preliminary evidence of where the informal dynamics have affected the highest judicial review body in each country: in the composition of the bench, the day-to-day workings of the court or (more difficult) actual decision-making in constitutional cases. Comparing two courts that differ institutionally – Indonesia's Constitutional Court and the Philippines' Supreme Court – and illustrating how informal dynamics permeate these different court structures highlights the critical

12 Nick Cheesman, *Opposing the Rule of Law: How Myanmar's Courts Make Law and Order* (Cambridge: Cambridge University Press, 2015); Sebastiaan Pompe, *The Indonesian Supreme Court: A Study of Institutional Collapse* (Ithaca, NY: Cornell University, 2005); David M. Engel, *Code and Custom in a Thai Provincial Court: The Interaction of Formal and Informal Systems of Justice* (Tucson, AZ: University of Arizona Press, 1978); David M. Engel and Jaruwan Engel, *Tort, Custom, and Karma: Globalization and Legal Consciousness in Thailand* (Palo Alto, CA: Stanford University Press, 2010).

13 Laarni Escresa and Nuno Garoupa, 'Testing the logic of strategic defection: The case of the Philippine supreme court – An empirical analysis (1986–2010)', (2013) 21 *Asian Journal of Political Science* 189–211; Laarni Escresa and Nuno Garoupa, 'Judicial politics in unstable democracies: The case of the Philippine Supreme Court, an empirical analysis 1986–2010', (2012) 3 *Asian Journal of Law and Economics* 1–37.

14 Diana Kapiszewski, Gordon Silverstein and Robert A. Kagan, 'Expanding judicial roles in new or restored democracies', in Diana Kapiszewski, Gordon Silverstein and Robert A. Kagan (eds.), *Consequential Courts: Judicial Roles in Global Perspective* (Cambridge: Cambridge University Press, 2013) 1–44; Pablo Spiller and Rafael Gely, 'Strategic judicial decision-making', in Keith E. Whittington, R. Daniel Kelemen and Gregory A. Caldeira (eds.), *The Oxford Handbook of Law and Politics* (Oxford: Oxford University Press, 2010) 35–43.

importance of these dynamics in South East Asia. The chapter concludes with a discussion of what this relational perspective implies for the study of judicial and constitutional politics in the region and beyond.

II Towards a Relational Understanding

How to explain judicial behaviour – what motivates judges to decide cases as they do and what forces are likely to influence their decisions – is at the centre of the scholarship that has emerged in response to traditional normative studies of how judges ought to decide cases.[15] But as recent scholarly contributions related to courts in the Global South have highlighted, there is an urgent need to give more attention to the informal, relational aspects of the work of judges.[16]

1 Traditional Approaches

Legalistic, attitudinal and strategic rational approaches have long dominated studies of judicial politics – approaches that come with very different assumptions about what motivates and influences a judge's decision.[17] For instance, legalistic accounts assume that judges apply the law in conformity with precedent and legal norms; hence, legal considerations principally guide the behaviour of judges, and law and legal mechanisms constrain each judge's actions.[18] Attitudinal models, by contrast, downplay the influence of law to argue that ideological positions and policy preferences shape the decisions of judges and courts, especially courts of last resort.[19] Dominant strategic rational models share the notion of judicial preferences, though these models also acknowledge that in imposing policy preferences, judges must take into account the preferences of other political and institutional actors so that they might deviate

[15] Lawrence M. Friedman, 'Judging the judges: Some remarks on the way judges think and the way judges act', in John N. Drobak (ed.), *Norms and the Law* (Cambridge: Cambridge University Press, 2006), 139–160.

[16] Trochev and Ellett, note 9.

[17] Jeffrey A. Segal, 'Judicial behavior', in Keith E. Whittington, R. Daniel Kelemen and Gregory A. Caldeira (eds.), *The Oxford Handbook of Law and Politics* (Oxford: Oxford University Press, 2010) 19–33.

[18] Michael A. Bailey and Forrest Maltzman, *The Constrained Court: Law, Politics, and the Decisions Justices Make* (Princeton: Princeton University Press, 2011).

[19] Jeffrey A. Segal and Harold J. Spaeth, *The Supreme Court and the Attitudinal Model Revisited* (Cambridge: Cambridge University Press, 2002).

from their preferred outcome in light of prospective responses or in order to secure the most acceptable outcome.[20] In short, traditional models of judicial behaviour all assume, to different degrees, that considerations of policy – particularly legal policy – substantially influence the choices of higher court justices.[21]

These models have proved useful, and they increasingly incorporate ideas from each other.[22] However, there is debate about their empirical and theoretical reach. Most, having arisen in Western democracies, assume that political and legal systems are solidly institutionalized so that they exert constraints on judges via accepted legal mechanisms and doctrines (legalistic models), ideological and policy preferences along party lines (attitudinal models) or strategic behaviour responding to other political institutions (strategic rational models). Unfortunately, these assumptions travel only with difficulty to countries in South East Asia (or the entire Global South, for that matter), given that institutions there are weak and complex and informal practices introduce much greater uncertainty.[23] Moreover, the singular focus on the legal policy preferences of judges has been criticized even in Western settings, where scholars have suggested that judges may pursue a host of goals beyond legal policy, such as personal standing with public and legal audiences,[24] career considerations and personal aspects of workload and leisure time[25] or maintaining collegial relations on the bench.[26]

Taking justices as human beings, these scholarly contributions have helped to supplement dominant models with explanations of why there is often divergence from leading models.[27] But is the new emphasis on universal human traits sufficient by itself? A host of other informal norms – e.g., loyalty, authority, reciprocity, personal benefit – might compete with such notions as standing with legal and public audiences. Similarly, it must be acknowledged that judges are embedded in wider

[20] Lee Epstein and Jack Knight, *The Choices Justices Make* (Washington, DC: CQ Press, 1998); Spiller and Gely, note 14 at 35–43; J. Mark Ramseyer, 'The puzzling (in)dependence of courts: A comparative approach', (1994) 23 *Journal of Legal Studies* 721–747.

[21] Baum, note 9.

[22] Ibid.

[23] Helmke, note 8; Staton, note 8; Spiller and Gely, note 14.

[24] Baum, note 9.

[25] Richard A. Posner, *How Judges Think* (Cambridge, MA: Harvard University Press, 2008).

[26] Friedman, note 15.

[27] Baum, note 9; Lawrence Baum, *The Puzzle of Judicial Behavior* (Ann Arbor, MI: University of Michigan Press, 1997).

circles of social interaction in terms of, for instance, the judicial hierarchy, other political institutions and the public at large.[28] That is why judicial behaviour might best be understood as an outcome of interactions amongst judges as well as their interactions with other social actors – informal relations shaped by their sociocultural context.[29]

2 *A Relational Turn?*

A distinct new line of inquiry about judicial politics is emerging that seeks to rethink the relationship-based behaviour of judges. Drawing on ample anecdotal evidence of the influence of networks on judges in Africa, Asia and Latin America, this new scholarship has used a relational perspective on judicial behaviour to explain variations in such outcomes as judicial autonomy, ideational diffusion, patronage appointments and even the actual decisions of judges.[30] This relational turn recognizes the important dimension of informality in less institutionalized settings, especially the critical role of informal relationships in animating judicial behaviour.

But what does this relational turn in scholarship entail? Three questions seem critical: (1) Which types of networks matter for judicial actors? (2) What informs the ties between judges and other social actors? (3) Perhaps most important, how do informal relational dynamics affect how judges behave? With the debate in flux, the observations made here should be recognized as preliminary, at best.

There are innumerable types of networks, defined here as groups or systems of social interactions and personal relationships adapted to social circumstances.[31] Evidence, both anecdotal and empirical, suggests that the types of networks most relevant for the judiciary are those based on friendship, recruitment to judicial positions, political interests (partisan or ideological), patronage and clientelism and those based on cultural, regional or religious ties. Such networks generally form through repetitive interaction (e.g., socialization in law school, shared years on the bench, membership in legal associations); they might differ in the extent to which

28 Friedman, note 15.

29 Ingram, note 9; Ellett, note 2.

30 Staton, note 8; Ellett, note 2; Marites Vitug, *Shadow of Doubt: Probing the Supreme Court* (Quezon City: Public Trust Media Group, 2010); Vitug, note 6.

31 For a good overview, see John Scott, *Social Network Analysis* (London: SAGE Publications Inc., 2013).

they are formally recognized (e.g., alumni associations, legal fraternities and sororities) or if they are mainly informal (e.g., friendships); in either case, the relationship dynamics are, in essence, guided by informality.

Similarly, the ties between actors in these networks can be characterized by different intra-personal dynamics or combinations thereof, such as reciprocity, self-presentation, individual benefit, ideational affinities or authority and loyalty. For instance, it might be expected that a friendship network will be dominated by aspects of self-presentation or ideational affinities; career development networks might be motivated by aspects of reciprocity or individual benefits; networks based on patronage and clientelism might largely be characterized by authority and loyalty, often reinforced by shared regional, cultural or kinship ties. Formalized network theory suggests that the more overlapping ties there are between actors or groups, the stronger not only the ties but also the network itself.[32]

The literature – some journalistic, some academic – suggests areas where networks have influenced the workings of judges. For instance, networks have been found to play out forcefully in the composition of the bench, but particularly in the executive that often makes the final decisions about judicial appointments.[33] In fact, even where judicial commissions are charged with preparing shortlists or a multitrack appointment process is in place, networks actively seek to influence selections.[34] Friendships or ideational affinities might also influence the decisions judges make on the bench, help diffuse ideas or create reform coalitions within the judiciary.[35] Similarly, patronage relationships often affect judicial assignments and decisional deference to other branches of government; they also operate after retirement, when justices are rewarded with government appointments.[36] Finally, international networks of clerks and justices might prove critical to the diffusion of ideas within the judiciary, and

32 Mark S. Granovetter, 'The strength of weak ties', (1973) 78 *American Journal of Sociology* 1360–1380.

33 Druscilla Scribner, *Limiting Presidential Power: Supreme Court-Executive Relations in Argentina and Chile* (San Diego, CA: University of California, 2004); Kate Malleson and Peter H. Russel (eds.), *Appointing Judges in an Age of Judicial Power: Critical Perspectives from Around the World* (Toronto: Toronto University Press, 2006).

34 Y. T. Chua, B. B. Cruz, M. G. Ordenes-Cascolan, L. Rimban, J. Santiago and E. Tordesillas, *Political economy analysis of judicial appointments in the Philippines* (*VERA Files*, 2012).

35 Matthew Ingram, 'Networked justice: Judges, the diffusion of ideas, and legal reform movements in Mexico', (2016) 48 *Journal of Latin American Studies* 739–768.

36 Manuel A. Gomez, 'Knowledge and social networks in the construction of elite lawyers in Venezuela', (2009) 23 *Sociologica del Diritto* 113–135; Llanos et al., note 9.

Table 3.1 *Network influence in the judiciary*

Type of network	Characteristics of relational ties	Potential outcomes of interest for judicial behaviour
Professional/recruitment	Goal-oriented; individual benefit	Judicial appointments
Friendship-based	Shared experiences; self-presentation; reciprocal; durable	On- and off-bench loyalties
Ideational	Shared ideas; reciprocity	On-bench factional voting; internal reform dynamics
Political	Ideological; partisan	On-bench voting; on-bench pursuit of policy preferences
Sociocultural	Primordial loyalties based on regional, religious or cultural traits	On- and off-bench loyalties
Patronage/clientelism	Exchange-focused, dyadic, contingent, asymmetric, iterated, authority	Delivery of judicial decisions in exchange for rewards; indebtedness, etc.

alliances between judges and societal actors are considered critical to determining how much autonomy judges actually have.[37]

In short (see Table 3.1), different types of networks impact judicial behaviour based on a variety of very different relational ties, across a variety of areas – e.g., when judges decide to protect institutional independence or influence decisions within a collegiate court, or in terms of internal organization and performance, how careers progress on and off the bench and even after retirement.

A few qualifiers are in order: This list should not be considered comprehensive; it is simply a preliminary outline to capture the relational dimension emerging in the judicial politics literature. It should also be clear that judicial actors are often part of several overlapping networks and that they might move in and out of networks over time or due to personal circumstances. Networks might not all be equally tight so that they might not all affect judicial behaviour to the same degree. In fact, friendship or

[37] Trochev and Ellett, note 9.

kinship networks might be expected to bind more forcefully than professional or political ties, but whether friendship networks have similar relevance to judicial behaviour will depend greatly on the circumstances.

These qualifications also relate to the methodological challenges that come with the relational perspective, particularly as far as measurement and causal inferences are concerned. It has been demonstrated that there are many ways to study the relational aspects of judicial behaviour, from formal network analysis to qualitative accounts of judicial dynamics and behaviour.[38] The purpose here, however, is simply to consider the main conceptual dimensions of this new line of inquiry using two case studies to illustrate how it can help explain the dynamics of judicial behaviour in South East Asia.

III Informal and Relational Dynamics in Action: Indonesia and the Philippines

The Supreme Court of the Philippines and the Indonesian Constitutional Court illustrate some of the points already raised. Both are charged with constitutional adjudication in a weakly institutionalized presidential system marked by fluid party structures and dominance by traditional elites.[39] Though the Indonesian constitutional court was formed in 2001 as a specialized Kelsenian-type court solely to adjudicate constitutional questions, and the Philippine Supreme Court is an apex court whose powers were greatly expanded after the 1986 democratic transition, both have also had to deal with similar challenges to legal professionalism. Chief justices in both countries have been impeached for abuse of office and corruption, in the Philippines in 2012 and in Indonesia in 2014. Demonstrating how similar patterns of informality play out in very different judicial institutions illustrates the importance of these understudied factors.

1 *How Do Networks Form? The Bench and Beyond*

As a look at the bench confirms, both courts are still deeply embedded in national elite structures. While it is estimated that the Philippines has

[38] For a good overview, see Ingram, note 9.

[39] Björn Dressel, 'The Philippines: How much real democracy?' (2011) 32 *International Political Science Review* 529–545; Marcus Mietzner, 'Political conflict and democratic consolidation in Indonesia: The role of the constitutional court', (2010) 10 *Journal of East Asian Studies* 397–424.

Table 3.2 *Composition of the Philippine Supreme Court Bench, 1987–2016*

President:		Aquino I	Ramos	Estrada	Arroyo	Aquino III
No. of appointments		24[40]	14	6	21	6
Gender	Male (%)	83	100	50	81	66
	Female (%)	17	0	50	19	33
University	University of Philippines (%)	71	43	33	38	33
	Ateneo (%)	13	0	17	24	50
	Santo Tomas (%)	8	0	50	5	0
	Far Eastern (%)	0	14	0	10	0
	Quezon (%)	4	14	0	10	0
	Other (%)	4	14	0	19	17
Prior position	Judicial (%)	50	71	83	67	33
	Academe (%)	21	7	0	5	33
	Executive (%)	0	7	0	14	33
	Private (%)	25	14	0	14	0
	Other (%)	4	0	17	0	0
Region	Luzon (%)	75	86	83	81	83
	Visayas (%)	21	14	17	10	17
	Mindanao (%)	4	0	0	10	0

Source: Supreme Court website – justice profiles.

about 105 law schools, over the last three decades (1987–2015), appointments to the male-dominated supreme court have featured graduates of only six law schools, of which two, Ateneo de Manila University and the University of the Philippines, account for about 64 per cent of the justices who have served since 1986 (Table 3.2). Some regions, like Luzon, are over-represented relative to the population; others, like Mindanao, are under-represented – an illustration of the traditional bias of elite socialization in the capital, Manila, and surrounding Luzon. A majority of justices have been appointed from within the judiciary (61 per cent), followed by academe (13 per cent) and the executive branch (11 per

[40] Five of these were reappointments from the Marcos period.

Table 3.3 *Composition of the Constitutional Court Bench in Indonesia, 2003–2016*

President:		Megawati	SBY	Jokowi
No. of appointments		9	14	4
Gender	Male (%)	100	93	100
	Female (%)	0	7	0
University	UI (%)	22	7	0
	Hasanuddin (%)	22	21	0
	U. Islam Indonesia (%)	0	7	25
	Gadjah Mahda (%)	11	7	0
	Udayana (%)	11	0	25
	Other (%)	33	64	50
Prior position	Judicial (%)	33	29	50
	Academe (%)	11	21	50
	Executive (%)	33	21	0
	Parliament (%)	22	29	0
Region	Java (%)	44	43	25
	Sumatra (%)	33	14	50
	Kalimantan (%)	0	7	0
	Sulawesi (%)	22	21	0
	Nusa Tenggara (%)	0	14	25

Source: Constitutional Court website – justice profiles.

cent). The numbers fluctuate considerably across presidents – a sign of the influence of the president on appointments.

From a look at shared years on a lower court, such as the court of appeals (55 per cent), overlapping periods in law school (38 per cent) and memberships in law school alumni associations, most justices on the highest bench are likely to have known each other previously through professional and social networks.

The pattern is slightly more diverse for the constitutional court in Indonesia (2003–2016; Table 3.3). While the bench there is even more male-dominated, the twenty-three justices to date have been trained at sixteen different institutions, with the highest number from Islam Indonesia University (14 per cent). This is somewhat remarkable given that Indonesia has only twenty-two law schools. There is also more diversity in terms of the professional background of appointees, with a majority coming from the judiciary (43 per cent), followed by academe (21 per cent) and the executive branch (18 per cent) – perhaps because parliament, the executive and the supreme court each select a third of the justices. As for the regional background of justices, the most populous regions, like Java, are actually under-represented relative to the population, though not in absolute terms, and regions like Sumatra and Kalimantan are slightly over-represented.

This might suggest weaker ties between justices, except that constitutional court justices share many overlapping pre-appointment network affiliations in terms of, e.g., concurrent years on the lower court bench (37 per cent) or in parliament (20 per cent) or membership in Islamic student organizations such as *Himpunan Mahasiwa Islam* (16 per cent). The fact that each justice must also have earned a PhD reinforces linkages with academe; often academics who become justices have been supervisors or readers of the theses of constitutional court justices. Though in some ways the multitrack appointment system has allowed for greater diversity on the bench, it may also have meant that deeper institutional ties are transferred onto the bench.

Because in both the Philippines and Indonesia, justices on the highest courts are selected from within a small elite group, their social and professional networks overlap. While the ties do not necessarily imply friendship, they do suggest important connections not only on the bench but also beyond. As far as the latter is concerned, it might be helpful to think about continuums along the lines of (a) public to secret and (b) ideational to material. Consequently, many of these ties may lie dormant, only being activated at critical moments, which means they would have different importance at different times. For instance, high-profile political cases might mobilize political connections between judges and the executive, ministers or party affiliates that have been formed through joint political activities or similar ideational interests, whereas civil law matters might draw on connections with lawyers and the legal complex based more broadly on material interests.

2 *The Effects of Networks*

Tracing how informal networks affect judicial behaviour is not easy. Here, we look at appointments, moments of crisis and judicial decisions to extract critical insights into the relational aspects of judicial behaviour.

Networks and Appointments

Although in both countries, the president appoints the justices, the nomination processes are quite different. While Indonesia's Constitutional Court justices are nominated by all three branches of government (executive, legislative and judiciary), in the Philippines, the supreme court justices are nominated by the Judicial and Bar Council (JBC), an independent commission composed of four *ex-officio* members (the chief justice, the secretary of justice, and one member each from the upper and lower house) and four regular members (a law professor, a retired supreme court justice, a member of the Integrated Bar of the Philippines and a representative of the private sector). Yet, appointment to both courts has traditionally been the focus of the activities of networks seeking to influence the composition of the bench.

In the Philippines, the JBC was created by the 1986 constitution to insulate judicial appointments from politics and ensure that appointees are of proven competence, probity and independence. This was a deliberate turn away from the previous practice of confirming presidential appointees by the parliamentary Commission on Appointments (CA), which was seen as favouring judges who relied on a backer (*padrino*) on the CA to secure appointment rather than being recruited on merit.[41] Yet, it is questionable whether the JBC has managed to insulate itself from the traditional informal channels shaping judicial appointments.

For one thing, the executive still has considerable influence over the JBC through control of the political appointees (secretary of justice, upper and lower house members) or because regular members often lobby for another term and, thus, end up owing gratitude, if not loyalty, to the president. Given various informal ties, too, it is not uncommon for JBC members to be called by presidential staff or political brokers to influence the shortlist of candidates. One JBC member has said, 'In all nominations, there were so many calls. I am not sure whether they were really relaying the president's instructions.'[42]

Once the JBC shortlist is submitted to the president, networks also lobby the president and staff for individual candidates. As one observer remarked, 'Nominees go to politicians, bishops, priests or close to those

[41] Vitug, note 6 at 208; Chua et al., note 34. For the background of justices up to 1970, see C. Neal Tate, *The Social Background, Political Recruitment, and Decision Making of the Philippine Supreme Court Justices, 1901–1986* (PhD Dissertation, Tulane University, New Orleans, LA, 1970).

[42] Chua et al., note 34 at 39.

in power . . . it really pays if you have a backer or if the president knows you.'[43] Presidential advisors are reported to prepare spreadsheets for the executive that list not only the nominees' qualifications and integrity but also influential backers and affiliations.[44] This parallel screening process is often conducted by the inner circles of presidential advisors, which in the past, have included family members and close friends, as under Presidents Estrada (1998–2001) and Macapagal-Arroyo (2001–2012).[45,46]

The result of these informal processes has been a severely compromised nomination process which has ignored concerns about the integrity of executive candidates and seen inflation in the number of candidates shortlisted against the rules.[47]

Meanwhile, a study of presidential nominations to the supreme court between 1988 and 2008 found that of 208 candidates submitted by the JBC, effectively, only eighty were nominated because a majority were nominated several times, which suggests a shallow pool of qualified candidates and raises concerns about the diversity of the bench.[48]

Combined with efforts by Ramos and Arroyo to bypass constitutional limits on judicial appointments at the end of their terms ('midnight'

[43] Ibid. See also Vitug, note 30; there are reports that former Chief Justices Panganiban and Puno both mobilized support from the Catholic Church and the Masons; Associate Justice Velasco garnered endorsement from Cebu Archbishop Vidal, and Associate Justice Ruben Reyes claimed public support from free church Igelsia ni Cristo and Catholic charismatic renewal group El Shaddai.

[44] See Purple Romero, 'Besides JBC, palace has judicial search committee', *Rappler*, 2012, June 2, at www.rappler.com/nation/6343-there-s-jbc,-then-there-s-malacanang-s-judicial-search-committee (accessed 6 October 2017).

[45] Vitug, note 30 at 118.

[46] This process can be mutually reinforcing, as Justice Villarama pointed out: 'I would be lying if I said that I did not look for connections [to the Palace]. Friends pushed for me. Justice Peralta guided me. But there was no single factor responsible for my success this time. It was convergence' (Vitug, note 30 at 106).

[47] One problematic case is that of Justice Velasco, an Arroyo appointee, who is still haunted by claims of ethics violations; a similar controversy recently erupted over Aquino's appointment of Jardeleza, who was shortlisted by the JBC despite resistance from C. J. Sereno, who accused Jardeleza of lack of integrity and committing acts tantamount to treason when he 'deliberately' pushed for the exclusion of Itu Aba, the largest island in the Spratly Group of Islands, for discussion in the memorandum (or memorial, in international law) submitted to the United Nations backed tribunal.

[48] On the average, nominees were included in the list two and a half times; see Dante B. Gatmaytan and Cielo Magno, 'Averting diversity: A review of nominations and appointments to the Philippine Supreme Court (1988–2008)' (2011) 6 *Asian Journal of Comparative Law* 1–18.

appointments), it seems fair to conclude that informal network activities often directly compete with, if not overshadow, the formal rules – which undermines the legitimacy of the JBC and its nomination process.[49]

In Indonesia, the pattern is similar, but the structures are very different. Different branches of government each nominate a third of the candidates for the top bench; all must pass minimum age and educational criteria, and the president is bound to choose from those nominated. As a result, the networks are mainly active within the nominating institutions. For instance, given that constitutional court judges must have a PhD, there were fewer than twenty applications from within the judiciary in 2014, most of them from lower-level high court judges rather than the supreme court bench. Since 2014, this process has involved a fit and proper test, suggesting that selection by the SC leadership had in the past been highly discretionary, leading to public perceptions that the supreme court candidates for the constitutional court bench had been of low quality because of the traditional rivalry between the two courts.[50]

Informality and relational aspects are also quite evident in the nomination processes of the legislature and the executive. Parliamentary Committee IV selects nominees, who undergo a fit and proper test before trying to muster support from the twenty or so political parties represented on the committee. Political horse-trading is common; many of those involved readily admit that what matters is less the quality of a candidate than whether he (usually) can claim support from political networks in the form of either political party affiliation or backing from such influential organizations as Nahdlatul Ulama (NU), Muhammadiya or the Islamic Student Association (HMI, *Himpunan Mahasiwa Islam*). It is, thus, not surprising that of nine nominees from parliament since 2003, seven have been members of either parliament or the executive branch – political networks in action.

Similarly, presidential nominees need to gain favour with the president or vice president or their close advisors, who, in turn, might have favoured politically connected second-rate candidates such as Associate Justice Patrialis Akbar, the former minister of justice, who was arrested

[49] See Artemio Panganiban, 'Reforming the judicial and bar council', in Artemio Panganiban (ed.), *With Due Respect: Selected Columns from the Philippine Daily Inquirer* (Manila: Inquirer Books, 2012), 105–108.

[50] Some have suggested that the new rules are not just a reaction to public pressure but were also meant to keep certain internal candidates out. This is possible, since the fit and proper test has remained ill-defined (interview, supreme court justices and staff, 2015, August 10).

early in 2017 on corruption charges (see the section Informal Networks and Judicial Decision-Making for a full discussion of the case). However, a more centralized decision-making process has also brought greater public scrutiny, which in turn, has produced a more diverse profile for the eight presidential nominees so far – though the majority had a scholarly background. Nevertheless, coordination on candidates between parliament and executive is not uncommon, particularly when the president's party has a majority in parliament: candidates can be nominated from either side, according to political expediency.

In short, both countries demonstrate the powerful influence of relational aspects such as political affiliation or ties of loyalty and authority on the nomination process. These aspects often directly compete with, or may even supplant, the official channels, which clearly affects the composition of the bench and, sometimes, its quality and performance (see The Eroding Effects of Informal Networks).

The Eroding Effects of Informal Networks

The impeachment of the chief justice of the Philippines Supreme Court in 2012, and of his counterpart on Indonesia's Constitutional Court in 2014, are vivid illustrations of the negative consequences that relational ties can have on the functioning of the judiciary.

At first glance, it might seem that doubts about the impartiality of judgments in politically charged cases, as much as outright corruption, were at the centre of the impeachment proceedings in both cases. For instance, in the Senate hearings, Chief Justice Renato Corona in the Philippines faced eight different charges[51] for betrayal of public trust and violation of the constitution; his conviction was ultimately based on failure to 'disclose assets, liabilities, and net worth as required under the constitution' in relation to PHP 180 million ($4 million) in assets – personal funds that were fifty times more than the income he declared and far more than the income of PHP 27 million that might be expected over ten years of service; moreover, some deposits coincided suspiciously

[51] These charges were partiality and subservience in cases involving the Arroyo administration; failure to disclose assets publicly; failure to meet the stringent constitutional standards for judges; disregarding the principle of separation of power; arbitrariness and partiality in consistently disregarding the principle of *res judicata*; arrogating to himself authority and jurisdiction to improperly investigate a justice; partiality in temporarily granting a restraining order in favour of former president Arroyo; and failure to account for the Judiciary Development Fund.

with major supreme court decisions, some of which were reversals.[52] Akil Mochtar, chief justice of Indonesia's Constitutional Court, was convicted of taking IDR 57 billion ($5.1 million) in payments related to local election disputes and laundering another IDR 160 billion ($14 million) during his five years on the court – activities that brought him an unprecedented life sentence.[53]

What could easily be dismissed as the personal failings of these individuals ignores the part played by informal networks and relational aspects in promoting the outcomes. For instance, doubts were raised early on about Corona's political connections to President Arroyo (2001–2012), for whom he had served as legal counsel, acting executive secretary and presidential chief of staff (2001–2002) before he was nominated to the supreme court bench in 2002. Those concerns were aggravated when the president elevated Corona to chief justice in 2010, two days after the 2010 election made Benigno Aquino III president and a month before Arroyo's term expired; this was widely seen as a breach of the constitutional prohibition of midnight appointments.[54] Concerns about the possibility that the court was biased – Aquino had appointed an unprecedented fifteen supreme court justices – were apparently confirmed when the court declared unconstitutional several executive orders issued by the new Aquino administration that had charged former president Arroyo with grave abuse of discretion and plunder – thus derailing the reform efforts of the new administration and prompting the impeachment process against Corona.

The political context aside, informal networks and relational loyalties clearly had powerful effects here both on and off the bench. For instance, despite concerns about shortcomings in his educational qualifications, it appeared that Corona was probably chosen from the JBC shortlist due to his close ties with the president. His voting record on the bench in favour of President Arroyo in 125 high-profile political cases (84 per cent)[55] put him

[52] Vitug, note 6 at 254.

[53] See Haeril Halim, 'Historic sentence for Akil' (2014, July 1) *Jakarta Post*, at www.thejakartapost.com/news/2014/07/01/historic-sentence-akil.html (accessed 6 October 2017).

[54] However, in *De Castro* v. *JBC* (2010, March 17), the supreme court approved the appointment in a 9:3 decision – a vote widely seen as coming from a stacked court (see Artemio Panganiban, 'Midnight chief justice', note 49 at 71–75.

[55] Two data sets are used in the section Informal Networks and Judicial Decision-Making. The first is based on 125 high-profile cases used by Escresa and Garoupa, note 13; the other is based on forty-seven narrower megapolitical cases collected by myself.

in the top decile of pro-government votes in a 1986–2010 supreme court sample,[56] and after he became chief justice, evidence of payments into his account in close proximity to high-profile cases added weight to concerns that patron–client dynamics were influencing outcomes.[57] During the impeachment proceedings, a majority of Corona's supporters had connections with his alma mater, Ateneo, and its fraternities, whereas opponents were largely connected with the University of the Philippines Law School.[58]

The dynamics surrounding the impeachment of Indonesia's Chief Justice Akil Mochtar were similar. Long associated with the Golkar party (1999–2008) in the lower house, Mochtar was elected to the bench by his parliamentary peers despite previous accusations (which could not be substantiated) that he had accepted kickbacks of IDR 680 million for projects in West Kalimantan when he was chair of the House of Representatives Commission overseeing legal affairs (2004–2006). He later relied on his former colleagues in parliament to be re-elected for another five-year term in 2013 despite rumours that he had accepted IDR 1 billion during disputes over the election of the Simalungun regional head – an accusation that the then Chief Justice Mohammad Mahfud pursued only hesitantly. His peers on the bench then elected Mochtar chief justice in 2013.

However, the local election cases that began to dominate the bench in 2009 were what proved how deeply his situation was embedded in political loyalties and expectations from his past. In 2013, anti-corruption investigators caught him red-handed accepting about IDR 3 billion ($250,000) in bribes from a businessman and a Golkar lawmaker, thus demonstrating his continuing difficulties in detaching himself from Golkar political loyalties. Revelations that he had accepted bribes of roughly IDR 57 billion ($5.1 million) in local election disputes and laundered IDR 160 billion ($14 million) in his five years on the bench also reveal that his practice went far beyond his party circles (they may also have involved colleagues, given that decisions in electoral matters must be heard by at least three justices).[59]

56 Ibid., at 26–27.

57 Vitug, note 6 at 252–254.

58 Jay B. Rempillo, 'Outpouring of Support for Chief Justice Renato Corona' (2012, December 16) *Bantay Hustisya* 2012, at https://bantayhustisya2012.wordpress.com/2012/01/16/outpouring-of-support-for-chief-justice-renato-corona/ (accessed 6 October 2017).

59 See Peter Alford, 'Corrupt judge Akil Mochtar destroyed Indonesian court's authority: judge' (2014, July 1) *The Australian*, at www.theaustralian.com.au/news/world/corrupt-judge-akil-mochtar-destroyed-indonesian-courts-authority-judge/story-e6frg6so-1226973354693 (accessed 6 October 2017).

Both impeachments thus illustrate not only corrupt practices but also the continuing importance of the informal connections and patron–client patterns that made it possible to circumvent safeguards for nominations and prevented insulation of justices from the ties that bind. Both sparked a major crisis and soul-searching within their institutions, though the resultant reforms have had limited success.[60] That professional standards have declined is also demonstrated, if less dramatically, by bribery allegations against Justice Ynares-Santiago in 2007,[61] the leaking of a decision by Justice Reyes and the plagiarism scandal involving Justice del Castillo at the Philippines Supreme Court in 2010, triggered by a research assistant recruited from his alma mater and working for his wife's law office.[62]

Informal Networks and Judicial Decision-Making

Linking informal networks to actual decisions made by justices is very difficult. Deliberations are not made public, and justices certainly do not openly discuss informal influences. However, it is possible to marshal evidence from interviews and secondary sources to support the argument that informal relationships on and off the bench do influence actual decisions and, thus, relate to professional ethics and independent behaviour on the bench.

For instance, informal dynamics of seniority and hierarchy are well documented for the Philippines Supreme Court, including the power of the chief justice to set the agenda, which might facilitate majority decisions, particularly in en banc cases, where voting is formal.[63] Informal

[60] A presidential order by Indonesia's president after Akil Mochtar was arrested, stipulating that constitutional court justices had to be unconnected to a political party connection for the five years prior to appointment, was rejected by the constitutional court in 2014; similarly, criticism of the JBC in the Philippines has largely faded; evidence of pork-barrel allocations in favour of the MPs supporting the Corona impeachment has diverted attention away from the central issues.

[61] Related to a package received by her office that contained 10 million pesos ($225,000), which some suggested was related to cases written by Ynares-Santiago, such as the dismissal of graft allegations against PIATCO chairman Henry Go and a prime land dispute; see Mike Frialde, 'SC to tackle P10-M bribery charge against justice' (2007, September 25) *Philstar*, at www.philstar.com/headlines/16274/sc-tackle-p10-m-bribery-charge-against-justice (accessed 6 October 2017).

[62] See 'Ex-Ateneo prof behind SC plagiarism scandal?' (2010, October 28) *ABS-CBN News*, at www.abs-cbnnews.com/nation/10/27/10/ex-ateneo-prof-behind-sc-plagiarism-scandal (accessed 6 October 2017).

[63] Vitug, note 30; Vitug, note 6.

leadership often transcends formal roles, as illustrated by Associate Justice Carpio (2001–current) who is widely perceived as an opinion leader for the current bench, which raises speculation about how much the Chief Justice, Sereno (2012–current), can steer a bench made up of distinct factions.[64] With the court still dominated by Arroyo appointees, frictions between old and new justices have been common[65] – some of the former have formed a voting bloc that clearly favours Arroyo,[66] especially in support of the widely controversial sanctioning of midnight appointees.[67] It may also be noteworthy that Carpio and Carpio-Morales (cousins) have a 100 per cent congruent voting record in high-profile cases. Moreover, it was widely interpreted that reports that Associate Justice Ynares-Santiago (1999–2009) burst into tears when providing the crucial swing vote in an 8:7 decision dismissing the People's Initiative for Charter Change (*Lambino et al.* v. *COMELEC*) – a vote that pitted her against former classmate and close friend Chief Justice Puno – was a symptom of informal loyalties playing out.[68]

There is also growing empirical evidence that off-bench loyalties and personal connections matter to judicial decision-making. For instance, a study of 125 critical supreme court cases has shown that if justices have been appointed by the incumbent administration, the chance of their

[64] Speculations on factions and infighting is rife; see Aries Rufo, 'Jardeleza's SC entry and Sereno's eroding clout' (2014, August 20) *Rappler*, at www.rappler.com/newsbreak/66794-jardeleza-sc-sereno-clout; see also Jomar Canlas, 'Infighting Looms at the High Court' (2014, January 5) *Manila Times*, at www.manilatimes.net/infighting-looms-at-high-court/65403/ (accessed 6 October 2017).

[65] See the recent public exchange between Justice Bersamin and Justice Leonen, newly appointed by Aquino, over the decision to grant bail to Senator Enrile, in which Bersamin filed a complaint against Leonen for gross distortions when Leonen dissented, in sharp words, 'War of SC justices: Bersamin files complaint vs Leonen' (2015, August 24) *Rappler*, www.rappler.com/nation/103599-war-supreme-court-justices-bersamin-leonen (accessed 6 October 2017); for some, the issue is less about factional than generational differences about the transparency of the court (see Raul J. Palabrica, 'Generation gap in the Supreme Court' (2015, September 1) *Inquirer*, at http://opinion.inquirer.net/88123/generation-gap-in-the-supreme-court (accessed 6 October 2017).

[66] Much has been written (see especially Vitug, note 6 at 45) about the pro-Arroyo voting record of Justices Corona (84%), Tinga (57%), Chico Nazario (71%), Velasco (75%) and Nachura (100%). Moreover, in cases relevant to the Arroyo administration, Tinga and Corona voted similarly 85% of the time, compared to 71% for the whole group.

[67] *Arturo M. De Castro* v. *Judicial and Bar Council*, et al. G.R. No. 191002, G.R. No. 191032, G.R. No. 191057, A.M. No. 10-2-5-SC, G.R. No. 191149, G.R. No. 191342.

[68] Interview with a supreme court justice privy to internal debate; see also Vitug note 6 at 43. The common voting record of Puno and Ynares-Santiago in our selection of high-profile cases was 61%.

voting for the administration rises about 66 per cent compared to those not appointed by the incumbent; the study did not find a statistically significant endorsement of the widely perceived first-year syndrome in which new appointees vote more often for the incumbent than they do later in their terms.[69] But informal ties not captured by such studies certainly play out. For instance, President Arroyo paid the hospital bill of Chief Justice Corona, and Corona's wife was appointed to a lucrative private-sector position while he was on the bench – favours that not only fostered gratitude that he admitted but that many saw as being repaid with an 84 per cent record of voting in support of the increasingly beleaguered president.[70]

It is also common for intermediaries and brokers to approach justices about cases – a process facilitated by family ties, fraternity memberships or social ties. For instance, veteran lawyer Estelito Mendoza has become known for his highly successful interventions with the supreme court, including a highly controversial reversal of what was considered a final decision after he sent the court several letters.[71] He had not only taught several supreme court justices in law school and mentored many when he was solicitor general and justice secretary under Marcos, but he had also maintained close friendships with some. An example is the fact that Mendoza's wife was wedding godmother to the daughter of former Chief Justice Puno; it is perhaps noteworthy that Puno had an 11:2 record of voting in favour of Mendoza's clients.[72]

Lobbying through personal connections is a common practice to sway a motion of reconsideration, an en banc hearing or a favourable outcome

[69] Escresa and Garoupa, note 13.

[70] Similarly, Associate Justice del Castillo – then on the Court of Appeals – benefited from Arroyo's intervention to see a US heart surgeon; in an OpEd in the *Philippines Star*, he thanked the president, saying 'Her single indiscriminate act of kindness in my momentary blow is something of eternal value, let alone something that highlights how admirable she is', cited in Vitug, note 30 at 97.

[71] See 'SC spokesman-UP law professor exchange on Estelito Mendoza letters' (2011, October 18) *GMA News*, at www.gmanetwork.com/news/story/235816/news/nation/sc-spokesman-up-law-professor-exchange-on-estelito-mendoza-letters (accessed 6 October 2017).

[72] Vitug, note 6 at 118–119; Estelito Mendoza taught former chief justices Davide and Puno in law school, and as secretary general/justice secretary during the Marcos years, Mendoza was most likely in touch with many justices who passed through his department. Justice Kapunan was even asked to excuse himself from decisions involving Mendoza; see Marites Dañguilan Vitug, 'The ties between Lucas Bersamin and Estelito Mendoza' (2015, August 31) *Rappler*, at www.rappler.com/newsbreak/inside-track/104306-ties-lucas-bersamin-estelito-mendoza (accessed 6 October 2017).

(lawyers actually pride themselves on lobbying), and reportedly, even former presidents call in to influence votes,[73] so it is not surprising that lobbying is often seen to affect decisions in crucial cases:

> Through the years, it has become obvious that justices flip flop because they do not study the case – for lack of time or neglect – and completely rely on the ponente [the writer of the opinion]. When an MR [Motion for Reconsideration] comes their way and litigants, through emissaries, call the Justices' attention [to it] or lobby with them, they then take a closer look at the case. This appears to be common. They have been approached. This is the shorthand explanation for this phenomenon.[74]

There is similar evidence of informal influences on Indonesia's Constitutional Court, though it is perhaps less pronounced because the institution is much younger. In fact, both multitrack appointments and the more open deliberative culture instilled by the first chief justice, Assidiqie (2003–2008), seem to have prevented the definitive formation of hierarchies and factions amongst justices,[75] though as court decisions have been becoming shorter, dissent is less pronounced and the quality of decisions more questionable.[76,77] Nevertheless, it is common for political actors, often using intermediaries, to try to approach justices not only directly but also through court staff and even family members, particularly during the run-up to elections.

For instance, election candidates met with the daughter and the brother of Associate Justice Arsyad and bribed them to convince the judge to sway the court's decision in certain election cases; though

[73] President Ramos is reported to have called Justice Quisimbing in the PIRMA case, and Estrada reportedly called Justice Ynares-Santiago, his appointee, during the PIRMA case to influence a term extension.

[74] Vitug, note 30 at 142.

[75] Stefanus Hendrianto, 'The rise and fall of heroic chief justices: Constitutional politics and judicial leadership in Indonesia' (2016) 25 *Pacific Rim Law and Policy Journal* 489.

[76] Simon Butt, 'Jurisdictional expansion, self-limitation and legal reasoning in the Indonesian Constitutional Court', in Dri Utari Christina Rachmawati and I. Hasani (eds.), *Masa Depan Mahkamah Konstitusi RI: Naskah Konferensi Mahkamah Konstitusi dan Pemajuan Hak Konstitusional Warga (Future of the Constitutional Court: Conference Proceedings on the Constitutional Court and the Advancement of Citizens' Constitutional Rights)* (Bendungan Hilir, Indonesia: Pustaka Masyarakat Setara, 2013), 55–79; see also Simon Butt, *The Constitutional Court and Democracy in Indonesia* (Leiden: Brill Nijhoff, 2015).

[77] The average number of words in decisions has declined from 4,535 under Chief Justice Assidiqie to 3,387 under Chief Justice Mahfud; dissenting opinion also declined from 37% under Chief Justice Assidiqie to 13.7% in the Mahfud period and 10.2% post-Mahfud. Meanwhile, the ambiguous use of 'conditional' constitutional rulings went up from 35% in the first period to 60.4% in the last.

Arsyad denied being present at the meetings, he ultimately resigned.[78] Another major blow to the reputation of the Constitutional Court was the arrest in January 2017 of Associate Justice Patrialis Akbar, a former member of the National Mandate Party (PAN), whose appointment to the court by the president had been highly criticized because of his poor performance as minister of justice. The KPK charged him with receiving bribes of IDR 266 million ($20,000) from a prominent beef importer in order to sway the court's review of the *Animal Husbandry Law II* case.[79] Perhaps in an attempt to restore trust in the institution, in April 2017, he was replaced by highly regarded law professor Saldi Isra.[80]

As highlighted in this latest case, such approaches seem to be facilitated by the political background of many justices, though at times, they might also have provided avenues for well-connected chief justices to influence the president or lawmakers to help implement court decisions. It was widely speculated that the notable dissent of Justice Roestandi in the high-profile KPI case was largely attributable to his military background and connections, and the regional affinities and networks of Justice Palguna were seen as having influenced his dissent in the Bali Bomber case – speculations vigorously denied by both.[81] Recent reversals in high-profile cases such as that of the oil and gas law have also prompted speculation that the clout of the petitioner (a major Islamic organization, Muhammadiyah) influenced the court's sudden reversal,

[78] Ina Parlina, 'Justice quits over family bribery scandal' (2011, February 12) *Jakarta Post*, at www.thejakartapost.com/news/2011/02/12/justice-quits-over-family-bribery-scandal.html (accessed 6 October 2017).

[79] 'Beef importer Basuki reportedly confesses to bribing Constitutional Court aide' (2017, January 27) *Jakarta Post*, at www.thejakartapost.com/news/2017/01/27/beef-importer-basuki-reportedly-confesses-to-bribing-constitutional-court-aide.html (accessed 6 October 2017; 'KPK names MK Justice Patrialis Akbar suspect in the bribery case' (2017, February 27) *Jakarta Post*, at www.thejakartapost.com/news/2017/01/27/kpk-names-mk-justice-patrialis-akbar-suspect-in-bribery-case.html (accessed 6 October 2017).

[80] Muhammad Tanziel Aziez, 'High hopes for Saldi Isra to restore trust in Constitutional Court' (2017, April 11) *Indonesia at Melbourne*, at http://indonesiaatmelbourne.unimelb.edu.au/high-hopes-for-saldi-isra-to-restore-trust-in-constitutional-court/ (accessed 6 October 2017).

[81] In his article 'Why I gave a dissenting opinion', Justice Roestandi defended his decision: 'So, not because I am a former military member I became a dissenter!' thus denying claims that his dissent was a form of the revenge of the armed forces against its historical enemy, the PKI. Similarly, Justice Palguna denied that his Balinese background explained his dissent against the retroactive application of the Human Rights Court Law, though he said that he 'was tortured by the decision' but was glad to realize that his position had not changed from an earlier principle developed in law school, interview, 2015, August 12.

much to the detriment of the economic platform of president Widodo.[82] However, more empirical research is needed to substantiate this claim.

In both cases, there is considerable evidence that informal connections were mobilized to lobby justices in environments marked by repeated crossover of actors between different branches of government. Thus, rather than outright corruption, informal ties of loyalty, friendships and social interactions often influence judicial discretion and decisions more than professional norms and codes of judicial ethics.

IV Conclusion

This chapter has drawn attention to new scholarship about judicial politics that illuminates how relational and informal aspects inform judicial behaviour and judicial performance generally. The recent relational turn in this scholarship arises from the empirical realities in many countries not only in Asia but throughout the Global South; it recognizes that judges remain deeply embedded in personal networks and hybrid judicial institutions, and outcomes often deviate from expected legal practice due to, among other factors, persistent sociocultural patterns of obligation, reciprocity and authority.

South East Asia is a particularly suitable place to explore this relational perspective. Since independence, judicial and legal sectors there have experienced both rapid growth and continuing professionalization.[83] Scholarship has traditionally analysed the region in terms of patterns of patronage and clientelism and continues to stress – though often only implicitly – the importance of informal rules and cultural patterns in institutional and societal interaction, despite rapid modernization of the judicial and legal sectors.[84] In fact, as our discussion of top courts in the Philippines and Indonesia makes clear, informal norms based on loyalty, friendship and patron–client ties influence such diverse areas as judicial appointments, professionalism on the bench and even judicial decision-making.

[82] See Jeffrey Hutton, 'Muslim NGO lawsuits threaten Indonesia president's reformist agenda' (2015, April 1) *Christian Science Monitor*, at www.csmonitor.com/World/Asia-Pacific/2015/0401/Muslim-NGO-lawsuits-threaten-Indonesia-president-s-reformist-agenda (accessed 6 October 2017).

[83] Dezalay and Garth, note 9.

[84] Insightful contributions in this regard include Cheesman, note 12; Pompe note 12; Engel, *Code and Custom*, note 12; Engel and Engel, note 12.

This is not to suggest that legal norms and professional conduct do not matter. Legal education has proliferated to meet the demands of a growing legal profession, and law and bar associations have become vocal about enhancing legal professionalism.[85] Meanwhile, judicial reforms, some in process for more than a quarter century, have gradually improved the workings of the judiciary, especially the training of judges. And many judges, particularly in the highest courts, wish to be recognized by both domestic and international audiences for their professional ethics and legal craftsmanship.[86] As illustrated by the public reactions to recent scandals in South East Asia, ranging from outright corruption to plagiarism and ethical failings, these problems have often led to soul-searching and efforts to reconstitute the legitimacy of judicial institutions – efforts that, as illustrated by Indonesia and the Philippines, are not yet fully effective.

Judges in the region thus often find themselves impaled on the horns of a dilemma: On the one hand, law and legal discourse increasingly matter, and justices, particularly on the highest courts, have been able to increasingly shape the national legal landscape. On the other hand, as highlighted by the recent impeachments of chief justices in the Philippines and Indonesia and the unpredictable jurisprudence related to high-profile constitutional and political cases, courts are still deeply rooted in the sociocultural context. Thus, justices in the region have to straddle the expectations generated by relational ties, on the one hand, and aspirations for greater professionalization and adherence to legal norms, on the other. As an interviewee in Indonesia said, 'I am not worried about being offered money, because I know I won't take it, but I am worried about my friends calling me.' In sum, how effectively judges can untie themselves from the ties that bind is the key to better understanding judicial behaviour in the region, particularly in high-profile political cases.

Empirical study of the relational turn in the study of judicial politics entails a multitude of methodological challenges. As illustrated here, much of the evidence is naturally anecdotal; judges are hardly likely to admit publicly to the personal pressures they face. Meanwhile, statistical analysis often dismisses the factors discussed here as unobservable and

[85] Halliday et al., note 10.

[86] Fritz Siregar, 'The political context of judicial review in Indonesia', (2015) 2 *Indonesia Law Review*, 208–237.

accounts for them as, at best, deviations from standard accounts.[87] Yet, a variety of techniques are emerging that, alone or in combination, can bring these dynamics into the open, such as in-depth qualitative accounts and use of network theory to capture personal ties in a more quantifiable way.

It has become necessary to push the scholarly agenda beyond the traditional legalistic, attitudinal and strategic rational accounts that have come to dominate the judicial politics field. By drawing attention to the tension between legal professionalism and informal networks and norms, it may be possible to address the puzzling behaviour of courts as the judicialization trend unfolds in South East Asia. What is needed is a new research agenda that deals with the informal and relational aspects that affect judicial behaviour – something long overdue and clearly more than ever necessary.

[87] Escresa and Garoupa, note 13.

4

Towards More Intra-Asian Judicial Cooperation in the Constitutional Sphere

MAARTJE DE VISSER

I Introduction

On 14 August 2015, the Association of Asian Constitutional Courts and Equivalent Institutions unanimously agreed to welcome Myanmar's Constitutional Tribunal and the constitutional chamber of the Supreme Court of Kyrgyzstan as new members.[1] That same year, the dedicated International Affairs Division of the Korean Constitutional Court took care of the logistical arrangements attendant on hosting judges from the US Supreme Court and the European Court of Human Rights (ECtHR) to Seoul.[2] For its part, the Japanese Supreme Court gives one-third of its bench the opportunity to go on a week-long working visit to a judicial institution elsewhere on a yearly basis.[3] The Hong Kong Court of Final Appeal counts distinguished judges from other common law jurisdictions amongst its membership, who can partake in hearing appeals involving constitutional matters.[4] For Taiwan's Council of Grand Justices, foreign constitutional materials are consulted 'in almost every case',[5] and explicit references to out-of-state approaches, while decidedly less common, are said to be on the rise.[6] Further examples could easily be added to this list,

[1] For further details, see the Association's website at www.aaccrd.org/en/aboutUs.do (accessed 6 October 2017).

[2] On 3 August and 22 June, respectively, as mentioned on the dedicated Visits by Foreign Dignitaries page of the Korean Constitutional Court (see english.ccourt.go.kr/cckhome/eng/index.do) (accessed 6 October 2017).

[3] David Law, 'Judicial comparativism and judicial diplomacy' (2015) 163 *University of Pennsylvania Law Review* 927–1036, 961.

[4] Cf. Art. 82 of the Basic Law of the Hong King SAR of the Republic of China 1997 and s. 5(3) of the Hong Kong Court of Final Appeal Ordinance (Cap. 484).

[5] David Law and Wen-Chen Chang, 'The limits of global judicial dialogue' (2011) 86 *Washington Law Review* 523–567, 560.

[6] Wen-Chen Chang and Jiunn-rong Yeh, 'Judges as discursive agent: The use of foreign precedents by the Constitutional Court of Taiwan', in Tania Groppi and Marie-Claire

but the general point will be clear: much like their counterparts in other regions, Asian judges with a constitutional mandate are cognisant of the fact that they operate in what Vicki Jackson calls 'an increasingly transnational legal environment',[7] and one of the ways in which they respond to this legal reality is through more intense interactions with foreign judges.

That is the topic of the present chapter, which offers an examination of the phenomenon of cross-border judicial cooperation in the Asian setting.[8] The main argument that I seek to develop is that this is, on balance, a desirable practice that ought to be cultivated in light of maintaining a steadfast commitment to, and the best possible implementation of, constitutional values. At the same time, David Law and Wen-Chen Chang have correctly pointed out that those who champion regional judicial dialogues must take seriously the institutional and other structural factors that determine the incentives and opportunities for such dialogues to take place.[9] I will, therefore, also examine the extent to which it is actually possible for Asian judges to nurture their ability to develop ties with judges in other countries.

The remainder of this chapter proceeds as follows. In Section II, I present a brief overview of the different modalities of cross-border judicial cooperation, ranging from formal and direct avenues for contact to more informal and indirect modalities. This is followed, in Section III, by a discussion of the reasons as to why constitutional courts should actively establish ties with their counterparts in other jurisdictions and the benefits this is expected to yield. While inter-court relationships raise important normative questions regarding the legitimacy of this practice, I contend that the practical impediments to cross-border judicial cooperation are, at present, more relevant and serious, yet also more difficult to satisfactorily address in the short to medium term. In that vein, I confront, in Section IV, the challenges

Ponthoreau (eds.), *The Use of Foreign Precedents by Constitutional Judges* (Oxford: Hart Publishing, 2013) 373–391, 391.

7 Vicki Jackson, *Constitutional Engagement in a Transnational Era* (New York: Oxford University Press, 2010) 1.

8 In keeping with the theme of this volume, the focus will be on interactions amongst courts with a constitutional mandate, although I acknowledge that this practice is not confined to those echelons of the judiciary. In the particular Asian context, consider e.g., the working committee of the ASEAN Chief Justices Meeting on child customary disputes or the Asian Judges Network on the Environment.

9 Law and Chang, 'Limits of Dialogue', 575.

that must be overcome to increase the incidence and quality of cooperation amongst Asian constitutional courts.

II Modes of Transnational Judicial Contact

At the outset, it should be noted that various forms of transnational judicial contact are said to exist. A distinction is usually drawn between direct, face-to-face interactions, on the one hand, and on the other hand, indirect engagement through the medium of judicial decisions or other written texts. Each of these categories, in turn, encompasses a range of judicial behaviours.

Several avenues for actual judge-to-judge dialogues can be identified, as alluded to in the examples offered at the opening of this chapter. It is common for judges to meet each other when hosting delegations from foreign courts or when travelling abroad to visit courts elsewhere. We have seen that this happens in Hong Kong as a matter of course, and the Korean and Indonesian constitutional courts in particular regularly trot the globe for work-related reasons. By way of illustration, in 2015, a delegation of the Indonesian Constitutional Court visited its Turkish counterpart, which has also welcomed visitors from Algeria, Kyrgyzstan and Croatia.[10] Further opportunities for face-to-face contact are provided by attending conferences organized by law schools, international bodies or courts themselves, typically to mark their more significant anniversaries. For instance, in October 2015, judges from, amongst others, the Thai, Malaysian and Korean courts participated in a conference on the role of constitutional courts in giving effect to the separation of powers and human rights to mark the twentieth anniversary of the Uzbek court.[11]

In terms of the range of participants and frequency of contact, court visits and conference participation enable a relatively *ad hoc* and unstructured form of dialogue. This explains why they have, in recent years, been complemented by the establishment of (quasi) formal platforms that allow for regular and repeated interaction amongst the same set of judges. Here, one can think of the conclusion of bilateral memoranda of understanding on a diverse range of judicial matters. Within Asia, the

[10] See the News and Events page of the Turkish Constitutional Court (at www.constitutionalcourt.gov.tr) (accessed 6 October 2017).

[11] Reported *inter alia* on the News page of the website of the Permanent Mission of the Republic of Uzbekistan to the United Nations.

Korean Constitutional Court is undoubtedly at the vanguard: it has agreed to MOUs with its counterparts in Bulgaria, Turkey and Thailand that, *inter alia*, envisage the strengthening of institutional capacities and the ability to conduct comparative law research.[12] It has also signed an MOU with the constitutional court of Mongolia to 'help lay the foundation for the development of IT services and procedures [at that court]'.[13] To be clear, such bilateral agreements do not always involve Seoul as one of the signatories: in 2014, the Indonesian and Thai constitutional courts similarly sought to promote cooperation between them by means of an MOC that allows for joint training programs, research projects and the exchange of knowledge 'on the subjects of mutual interest'.[14]

Official judicial networks, such as the Association of Asian Constitutional Courts,[15] mentioned earlier, offer a further platform for more structured judge-to-judge contact. This organization saw the light in 2010, and builds on earlier informal meetings amongst constitutional justices in the region.[16] As of this writing, the AACC's membership has more than doubled from its original seven members, and today, it includes courts with a constitutional mandate from Azerbaijan, Indonesia, Korea, Kazakhstan, Kyrgyzstan, Malaysia, Mongolia, Myanmar, Pakistan, the Philippines, the Russian Federation, Tajikistan, Thailand, Turkey and Uzbekistan, as well as the Independent Commission for Overseeing the Implementation of the Constitution of Afghanistan. The AACC has, then, embraced a broad definition of 'Asia', and it has been candid about its ambition to become a well-established judicial association to which many, if not all, courts with constitutional jurisdiction in the region belong.[17] The AACC, and the great majority of its

[12] In 2011, a special Constitutional Research Institute was set up at the Korean Constitutional Court, which has one directorate devoted to comparative research; however, the other directorates also consider relevant foreign systems and approaches in their work.

[13] See the press release, 'The court offers assistance for the development of Mongolian constitutional justice system' (2015) *Constitutional Court of Korea*, http://english.ccourt.go.kr/cckhome/eng/introduction/news/newsDetail.do?bbsSeq=43 (accessed 7 July 2015).

[14] Memorandum of Cooperation between the Constitutional Court of the Republic of Indonesia and the Constitutional Court of the Kingdom of Thailand, art. 2.

[15] The AACC has a dedicated website that can be found at www.aaccei.org (accessed 20 April 2018).

[16] A more detailed account of the AACC's genesis and functioning can be found in Maartje de Visser, 'We all stand together: The role of the Association of Asian Constitutional Courts and Equivalent Institutions in promoting constitutionalism' (2016) 3 *Asian Journal of Law and Society* 105–134.

[17] See its 2012 Seoul Declaration, paragraph 4, and its 2014 Istanbul Declaration, paragraph 3. Both texts can be found on the AACC's website.

members,[18] have, in turn, acceded to the World Conference on Constitutional Justice, which aims to facilitate a 'judicial dialogue between constitutional judges on a global scale'.[19] Both the AACC and the World Conference envisage the organization of regular conferences, symposia and seminars to allow for real-time networking.[20] Besides allocating time for serious reflection and debate on constitutional topics, their respective conference programs also typically feature a series of social–cultural events, the importance of which cannot be underestimated: these help members gain further appreciation for the environment in which one of their own performs its constitutional functions, and personal relations flourish more under the mellowing influence of wine and good cheer than during speeches in sterile hotel function rooms. The AACC further makes itself available to provide technical assistance to improve judicial independence[21] and pursues cooperation with other organizations related to constitutional matters.[22] These include associations of constitutional courts in other regions, and representatives of such groupings typically attend the biennial AACC congress. The AACC chair, for its part, reciprocates by participating in some of the events hosted by other networks of constitutional courts. This, one can surmise, allows for the sharing of best practices and mutual learning concerning the development of transnational judicial alliances and the directions that they may take. The importance of doing so should not be underestimated when one realizes that the setting up of regional judicial networks is a recent phenomenon[23] and that there is, accordingly, no traditional blueprint that courts can follow in this regard. Furthermore, in 2012, the AACC

[18] Using the definition of 'Asia' provided by the UN Statistics Division, the World Conference includes courts from central Asia (Tajikistan, Uzbekistan), Eastern Asia (South Korea, Mongolia), Southern Asia (Pakistan), South Eastern Asia (Indonesia, Thailand) and Western Asia (Armenia, Azerbaijan, Cyprus, Georgia, Israel, Lebanon and Turkey).

[19] More information can be found on its website at www.venice.coe.int/WCCJ/ (accessed 6 October 2017).

[20] AACC Statute, Art. 4(a) and (b).

[21] Ibid., Art. 4(d).

[22] Ibid., Art. 4(e).

[23] Europe has been the forerunner: The Conference of European Constitutional Courts was established in 1972. In 1997, the Union of Arab Constitutional Courts and Councils saw the light of day, followed in 2003 by the Southern African Chief Justice Forum and the launch of the Latin American Conference of Constitutional Justice in 2005. In 2011, the Conference of Constitutional Jurisdictions of Africa was established, and in 2015, that region also witnessed the founding of the Network of Constitutional Courts and Councils of West and Central Africa.

concluded a cooperation agreement with the Venice Commission[24] (the Council of Europe's advisory body on constitutional matters[25]). The agreement gives AACC courts the option to contribute to the latter's CODICES database, which holds full-text files on landmark constitutional rulings, with headnotes in English or French. They are, furthermore, given access to the Venice Forum, a closed-off section for constitutional judiciaries on the Commission's website, which allows courts to enter into direct contact with one another through electronic means and ask concrete questions, including for the purpose of adjudicating pending cases.[26]

Turning to the second broad variety of judicial contact – indirect engagement with constitutional approaches practised elsewhere through the medium of a written text – scholars have observed that, like their counterparts in other regions, Asian constitutional courts are no strangers to the use of foreign opinions in their decision-making. Foreign precedents are used as a source of inspiration,[27] and they can play the role of providing probative arguments as well as supporting *a contrario* lines of reasoning,[28] with emphasis being placed on the uniqueness of the domestic constitutional experience. The absence of comprehensive data about citation practices makes it difficult to be categorical about the identity of the suppliers of foreign decisions, but it would appear that non-Asian courts – notably the US Supreme Court and, to a lesser extent, the German *Bundesverfassungsgerichtshof* – are particularly influential,

[24] Cooperation Agreement between the Association of Asian Constitutional Courts and Equivalent Institutions and the European Commission for Democracy through Law of the Council of Europe (Venice Commission), Seoul, 22 May 2012.

[25] The Venice Commission's work has progressively extended beyond continental Europe, and in 2002, it extended its membership to non-European states. South Korea successfully applied to join this organization in 2006, and its representative on the commission has been elected as vice-chair of the Council on Constitutional Justice.

[26] According to the Venice Commission's 2015 annual report (available on its website at pp. 41–42), the forum dealt with thirty-four comparative law research requests that year pertaining *inter alia* to the adoption of children by same-sex partners and the reimbursement of legal costs related to adoption proceedings. The forum also includes a newsgroup that enables courts to inform one another about significant rulings that they have handed down and issue requests for general information.

[27] E.g., the decisions of the Indian Supreme Court in *Chiranjit Lal* v. *Union of India* (1950) 1 SCR 869; *Golak Nath* v. *State of Punjab* (1967) 2 SCR 762; *Kesavananda Bharati* v. *State of Kerala* (1973) 4 SCC 225.

[28] E.g., the decision of the Indian Supreme Court in *State of Travancore-Cochin* v. *Bombay* (1952) SC 366.

more so than those from neighbouring jurisdictions.[29] This means that, at least for the moment, the use of foreign precedents has only a limited intra-regional dimension and, thus, does little to foster engagement amongst Asian courts *inter se*. I suspect that any change in this respect will be some time in the making, not least because it requires a change in perception as to which court(s) deserve(s) to be regarded as the proverbial Hercules in constitutional adjudication. Typical reasons for judges to consult the work of their counterparts in other countries include learning about new or additional ways to tackle the problem before them and seeking to borrow some of the authority that vests in the foreign court, including in the eyes of its own interlocutors.[30] This presupposes that the donor court has built up a comprehensive body of case law addressing (almost) the full spectrum of constitutional questions and enjoys a solid reputation and respect by the other branches of government, to boot, domestically as well as further afield. An important element in realizing these qualities is, in general, the passage of time,[31] whereas – to paraphrase Judge Calabresi's observation – most of Asia's courts with a constitutional mandate have not yet reached the stage of parenthood.[32]

[29] Cf. Law, Judicial Comparativism, 1024.

[30] Developed in more detail below. See also, e.g., Albert H. Y. Chen, 'International human rights law and domestic constitutional law: Internationalisation of constitutional law in Hong Kong' (2009) 4 *National Taiwan University Law Review* 272–273, 273. The reverse situation has famously been mentioned by Justice Breyer: he explained that his controversial citation of a decision of the Supreme Court of Zimbabwe in *Knight* v. *Florida*, 528 U.S. 990, 996 (1990) was inspired by a desire to show support to beleaguered judges in their relationship with their legislators in transitional democracies, although he later admitted that this particular choice – but not the underlying rationale – might have been a 'tactical error' (Norman Dorsen, 'The relevance of foreign legal materials in U.S. constitutional cases: A conversation between Justice Antonin Scalia and Justice Stephen Breyer' (2005) 3 *International Journal of Constitutional Law* 519–541, 528).

[31] South Africa would appear to be an exception to this rule, with its constitutional court relatively quickly establishing a solid international reputation, in particular for its extensive engagement with foreign constitutional materials (authorized by South African Constitution, Art. 39(1)(c)). Its own jurisprudence and notably its progressive rulings in the area of social and economic rights has, in turn, been a source of inspiration for courts elsewhere.

[32] In his opinion in *United States* v. *Then*, 56 F. 3d 464, 469 (2d Cir. 1995), he wrote that 'Since World War II, many countries have adopted forms of judicial review, which – though different from ours in many particulars – unmistakeably draw their origin and inspiration from American constitutional theory and practice. . . . These countries are our "constitutional offspring" and how they have dealt with problems analogous to ours can be very useful to us when we face difficult constitutional issues. Wise parents do not hesitate to learn from their children.'

Amongst this cohort, the Korean Constitutional Court is most obviously committed to competing in this judicial popularity contest, which has given rise to 'a multi-pronged strategy aimed at winning regional and global influence'[33] – some elements of which we have already seen.

Judges may also engage with foreign courts and their case law in an even more indirect manner through extrajudicial writings on constitutional questions. There is as yet very little evidence of such a practice in Asia, in contrast to Europe or the United States.[34] The incidence of judges donning their writing hat for academic purposes can be accounted for in several ways: their affinity with the scholarly discourse (which, in turn, is linked to the arrangements for the selection of constitutional justices[35]), the cultural appropriateness of sitting judges writing academic treatises on points of (foreign) law and the existence of pan-regional courts with the power to issue rulings that affect domestic constitutional law, thereby creating incentives for national courts to propagate alternative accounts, including by means of scholarly contributions.[36]

In the remainder of this chapter, I will focus on direct judge-to-judge interactions, while I acknowledge that these should not be conceived of as hermetically separate from indirect forms of foreign engagement.[37] Meetings at conferences or in the context of judicial delegations have often been treated superficially, if at all, in the literature, which has grown enamoured of studies of judicial citation practices. To be sure, there is, unsurprisingly, a great deal of common ground when analysing both

[33] Law, 'Judicial diplomacy', 1024.

[34] Although judges can, and do, write extrajudicially on other topics. Singapore's chief justice has, for instance, published on a variety of international issues: Sundaresh Menon, 'Transnational commercial law: Realities, challenges and a call for meaningful convergence' (2013) 13 *Singapore Journal of Legal Studies* 231–252; Sundaresh Menon, 'International terrorism and human rights' (2014) 4 *Asian Journal of International Law* 1–33.

[35] See, e.g., Myanmar Constitution, Art. 333(d)(iv); Timor-Leste Constitution, Art. 125(2); Turkish Constitution, Art. 146.

[36] See, e.g., Andras Voßkuhle, 'Multilevel cooperation of the European constitutional courts: Der Europäische Verfassungsgerichtsverbund' (2010) 6 *European Constitutional Law Review* 175–198; Mark Bossuyt and Willem Verrijdt, 'The full effect of EU law and of constitutional review in Belgium and France after the *Melki* judgment' (2011) 7 *European Constitutional Law Review* 355–391; Rt Hon Lady Justice Arden, 'Peaceful or problematic? The relationship between national supreme courts and supranational courts in Europe' (2010) 29 *Yearbook of European Law* 3–20.

[37] For instance, the choice as to the citation of a particular foreign case or court may be precipitated by face-to-face meetings with the members of that judicial institution, and vice versa. Using foreign decisions in domestic adjudication may motivate judges to orchestrate personal encounters with the authors of those judgments.

types of judicial practices, but the immediate and synchronous quality of oral exchanges, and the kind of socialization processes that may take place in their wake, also raise issues peculiar to these modes of contact and, hence, merit attention in their own right.

III The Case for Direct Judge-to-Judge Contact across Borders

With judges increasingly willing to travel and actually interact with one another, the question of the desirability of this particular variety of judicial dialogue looms large. For reasons that I will elaborate below, my own view is that this is a welcome practice that should be extended spatially and intensified along personal and subject-matter dimensions in the future.

1 *Improve the Quality of Domestic Constitutional Adjudication*

The most intuitive, and indeed, the most frequently voiced, argument in favour of transnational judicial engagements is that these contribute to better performance of the participating judge's mandate by offering access to greater knowledge and expertise.[38] While the well-known adage 'one is never too old to learn' suggests that mature courts also may benefit from hearing about foreign constitutional approaches, Jeffrey Goldsworthy has noted that younger courts charged with enforcing a constitutional text of a more recent vintage 'have a [comparatively] greater need to seek guidance elsewhere'.[39] This would be a fair characterization of the situation in which a large portion of Asian courts with a constitutional role find themselves. From this viewpoint, bilateral visits, including those organized pursuant to an MOU, are valued for their educational potential, and participation in organizations like the AACC is sought after for the access it provides to additional resources on the myriad ways in which constitutional justice can be dispensed.[40]

[38] See, e.g., Gabor Halmai, 'The Use of Foreign Law in Constitutional Interpretation', in Michel Rosenfeld and Andras Sajó (eds.), *The Oxford Handbook of Comparative Constitutional Law* (Oxford: Oxford University Press, 2012) 1333; Anne-Marie Slaughter, 'Judicial globalization' (2000) 40 *Virginia Journal of International Law* 1103–1105, 1103.

[39] Jeffrey Goldsworthy, 'Constitutional interpretation', in Rosenfeld and Sajó (eds.), *Handbook of Comparative Constitutional Law*, 709.

[40] Cf. the preamble to the AACC Statute (identifying a 'need of sharing experiences, exchanging information, and discussing issues of mutual concern over constitutional

The impact of the availability of foreign ideas on domestic constitutional adjudication may be felt at the level of decision-making. As prominent scholars such as Anne-Marie Slaughter have predicted, learning about different approaches to classic and novel constitutional issues alike may sharpen judges' minds and broaden their horizons, which can enhance the quality of substantive decisions.[41] Legal realists will presumably agree: a judge's exposure to foreign constitutional materials and opinions may, much like his educational or religious background, shape his persuasions and world views, which in turn, can affect the manner in which he interprets domestic law (although these scholars may not necessarily characterize such an outcome as qualitatively better). Indeed, several of the protagonists themselves have admitted that they cherish opportunities to take cognizance of approaches adopted elsewhere, which are treated as an additional source of practical wisdom that can aid in the difficult business of judging hard constitutional questions.[42] This focuses attention on the debate that rages most notably in the United States about the propriety of foreign cross-citations. Critics either deny the relevance of foreign law due to local particularities, object to the manipulation of the selection of sources ('cherry-picking') that such a practice often entails or resist the judicial importation of ideas from elsewhere as undemocratic on the grounds that these do not originate from within the domestic body politic and do not respect the autochthonous nature of the constitution.[43] Given the focus of this chapter on direct as opposed to indirect engagements, this is not the place to enter into and add to that debate. A few brief comments are warranted at this juncture, however,

practice and jurisprudence *for the development of the Asian constitutional courts and equivalent institutions*' (emphasis added).

[41] Anne-Marie Slaughter, *A New World Order* (New Haven, CT: Princeton University Press, 2004) 99.

[42] See, e.g., Aharon Barak, 'A judge on judging: The role of a supreme court in a democracy' (2002) 116 *Harvard Law Review* 19, 111; Michael Kirby, 'Transnational judicial dialogue, internationalisation of law and Australian judges' (2008) 9 *Melbourne Journal of International Law* 171–189, 184; Guy Canivet, 'Trans-judicial dialogue in a global world', in Sam Muller and Sidney Richards (eds.), *Highest Courts and Globalisation* (The Hague: TMC Asser Press, 2010) 29–30.

[43] For an overview with more references, see Jackson, Constitutional Engagement, ch. 1; Sujit Choudhry, 'Migration as a new metaphor in comparative constitutional law', in Sujit Choudhry (ed.), *The Migration of Constitutional Ideas* (Cambridge: Cambridge University Press, 2006) 1–13; Michel Rosenfeld, 'Comparative constitutional analysis in United States adjudication and scholarship', in Rosenfeld and Sajó (eds.), *Handbook of Comparative Constitutional Law*, 38–53.

given the often-assumed correlation between increasing the frequency of actual judicial dialogues and the practice of foreign cross-citation.

Cheryl Saunders has observed that none of the concerns that animate the US polemic are, at present, perceived as pertinent in Asia, be it in the opinions of concurring or dissenting judges or in scholarly work.[44] Moreover, there are, in my view, several factors at play in this region that are likely to soften the tone and significance of any such debate should it erupt in the future. It has been relatively common for constitution-making or amending projects in Asia to involve a consideration (and, in a number of cases, also adoption) of foreign ideas and practices,[45] including framing domestic bills of rights in language reminiscent of international rights instruments.[46] This not-exclusively-homegrown pedigree of the constitutional text could be treated as a permit to continue the practice of looking beyond borders in constitutional interpretation.[47] Zaid Al-Ali and Arun Thiruvengadam add that, outside of the United States, consideration of foreign decisions has been used to 'enhance particular aspects of [the] domestic constitutional culture', not place it in jeopardy.[48] Also, a fair proportion of Asian constitutional

[44] Cheryl Saunders, 'Judicial Engagement', in Rosalind Dixon and Tom Ginsburg (eds.), *Comparative Constitutional Law in Asia* (Cheltenham, UK: Edward Elgar, 2014) 80–101, 88.

[45] See, e.g., the case studies on China and Japan in ch. 1 of Wen-Chen Chang, Li-ann Thio, Kevin Y. L. Tan and Jiunn-rong Yeh, *Constitutionalism in Asia: Cases and Materials* (Oxford: Hart Publishing, 2014); H. Kumarasingham (ed.), *Constitution-Making in Asia: Decolonisation and State-Building in the Aftermath of the British Empire* (Oxford: Routledge, 2016).

[46] On this, see, e.g., Paul Lauren, *The Evolution of International Human Rights: Visions Seen*, 2nd edn. (Philadelphia: University of Pennsylvania Press, 2003) at 234.

[47] Going further, Jackson, *Constitutional Engagement*, page 86 suggests that national constitutional provisions that insist that limitations of human rights must be necessary in a free and democratic society 'virtually *require* some comparison with other free and democratic countries' (emphasis added). Such clauses can, for instance, be found in the Turkish constitution (Art. 13 provides that restrictions must 'not be in conflict with … the requirements of the democratic order of the society') and the Indonesian constitution (Arts. 28I(5) and 28J(2) refer to limitations 'in accordance with the principle of a democratic and law-based state'). In a comparable vein, other Asian constitutions proclaim adherence to universally recognized principles of international law (see, e.g., Philippines Constitution, Art. II(2); Mongolian Constitution, Art. 10(1)), which could be interpreted as authorizing – if not mandating – an examination of foreign sources to uncover what these principles are.

[48] Zaid Al-Ali and Arun Thiruvengadam, 'The competing effect of national uniqueness and comparative influences on constitutional practice', in Mark Tushnet, Thomas Fleiner and Cheryl Saunders (eds.), *Routledge Handbook of Constitutional Law* (London: Routledge, 2013) 427–442.

judges operate in countries that adhere to the civil law tradition, where legal culture generally inhibits explicit references to foreign materials to a greater extent than in common law decisions – with the corollary that there is simply less fuel for malcontents to avail themselves of.[49]

The assumption so far has been that as occasions for real-life interactions multiply, so too will the effect of foreign approaches in domestic constitutional adjudication increase, including the incidence of citation of out-of-state materials. Some appear to doubt the accuracy of this narrative. Based on his personal observations with judicial networking in the European context, Michal Bobek argues that the practical utility of face-to-face encounters for deciding specific cases is 'very, very limited'.[50] He suggests that this is so for two reasons: judges 'prefer to talk amongst themselves about anything other than their cases', and the substantive information that is nevertheless shared 'tends to be superficial, selective, and random'.[51]

Two points can be made in response. On the one hand, Asian judges are able to participate in meetings specifically designed to enable the sharing of insights as to how to solve certain types of cases, which helps to alleviate the drawbacks identified by Bobek. The clearest example at present is the annual AACC Summer School on Constitutional Law that has been hosted by the Turkish Constitutional Court from 2013 onwards that focuses on the interpretation and application of specific fundamental rights such as equality, freedom of expression and the right to respect for family life. Almost all AACC member courts send judges or supporting personnel (such as research judges or advisers), who are expected to present their constitutional framework and highlight important considerations that their judicial institution considers in adjudicating issues pertaining to the fundamental right under discussion. In addition, the participants attend lectures given by experts in the field. On the other hand, if it is indeed the case that judge-to-judge interactions generally have only a minimal impact on the development of domestic constitutional case law – and this is a claim that remains to be convincingly

[49] On the relevance of this distinction in analysing the use of cross-citations, see Tania Groppi and Marie-Claire Ponthoreau, 'Conclusion. The use of foreign precedents by constitutional judges: A limited practice, an uncertain future', in Groppi and Ponthoreau (eds.), *Foreign Precedents*, 412–414.

[50] Michal Bobek, *Comparative Reasoning in European Supreme Courts* (Oxford: Oxford University Press, 2013), 49.

[51] Ibid.

proven – it means that unease about the use of foreign references is not a good reason to object to real-time contact and networking.

Now, even if actual dialogues are not very helpful for decision-making, other grounds can be marshalled in support of the practice. They can expose participants to new ideas on the organizational arrangements pertaining to constitutional adjudication: for example, one of the AACC's functions is promoting 'the exchange of views on ... structural and operational issues'.[52] Circulation of this kind of practical wisdom is valuable because it may enhance the efficiency and transparency of court proceedings, which is one strategy that a court can use to secure its legitimacy in the eyes of its domestic stakeholders. Again, this may resonate with a sizeable number of Asian courts in view of their relatively recent genesis.

2 *The 'Brotherhood' of Justices*

A second factor in favour of cross-border judicial dialogues focuses on the socializing and psychological effects attendant with direct contact. In line with Maslow's idea that humans need to feel a sense of belonging, such contact means that judges are put in a position whereby they can satiate a desire for kinship and common purpose in the sense of upholding fundamental constitutional values like justice and the rule of law. The knowledge of being part of a wider, like-minded community of judges may provide moral support to faithfully discharge their mandate and resist the temptation of pandering to public or political pressure.[53] For instance, the Indonesian Constitutional Court has received praise for swiftly establishing a reputation of independence,[54]

[52] AACC Statute, Art. 4(e).

[53] Cf. the keynote speech delivered by Christoph Grabenwarter 'Separation of Powers and the Independence of Constitutional Courts and Equivalent Bodies', 2nd Congress of the World Conference on Constitutional Justice (16 January 2011, Rio de Janeiro), in which he noted that '[multilateral cooperation] initiatives assist the constitutional court to hold an independent position in the internal separation of powers'.

[54] E.g., Simon Butt, *The Constitutional Court and Democracy in Indonesia* (Leiden, The Netherlands: Koninklijke Brill, 2015) 6; Fritz Siregar, 'Indonesian constitutional politics' (2013, October 20) *I-CONnect Blog*; Nadirsyah Hosen, 'Promoting democracy and finding the right direction: A review of major constitutional developments in Indonesia', in Albert H. Y. Chen (ed.), *Constitutionalism in Asia in the Early Twenty-First Century* (Cambridge: Cambridge University Press, 2014) 322–342, 328.

and its experience has, accordingly, been held up as worthy of study and, potentially, emulation by other courts in emerging democracies such as Myanmar.[55]

One possible corollary is a sense of transnational solidarity. This may be illustrated by considering events in Hungary in the early 2010s. Following governmental tinkering with the organization of Hungary's judiciary, the president of the Hungarian Supreme Court, Mr. Andras Baka, was forced to relinquish his post.[56] The relevant regional judicial forum, the Network of Presidents of the Supreme Judicial Courts of the EU, showed its concern about this turn of events in a variety of ways: it asked its members to call upon their ministers of foreign affairs to intervene, repeatedly met with European Commission officials to share arguments that could be useful in EU infringement proceedings directed at the relevant Hungarian measures[57] and proceeded to appoint Mr. Baka as honorary president of the network. These expressions of transnational solidarity were clearly perceived as meaningful by the latter: 'I admit that the support of my distinguished colleagues was always, and still is, really precious for me on a personal level. At the same time, and much more importantly, I perceive this decision as a sign of concern for our commonly shared values and principles.'[58] The response by the then president of the network further exemplifies the value attributed to the moral dimension of inter-court contact: '[E]ven if the content of these words of Andras Baka is the sole result of our interventions, I am already very pleased. We have done what we should and could do.'[59]

[55] E.g., chapter 11 by Andrew Harding in this volume; Gabriela Marti, 'The role of the constitutional tribunal in Myanmar's reform process' (2015) 10 *Asian Journal of Comparative Law* 153–184.

[56] Under the Transitional Provisions of the new Fundamental Law of Hungary, the supreme court would be succeeded by the Curia on 1 January 2012, and this also resulted in the premature termination of the mandate of the former's president.

[57] The matter was eventually litigated before the Court of Justice of the European Union as Case C-286/12, *European Commission* v. *Hungary* [2013] ECR 687. In addition, Mr. Baka brought proceedings in his personal capacity against the Hungarian State before the ECtHR, citing an infringement of his right to access to court: App no 20261/12 *Baka* v. *Hungary* (ECtHR, Grand Chamber, 23 June 2016).

[58] Recounted by Geert Corstens, 'Judges for Judges', speech delivered on 10 December 2012 (in Dutch) (copy on file with author).

[59] Ibid.

3 *Raising Asia's Voice on the International Plane*

Lastly, and adopting a more long-term perspective, real-time personal interactions can help nurture a stronger and more concerted Asian contribution to the global constitutional discourse. This discourse has, from the outset, been dominated by how European and North American countries have given effect to the ideals of constitutionalism and constitutional justice. In more recent years, the attitudes of non-Western states towards these ideals have begun to capture the imagination. This is an opportune turn of events: the story of the developments in Asia offers 'useful and fascinating case studies of [the successes and challenges in] the achievement of constitutionalism'[60] and advances our thinking by highlighting 'blind spots or missing categories in existing constitutional scholarship'.[61] Judge-to-judge dialogues are a potentially profitable means to raise awareness about the manner in which constitutional justice is administered in other parts of the world. We have seen that Asian courts regularly host visitors from non-Asian judicial institutions and, in turn, send delegations to courts outside the region. In addition, the AACC statute provides that observers may attend its biennial congresses, and in the past, courts from *inter alia* South Africa, Germany, Bulgaria, Armenia and Austria were accordingly able to hear AACC members' views on a range of substantive and procedural constitutional themes. The AACC's own accession to the World Conference on Constitutional Justice enables this organization to represent at least part of Asia on the world stage and share how its members understand constitutional evergreens. Different from the grounds canvassed above, under this rationale, judicial gatherings are not valued primarily for the contribution they can make to successful constitutional adjudication in Asian states: courts and others interested in constitutional justice who are located outside this region are the intended beneficiaries.

IV Coping with Normative and Practical Challenges

Assuming that one is convinced that cross-border judicial contact is worthwhile for any single or combination of the reasons set out in the

60 Albert H. Y. Chen, 'The achievement of constitutionalism in Asia: Moving beyond constitutions without constitutionalism', in Chen (ed.), *Constitutionalism in Asia*, 1–31, 3.

61 Rosalind Dixon and Tom Ginsburg, 'Introduction', in Dixon and Ginsburg (eds.), *Comparative Constitutionalism in Asia*, 1–22, 12.

previous section and that it ought to be nurtured, there are several normative and practical challenges to contend with.

As for the former type, inter-court relationships may pose a challenge to the traditional view of the position and functioning of constitutional courts. In our constitutional traditions, judges express their views through the decisions they hand down. Their *individual* personalities are supposed to be irrelevant – justice is blind, as the old adage has it. The realization that judges cross the boundaries of their domestic legal system to meet their counterparts, share information and debate common problems is a powerful reminder that this view is a legal fiction. It highlights as an important issue how to evaluate the impact of inter-court contact in shaping judicial beliefs and identities. David Law argues that judges increasingly pursue diplomatic objectives in the exercise of their functions that are targeted at their counterparts in other jurisdictions. He calls this an exercise of 'power politics' and notes that '[t]he more that courts interact with one another . . . the more likely it becomes that they will behave in ways intended to influence those in other countries.'[62] In Asia, the Korean Constitutional Court exemplifies this line of thinking. To illustrate, the press release on the occasion of the conclusion of the MOU with the Mongolian court proudly declares that the Korean Constitutional Court's international profile in the field of constitutional justice has resulted in 'an increasing number of courts . . . making requests for assistance with the development of their IT service and procedures in an effort to benchmark the Korean system *even in the area of information technology* (emphasis added)'.[63] Assuming that courts will have a modicum of success in constructing influence, and depending on the area in which such influence manifests itself (e.g., at the level of adjudicatory approaches or operational strategies), the upshot will be that we must reflect on our understanding of internal judicial independence and, concomitantly, on how this value ought to be enforced for travelling judges.

In a related vein, Frishman cautions that direct transnational contact amongst judges will induce them to behave in a concerted fashion, including as regards their self-perception and the manner in which they accordingly present themselves vis-à-vis their domestic audiences.[64]

[62] Law, 'Judicial Diplomacy', 1022–1023.

[63] Constitutional Court of Korea, 'Court offers assistance for the development of Mongolian constitutional justice system'.

[64] Olga Frishman, 'Should courts fear transnational engagement?' (2016) 49 *Vanderbilt Journal of Transnational Law* 1.

This, she fears, could create a disconnect between the court and (at least some of) its national interlocutors, thereby decreasing its social legitimacy. While there is as yet no evidence of Asian courts displaying such conduct, transnational judicial contact may thus have consequences for their position and effectiveness on the domestic plane – the ramifications would have an impact that would be felt particularly keenly in a region like Asia, where constitutional justice is not as ingrained and a natural part of the sociopolitical consciousness as in most parts of Europe and North America. As such, and although my overall position is supportive of regional judicial dialogues, I recognize that it is clearly important that the further cultivation of such a practice be balanced with the need for judges to remain attuned to their local environment, not least to give effect to the notion of accountability.

Picking up on that last notion, it is noteworthy that very few Asian courts currently provide information about their international dealings. It is accordingly difficult for domestic stakeholders (and interested academics) to learn whether a court is a member of a regional alliance, how often it receives judicial delegations or goes on visits and the objectives and outcomes of such trips.[65] This, I think, ought to be rectified. While it is desirable to retain a sufficient degree of confidentiality about the precise content of intra-judicial discussions so as to facilitate a free and frank exchange of views, there is, in my view, no good reason for courts to refrain from disclosing – ideally through a combination of press releases at the relevant point in time and a dedicated portion in their annual report – when such meetings take place, who participates or the text of any judicial cooperation agreements that have been concluded (such as MOUs). On the contrary, greater clarity on such matters would accord well with values such as transparency and provide much-needed empirical data for a better analysis of the nature and possible normative consequences of direct dialogues. Relatedly, some of the court's municipal audiences may think that the reason for not sharing such information is a desire to conceal the enormous significance and impact that judges ascribe to such face-to-face gatherings, which could confirm feelings of unease about perceptions of a

[65] An excellent example is set by the UK Supreme Court, whose annual reports (available on its website at www.supremecourt.uk) (accessed 6 October 2017) include a separate section on that court's international relations, where one can find information about the identity of the visitors hosted in London, trips undertaken by UKSC justices and the costs involved.

growing power of unaccountable judges, again with possible detrimental consequences for the court's social legitimacy.

Yet, while these issues clearly have a certain *gravitas*, they are – at least for now – more of an academic concern. In fact, the more pressing challenge is how to stimulate the frequency with which Asian judges actually interact with one another and the quality of their exchanges. Put differently, a normative debate about transnational direct contact presupposes a certain kind of usage of regional forums such as the AACC and bilateral meetings that has not (yet) been achieved as a matter of judicial practice. So, what are some of the more relevant impediments in this regard, and how might these be alleviated?

There is, first, the question of incentives to forge ties with foreign courts, including by joining the AACC. While the latter's membership has more than doubled in the five years since its establishment, a much larger proportion of Asian courts have so far refrained from joining this regional association. Any decision to that effect obviously cannot be rationalized with reference to a single factor: for instance, Japanese judges have claimed to not be aware of the AACC's existence; the Taiwanese Council of Grand Justices has so far refrained from pursuing membership for fear of being asked to leave the association in the eventuality that China's Supreme People's Court was to join; and an application by the Hong Kong Court of Final Appeal would not stand much chance of success given the requirement that AACC members must perform constitutional review in 'a sovereign country in Asia'.[66]

Yet, part of the explanation must arguably be sought in the belief among some courts or members thereof that there is no serious need to establish regular and structured interactions with counterparts in neighbouring jurisdictions. This focuses attention on the impact of the existence of other regional organizations committed to advancing constitutional ideals like the rule of law, democracy and human rights. By way of example, in 2015, the Conference of Constitutional Jurisdictions of Africa (CCJA) concluded a cooperation agreement with the African Union that provides for regular consultations between the former and the AU Commission, including in relation to relevant constitutional matters.[67] What is more, the CCJA is co-opted in the design and implementation of joint programs 'aiming at promoting democracy,

[66] AACC Statute, Art. 6(1)).

[67] Memorandum of Understanding between the Commission of the African Union and the Conference of Constitutional Jurisdictions of Africa (2015), Addis Ababa, 2 April 2015.

good governance, human and peoples' rights, constitutionalism, free and fair elections and rule of law in the African Union Member States'.[68] Such partnerships may entice courts to join regional judicial associations, notably if their state is a member of the relevant political organization that the cooperation agreement is concluded with. Similarly, all European constitutional courts are confronted by the influence that EU law exerts on domestic constitutional frameworks and on the municipal understanding of shared constitutional rights and values, and this serves as a powerful catalyst for these institutions to participate in the Conference of European Constitutional Courts.[69] Much the same can be said about the existence and functioning of regional human rights courts such as the ECtHR, the Inter-American Court of Human Rights (IACHR) and the African Court on Human and Peoples' Rights.[70]

Matters are presently very different for Asian courts with a constitutional mandate. There is the Association of Southeast Asian Nations (ASEAN), which has as one of its objectives '[t]o strengthen democracy, enhance good governance and the rule of law, and to promote and protect human rights and fundamental freedoms'[71] – the implementation of which has so far resulted in the adoption of an ASEAN Human Rights Declaration and the establishment of the ASEAN Intergovernmental Commission on Human Rights.[72] However, the latter's decidedly modest competences and non-judicial character do not make it a promising partner for Asian constitutional courts to establish contact with. The general rule of non-intervention that continues to characterize ASEAN

[68] Ibid., Art. 1.

[69] Several of its congresses have been devoted to the interplay between national and European legal orders; see, for instance, the XIIth Congress (2002, Brussels) on 'The relations between the constitutional courts and other national courts, including the interference in this area of the action of European courts' and the XVIth congress (2014, Wien) on 'Co-operation of Constitutional Courts in Europe – Current Situation and Perspectives'.

[70] The ECtHR is particularly conscious of its role as a catalyst for cross-border judicial contact: it hosts annual seminars entitled 'Dialogue between Judges' to mark the opening of the judicial year, where its members and members of national highest courts discuss themes of common interest.

[71] ASEAN Charter, Art. 1(7).

[72] Tan Hsien-li, *The ASEAN Intergovernmental Commission on Human Rights: Institutionalising Human Rights in Southeast Asia* (Cambridge: Cambridge University Press, 2011), and for a more recent study that advocates the establishment of an ASEAN court of human rights, Hien Bui, 'The ASEAN human rights system: A critical analysis' (2016) 11 *Asian Journal of Comparative Law* 111–140.

cooperation[73] has further meant that the organization's rules and policies have not had the kind of effect on domestic constitutional law that could otherwise have galvanized national judicial guardians. What is more, ASEAN is not envisaged as a pan-regional association in the image of the EU or the African Union: its geographic coverage is, as can be clearly seen from its nomenclature, restricted to only a relatively small part of the greater Asian region and excludes a number of the countries that AACC members hail from. This further circumscribes its potential as a logical rallying point or interlocutor for pan-regional judicial dialogues.

Some changes could be afoot, however. There is judicial interest in the replication of an institution like the ECtHR or the IACHR in Asia. During the third Congress of the World Conference on Constitutional Justice in 2014, the prospect of an Asian court of human rights was warmly endorsed by the judges in attendance,[74] and as of this writing, the Korean Constitutional Court is actively exploring how it can promote and steer a region-wide discussion in this regard to prepare the ground for the eventual creation of such an international court.[75] These efforts should be taken as an encouraging sign, even though it should be clear that there must be no expectation that they will bear fruit in the short to medium term, given the significant political and other hurdles that will have to be overcome in making an Asian human rights court a reality.

Secondly, the AACC has so far not realized the added value it could generate for its members as a permanent forum for judicial contact – which, in turn, could incentivize other courts to join, even in the absence of a strong regional integration impetus.[76] In fact, the claim made by one of its individual members that the AACC is 'one of the leading organisations in Asia in the field of constitutional justice'[77] is better seen as

[73] See, e.g., ASEAN Charter, Art. 2(e); Treaty of Amity and Cooperation in Southeast Asia (signed on 24 February 1976, entered into force 21 June 1976), Art. 2. Also, Linjun Wu, *East Asia and the Principle of Non-Intervention: Policies and Practices* (Baltimore, MD: Maryland Series in Contemporary Asian Studies 2000) 1.

[74] Seoul Communiqué, adopted at the culmination of the 3rd Congress of the World Conference on Constitutional Justice (Seoul, 30 September 2014).

[75] For a critical analysis of this proposal with an emphasis on the importance of inter-court relations, see Maartje de Visser, 'Cultivating judicial conversations on human rights protection under the auspices of a regional rights regime' (2017) 1 *Asian Yearbook of Human Rights and Humanitarian Law* 192–291.

[76] In more detail on the AACC's present limitations, see de Visser, 'We All Stand Together'.

[77] Haşim Kiliç, 'Welcome Message for the 2nd Congress of the AACC', on file with the author.

aspirational in nature than descriptively accurate. As we have seen, its main contribution to relationship-building is through the organizing of congresses, and there are limits to what these gatherings have achieved. AACC congresses take place every alternate year, with members having only two days to meet, debate and socialize. While attractive at first blush, increasing the frequency or duration of these congresses is likely to encounter financial and other obstacles. A more promising strategy entails making changes to the manner in which the congresses function so as to encourage the sharing of experiences and mutual learning to the fullest extent. The topics for debate have until now been pitched at a high level of generality, with the concomitant risk of participants not necessarily canvassing the same issues in their contributions.[78] When an intervention does not address a specific aspect of the general theme, the audience is left to wonder whether this is because that aspect does not play out in the country in question or because it is not perceived as problematic, and if so, why this is the case. Matters are exacerbated by the limited time available for the sharing of views – the average time allocated for discussion for each theme during the second congress was only one-and-a-half hours – and the fact that the program, accordingly, does not contemplate every member court taking the floor to address the gathering during each session.

In selecting the congress theme, AACC members ought instead to opt for depth over breadth. A more carefully delineated topic is conducive to a more focused discussion by nudging participants to exchange views on relevant (legal–technical) particulars rather than delivering constitutional platitudes. The AACC could further benefit from using questionnaires to collect and disseminate information about the constitutional praxis of its members. This methodology has been successfully employed by other judicial alliances, including the World Conference on Constitutional Justice that can count nine of the current sixteen AACC courts amongst its membership. Each AACC court would be expected to prepare a national report setting out how the various facets of the overall theme are regulated or dealt with in its jurisdiction, ideally illustrated with examples drawn from its body of case law. These national reports would then form the basis of the debate during the

[78] The theme of the inaugural congress was 'Constitutional justice in Asia at present and in the future'; during the second congress, themes ran the gamut from the protection of human rights to difficulties facing courts with a constitutional mandate to constitutional interpretation and the role of courts in protecting the constitutional order.

actual congress, thereby better enabling participants to identify and make sense of differences and similarities in approach. To further facilitate this process, the host court could be tasked with compiling a general report, to be circulated amongst the AACC members in advance, that synthesizes the national reports and pinpoints the most varied, contested or unsettled issues. Proceeding in this manner does not appear to be excessively costly in terms of resources, while it could yield considerable benefits in terms of the quality and usefulness of these gatherings.

The preceding discussion has, so far, glossed over two essential prerequisites for effective transnational judicial contact: resources and linguistic capabilities. In fact, the presence – or more likely in this region, absence – of these factors will decisively shape the extent and success of direct judicial networking in the short to medium term. Sending or receiving judicial delegations or allowing justices to participate in meetings hosted by regional associations is costly, not only in terms of funding travel, accommodations and dining expenses but also – and perhaps even more so – in terms of demands on court personnel. Direct transnational judicial interaction entails judges spending time away from the bench and could give rise to or exacerbate a case backlog. If a court has only a limited budget or is understaffed, then its members will simply not be able to participate in personal meetings in other states. Lacking the power of the purse, courts here are at the mercy of the political institutions, and in developing economies, increasing court budgets will not rank amongst the chief spending priorities. Further, mastery of English appears essential for meaningful and real discursive dialogues with foreign counterparts, including through the AACC, which conducts all its activities in this language.[79] Notably, older Asian judges who have not been abroad for their studies or other reasons may, thus, face a very real linguistic barrier[80] that might only be mitigated, or perhaps overcome, as and when younger generations who have had exposure to several languages succeed them on the bench.

79 AACC Statute, Art. 5(1). Upon request, simultaneous translation can be arranged during the biannual congresses, to be paid for by the member court in question.

80 This may explain why the Cambodian constitutional court has, to date, decided to forego membership in the AACC and has joined the *Association des Cours Constitutionnelles ayant en Partage l'Usage du Français* instead.

V Final Remarks

As constitutional justice becomes more firmly entrenched in Asia, there is every reason to expect that this will result in a growing interest in cross-border judicial cooperation amongst judges as well as within the academic community. This is a welcome development, notably because the cultivation of an epistemic community amongst courts in the region serves important instrumental aims related to their role as constitutional guardians. Yet, talk of comity and friendship amongst like-minded legal professionals who cherish each other's company should not blind us to the fact that judges simultaneously act as their state's representative when operating in a transnational setting. They can be expected to be mindful of relevant geopolitical dynamics and domestic sensitivities, and this is likely to influence decisions as to which court(s) to ally with – either through bilateral visits or MOUs or through the issuing of invitations to join official judicial networks. For their part, domestic political institutions can, and do, affect the impetus to pursue transnational contact through the ties that they forge with other states; and they shape the institutional environment of courts, thus determining *inter alia* whether these institutions will even be equipped to participate in a regional or global judicial discourse. Even assuming willingness and an open-minded mentality on the part of the protagonists, patience will, thus, be key for those committed to the flourishing of strong and truly pan-Asian judicial relationships.

5

An Evolving Court with Changing Functions

The Constitutional Court and Judicial Review in Taiwan

JIUNN-RONG YEH AND WEN-CHEN CHANG*

I Introduction

Judicial review of parliamentary acts on constitutional grounds has become a global phenomenon in recent decades. As this chapter will show, Taiwan stands as no exception to this trend. Taiwan's Constitutional Court, also known as the Council of Grand Justices, was created in 1948 and has since evolved into *a* powerful, if not *the most* powerful, institution in Taiwan's constitutional development.[1]

The rise of Taiwan's Constitutional Court, however, has not been without hurdles. Prior to the late 1980s, Taiwan was placed under the authoritarian governance of a single political party, the Kuomintang (KMT).[2] The Republic of China (ROC) Constitution, enacted on the Chinese mainland in 1946, was substantially suspended as a result of the KMT government's relocation to Taiwan in 1949 and the ensuing warfare between the KMT and the Chinese Communist Party on the mainland.[3] A martial law decree was declared, which was eventually lifted in 1987.[4] Despite those gloomy years, the Constitutional Court was sustained institutionally and continued to exercise – albeit not without substantial constraints – the powers of constitutional interpretation and judicial review.[5] The functions of the Constitutional Court became

* The authors would like to express our gratitude for the superb research assistance by Yu-Teng (Eton) Lin and Yu-Cheng (Jason) Yeh. All errors are, of course, ours.

1 Tom Ginsburg, *Judicial Review in New Democracies: Constitutional Courts in Asian Cases* (Cambridge: Cambridge University Press, 2003) 106–157; Jiunn-rong Yeh, *The Constitution of Taiwan: A Contextual Analysis* (Oxford: Hart Publishing, 2016) 1–2.

2 Yeh, ibid., 1–2.

3 Ibid., 28–30.

4 Ibid., 30–36.

5 Ibid., 171–174; Ginsburg, note 1 at 124–144.

full-blown in the late 1980s and 1990s when the democratization and constitutional reforms were undertaken.[6]

In May 2000, the success of democratic transition brought about the first peaceful transfer of government powers, after a presidential election, from the KMT to the long-time opposition, the Democratic Progressive Party (DPP). Because the KMT still held a strong parliamentary majority, a period of divided government began in which confrontational politics between the KMT and DPP required judicial resolution from time to time.[7] To meet these daunting challenges, the Constitutional Court developed a variety of sophisticated strategies, including judicial facilitation of political dialogue, essential to maintaining stability in the time of political turbulence.[8]

The years of divided government were put to an end in May 2008, when the KMT won back the presidency and continued to control the parliament. The KMT's regained political dominance placed the DPP and other members of the political oppositions onto the sidelines, and as a result, sharply reduced the number of politically charged cases entering the judicial docket. In May 2016, the DPP won back the presidency with the first woman president, and also for the first time, secured a parliamentary majority. The unitary government has thus continued, but this time, with the DPP as the ruling party.

Since the end of divided government in 2008, the Constitutional Court has rendered interpretations in about a hundred cases.[9] Among these cases, only three cases were of high political profile,[10] compared to more than a dozen such cases in the period between 2000 and 2008.[11] Perhaps, for some observers, the Constitutional Court's diminishing role in high politics was a sign of its 'gradual constitutional irrelevance', and even

[6] See notes 54–59 and accompanying text. See also Yeh, note 1 at 167–168.

[7] Jiunn-rong Yeh, 'Presidential politics and judicial facilitation of political dialogue between political actors in new Asian democracies: Comparing the South Korean and Taiwanese experiences' (2010) 8 *International Journal of Constitutional Law* 911–949.

[8] Ibid. See also Yeh, note 1 at 174–191.

[9] There are, altogether, 105 interpretations, from *Interpretation No 643* to *Interpretation No 747*, as of the time of writing in May 2017.

[10] These are *Interpretation Nos 721* (regarding constitutionality of constitutional revision on parliamentary redistricting), *729* (regarding the parliament's investigatory power over cases under criminal investigation) and *735* (regarding whether it is constitutional to hold a vote of no confidence against the Premier in an extraordinary parliamentary session convened for other purposes).

[11] There are *Interpretation Nos 520, 541, 543, 550, 553, 613, 627, 632, 633* and *645*. For detailed analyses of these cases, see Yeh, note 7 at 931–938.

'a shift away from judicial activism towards a nominal institution'.[12] The reality, however, is the opposite.

The Constitutional Court has been extensively engaged in constitutional interpretation and dispute resolution regarding constitutional rights and fundamental freedoms. Nearly all cases decided since 2008 were about fundamental rights and freedoms, and in more than half of these cases, the Constitutional Court declared the impugned statutes or government acts unconstitutional on the grounds of violation of rights.[13] One of the most recent landmark decisions was *JY (Judicial Yuan) Interpretation No 748*, in which the Constitutional Court held that the failure of the Civil Code provisions in not allowing same-sex marriage was in violation of the equal right to marriage.[14] Also notably, in many decisions involving fundamental rights and freedoms, the Constitutional Court exhibited greater willingness than before in making references to international human rights law as well as foreign jurisprudence – a feature we identified elsewhere as part of transnational constitutionalism.[15]

Aside from the introduction (Section I) and conclusion (Section V), this chapter has three main sections. Section II discusses the Constitutional Court's powers, jurisdiction and adjudicative procedure. Section III explores the process by which the Constitutional Court has successfully transformed itself and eventually made significant contributions to Taiwan's democratic transitions. Section IV highlights the court's key decisions in the last decade, from 2007 to 2017, the majority of which were concerned with fundamental rights and freedoms, including personal freedom, due process guarantee, freedom of expression, press freedom and the rights of women and minorities.

[12] Ming-Sung Kuo, 'Moving towards a nominal constitutional court? Critical reflections on the shift from judicial activism to constitutional irrelevance in Taiwan's constitutional politics' (2016) 25 *Pacific Rim Law & Policy Journal* 605–634.

[13] The cases in which declarations of unconstitutionality were made in whole or in part against impugned acts include *Interpretation Nos 644, 645, 649, 650, 653, 654, 655, 657, 658, 661, 662, 663, 664, 666, 669, 670, 673, 674, 677, 680, 685, 687, 692, 694, 696, 701, 702, 703, 704, 705, 706, 707, 708, 709, 710, 711, 712, 713, 715, 716, 718, 722, 723, 724, 730, 731, 732, 733, 734, 737, 739, 744, 745, 746* and *747*.

[14] *JY Interpretation No 748* (2017).

[15] Jiunn-rong Yeh and Wen-Chen Chang, 'A decade of changing constitutionalism in Taiwan: Transitional and transnational perspectives', in Albert H. Y. Chen (ed.), *Constitutionalism in Asia in the Early Twenty-First Century* (Cambridge: Cambridge University Press, 2014) 141–168 at 152–163.

There is no doubt that the Constitutional Court has continued to occupy a central place in the development of constitutionalism in Taiwan. Its key focus, however, is no longer on power politics, as it was in the past decades of democratic transition and divided government. Instead, the Constitutional Court has turned to engaging itself extensively in the constitutional resolution of rights disputes placed before it by vibrant civil society groups, embarking on the journey of the development of civil constitutionalism.[16]

II The Court's Powers and Procedures

Although now recognized as a successful institution, the Constitutional Court was not envisaged by the ROC Constitution, which mentioned only the Judicial Yuan as the state's highest judicial organ and grand justices appointed to serve in the Judicial Yuan.[17] In 1948, the Council of Grand Justices was created under the Judicial Yuan to exercise the power of constitutional interpretation; the council was institutionally separated from other final courts of civil, criminal and administrative litigation. A centralized model of judicial review of legislative and administrative acts – albeit not specified in the constitution – was thus established. The powers, jurisdiction and adjudicative procedure of the council were subsequently stipulated in the Council of Grand Justices Act, enacted in 1958, which was replaced by the Constitutional Interpretation Procedure Act in 1993.[18] Since the 1993 Act, the Council of Grand Justices was rechristened the Constitutional Court.

Unlike the Asian constitutional courts established during the period of democratic transition in the late 1980s and 1990s,[19] Taiwan's Constitutional Court was a much earlier creation, though without explicit constitutional specification. Yet, as the following illustrates, much of the Constitutional Court's powers and jurisdiction were altered or added later in the course of its development, especially during the democratic

[16] See Jiunn-rong Yeh, 'Marching towards civic constitutionalism with sunflowers' (2015) 45 *Hong Kong Law Journal* 315; Yeh, note 1 at 244–246.

[17] Yeh, note 1 at 157–159.

[18] The official English translation of the Act is available at www.judicial.gov.tw/constitutionalcourt/en/p07.asp (accessed 3 July 2018).

[19] Andrew Harding, Peter Leyland and Tania Groppi, 'Constitutional courts: Forms, functions and practice in comparative perspective', in Andrew Harding and Peter Leyland (eds.), *Constitutional Courts: A Comparative Study* (London: Wildy, Simmonds & Hill Publishing, 2009) 1–29 at 12.

transition and constitutional reforms in the 1990s. The key to understanding the court's changing powers and its present status lies in the evolution of its role in the course of Taiwan's democratic transition.

1 *Powers and Jurisdictions*

The Constitutional Court's two primary powers, which were vested in the Grand Justices by the ROC Constitution, are the power to interpret the constitution and the power to unify legal interpretations.[20] Before the 1980s, the majority of interpretations rendered by the Constitutional Court involved unifying statutory interpretations. However, since the late 1980s, constitutional interpretations have dominated the Constitutional Court's docket.

The court's power of constitutional interpretation encompasses the following four principal types of jurisdiction, similar to those of European-style constitutional courts: abstract review, concrete review, individual complaint and competence dispute.[21] A constitutional organ or one of the central or local government agencies may request abstract review whenever doubts arise over the constitutionality of relevant laws or ordinances.[22] Furthermore, since the enactment of the Constitutional Interpretation Procedure Act of 1993, members of the Legislative Yuan (Taiwan's legislature, or parliament) may petition the Constitutional Court, requesting an interpretation of constitutional provisions or a ruling on the constitutionality of laws, provided that the petition is supported by at least one-third of the total number of legislators.[23] This channel allows a legislative minority to levy a constitutional challenge to the final enactment of laws, but the Constitutional Court has indicated that legislators should endeavour to revise the impugned law prior to petitioning the Constitutional Court.[24]

The power of concrete review was not granted to the Constitutional Court either by the constitution or by statute. Rather, the Constitutional Court itself created this authority through *JY Interpretation No 371*.[25] This interpretation addressed the questions of whether the court had the

[20] Art. 78, Constitution of the Republic of China (1947).
[21] Wen-Chen Chang, Li-ann Thio, Kevin Y. L. Tan and Jiunn-rong Yeh (eds.), *Constitutionalism in Asia: Cases and Materials* (Oxford: Hart Publishing, 2014) 328–335.
[22] Art. 5, Constitutional Interpretation Procedure Act (1993).
[23] Art. 5(1)(3), Constitutional Interpretation Procedure Act (1993).
[24] *JY Interpretation No 603* (2005).
[25] *JY Interpretation No 371* (1995).

exclusive power of judicial review, or whether ordinary courts had concurrent jurisdiction to review the constitutionality of statutes while adjudicating concrete legal disputes. In response, the Constitutional Court asserted its exclusive power of judicial review, while reserving for the ordinary courts a referral power in cases in which the constitutionality of laws or regulations may be at issue.[26] According to the Constitutional Court, '[I]n trying a case where a judge, with reasonable assurance, has suspected that the statute applicable to the case is unconstitutional, the judge may suspend the pending procedure on the grounds that the constitutionality of the statute is a prerequisite issue and petition the Constitutional Court for interpretation.'[27]

The 1958 Council Act granted the Council of Grand Justices the jurisdiction over individual complaints. Since then, any individual, legal entity or political party may file a constitutional petition with the Constitutional Court if they believe their constitutional rights have been infringed, all other remedies provided by law for such infringement have been exhausted and they have doubts about the constitutionality of laws or regulations applied in a final judgment by a court of last resort. However, remedies for such infractions available through the Constitutional Court are limited to the review of the constitutionality of the impugned laws and regulations. The Constitutional Court cannot resolve the case or provide any direct remedies. Yet, if the Constitutional Court invalidates the impugned statute or ordinance, the petitioner will then be entitled to a retrial or an extraordinary appeal to the ordinary courts, in accordance with such decision.[28]

The Constitutional Court's final area of jurisdiction is the resolution of disputes over the respective competence of official bodies. According to the Constitutional Interpretation Procedure Act, government organs, the central government and local governments may petition the Constitutional Court for competence resolution should they have doubts about their respective jurisdiction or encounter conflict with other organs of government.[29] Throughout the period of Taiwan's democratic transition, the Constitutional Court has played a pivotal role in resolving competence disputes between the executive and legislative branches and among the different levels of government.[30]

[26] Ibid.
[27] Ibid.
[28] *JY Interpretation No 185* (1984) and *JY Interpretation No 725* (2014).
[29] Art. 5, Constitutional Interpretation Procedure Act (1993).
[30] Yeh, 'Presidential Politics', note 7 at 935–938.

In addition to the above primary powers, the Constitutional Court enjoys such ancillary powers as the adjudication of impeachment proceedings and dissolution of unconstitutional political parties.[31] Taiwan's constitutional revision of 2005 conferred on the Constitutional Court the power to adjudicate the impeachment of the president and vice president should the Legislative Yuan approve the motion of impeachment.[32] The constitutional revision of 1992 established the Constitutional Court's power to dissolve political parties whose 'goals or activities endanger the existence of the Republic of China or the nation's free and democratic constitutional order'.[33] To date, neither presidential impeachment nor dissolution of unconstitutional political parties have been presented to the Constitutional Court.

The avenues to gain access to the Constitutional Court have increased incrementally through laws and judicial interpretations. In particular, the breadth of the Constitutional Court's jurisdiction has served an important role in Taiwan's democratic transition. All in all, the court has gained diverse opportunities to play a role in a number of high-profile cases involving citizens' rights and political matters and has helped steer the process of democratization.

2 *Adjudication Procedure*

Procedurally, the Constitutional Court's rules for rendering interpretations and issuing opinions are provided by the Constitutional Interpretation Procedure Act of 1993, which replaced the Council Act of 1958. Among other changes, the 1993 Act established more trial-like procedures for the Constitutional Court. Before 1993, the Constitutional Court adjudicated cases without hearing oral arguments and relied solely on written submissions from petitioners and government agencies. Under the 1993 Act, however, the court has the discretion to hold an oral hearing.[34] Upon the request of petitioners or the justices, the Constitutional Court may order the petitioners, relevant parties or government agencies to submit briefs and other relevant documents. Occasionally, the

[31] Tom Ginsburg, 'Ancillary powers of constitutional courts', in Tom Ginsburg and Robert A. Kagan (eds.), *Institutions and Public Law: Comparative Approaches* (New York: Peter Lang Publishing, 2004) 225.

[32] Art. 2, Additional Articles to the Constitution of the Republic of China (2005).

[33] Art. 5(5), Additional Articles to the Constitution of the Republic of China (2005).

[34] Art. 13, Constitutional Interpretation Procedure Act (1993).

court may also convene informal sessions in which legal scholars or other experts are invited to provide relevant legal or policy analyses, particularly on comparative constitutional studies.[35]

A panel of three Grand Justices carries out a preliminary review to determine whether to admit or dismiss the petition. The panel's draft decision is then submitted to the Constitutional Court for deliberation.[36] The quorum required to render an interpretation depends on the nature of the interpretation at issue. To render an interpretation or to rule on the constitutionality of statutes, a quorum is defined as two-thirds of the Grand Justices currently in office, and two-thirds of those present are required for consent to the decision. For matters regarding the constitutionality of administrative rules, a quorum is similarly defined as two-thirds of the incumbent Grand Justices, but the votes of only half of those present are necessary for consent to a decision. For matters regarding a unified interpretation of laws or administrative rules, the number of Grand Justices required to constitute a quorum is reduced to half of the incumbents, and half of those present are required for consent. The most stringent requirements govern the dissolution of an unconstitutional political party. For such matters, a quorum is comprised of at least three-quarters of the incumbent Grand Justices, and two-thirds of those present are required for consent.

Notably, the rules concerning quorums required for interpretations by the Constitutional Court have undergone significant changes. The first-term Council relied on its self-enacted rules for rendering interpretations. During this period, interpretations required only a simple majority for passage. The 1958 Council Act altered this simple majority rule by requiring the presence of three-quarters of the Grand Justices to constitute a quorum, and three-quarters of those present to pass a constitutional interpretation. This high threshold was a reprisal enacted by the Legislative Yuan in an effort to paralyse the Constitutional Court as a result of the Legislative Yuan's dissatisfaction with *JY Interpretation No 76*, which held that the National Assembly, the Legislative Yuan and the Control Yuan all stood on equal footing as parliamentary institutions.[37]

[35] David Law and Wen-Chen Chang, 'The limits of global judicial dialogue' (2011) 86 *Washington Law Review* 523–567 at 563.

[36] Arts 10 and 11, Constitutional Interpretation Procedure Act (1993).

[37] Jiunn-rong Yeh, 'The Cult of *Fatung*: Representational manipulation and reconstruction in Taiwan', in Graham Hassall and Cheryl Saunders (eds.), *The People's Representatives: Electoral Systems in the Asia-Pacific Region* (Sydney: Allen & Unwin, 1997) 23–37.

After the Constitutional Court passes an interpretation, concurring or dissenting justices may provide their own separate opinions within five days. The Constitutional Court's majority interpretation, as well as concurring and dissenting opinions, are then released to the public.[38] The number of concurring and dissenting opinions has risen sharply since the late 1980s.[39] Especially in recent years, it has not been uncommon for one interpretation to be accompanied by six to seven individual concurring or dissenting opinions.[40]

III The Road to Transformation

The establishment of the Council of Grand Justices coincided with the constitutional crisis that resulted from the ROC government's retreat to Taiwan. The early years of the Council saw itself more as a legal advisor to the government[41] rather than an impartial adjudicator of constitutional disputes. The Council did not become an effective judicial institution until the Martial Law Decree was lifted in 1987 and the subsequent political liberalization and democratic transition began.[42]

1 The Rubber Stamping Court

Before the 1980s, the Constitutional Court's impact was limited due to authoritarian governance. For the most part, the court served as a legal advisor to the government, rendering decisions that unified interpretations of statutes or ordinances. However, in a few cases, the court was called upon to resolve constitutional crises that resulted from the ROC government's retreat from the Mainland to Taiwan.

JY Interpretation No 31, rendered in 1954, was one of the Constitutional Court's first infamous decisions, occurring at a time when the

[38] Art 17, Constitutional Interpretation Procedure Act (1993).

[39] Wen-Chen Chang and Jiunn-rong Yeh, 'Judges as discursive agent: The use of foreign precedents by the Constitutional Court of Taiwan', in Tania Groppi and Marie-Claire Ponthoreau (eds.), *The Use of Foreign Precedents by Constitutional Judges* (Oxford: Hart Publishing, 2013) 373–391 at 382–384.

[40] See www.judicial.gov.tw/constitutionalcourt/en/p07.asp (accessed 3 July 2018).

[41] See Yueh-sheng Weng, 'Interpretations of the constitutional court and the developments of rule of law and democratic constitutionalism in Taiwan', in Dirk Ehlers, Henning Glaser and Kittisak Prokati (eds.), *Constitutionalism and Good Governance: Eastern and Western Perspectives* (Baden-Baden: Nomos, 2014) 321–360.

[42] Tom Ginsburg, 'Confucian constitutionalism? The emergence of constitutional review in Korea and Taiwan' (2002) 27 *Law & Social Inquiry* 763–799.

KMT government was determined to 'take back the Mainland' and assert its legitimacy to govern as the only government of the whole of China.[43] When the first-term tenure of legislative representatives expired in 1954 and no election could be held on the Mainland to fill the vacancies, a constitutional solution was required. The court extended the representatives' terms, ruling that 'the nation was under crisis and the country could not hold the election for the second term legally'.[44] As a result of the court's ruling, those first-term representatives continued to serve for the next four decades, resulting in distortions of representation. Following the death of some of those representatives, legislative measures were undertaken to fill their vacancies by holding supplementary elections or by adding more seats for representatives elected locally in Taiwan. Occasionally, the Constitutional Court was called upon to provide legitimacy for these politically expedient solutions. For instance, in *JY Interpretation No 85*, the Constitutional Court ruled that the calculation of the total number of members of the National Assembly for the purpose of the quorum should be based on those who were able to convene.[45] Likewise, in *JY Interpretation Nos 117* and *150*, the Constitutional Court affirmed the constitutionality of adding extra seats to both the Legislative Yuan and the National Assembly by means of legislative enactments.[46]

Prior to the 1980s, the Constitutional Court rarely asserted itself as the guardian of the constitution. On rare occasions, however, the court nevertheless risked undermining its own institutional authority by standing in opposition to other branches of government. In *JY Interpretation No 86*, which was decided in 1960, the court held that the law that allowed the Ministry of Justice to supervise the lower courts was inconsistent with the constitution and required all courts to be placed under the Judicial Yuan.[47] However, this decision was ignored by the government, and the impugned law was not revised until 1980, two decades following the original decision.

Ginsburg and Moustafa have argued that courts in an authoritarian context may still provide social-control functions such as controlling administrative agents, legitimizing controversial policies and providing

[43] Yeh, note 37 at 23.
[44] *JY Interpretation No 31* (1954).
[45] *JY Interpretation No 85* (1960).
[46] *JY Interpretation No 117* (1966); *JY Interpretation No 150* (1977).
[47] *JY Interpretation No 86* (1960).

credible commitments in the economic sphere.[48] Prior to the 1980s, Taiwan's Constitutional Court had, indeed, performed such functions.[49] For example, when faced with disputes arising from controversial issues such as land reform and redistributive measures, the court was called upon to deal with the technical and interpretive aspects of issues concurrently in order to lend a legitimacy to the disputed policy.[50]

Apart from legitimating social and political policies, the Constitutional Court also began to bolster its own institutional authority, particularly in the early 1980s, when it rendered several decisions that reinforced the legal standing of its own interpretations. For instance, in *JY Interpretation No 177*, the court stressed that 'an Interpretation given by this Yuan in response to a petition shall also be applicable with respect to the legal action of the petitioner, in respect of which the original petition was made'.[51] Further, in *JY Interpretation No 185*, the court made it clear that its interpretations 'shall be binding upon every institution and person in the country, and each institution shall abide by the meaning of these interpretations in handling relevant matters'; any 'prior precedents which are contrary to these interpretations shall automatically be nullified'.[52] More importantly, the court fashioned a remedy that had previously been unavailable to successful petitioners. The court stated in *JY Interpretation No 185* that 'in the case of a final and irrevocable judgment where the statute or ordinance or the interpretation of such a statute or ordinance applied in rendering such judgment is deemed contrary to the Constitution ... the party against whom such final and irrevocable judgment is entered shall be entitled to apply for a retrial or an extraordinary appeal on the basis of said interpretation'.[53] As expected, individuals' petitions to the Constitutional Court rose sharply after this interpretation.

[48] See Tamir Moustafa and Tom Ginsburg, 'Introduction: The functions of courts in authoritarian politics', in Tom Ginsburg and Tamir Moustafa (eds.), *Rule by Law: The Politics of Courts in Authoritarian Regimes* (Cambridge: Cambridge University Press, 2008) 1–22.

[49] See Wen-Chen Chang, 'The governing functions of the constitutional court and administrative courts of ROC', in Jau-Yuan Huang (ed.), *The Legacy and Sustainability of Rule of Law* [Fachi te Chu'ancheng yu Yunghsu] (Taipei: Sharing, 2013) 75–108 (in Chinese).

[50] The court dealt with such issues in various interpretations, such as *JY Interpretation Nos 78, 124* and *125*.

[51] *JY Interpretation No 177* (1982).

[52] *JY Interpretation No 185* (1984).

[53] Ibid.

2 *The Tipping Point of Change*

Political liberalization and democratization in the late 1980s and early 1990s placed the Constitutional Court at the centre of Taiwan's transitional politics. Perhaps the most prominent case was *JY Interpretation No 261*, in which the Constitutional Court ordered 'those first-term national representatives who have not been re-elected on a periodical basis to cease the exercise of their powers no later than December 31, 1991'.[54] The court went even further, requiring the government 'to hold, in due course, a nationwide second-term election of the national representatives including a certain number of representatives-at-large . . . so that the constitutional system will function properly'.[55] *JY Interpretation No 261*, together with other reform measures, made possible Taiwan's unprecedented political and constitutional reforms of the 1990s and early 2000s. Political disputes and controversies that have arisen from these reforms continue to demand judicial resolution. The pinnacle of the Constitutional Court's institutional power and strength was reflected in *JY Interpretation No 499*, in which the court invalidated in its entirety the constitutional revision of 1999.[56] The Constitutional Court's institutional prominence grew during the 1990s, transforming it into an even more indispensable judicial authority as it entered the new millennium.

During the period of divided government between 2000 and 2008, in which the DPP held the executive powers and the KMT dominated the parliament, serious political confrontations required judicial resolution. The Constitutional Court became a primary political mediator of highly charged political disputes; it adopted what we call a 'dialectic approach' in facilitation of political dialogues.[57] For example, in a constitutional dispute concerning the suspension of the construction of a nuclear power plant, the Constitutional Court held that the DPP-led government should negotiate with the KMT-dominated parliament to resolve the issue.[58] In another case where a KMT-led local government had a financial dispute with the DPP-led central government concerning the national health insurance programme, the Constitutional Court adopted a similar pro-dialogue approach and

[54] *JY Interpretation No 261* (1990).
[55] Ibid.
[56] *JY Interpretation No 499* (2000).
[57] Yeh, note 30; Wen-Chen Chang, 'Strategic judicial responses in politically charged cases: East Asian experiences' (2010) 8 *International Journal of Constitutional Law* 885–910.
[58] *JY Interpretation No 520* (2001).

emphasized that both governments needed to negotiate with one another in order to reach a consensus.[59]

3 *The Overall Performance*

The impact of the Constitutional Court's functional transformation is best demonstrated by examining the number of petitions it has received over the course of its existence. According to the statistics, the number of petitions to the court has risen sharply, as follows: 658 petitions in the first term (1948–1958), down to 355 in the second (1958–1967), rising to 446 in the third (1967–1976), dramatically increasing to 1,145 in the fourth (1976–1985), roughly doubling to 2,702 in the fifth (1985–1994), and falling slightly to 2,334 in the sixth (1994–2003).[60] In the sixth term, the Constitutional Court received a yearly average of nearly 250 petitions. Since 2003, this yearly figure has more than doubled to an average of 520 petitions.[61]

In addition, among the petitions submitted to the Constitutional Court, the majority have originated from individuals concerned about infringement of their constitutionally protected rights by impugned laws or regulations. According to the statistics, altogether, there were 7,640 petitions from the court's first to its sixth terms (1948–2003). Of these, 6,825 (89.33 per cent) were from individuals, and 815 (10.67 per cent) were from government agencies.[62] Following its first and second terms, the court consistently received 90 per cent or more of its petitions from individuals over the course of its subsequent terms – a trend that supports the view that one of the Constitutional Court's paramount functions has been to safeguard the fundamental rights and freedoms of individuals.[63] Furthermore, the fact that the court issued a majority of its interpretations in the years since the 1980s tends to support the theory that increased political liberation and democratization have dramatically increased the efficiency of the court.

[59] *JY Interpretation No 550* (2002).

[60] See www.judicial.gov.tw/constitutionalcourt/en/p07.asp (accessed 3 July 2018).

[61] The number of petitions to the Constitutional Court has been on a steady rise since 2003. In 2003–2007, the annual numbers of petitions were 459 (in 2003), 465 (in 2004), 524 (in 2005), 500 (in 2006) and 549 (in 2007). There were 913 petitions in 2012, 896 petitions in 2013, 840 petitions in 2014, 745 petitions in 2015 and 827 petitions in 2016. More detailed information is available at www.judicial.gov.tw/constitutionalcourt/en/p07.asp (accessed 3 July 2018).

[62] See www.judicial.gov.tw/constitutionalcourt/en/p07.asp (accessed 3 July 2018).

[63] During the first term, 65.65% of the petitions were from government agencies, while 34.35% were from individuals. In the second term, 19.44% of the petitions were from government agencies, while 80.56% were from individuals. See www.judicial.gov.tw/constitutionalcourt/en/p07.asp (accessed 3 July 2018).

The Constitutional Court's functional transformation is further reflected in the number of uniform or constitutional interpretations. During its first three terms, the court dealt mostly with the uniform interpretation of statutes or ordinances in the context of the 'Temporary Provisions Effective During the Period of National Mobilization for Suppression of the Communist Rebellion' (*hereinafter* 'Temporary Provision') and the imposition of martial law. During this period, the court could act only as a legal advisor to resolve technical legal issues for the authoritarian government.[64] In its fourth term, the court broke away from this limited role, with the number of its constitutional interpretations surpassing the number of uniform interpretations. Since its fifth term, the court has delivered far more constitutional interpretations than before. In fact, constitutional interpretations have constituted more than 90 per cent of the interpretations rendered by the court. Thus, this shift has signalled the Council of Grand Justices' transformation into a genuine and effectively functional constitutional court.

The final indicator of the transformative Constitutional Court is the number of interpretations in which the impugned statutes or ordinances were deemed unconstitutional. The Constitutional Court's first three terms produced only one interpretation with a declaration of unconstitutionality. The fourth term had only four such findings of unconstitutionality. The number of unconstitutional findings rose dramatically in the court's fifth term, with a finding of unconstitutionality in 42 out of a total of 149 constitutional interpretations (28.2 per cent). The ratio of unconstitutional findings climbed again in the court's sixth term (75 out of 191 constitutional interpretations, or 39.3 per cent) and again rose to a record high (67 interpretations out of 135 constitutional interpretations, 49.6 per cent) in the period from 2003 to 2013. The Constitutional Court has unequivocally become a powerful constitutional institution, signalled by the fact that the court has struck down nearly half of the challenged statutes and regulations that have come before it. The record high number of unconstitutional findings in the last decade may suggest that the court has become even more uninhibited in exercising its final decision-making authority.

IV Notable Decisions from the Last Decade

As discussed in the introductory section of this chapter, confrontational politics ended in 2008 when the KMT came to control both the executive

[64] Weng, note 41 at 321–360.

and legislative powers. The unitary government has since continued, as in 2016, the DPP won back the presidency with the first woman president and secured a parliamentary majority for the first time. The unity of the executive and legislative branches has seen a decline in the number of politically high-profile cases entering into the Constitutional Court's docket.[65] At the same time, the number of individuals' petitions challenging legislative or executive acts on grounds of violation of constitutional rights continued to rise steadily,[66] and the Constitutional Court has responded to these rights challenges with a high number of declarations of unconstitutionality.[67] A recent example was the decision on same-sex marriage on 24 May 2017, in which the Constitutional Court held unconstitutional the Civil Code provisions that failed to recognize gay couples' equal right to marriage.[68]

The following discussion will highlight notable decisions from the last decade, most of which were concerned with constitutional rights, including personal freedom, due process guarantee, freedom of expression, press freedom and the rights of women and minorities. Apart from these rights decisions, one other decision is also worthy of special mention. This is *JY Interpretation No 721*,[69] in which the Constitutional Court for a third time in its history reviewed the constitutionality of a constitutional amendment. However, unlike the previous decisions, this time, the Constitutional Court sustained the impugned constitutional amendment.

1 *Personal Freedom and Due Process Guarantee*

Article 8 of the ROC Constitution provides a strong guarantee for the protection of personal freedom, prescribing that 'no person shall be tried or punished otherwise than by a law court in accordance with the procedure prescribed by law', and that 'any arrest, detention, trial, or punishment which is not in accordance with the procedure prescribed by law may be resisted'. Since the early 1990s, the Constitutional Court has read this provision as demanding both substantive and procedural due process guarantees in circumstances where individuals' physical freedoms are

[65] See notes 9–10 and accompanying text.
[66] See notes 61–62 and accompanying text.
[67] See notes 13–15 and accompanying text.
[68] *JY Interpretation No 748* (2017).
[69] *JY Interpretation No 721* (2015).

encroached upon by the exercise of government powers.[70] According to the court, any measures restraining physical freedom must be carried out in accordance with the procedure prescribed by law, and the content in those measures must be proper in substance and comply with the principles of statutory prescription (alternatively translated as 'legislative reservation') and proportionality in Article 23 of the constitution.[71]

Although Article 8 expressly refers to the restraint on physical freedom in a criminal context, the Constitutional Court has nevertheless applied it in much broader contexts, including administrative and disciplinary contexts. For the court, physical freedom is the foundation of all freedoms, and thus, any measure imposed by the government to restrain the physical freedom of a person, irrespective of whether or not he or she is a criminal suspect or defendant, must comply with necessary judicial procedure as well as other due process guarantees.[72] In addition, the Constitutional Court has also extended the application of due process requirements – albeit not expressly stipulated in the constitution – beyond physical freedoms. In cases concerning violation of the right to work or to serve in the government, or concerning infringement of property rights, the Constitutional Court has required the provision of due process guarantees, such as the right to be heard and the right to seek timely judicial remedies.[73]

In the last decade, the Constitutional Court continued to adopt a broad reading of Article 8 and generously extended due process guarantees to various contexts. Most remarkable was *JY Interpretation No 708*, made in 2013, in which the Constitutional Court declared that the protection of physical freedom alongside due process guarantees in Article 8 should not only apply to ROC nationals but also to foreigners.[74] According to the court, the protection of the physical freedom of each individual – regardless of his or her nationality – is a common principle in modern society, thus the guarantee of physical freedom with due process must extend to foreign nationals in Taiwan. As a result, the Constitutional Court held that the impugned provisions concerning deportation proceedings were unconstitutional for lack of prompt and effective judicial remedies provided for foreigners being deported. In addition, the Constitutional Court extended

[70] *JY Interpretation No 384* (1995).
[71] For further explanation of these principles as they have been developed in Taiwan, *see* Yeh, note 1 at 184–186.
[72] *JY Interpretation No 396* (1996).
[73] For example, *JY Interpretation No 409* (1996); *JY Interpretation No 462* (1998).
[74] *JY Interpretation No 708 (2013).*

the protection of physical freedom and due process guarantees to those from Mainland China in *JY Interpretation No 710*. As the relevant statutory provisions failed to provide deported mainlanders with due process guarantees, they were found unconstitutional; the court prescribed that they would lose effect in two years' time.[75]

Also notable is the recent extension of due process guarantees to circumstances of infringement of the right to adequate housing, freedom of residence and property rights in the contexts of urban renewal, city planning and property takings. In 2013, the Constitutional Court held in *JY Interpretation No 709* that the Urban Renewal Act was inconsistent with due process guarantees required by the constitution as it failed to establish an appropriate body to review urban renewal plans and to ensure that interested parties would be informed of all relevant proceedings and of the opportunity to present their opinions in a timely manner.[76] In addition, the required proportion of persons entering into an agreement needed for an urban renewal application was also found unconstitutional.[77] This interpretation was a landmark decision, because the Constitutional Court, for the first time, held that due process guarantees must apply to a variety of fundamental rights and the detailed requirements of due process must correspond to 'the types of fundamental rights involved, the strength and scope of the restrictions on rights, the public interests pursued, the proper function of the determining authority, as well as the existence of alternative procedures and their costs'.[78] Clearly, the Constitutional Court has extended due process guarantees well beyond Article 8.

It was not at all a surprise that the Constitutional Court decided to apply due process to broader contexts other than restraint of physical freedoms. In Taiwan, recent years have seen stronger protests against urban renewals or redistricting plans and the government taking private properties. In the Constitutional Court's view, due process requirements may create a better set of mechanisms under which various stakeholders and government can communicate with one another and mediate conflicting interests, given the scarcity of land and related resources. Based on the same due process guarantees, the Constitutional Court subsequently held unconstitutional a provision of the Land Expropriation Act, because it did not give the

[75] *JY Interpretation No 710 (2013).*
[76] *JY Interpretation No 709 (2013).*
[77] Ibid., para. 1 of the court's ruling.
[78] Ibid., para. 4 of the court's reasoning.

landowner sufficient time to choose a method of compensation.[79] The court also decided to change an earlier interpretation so as to permit those whose rights would be affected by alteration of an urban plan to lodge an administrative appeal.[80] In a recent case, the Constitutional Court stipulated limits to government takings of private property for purposes of public transportation, demanding the relevant statute be written more specifically and with better procedures of notice.[81]

In exceptional situations, however, the Constitutional Court may be less demanding on due process protection even if physical freedom is substantially restrained. When the Severe Acute Respiratory Syndrome (SARS) crisis hit Taiwan in 2003, a special law was enacted to permit the government to impose compulsory quarantine on those who had contact with patients of contagious disease or suspected of being infected in order to control the spreading of SARS. The constitutionality of compulsory quarantine was challenged, and in 2011,[82] the Constitutional Court sustained such an extraordinary measure. For the court, the purpose of compulsory quarantine was to safeguard the life and health of individuals, and given the special needs of the circumstances, compulsory quarantine was a reasonable and necessary measure and consistent with due process requirements in the constitution.[83]

2 *Freedom of Expression and Prior Restraint*

The guarantee of freedom of expression is essential to the effective functioning of democracy. In the course of the democratic transition in the 1990s, Taiwan's Constitutional Court has strived to restore the freedom of expression that was substantially suppressed by the previous authoritarian governance.[84] In a landmark decision in which several provisions restricting the right of free assembly and parade were

[79] *JY Interpretation No 731 (2015).*

[80] *JY Interpretation No 742 (2016).* The earlier interpretation was *JY Interpretation No 156 (1979)*, which did not allow those whose interest was affected by an alternation of an urban plan to lodge administrative appeals because such an alteration was not deemed as directly affecting the rights of interested parties.

[81] *JY Interpretation No 743 (2016).*

[82] The applicant of this case was quarantined in 2003 during the SARS crisis. He then litigated his case to the Taipei High Administrative Court in 2004, and to the Supreme Administrative Court in 2006, but failed in both courts. Later, in 2007, the applicant petitioned the Constitutional Court, challenging the legal basis for compulsory quarantine.

[83] *JY Interpretation No 690 (2011).*

[84] Weng, note 41 at 321–360; Yeh, note 1 at 213.

invalidated, the Constitutional Court stressed that 'based on the idea that sovereignty lies with the people, the people shall enjoy the right to freely discuss and fully express their opinions so that facts will be sought after and the truth will be discovered, and that the public will shall be formed by means of the democratic process to propose policies and enact laws.'[85] Thus, 'the freedom of expression is the most important fundamental human right in practicing democracy' and the purposes of protecting free speech 'are to respect the dignity of an individual's independent existence and his or her autonomy to freely engage in activities'.[86]

Influenced by the First Amendment jurisprudence of the United States, the Constitutional Court has adopted the distinction between content-based and content-neutral restrictions and the differentiation between high-value and low-value speech.[87] Content-neutral restrictions – such as time, place or manner restrictions on public gatherings or parades – may be reasonably justified, but content-based restrictions must be subject to more stringent review.[88] In addition, the Constitutional Court has deemed commercial speech of drug advertisement[89] and obscene speech of erotic novels and comics[90] to be within the scope of protected speech. Yet, due to the low-value nature of both types of speech, their restrictions can be reasonably justified on the grounds of protecting public health and maintaining sexual morality or social decency.[91] In contrast, high-value speech must be protected and restrictions on it subject to the most stringent standards of review. The Constitutional Court has invalidated content-based restrictions in both the Assembly and Parade Act and the Civic Organizations Act that prohibited the formation of civic organizations and public gatherings and parades that advocate communism or secession of territory.[92]

More recent progress in the protection of free speech concerned the regulation of prior restraint. Unlike Japan and South Korea,[93] Taiwan's constitution does not expressly ban prior restraint, a method of

85 *JY Interpretation No 445 (1998).*
86 Ibid.
87 Yeh, note 1 at 209–221.
88 *JY Interpretation No 445 (1998).*
89 *JY Interpretation No 414 (1996).*
90 *JY Interpretation No 617 (2006).*
91 Yeh, note 1 at 212–213.
92 *JY Interpretation No 445 (1998); JY Interpretation No 644 (2008).* See also Yeh, note 1 at 210–211.
93 Article 21 of Japan's Constitution states that no censorship shall be maintained, and a similar ban also appears in the Constitution of South Korea. For further discussion, see Chang et al., note 21 at 643–644.

government censorship typically imposed on printing press or other forms of expression prior to publication. Since the abrogation in 1999 of the Publication Act, which had imposed prior restraint on printing press and publications for decades, there has been no government censorship imposed on any printing press or other forms of publication. Yet, prior restraint has continued in other areas of expression involving various forms of government censorship, such as a prior approval for public assembly[94] or drug advertisements.[95] This worried many as it may have chilling effects on freedom of expression in a democratic society.[96]

Since 2008, the Constitutional Court has gradually narrowed down the system of prior restraint involving government censorship of free speech. The first case was *JY Interpretation No 644*, in which the Constitutional Court unequivocally found content-based restrictions on the formation of civil organizations was unconstitutional.[97] The second case came at a time when the government was confronted with the Sunflower Movement that staged protests against a proposed trade agreement between Taiwan and China within the parliament building in Taipei for a month.[98] In *JY Interpretation No 718*, while the Constitutional Court continued to sustain the system of prior approval for public assembly and parade, it made an exception for simultaneous or urgent public assembly and parade, where a crowd may simultaneously gather due to a special cause without any prior organization.[99]

The last and most recent case involved the regulation of cosmetics advertisements, under which advertising cosmetics required prior government approval.[100] The Constitutional Court deemed such a regulation to be prior restraint – the most severe form of infringement of free speech, to be placed under a presumption of unconstitutionality. Since that presumption was applicable, a strict scrutiny must be exercised. First, the court would consider whether the restriction is for substantial public interest, which is to protect individuals from direct, immediate and irreparable harm to their life, body and health. Second, the court would consider whether there is any direct and absolute relationship between the restriction and the substantial public interest the former

94 Yeh, note 1 at 209–210.
95 *JY Interpretation No 414 (1996).*
96 Thomas I. Emerson, 'The doctrine of prior restraint' (1955) 20 *Law & Contemporary Problems* 648–671 at 655–660.
97 *JY Interpretation No 644 (2008).*
98 Yeh, 'Marching Toward Civic Constitutionalism', note 16 at 315.
99 *JY Interpretation No 718 (2014).*
100 *JY Interpretation No 744 (2017).*

purports to achieve. Third, the court would consider whether there is an immediate judicial remedy available for individuals thus harmed. This was the first time ever that Taiwan's Constitutional Court exercised the so-called strictest scrutiny to enhance the freedom of expression; as expected, the impugned regulation was held unconstitutional.[101]

3 *Press Freedom and the Media*

Since the democratization began in the late 1980s, Taiwan has seen a thriving and robust development of press and media. In 2017, Taiwan received an improved rating by Freedom House from 2 to 1 as a fully free country due to the demonstration of media independence.[102] The freedom of press and media is not expressly guaranteed in the ROC Constitution, but it has been achieved through a series of constitutional interpretations, some of which were fairly recent.

In *JY Interpretation No 364,* the Constitutional Court extended – for the first time – constitutional protection to freedom of press and media by unequivocally stating that 'the freedom of speech through radio and television is protected under Article 11 of the constitution', guaranteeing individual freedoms of speech, teaching, writing and publication.[103]

In 2006, when the Constitutional Court dealt with the constitutionality of an independent commission regulating public communications, it affirmed that the freedom of communication was within the protected scope of free speech as it was 'the freedom to operate or utilize broadcasting, television and other communications and mass media networks to obtain information and publish speeches.'[104] According to the Constitutional Court, because 'communications and mass media are the means and platforms by which public opinions are formed', the government is obligated to 'actively devise institutions to prevent information monopoly and to guarantee pluralistic views distributed via the platforms'.[105] Following this decision, in light of limited radio frequencies, the Constitutional Court also pointed out that the government 'should allocate radio frequencies fairly and reasonably to safeguard the freedom of expression'.[106]

[101] Ibid.

[102] Freedom House, 'Freedom in the World 2017', available at https://freedomhouse.org/report/freedom-world/2018/taiwan (accessed 3 July 2018).

[103] *JY Interpretation No 364 (1994).*

[104] *JY Interpretation No 613 (2006).*

[105] Ibid.

[106] *JY Interpretation No 678 (2010).*

Whether press freedom should also be extended to journalists was a key issue in *JY Interpretation No 689*, decided in 2011.[107] In this case, a journalist was fined for stalking a famous couple and challenged the constitutionality of the law on the basis of press freedom. The government, however, argued that the law was for the protection of individuals' privacy. The Constitutional Court eventually struck a balance between the two rights, narrowing the applicable scope of the provision in imposing a fine while sustaining it. According to the court, 'a journalist's stalking another person shall be considered to have legitimate reasons and shall not be subject to penalty by the aforementioned provision if, judging from the facts, a specific event is of concern to the public, of public interest, and newsworthy, and the stalking is not intolerable under the general social standard'.[108] Thus read narrowly, the provision at issue was not inconsistent with the constitution.

The court considered press freedom as indispensable to ensuring 'that news media can provide newsworthy and diverse information, promoting full and adequate flow of information to satisfy the people's right to know, formation of public opinion and achieving public oversight' in a democratic and pluralistic society. The freedom of press should include freedom of newsgathering for the purpose of providing the contents of news reports.[109] More importantly, according to the court, a citizen journalist should enjoy the same right as does a professional journalist, because the freedom of newsgathering does not only protect 'a journalist who works for a press institution but also protects an ordinary person who gathers information with the aim of providing newsworthy information to the public or promoting the discussion of public affairs to supervise the government'.[110]

With regard to the right of privacy, albeit not expressly guaranteed in the constitution, the court has deemed it to be an unenumerated constitutional right, which includes the rights of self-control of personal information in earlier decisions.[111] In the present case, the court reasoned that individuals also enjoy their privacy in a public place, but this right is not without limits. According to the court, 'whether stalking can be legally justified depends on whether the stalker has justifiable reasons based on an overall assessment of the factors, including the purpose, the

107 *JY Interpretation No 689 (2011).*
108 Ibid.
109 Ibid.
110 Ibid.
111 *JY Interpretation No 585 (2004); JY Interpretation No 603 (2005).*

circumstances of the relevant people, time, place and context, the extent to which the one being stalked is intruded upon and whether or not the intrusion caused by the stalking has exceeded the reasonable tolerance of the general public'.[112]

The tension between the rights of the press and individuals has also been shown in a few other decisions. For example, a balance was struck between the two by providing individuals with the right of access to the media, including a right to reply if confronted by erroneous reporting or unfair comments by the media.[113] As it was considered that the media was not ready for self-regulation by means of effective mechanisms, the Constitutional Court upheld the criminalization of defamation, albeit with narrowed construction and application.[114] In civil cases involving defamation, the Constitutional Court also found a court-imposed apology constitutional for balancing the right of reputation and freedom of expression.[115]

4 *Minority Rights and Women's Rights*

The most important advancement of fundamental rights in the last decade concerns the rights of minorities, including indigenous people, persons with disabilities, women and sexual minorities. While the ROC Constitution recognizes the right to equality by affirming that all citizens are equal before the law irrespective of sex, religion, race, class or party affiliation,[116] it does not specify in detail how to guarantee the rights of minorities.

In the course of constitutional reforms in the 1990s, human rights organizations and minorities' groups urged the inclusion into the constitution of a few additional provisions relating to special guarantees of minorities' rights. Yet, regrettably, the provisions that were eventually included were not in the form of rights but were instead in the form of policy declarations merely urging the government to take appropriate actions to protect minorities. For example, it was prescribed that the state should 'protect the dignity of women, safeguard their personal safety,

[112] *JY Interpretation No 689 (2011)*, para. 7 of the court's reasoning.
[113] *JY Interpretation No* 364 (1994).
[114] *JY Interpretation No 509 (2000)*.
[115] *JY Interpretation No 656 (2009)*; Jiunn-rong Yeh, 'Court-ordered apology: The function of courts in the construction of society, culture and the law', in Jiunn-rong Yeh (ed.), *The Functional Transformation of Courts: Taiwan and Korea in Comparison* (Taipei: National Taiwan University Press, 2015) 21–38.
[116] Art. 7 of the ROC Constitution.

eliminate sexual discrimination, and further substantive gender equality',[117] provide 'assistance in everyday life for physically and mentally handicapped persons',[118] 'actively preserve and foster the development of aboriginal languages and cultures', and 'safeguard the status and political participation of the aborigines'.[119] As mere policy declarations, these provisions have not been effective in enforcing the rights of minorities.

The recent progress in domestic incorporation of international human rights law,[120] however, altered the situation. In 2007, Taiwan's government acceded to the Convention on Elimination of All Forms of Discrimination against Women (CEDAW) and subsequently passed an implementation act to provide for its domestic legal effect.[121] In 2009, two human rights covenants – the International Covenant on Civil and Political Rights and International Covenant on Economic, Social and Cultural Rights – were also ratified, and an implementation act was enacted to provide for their legal effect.[122] In 2014, the Taiwanese Parliament further enacted implementation acts to incorporate into domestic law the Convention on the Rights of Persons with Disabilities (CRPD) and the Convention on the Rights of the Child (CRC). In the legislative process of incorporating these international human rights conventions, the rights of minorities were placed at the centre of public debate and eventually caught the attention of the Constitutional Court.

The first case concerning the rights of persons with disabilities in the Constitutional Court's docket was *JY Interpretation No 649*, in 2008.[123] What was challenged in this case was the constitutionality of preferential treatment provided in the Physically and Mentally Disabled Citizens Protection Act for vision-impaired individuals to enjoy a monopoly over massage business, with a fine imposed on those who were not vision-impaired and engaged in such business. The petitioners – who were not vision-impaired – argued that the act violated their right to equality as

[117] Sec. 6, Art. 10, Additional Articles to the ROC Constitution.
[118] Sec. 7, Art. 10, Additional Articles to the ROC Constitution.
[119] Secs. 11 and 12, Art. 10, Additional Articles to the ROC Constitution.
[120] Yeh and Chang, note 15 at 152–163. See also Wen-Chen Chang, 'An isolated nation with global-minded citizens: Bottom-up transnational constitutionalism in Taiwan' (2009) 4 *National Taiwan University Law Review* 203–235 at 222–233.
[121] Chang, 'An Isolated Nation', note 120 at 222–233 and note 66.
[122] The full title of this implementation act is 'The Act to Implement the International Covenant on Civil and Political Rights and the International Covenant on Economic, Social and Cultural Rights' [Kungmin Yu Chengchih Ch'uanli Kuochi Kungyueh chi Chingchi Shehua Wenhua Ch'uanli Kuochi Kungyueh Shihhsingfa].
[123] *JY Interpretation No 649 (2008).*

well as right to work. Eventually, the court ruled in the petitioners' favour, finding that the act failed to achieve any significant progress in improving the socio-economic conditions of vision-impaired people and also disproportionately encroached upon the equal right to work of those who were not vision-impaired.[124]

As regards the right of equality, the Constitutional Court reasoned that a law giving preferential treatment to vision-impaired persons would be consistent with the constitutional protection of equality only if 'it is to achieve an important public interest, without excessively restraining the rights of those who are not vision-impaired', and 'the protective measure for the vision-impaired has a substantial nexus with the objectives it intends to accomplish'.[125] As for the right to work, the court held that the right to work entails 'the freedom to engage in employment and to choose occupation'. Restrictions on the freedom to choose an occupation may sometimes be justified if the restrictions 'concern the subjective condition needed, which means professional capability or license to perform the specific occupation, and such capability or [license] status can be gained through training and fostering, such as knowledge, academic degree or physical capability'. 'No restrictions may be permitted without justification of important public interest'; restrictions 'must not violate the principle of proportionality'.[126] As the government was constitutionally mandated to assist persons with disabilities, the court accepted that the act was designed to achieve a significant public interest. Yet, for years, with the expansion and changing situation of the massage business, the protective measures adopted by the act were not effective in improving the living conditions of vision-impaired people; worse still, the impugned measures excessively encroached upon the equal right to work of those not vision-impaired.[127]

Turning now to indigenous rights, a landmark decision was made in 2014 involving a constitutional challenge to a provision of the Government Procurement Act requiring successful government procurement bidders – if hiring more than a hundred employees – to recruit

[124] Ibid., paras. 3, 5 of the court's reasoning.

[125] Ibid., para. 2 of the court's reasoning.

[126] Ibid., para. 2 of the court's reasoning. Similar lines of reasoning on the right of work and freedom to choose employment also appeared in *JY Interpretation Nos 404, 510, 584, 612, 634* and *639*. The most recent decision was *JY Interpretation No 711* (2013), where the Constitutional Court, applying the same standard of review, held unconstitutional the provisions of the Pharmacists Act limiting pharmacists to practising at a single location.

[127] *JY Interpretation No 649 (2008).*

indigenous people at a minimum level of 1 per cent of their employees.[128] Bidders who failed to do so would be required – as a substitute for the employment of indigenous people – to pay a fee to the Indigenous Peoples' Comprehensive Development Fund. This time, the Constitutional Court found the preferential treatment for indigenous people to be consistent with the right of equality, without violation of the principle of proportionality or infringement of property right.

Particularly noteworthy in this decision are the Constitutional Court's direct references to the United Nations' Declaration on the Rights of Indigenous Peoples as well as to a few constitutional provisions mentioned above.[129] In light of these instruments and provisions, the court stressed that the government is obligated to promote the employment of indigenous people and to improve their economic and social conditions.[130] It further explained that '[s]ince the level of indigenous people's education and professional skill is by and large relatively weak as compared to the competitiveness of the job market, their living conditions are thus affected. The scheme adopted by the regulations in dispute has therefore established a reasonable connection with the objectives anticipated to be achieved.'[131] As a result, the challenged provision was sustained.

Since the 1990s, women's rights have been substantially improved through constitutional interpretations made in cases of petitions by women's groups.[132] The Constitutional Court has invalidated laws that privileged fathers in the contexts of decisions as to household residence and child custody[133] and that allowed married sons, but not married daughters, of a veteran to inherit the right to government property that was originally enjoyed by the veteran.[134] One of the most important decisions concerning women's rights was *JY Interpretation No 666* in 2009.[135] In this case, the Constitutional Court applied the principle of substantive equality, holding unconstitutional a law that fined only those

[128] *JY Interpretation No 719 (2014).*
[129] Ibid., para. 3 of the court's reasoning.
[130] Ibid., para. 5 of the court's reasoning.
[131] Ibid., para. 6 of the court's reasoning.
[132] Yeh, note 1 at 218–221. For further discussion from a comparative perspective, see Wen-Chen Chang, 'Public interest litigation in Taiwan: Strategy for law and policy changes in the course of democratization', in Po Jen Yap and Holning Lau (eds.), *Public Interest Litigation in Asia* (Abingdon, UK: Routledge, 2011) 136–160.
[133] *JY Interpretation No 365 (1994); JY Interpretation No 452 (1998).*
[134] *JY Interpretation No 457 (1998).*
[135] *JY Interpretation No 666 (2009).*

engaging in sexual transactions for profit, but not those purchasing sex services. Relying on empirical studies showing that a predominant number of those engaged in prostitution were women of lower social and economic status, the Constitutional Court deemed the impugned provision a *de facto* discrimination against women and a violation of sex equality.[136]

A rather controversial decision on women's rights was *JY Interpretation No 728*, made in 2015.[137] In this case, a constitutional challenge was brought against the Statute Governing Ancestral Worship Guilds, which permitted such a guild to determine, by means of its internal regulations, who would be a qualified successor for the purpose of the worship guild. The petitioner was a married daughter who was not permitted to be a successor; she argued that the impugned provision constituted *de facto* discrimination against women, as most guilds assigned only men as successors. Unlike in the above-mentioned *JY Interpretation No 666*, the Constitutional Court in this case did not hold the *de facto* discrimination to be a violation of sex equality. Instead, the court sustained the impugned provision on the grounds of the freedom of association, property rights and freedom of contract enjoyed by the founders and their descendants, as an ancestral worship guild is an association formed by properties donated by the founders for the purpose of providing services for ancestral worship or other forms of worship.[138] Thus 'even though such a disputed provision may constitute differential treatment in substance, since it is not arbitrary, it is not in conflict with the principle of sex equality embodied in Article 7 of the constitution, nor does it infringe women's right to property.'[139]

Perhaps aware of possible criticism of this decision, in the last part of the Interpretation, the Constitutional Court urged the government to 'conduct a timely review and modification of the related law to ensure it is keeping pace with time, especially taking into consideration the state's positive duty to protect women' under Articles 2 and 5 of CEDAW that had been domestically incorporated, as well as other constitutional provisions.[140] The reference to related CEDAW provisions, however, has not put down the anger of women's groups contending that the court has yielded too much to tradition and religion.

[136] Ibid., para. 3 of the court's reasoning.
[137] *JY Interpretation No 728 (2015).*
[138] Ibid., para. 2 of the court's reasoning.
[139] Ibid., para 2 of the court's reasoning.
[140] Ibid., para 2 of the court's reasoning.

In line with the rising demands for equal rights of minorities, the demand for recognition of same-sex marriage also caught the Constitutional Court's attention.[141] One gay man, Chia-Wei Chi, had sought to register his gay marriage for years. With the legal assistance provided by the Taiwan Alliance to Promote Civil Partnership Rights (TAPCPR)[142] and their leading gay rights lawyers, Chi lodged his case before the Constitutional Court. Meanwhile, facing repeated requests for same-sex marriage registration, the Taipei city government also petitioned the Constitutional Court for clarification of the legal position. The Constitutional Court consolidated these two cases and held an oral hearing on 24 March 2017. Both pro- and anti-gay marriage groups rallied before the court's building, and a few anti-gay marriage activists came every morning to voice their positions.

On May 24, two months after the oral hearing, the Constitutional Court issued *JY Interpretation No 748*, unequivocally holding that the provisions in the Marriage Chapter of the Civil Code that 'do not permit two persons of the same sex to create a permanent union of intimate and exclusive nature for the committed purpose of managing a life together' were 'in violation of both the freedom of marriage as protected by Article 22 and the right to equality as guaranteed by Article 7 of the Constitution'.[143] In order to remedy such a legislative failure, the court demanded that 'the authorities concerned shall amend or enact relevant laws within two years'. Unprecedentedly, the court added that 'if relevant laws are not amended or enacted within the said two years, two persons of the same sex who intend to create the said permanent union shall be allowed to have their marriage registration effectuated at the authorities in charge of household registration by submitting a written document signed by two or more witnesses in accordance with the Marriage Chapter of the Civil Code'.[144]

This was the first time that the Constitutional Court provided a direct and specific remedy for legislative omission. As it might seem to be overstepping the limits of its role, the Constitutional Court struck a

141 *JY Interpretation No 748* (2017). An official press release in English of a summary of this case is available at http://jirs.judicial.gov.tw/GNNWS/NNWSS002.asp?id=267570&flag=1&regi=1&key=&MuchInfo=&courtid (accessed 3 July 2018).

142 The organization's mission statement and recent activities are available at https://tapcpr.org/.

143 *JY Interpretation No 748* (2017). The official translation of the ruling is available at http://jirs.judicial.gov.tw/GNNWS/NNWSS002.asp?id=267570&flag=1&regi=1&key=&MuchInfo=&courtid (accessed 3 July 2018).

144 Ibid.

balance by letting the legislative authority 'determine the formalities for achieving the equal protection of the freedom of marriage'.[145] In other words, while affirming that the equal right to marriage of gay couples is a constitutional right and must be ensured, the Constitutional Court left it open for the legislature to decide what format – marriage, union, partnership, among others – of that equal protection would be adopted and through what legislative measures – amending the Marriage Chapter of the Civil Code, adding a special chapter to the Civil Code, or enacting a special law, among others – it would be implemented. If the legislature fails to deliver, then the direct remedy provided by the court – a form of marriage for gay couples in accordance with the present Marriage Chapter of the Civil Code – would be effectuated. This balanced judicial strategy proved to be successful, as pro-gay marriage groups secured the constitutional recognition of equal right of marriage for gay couples, and anti-gay marriage groups – albeit disappointed – felt that they could continue to fight for their position in future legislative deliberations. The next day after the Constitutional Court's decision, all rallies on this issue moved to the front yard of the legislature.

5 *Judicial Review of the 2005 Constitutional Revision*

As discussed above, Taiwan's Constitutional Court was pivotal in steering the process of democratic transition and constitutional reforms during the 1990s. The most important decisions were *JY Interpretation No 261*, in which the court ordered national representatives who occupied parliamentary seats for decades to leave office by a designated date, and *JY Interpretation No 499*, in which the court invalidated the constitutional revision of 1999 on both procedural and substantive grounds.[146] In recent years, as politics returned to normal, high-profile cases like these have not come before the court. One exception, however, was *JY Interpretation No 721*, in which the constitutionality of the 2005 constitutional revision was challenged.[147]

The constitutional revision of 2005 changed the parliament's electoral rules, among other things. A new electoral system was adopted under which each eligible voter would have two votes – one for a candidate standing in a single district election, and the other for a political party

[145] Ibid.
[146] See notes 53–55 and accompanying text.
[147] *JY Interpretation No 721 (2015).*

competing for seats to be allocated by proportional representation. A 5 per cent threshold of all ballots must be met in order for any political party to be allocated any proportional representation seat. In this case, the petitioner was a small political party standing for the 2008 parliamentary election but failing to pass the 5 per cent threshold.

In dealing with the constitutional challenge, the Constitutional Court reiterated the criteria by which the constitutionality of a constitutional amendment should be judged.[148] First, a constitutional amendment must be enacted in accordance with constitutional due process. Second, since a constitutional amendment is enacted on the basis of powers bestowed by the constitution, it cannot alter 'the existing constitutional provisions of essential significance, such as the principle of the democratic republic, the principle of sovereignty of and by the people, the core contents of fundamental rights of people, and the principle of checks and balances of governmental powers.'[149]

Applying the above criteria, the Constitutional Court sustained the 2005 constitutional revision. According to the court, the reform of the electoral system in 2004 was supported by the general will of the people and did not encroach upon the essentially significant part of existing constitutional provisions. The court admitted that the 5 per cent threshold for political parties might result in a certain discrepancy between the percentages of ballots received by, and seats allotted to, various political parties and might be particularly disadvantageous to smaller political parties. Yet, the court recognized that this particular institutional reform was intended to avoid a clustering of small parties and fragmentation of parliamentary politics, which would impede the efficiency of legislative functions and the smooth interaction between the executive and the legislative powers. Eventually, the electoral rule was judged as not inconsistent with the constitution.[150]

V Conclusion

In the context of Taiwan's democratic transition, citizen outcry and political negotiation have been the main drivers of political reform under the constitutional order. The vibrant decisions of the Constitutional Court have contributed tremendously to the democratic transition

[148] They were first developed in *JY Interpretation No 499* (1999).
[149] *JY Interpretation No 721 (2015)*, para. 2 of the court's reasoning.
[150] Ibid., para. 3 of the court's reasoning.

beyond the changes ushered in through incremental constitutional revisions and the heightened political dynamics and civic engagement. Intriguingly, in a new democracy with a thin foundation of liberal constitutionalism, how could a constitutional court play such an important role in the flux of democratic transition and constitutional reform? Early constitutional mandate, the transitional context and learned judicial wisdom underpin much of the success of Taiwan's Constitutional Court. Moreover, the evolution of the court itself amidst the flux of political transition may explain the critical role the court has played in Taiwan's constitutional development.

Throughout its history, Taiwan's Constitutional Court has undergone dramatic institutional and functional transformations as it served the needs of Taiwan's citizenry. The Constitutional Court has contributed to the formation of a young constitutional democracy, especially during the height of democratization and constitutional reforms in the late 1980s and 1990s. In the years of divided government between 2000 and 2008, the court adopted a dialogic approach to facilitate political dialogue against the backdrop of confrontational politics. Since the end of divided government in 2008, the court has turned its attention to rights disputes. In May 2017, it became the first court in Asia to give constitutional recognition to gay marriage.[151]

Inspired by the enduring citizen engagement in constitutional discourse, the Constitutional Court has engaged itself extensively in constitutional resolution of rights disputes brought before it by vibrant civil groups, embarking on the journey of 'civil constitutionalism'. There is no doubt that the court has continued to occupy a central place in the development of constitutionalism in Taiwan. As has been the case in the past, it is expected that the court will continue to exert judicial powers as a strong check on the government, and its legitimacy and level of judicial scrutiny will continue to increase as the court responds to claims brought by civil groups, while wisely leaving some space for continuous dialogue between political branches and society at large.

[151] Cindy Sui, 'Taiwan's top court rules in favour of same-sex marriage', (2017, May 24) BBC News, www.bbc.com/news/world-asia-40012047 (accessed 3 July 2018).

6

Constitutional Court of Korea

Guardian of the Constitution or Mouthpiece of the Government?

CHAIHARK HAHM

I Historical Background

The establishment of the Constitutional Court of Korea was a result of the historic transition to democracy and the constitutional revision which took place in 1987. The court was formally opened and started receiving cases in 1988, after the National Assembly enacted the basic law setting forth its powers and organization, the Constitutional Court Act (CCA).[1] This was the first time in Korean history that a separate court for adjudicating constitutional matters was set up. Previous constitutions had provisions for institutions with the competence to deal with constitutional adjudication, but they were markedly weak and inactive. The founding constitution of 1948 provided for separate *ad hoc* committees for reviewing the constitutionality of laws and for adjudicating impeachment cases, but very few cases were referred to them. The constitution of 1960, adopted after the ouster of Syngman Rhee from the presidency, had articles for a constitutional court, but these were never implemented due to General Park Chung-hee's coup d'état the following year. Under the 1962 constitution adopted by the Park regime, the Supreme Court had the power of judicial review, but it hardly exercised that power. Park undertook another revision in 1972 and adopted the infamous *Yushin* constitution, which gave the powers of reviewing legislation and adjudicating impeachment cases to a nominal agency called the Constitutional Committee, which never heard any cases.[2] The same institution was

[1] Hŏnpŏp Chaep'anso Pŏp [Constitutional Court Act] (1988).

[2] When, in 1971, the Supreme Court struck down a couple of laws as unconstitutional, its justices were effectively removed by Park, who refused to renew their terms. After the

continued under the 1980 constitution adopted by the Chun Doo-hwan regime, but it remained similarly dormant.

The democratic transition of 1987 took place when Chun's authoritarian government was forced to relent in the face of massive nationwide protests on the part of students, laborers, teachers, small businessmen, professionals and even some law enforcement officers.[3] Foremost among the demands of the protesters was the revision of the constitution to allow for the election of the president through direct popular vote. The government agreed to this and a number of other measures designed to promote democracy and better protect individual rights.

Interestingly, however, during the actual constitutional revision process, the matter of constitutional adjudication seems to have been given rather low priority. Issues relating to the form of government (e.g., presidential versus parliamentary, the president's term of office, the president's re-electability, the scope of the president's emergency powers and the legislature's powers of oversight vis-à-vis the government) and the contents of the section on individual rights occupied the bulk of the drafters' attention. This may have been due to the fact that the people's expectations for an institution of constitutional adjudication were rather low, which was not surprising given the past experience with institutions of constitutional adjudication under previous constitutions.

Initial drafts proposed by various political parties in 1987 envisioned not providing for a separate court at all. The thinking seems to have been that if constitutional adjudication is to be encouraged, it should be done by strengthening the supreme court with powers of judicial review.[4] As deliberations progressed among the drafters, however, a proposal was

1972 constitutional revision, the Supreme Court was given the power to refer cases to the Constitutional Committee, but the court never dared to refer any cases.

[3] For the so-called June Democracy Movement of 1987 and its aftermath, see Carter Eckert, Ki-baik Lee, Young Ick Lew, Michael Robinson and Edward W. Wagner, *Korea Old and New: A History* (Seoul: Ilchokak, 1990), 375–387; John Kie-chiang Oh, *Korean Politics: The Quest for Democratization and Economic Development* (Ithaca, NY: Cornell University Press, 1999), 87–107. For an account of the constitutional revision process, see James M. West and Edward J. Baker, 'The 1987 constitutional reforms in South Korea: Electoral processes and judicial independence' (1988) 1 *Harvard Human Rights Journal* 135–176.

[4] As for the Supreme Court, the idea of gaining the power of judicial review appears to have elicited two opposite responses. On the one hand, it welcomed the idea primarily because it did not wish to see the creation of another court which could potentially become a competitor for judicial authority. On the other hand, it was rather apprehensive about exercising the power of judicial review (or adjudicating cases on impeachment and unconstitutional political parties) as these could potentially drag the Supreme Court into highly political disputes and jeopardize its independence.

made for the introduction of a system of constitutional complaints which would enable individual citizens to file claims to protect their constitutional rights against encroachment by state power. While the initiator of this proposal remains unclear, the idea was no doubt inspired by the German system of constitutional adjudication under the Federal Constitutional Court, particularly the *Verfassungsbeschwerde*, which was well known among Korean lawyers and scholars. Once this was agreed to, it became evident that constitutional complaints should not be handled by the Supreme Court and that a separate court must be created. The Constitutional Court was, thus, adopted by the drafters almost as an afterthought[5] and written into the new constitution in a chapter separate from the regular judiciary.

II Powers and Composition of the Constitutional Court

The constitution contains only three articles on the Constitutional Court. According to Article 111(1), the court has jurisdiction over five areas: (i) review of the constitutionality of statutes upon request by ordinary courts; (ii) impeachment cases; (iii) dissolution of political parties; (iv) competence dispute among different government agencies; and (v) adjudication of constitutional complaints as prescribed by law. Article 111(2) provides that there shall be nine justices at the Constitutional Court, that they must be qualified to sit on regular courts and that they shall be appointed by the president. Of the nine justices, Article 111(3) mandates that three shall be elected by the legislature (National Assembly) and three designated by the judiciary (chief justice of the Supreme Court). In the case of appointment of the head (president) of the Court, Article 111 (4) requires the consent of the legislature.[6]

Article 112(1) provides that justices of the Constitutional Court shall serve for a term of six years and that their terms may be renewed as

[5] Elsewhere, I have referred to the adoption of the constitutional court system in Korea as 'accidental constitutionalism'. Chaihark Hahm, 'Law, culture, and the politics of Confucianism' (2003) 16 *Columbia Journal of Asian Law* 253–301, 260.

[6] Although not required by the constitution, other justices must also undergo legislative scrutiny before their appointment. Chaihark Hahm, 'Beyond "law vs. politics" in constitutional adjudication: Lessons from South Korea' (2012) 10 *International Journal of Constitutional Law* 6–34, 25–26.

provided by law.[7] In order to guarantee the court's independence and political neutrality, Article 112(2) states that the justices may not join a political party or participate in political activities. Article 112(3) further guarantees the independence of the justices by limiting the cause for their dismissal to impeachment or imprisonment. Regarding the court's internal procedures, Article 113(1) provides that a concurrence of at least six justices is required for all types of cases except competence disputes. For further details on the court's internal affairs, Article 113(2) grants to the court the authority to establish rules regarding its own proceedings, internal discipline and administration. Exercising this authority, the court has adopted the Rules of Adjudication of the Constitutional Court. Finally, Article 113(3) leaves it to the legislature to further determine by statute the organization, operation and other necessary matters of the court. Pursuant to this provision, the National Assembly has duly enacted the CCA.

As can be seen, the constitution's provisions are, by necessity, very general and abstract, providing only a limited picture of the activities and functions of the court. The first thing to be noticed is that the constitution seems to combine a traditional judicial role with some more political functions.[8] Constitutionality review of statutes and constitutional complaints typically involve adjudication of claims brought by individuals who seek some form of remedy for alleged violations of their rights. These entail a rather conventional judicial function. According to the CCA, constitutionality review can be triggered only if the statute's constitutionality becomes an issue in a proceeding at a regular court. That is, ordinary courts must refer the issue to the Constitutional Court if there is doubt as to the constitutionality of a statute to be applied in the case at hand. The court cannot, in other words, review the constitutionality of statutes in the abstract, i.e., in the absence of a specific case or controversy. In this regard, the Korean court is unlike its putative model, the German Federal Constitutional Court.

As for the other three types of cases, they manifestly involve disputes that are of a considerably political nature. Ordering the dissolution of a political party is, in a sense, an inherently political act. Article 8 of the

[7] Despite this provision, the practice has become settled that justices are to serve only one six-year term. Except for a couple of justices appointed when the court was first established, no one has been reappointed.

[8] For a conceptual and historical discussion on the proper place of constitutional courts vis-à-vis the law/politics distinction, see Hahm, 'Beyond "law vs. politics"', note 6, 14–18.

Korean constitution provides that when the objective or activity of a political party violates the 'democratic basic order', it can be dissolved by a decision of the Constitutional Court. It is at least debatable whether this requires judicial reasoning or political calculus. Similarly, deciding on impeachment motions filed by the legislature against high-ranking public officials can be seen as a political act.[9] Adjudicating competence disputes among government agencies may seem less political, but it nevertheless requires an understanding of the proper distribution of power throughout the various units and levels of the government.

To be sure, in terms of the court's caseload, the five categories of adjudication are not of equal weight. As of January 2017, there had been only one case regarding dissolution of a political party and two impeachment cases, whereas in the competence dispute category, there had been eighty-seven cases, which is less than 0.3 per cent of the entire caseload since the court's founding. The vast majority of the cases (23,441 out of 30,043) have been constitutional complaints filed by individuals seeking redress for state violations of their constitutional rights.[10] Yet, 63 per cent of these constitutional complaints have been dismissed for lack of standing or other failure to comply with procedural requirements. Among the remaining cases that were decided on the merits, another 30 per cent of the total number of cases filed were rejected. Only 3 per cent of the constitutional complaints resulted in findings of violations of constitutional rights.

Constitutionality review of statutes comprises the next most frequent type of cases. The Constitutional Court Act provides two different routes by which the court can review the constitutionality of statutes. First, under Article 41 of CCA, an ordinary court may ask the Constitutional Court's determination if the outcome of a case at hand depends on the constitutionality of a statute to be applied in that case. The referral may be made at the request of the parties, or the court may do so *sua sponte*. To date, 869 cases of this type have been decided by the court. Among these, the impugned statutory provisions were held to be constitutional in 320 cases and unconstitutional in 273 cases, while in eighty-four other

[9] Historically, impeachment was a means for holding accountable officials who could not be tried through regular legal procedures. For background, see Raoul Berger, *Impeachment: The Constitutional Problems* (Cambridge, MA: Harvard University Press, 1974) 56–107.

[10] These numbers are taken from a chart found at the Constitutional Court's website: www.ccourt.go.kr/cckhome/kor/info/selectEventGeneralStats.do (accessed 3 July 2018).

cases, some other form of constitutional infirmity was found.[11] Secondly, according to Article 68(2) of CCA, in cases where the regular court denies a party's motion to refer the matter to the Constitutional Court, the party may then file a constitutional complaint with the court requesting a review of the constitutionality of the statute at issue. Although this takes the form of a constitutional complaint, it is, in substance, a constitutionality review of statute, and it is so treated by the court. There have been 5,643 cases of this kind filed at the court, of which more than half (3,209) were dismissed, and in about 35 per cent of the cases, the impugned statutory provisions were held to be constitutional. Only 5 per cent resulted in a finding of some form of constitutional infirmity.

III From Democratic Consolidation to Judicialization of Politics

As is shown by these numbers, the Constitutional Court is an extremely busy institution. Unlike the highest court of some other countries, it has no discretion to pick and choose cases. It is worth noting, however, that this popularity had to be earned. When the court was first established, it had hardly any business. Most of the general public did not know of the court's powers, and even those who knew were sceptical of whether it might actually exercise them. Many expressed doubts as to whether the court could accomplish anything meaningful. In some respects, such an attitude was not without reason because, originally, of the nine justices, only six were full time. Even the lawmakers who designed the court apparently felt that it would not have many cases to decide.

Over time, however, the court began to be inundated with cases. One justice who served during the earlier days of the court has written that the justices took deliberate care to discuss the actual merits of a case even if it could be dismissed on procedural grounds.[12] Obviously, this was possible because they did not have many cases to decide, but it was also an effort

[11] The Constitutional Court has developed the practice of issuing 'modified judgments' such as 'limited constitutionality', 'limited unconstitutionality', and 'not in conformity with the constitution'. This has led to some friction between the Constitutional Court and regular courts. Jong-ik Chon, 'The effect of constitutional adjudication on the judicial branch: The relationship between the constitutional court and the ordinary court', in Jiunn-rong Yeh (ed.), *The Functional Transformation of Courts: Taiwan and Korea in Comparison* (Göttingen, Germany: V&R unipress, 2015) 39–64, 9.

[12] Yi Shi-yun, 'Hŏnpŏp Chaep'an 10 nyŏn ŭi Hoego wa Chŏnmang' [A retrospective on ten years of constitutional adjudication]' (1999) 27 *Kongpŏp Yŏn'Gu* 107.

to convey to the general public the message that their claims would be given careful consideration by the court. Evidently, this proved a very successful marketing strategy. The system of constitutional complaints quickly became an extremely popular channel for citizens with grievances against the government to express their discontent and hopefully obtain redress.

The fact that the Constitutional Court was born in the context of Korea's transition out of authoritarian rule is also very significant. As the court was mandated by the new democratic constitution, it could be associated with the process of democratic transition. Unlike the Supreme Court, it was not burdened with a chequered past in terms of its record of protecting individual rights. The Constitutional Court built up a reputation as a key agent in the consolidation of Korea's fragile democracy. A number of its earlier decisions contributed to this. For example, with the case of the *Kukje* Corporation, which had been forced into bankruptcy during the Chun Doo-hwan administration, the court seemed to issue a constitutional reprimand against the high-handed economic and political practices of the past government.[13] Similarly, soon after its establishment, the court reviewed the notorious National Security Act and found that it was unconstitutional unless the law was given a narrow interpretation, as specified by the court itself.[14] While the practical effects of that decision are still being debated, the case was nevertheless symbolic in that it offered the court an opportunity to condemn the law's pernicious effects on the rule of law and citizens' enjoyment of their rights and freedom.

The court's involvement in a number of cases relating to 'transitional justice' has also contributed to the perception that it is a reliable ally of democracy. For example, during the presidency of Kim Young-sam, former presidents Chun Doo-hwan and Roh Tae-woo, who had come to power through a coup d'état, were tried and convicted of insurrection, mutiny and other charges. By clarifying constitutional issues arising from the criminal proceedings, the Constitutional Court is commonly regarded as having paved the way towards the eventual prosecution

[13] Const. Ct. 89 Hun-Ma 31 (29 July 1993). For an analysis of this case, see James M. West, '*Kukje* and Beyond: Constitutionalism and the Market' (1998) 3 *Segye Hŏnpŏp Yŏn'gu* 321.

[14] Const. Ct. 89 Hun-Ka 113 (2 April 1990).

and conviction of the ex-generals and, thus, having supported and promoted the pursuit of transitional justice in Korea.[15]

The court's popularity can be seen from a series of surveys asking the people's perception of the trustworthiness of various public and private organizations. Among the public organizations, the Constitutional Court has consistently ranked highest over a period of nine years.[16] Yet, the positive reputation coexists at present with increasing criticism about the court's alleged overreaching vis-à-vis the political process. There is increasing talk among scholars, journalists and commentators about the so-called judicialization of politics whereby the Constitutional Court is supposedly encroaching on areas that should be left to the people and their representatives.[17]

The year 2004 may perhaps be counted as the symbolic turning point when questions and dissatisfaction began to be expressed about the democratic propriety of 'nine unelected judges' deciding on momentous issues of national import. That year saw the much-noted case of impeachment of then-president Roh Moo-hyun.[18] Confronted with the spectacle of a judicial body adjudicating an essentially political squabble between the president and the opposition lawmakers, many citizens raised doubts as to whether the Constitutional Court was the proper venue for settling such disputes. What gave the justices, they asked, the right to decide whether a sitting president, who had been elected by the people, deserved to continue in office? In the same year, the court also decided the case of relocation of the nation's capital, in which it invoked the controversial notion of a 'customary constitution' to invalidate a law

[15] For a discussion of several Constitutional Court cases decided in the context of the trial of Chun and Roh, see Chaihark Hahm, 'Rule of law in South Korea: Rhetoric and implementation', in Randall Peerenboom (ed.), *Asian Discourses of Rule of Law: Theories and Implementation of Rule of Law in Twelve Asian Countries, France and the U.S.* (New York: Routledge, 2004) 385–416, 399–403; Kuk Cho, 'Transitional justice in Korea: Legally coping with past wrongs after democratization' (2007) 16 *Pacific Rim Law & Policy Journal* 579–612.

[16] From 2005 to 2013, a daily newspaper conducted surveys on the trustworthiness and influence of so-called power organizations in Korea. For the results of the most recent survey, see '*Yŏnghyangnyŏk K'ŏjin Kŏmch'al; Kuksech'ŏng Silloedo nŭn Twitkŏrŭm* [Prosecutors' influence rises: National tax office's trustworthiness recedes]' (22 August 2013) Joongang Ilbo.

[17] See, e.g., Jongcheol Kim and Jonghyun Park, 'Causes and conditions for sustainable judicialization of politics in Korea', in Björn Dressel (ed.), *The Judicialization of Politics in Asia* (New York: Routledge, 2012) 37–56 (employing Ran Hirshl's notion of mega-politics to describe the Korean Constitutional Court's involvement in political affairs).

[18] Const. Ct. 2004 Hun-Na 1 (14 May 2004).

passed by the legislature.[19] This decision sparked a series of criticism not only because the concept of customary constitution had never been accepted or even entertained by lawyers and scholars, but also because it seemed to enable the Constitutional Court to recognize any long-standing tradition as a source of constitutional authority whenever it suits its fancy. By implying that it could essentially create constitutional norms, the court seemed to be encroaching on the prerogative of the sovereign people as agents of constituent power.

Perhaps as a result of these and other decisions, in 2006, the court was embroiled in a political controversy over the appointment of the court's president. For months, the National Assembly, which must consent to the nominee for the position, engaged in a political war of attrition over whether the candidate was eligible for appointment.[20] Without going into the details of this controversy, suffice it to note that its timing suggests that it may have been a case of politicization of the court caused by the phenomenon of judicialization of politics. That is, having become aware that the Constitutional Court was exercising tremendous influence over political issues, lawmakers on both sides of the aisle may have wished to make sure that the court was led by someone with political views similar to their own. It was becoming clear that, with such awesome powers, the court had the potential to become the guardian of the constitution (*Hüter der Verfassung*), but this also meant that it could be used by the government as a powerful tool to pursue its own partisan agenda. Keenly aware of this, the opposition lawmakers sought to block the appointment of someone perceived to hold the same political views as the sitting president. While such politicization has, fortunately, not been repeated during the next rounds of appointment, it is safe to say that both the court and the politicians now know quite well that the possibility of such controversy is an integral part of the political environment in which the court operates.

IV Notable Decisions from the Last Decade

1 *Personal Freedom, Family Relations and Confucianism*

The Constitutional Court has somewhat of a reputation for being progressive in the area of family relations, especially when the principle of

[19] Const. Ct. 2004 Hun-Ma 554 (01 October 2004) (consolidated).
[20] For a discussion of this controversy, see Hahm, 'Beyond "law vs. politics"', note 6, 9–13.

equality is involved. In the past, it has held that the traditional head of household system is not in conformity with the constitution by violating the equality principle and the dignity of the individual.[21] It has also held that the traditional rule prohibiting marriage between persons of the same surname and same ancestral seat is inconsistent with the constitution.[22] These two decisions are commonly seen as having brought about revolutionary changes in individuals' relationships with their families. These rulings are considered particularly significant because they rejected the continuing relevance of Confucianism in the way family life is ordered. One is no longer to be identified as a subordinate member of a 'family' led by a household head, but as an autonomous individual. Similarly, the scope of one's potential marriage partners is no longer defined in accordance with an antiquated Confucian rule about family origins. Yet, the court has also shown a 'conservative' side when it comes to another aspect of the Confucian tradition, namely, filial piety. It has held that the criminal law provision stipulating heavier sentences for causing the death by battery of one's 'lineal ascendant' (i.e., parent, grandparent, great-grandparent, etc.) is constitutional because the rule promotes filial piety, a virtue still valuable in modern life, according to the court.[23]

In the recent decade, the court seems to have maintained this bifurcated approach. It has decided two cases in which seemingly unequal treatment of individuals was held to be justified when the virtue of filial piety was at issue. In one case, it held that it is constitutional for the law to prescribe heavier punishment for the murder of one's lineal ascendants.[24] It stated that filial piety is not merely some leftover from the feudal family system of a bygone era, but rather an 'essential constitutive part of the social ethics' of modern Korea. It also pointed to the marked depravity of the crime of parricide and the societal need for heightened condemnation of such heinous acts. In the second case, the court upheld a provision in the criminal procedure law which prohibits the filing of a criminal complaint against one's lineal ascendants.[25] It reasoned that the differential treatment resulting from this prohibition has reasonable grounds in that it is intended to promote the traditional ethical norm

[21] Const. Ct. 2001 Hun-Ka 9 (3 February 2005) (consolidated).
[22] Const. Ct. 95 Hun-Ka 6 (16 July 1997) (consolidated).
[23] Const. Ct. 2000 Hun-Ba 53 (28 March 2002).
[24] Const. Ct. 2011 Hun-Ba 267 (25 July 2013).
[25] Const. Ct. 2008 Hun-Ba 56 (24 February 2011).

of filial piety that is 'unique to Korea' and to discourage immoral acts of criminally accusing one's parents and grandparents.[26]

Where the notion of filial piety is not at issue, by contrast, the Constitutional Court seems to be heading in a more progressive direction.[27] In 2015, the court held that it is unconstitutional to criminalize adultery.[28] Noting the worldwide trend towards decriminalization of adultery and the change in the public's perception regarding the propriety of regulating such behaviour through the penal authority of the state, it reasoned that preservation of marriage and family should be sought via the free will and affection of the marriage partners rather than be enforced through punishment. The court concluded that the provision in the criminal law is unconstitutional because it imposes excessive restraint on individuals' right to sexual self-determination and infringes upon the right to privacy. This decision is significant not only because it sought to bring the law into line with social reality, but also because it shows the changes taking place in the Constitutional Court itself. This was the fifth case to be brought before the court that challenged the constitutionality of the crime of adultery.[29] The first decision was in 1990, and the court held that the provision was not unconstitutional. That decision was maintained in later cases decided in 1993 and 2001. In 2008, a majority of five justices found that it was not in conformity with the constitution, but since six votes are required to invalidate a law, the court had to conclude that the provision was constitutional. Finally, with this 2015 decision, there were seven justices who voted to strike down the provision.

Other cases regarding family relations also suggest that a change in the court's view may be imminent. While it is hard to track the process of change, as there were no previous cases on the same issue, the 2013 decision on the scope of persons eligible for adoption may be an example. In

26 For a critical reflection on this case, see Marie Seong-Hak Kim, 'Confucianism that confounds: Constitutional jurisprudence on filial piety in Korea', in Sungmoon Kim (ed.), *Confucianism, Law, and Democracy in Contemporary Korea* (New York: Rowman & Littlefield, 2015), 57–81.

27 Marie Seong-Hak Kim, 'In the name of custom, culture, and the constitution: Korean customary law in flux' (2013) 48 *Texas International Law Journal* 357–392, 373 (suggesting that practices that concern the dead have been more resilient to judicial change).

28 Const. Ct. 2009 Hun-Ba 17 (26 February 2015).

29 The movement to abolish the crime of adultery had a long history. In 1992, for example, the government itself prepared a bill to revise the criminal code in which the crime of adultery would be eliminated. This bill, however, was never adopted as law by the legislature.

this case, five justices thought it unconstitutional to disallow adoption by a single parent, but that number fell short of the six votes needed to strike down the provision in the Civil Code.[30] The 2012 decision on the criminalization of abortion may similarly reveal the possibility of a change in the court's future opinion.[31] In the first case ever on the constitutionality of punishing abortion, the justices were evenly split four to four. Defenders of the criminal law provision emphasized that the right to life does not depend on the ability to survive independently or on any intellectual capacity. By contrast, opponents claimed that the provision imposed excessive restraint on the mother's right to self-determination by failing to distinguish between the early stage of pregnancy, when the foetus is thought to feel no pain and when the risk to the mother's health is minimal, and later stages.

In this connection, it bears noting that in the case mentioned above regarding the ban on filing criminal complaints against one's lineal ascendants, five justices filed a dissenting opinion. For them, while the child–parent relationship may be an element to be considered in weighing the seriousness of a criminal act or the degree of culpability, it cannot be a basis for denying the right to request criminal investigation. In other words, although a majority of justices voted against the provision, it could not be invalidated because they were short one vote of the number needed to strike it down. This may suggest that even the virtue of filial piety may soon be deemed insufficient to justify the differential treatment of individuals based on their family status.

2 *Civil and Political Rights*

The Constitutional Court's jurisprudence on civil and political rights during the last decade may be described as fairly liberal on the whole. It issued a number of decisions that sought to expand the scope of the right to political expression and participation. For example, it held in 2009 that a provision in the Law on Assembly and Demonstration that banned outdoor assemblies at night-time (before sunrise or after sunset) was not in conformity with the constitution.[32] As a corollary, the

[30] Const. Ct. 2011 Hun-Ka 42 (26 September 2013). On historical changes in Korean laws on adoption and family succession, see Marie Kim, 'In the Name of Custom', note 27, 369–371.

[31] Const. Ct. 2010 Hun-Ba 402 (23 August 2012).

[32] Const. Ct. 2008 Hun-Ka 25 (24 September 2009).

provision that authorized punishment for violation of the above provision could not be defended, either. Similarly, the court held that a blanket restriction on the voting rights of prison inmates and convicts with suspended sentences was not constitutionally defensible.[33] It reasoned that disallowing voting for all convicted criminals without regard to the type or substance of the crime or to the degree of unlawfulness of the misdeed violates the principle of minimum restraint and infringes upon voting rights, and thereby violates the principle of universal suffrage.

In terms of freedom of expression, in 2012, the Constitutional Court issued a rather progressive decision concerning the right to post anonymous comments on the Internet.[34] It ruled unconstitutional a law that required Internet service providers who operated online boards to verify the identity of users who wished to submit posts on them. Media companies and operators of bulletin boards who violated this requirement were fined according to this law. This 'online real name system' had been established in response to a society-wide demand for regulating various abuses of the Internet, including libel and defamation, revelation of personal information and other verbal assaults. The main cause of such abuses was thought to be the anonymity of communication that was possible on the Internet. In a unanimous decision, the Constitutional Court held that requiring users to register their real name before they can post comments online infringes upon the freedom of expression, which is a fundamental value in a democratic society. Although it approved of the law's objectives and the appropriateness of the means chosen to achieve those objectives, the court said that the system resulted in an excessive restriction on the freedom of expression and privacy rights.

In a subsequent decision, however, the court held that the online real name system is constitutional during election periods.[35] It upheld a provision in the Law for Election of Public Officials that required Internet users to have their real name verified before expressing opinions either supporting or opposing political parties or candidates during periods of political campaign as defined by the law. The court was concerned that media websites and bulletin boards of portals might become conduits for spreading malicious and false information, which could have a considerable effect on election results. The court said that the measure is needed to guarantee fair elections and prevent the

[33] Const. Ct. 2012 Hun-Ma 409 (28 January 2014).
[34] Const. Ct. 2010 Hun-Ma 47 (23 August 2012).
[35] Const. Ct. 2012 Hun-Ma 734 (30 July 2015) (consolidated).

spreading of false and unverified information online. Further, it added that the system does not infringe upon the freedom of speech or privacy because no personal information is revealed other than names.

The Constitutional Court has tightly linked the issue of voting rights to the principle of popular sovereignty. In a series of decisions, it has suggested that if one is a member of the sovereign 'We the People' of Korea, then one should be granted the right to vote, regardless of one's place of residence or familiarity with the local conditions. Reversing its previous decision of 1999, in 2007, the court held that it is unconstitutional to deny the voting rights of overseas Koreans by predicating the right to vote on having a registered residence in Korea.[36] It reasoned that the right to vote in national elections is a fundamental right of the sovereign people and that any technical and administrative difficulty of allowing overseas nationals to vote cannot be a reason for denying their basic right. It further stated that even those with permanent residence in another country should be allowed to vote and that their exemption from such basic duties of nationals as tax payment and military duty cannot be grounds for excluding them from the vote because voting rights were never granted in exchange for the performance of such duties. As a result, the Law for Election of Public Officials was revised in 2009 to allow overseas citizens' participation in presidential elections and the party representation portion of general elections.

In a follow-up decision in 2014, the Constitutional Court reviewed the revised system of electing public officials.[37] It stated that electing members of the National Assembly from electoral districts is different from presidential elections or the party representation portion of general elections which are premised on a 'national constituency'. In district elections, voters must have some connection and familiarity with the district. It was, thus, not unconstitutional to require either a registered or established residence in the district. By contrast, in the case of a national referendum,[38] the court held that it was unconstitutional to exclude overseas citizens on grounds that they do not have a registered or established residence in Korea. It reasoned that connection or familiarity

[36] Const. Ct. 2004 Hun-Ma 644 (28 June 2007) (consolidated).

[37] Const. Ct. 2009 Hun-Ma 256 (24 July 2014) (consolidated).

[38] According to the constitution, national referendum is required for revising the constitution (Article 130). National referenda may also be called by the President on specific issues regarding 'foreign relations, national defense, national unification, and other important policy' related to the nation's continued existence (Article 72).

with a particular place in Korea was not required in order to cast a meaningful vote in a national referendum. One need not have an address in Korea to participate in national referenda.

That the Constitutional Court lays special importance on voting rights can also be seen in its decisions regarding the value of individual votes. In a 2014 decision, the court held that the electoral districting scheme adopted by the Law for Election of Public Officials was not in conformity with the constitution.[39] It pointed out that, given the population discrepancy among the electoral districts, a candidate in one of the more populous districts would not be elected even if he or she garnered more votes than a successful candidate from one of the less populous districts. This resulted in the violation of the voting rights and equality rights of voters in the more populous districts. The court, therefore, required that the districting schedule be revised to reduce the disparity among the districts. Furthermore, it set a specific guideline that the population of the most populous district should not be greater than twice the population of the least populous district. This was a departure from its earlier decision of 2001, in which the court had mandated the ratio of 3 to 1 as the upper limit for constitutionally tolerable population disparity among the districts.[40] Even at the time, the court stated that a ratio of 2 to 1 should be the ideal, and suggested that it might reconsider the standard of 3 to 1 upon passage of sufficient time and changes in the social conditions.

3 *Regulation of Political Parties*

In light of the centrality of political parties to modern representative democratic government, the Constitutional Court recognized that the freedom to establish and maintain political parties must be respected to the utmost degree, such that any law that restrains this freedom should be reviewed according to the strict criteria of proportionality. The court thus held unconstitutional a provision in the Law on Political Parties which stipulated automatic cancellation of registration for political parties that failed to garner less than 2 per cent of the entire votes cast

[39] Const. Ct. 2012 Hun-Ma 190 (30 October 2014) (consolidated).

[40] Const. Ct. 2000 Hun-Ma 92 (25 October 2001) (consolidated). This decision, in turn, had been a departure from an even earlier decision in which the court had specified the ratio of 4 to 1 as the tolerable level of disparity of the value of votes. Const. Ct. 95 Hun-Ma 224 (27 December 1995) (consolidated).

by the electorate in a general election.[41] It acknowledged that excluding from the political process parties that have no intention or ability to mediate the people's will may be a legitimate objective, and cancelling their registration may be an appropriate means for achieving that objective. Even so, the court pointed out that there are other, less intrusive, ways to accomplish the same objective, and that, in this case, the harm to the freedom to establish political parties was excessively grave compared to the benefit that might accrue to the public interest of contributing to democracy.

In evident contradiction to the court's solicitous attitude shown in the above decision towards smaller minor political parties, it decided in late 2014 to disband a fringe leftist party that had only five (out of three hundred) seats in the National Assembly.[42] This was the first time in Korean constitutional history that the procedure provided for in the constitution to dissolve a political party was utilized. According to Article 8(4) of the constitution, the government may bring such an action in the Constitutional Court if a political party's objectives or activities are contrary to the 'democratic basic order'. According to the government, the United Progressive Party's (UPP) platform of pursuing 'progressive democracy' was essentially the same as the goal of the communist North Korean regime, namely, the violent overthrow of the democratic government of the Republic of Korea. In an 8 to 1 decision, the court agreed with the government and ordered that the party be disbanded. It also held that, as a corollary to the dissolution of the party, the seats of its members in the National Assembly must be forfeited.

Realizing the gravity of its decision, the Constitutional Court issued an exceptionally long and detailed opinion in which it sought to show that the UPP posed a 'concrete danger of substantial harm' to the democratic basic order, which the court defined as a political order 'premised on a pluralistic worldview which presumes that all political viewpoints have relative truth-value and degrees of reasonableness', and which rejects all forms of violent and arbitrary rule and operates on democratic decision-making principles based on freedom and equality. The court found that the UPP's true objective was to implement 'progressive democracy' through violence and to ultimately achieve North Korean-style socialism in South Korea. It also found that the UPP's leaders are followers of North Korea and that their notion of progressive democracy is essentially

41 Const. Ct. 2012 Hun-Ma 431 (23 January 2014).
42 Const. Ct. 2013 Hun-Da 1 (19 December 2014).

the same as North Korea's 'revolutionary strategy' against South Korea. Given that the socialist regime of North Korea takes the party line as the absolute good and that its governance is essentially a one-man dictatorship or people's democracy based on their 'great leader theory', the court concluded that the UPP's objectives directly contradict South Korea's constitutional value of democratic basic order. This appears to be the court's implicit reply to the oft-heard criticism that outlawing a political viewpoint entails a form of intolerant 'value absolutism' and, as such, is inconsistent with democracy, which is premised upon pluralism and value relativism. The court's opinion seems to suggest that it was the UPP that was guilty of value absolutism, and that as a result, it was destroying the democratic ideals of pluralism and value relativism to which the South Korean constitutional order is dedicated. Next, citing a host of meetings by UPP members related to a criminal attempt at insurrection, irregularities and fraud in the UPP's internal election, as well as manipulation of polling data from an electoral district, the court also concluded that the party's activities constituted a rejection of the ideals of democracy such as parliamentarianism, rule of law and the system of election, as well as a negation of the very existence of the South Korean state.

Having found that the party's objectives and activities were contrary to the democratic basic order, the court then proceeded to analyse whether its dissolution might be a violation of the principle of proportionality, which must be observed whenever restrictions on the freedom of political parties are at issue. Pointing to the exceptionally grave danger posed by the UPP's objectives and activities, particularly in light of the special circumstances facing South Korea, it concluded that there was no other less intrusive means than dissolution that could properly address the danger, and that, in this case, the benefit to be derived from the dissolution (i.e., preservation of the values of democratic basic order such as popular sovereignty, fundamental rights, a multiparty system and separation of powers) was greater than the cost incurred by restricting the freedom of political parties. In sum, the proportionality principle was satisfied, and the UPP was ordered to be disbanded.

With these decisions on political parties, as well as those on the right to participate in elections, the court seems to be assuming the role of overseeing and safeguarding the integrity of the nation's political process. By disbanding the leftist UPP, in particular, it appears to be setting the parameters of political viewpoints allowable under the Korean constitution.

4 *Impeachment of the President*

In the space of a little over a decade, the Constitutional Court has twice decided on the fate of a sitting president. In the aforementioned 2004 case of Roh Moo-hyun's impeachment the court found that he had violated the constitution and laws on three counts: failing to remain neutral, as required by law, in relation to a general election; defying the ruling by the National Election Commission admonishing him to maintain neutrality; and promising to hold a confidence referendum contrary to the requirements of the constitution. The court held, however, that these acts did not amount to a grave enough threat to the constitutional order and reinstated him to the presidency.[43] Then, in 2017, the court found that President Park Geun-hye had betrayed the trust of the people by, *inter alia*, abusing her powers to enrich her personal friend, allowing this friend to influence state affairs, coercing corporations to donate funds to set up foundations for the same person's benefit and attempting to deny and cover up these actions when questioned by the legislature and the media. It concluded that these violations of the constitution and laws were grave enough to justify dismissing a democratically elected president from office.[44]

The 2004 decision was the first impeachment case ever decided by the Constitutional Court. Although the court declined to remove Roh from office, it attempted to provide a set of criteria to be employed in deciding impeachment cases. First, it proclaimed that a decision in impeachment proceedings must be solely the outcome of legal reasoning and involve no political consideration. This, it said, was required by Article 65(1), which states that the National Assembly may pass a resolution to impeach when the president and other public officials have 'violated the constitution or laws'. Mere maladministration or policy failures could not be a basis for impeachment. Then, it declared that despite the wording of this provision, not all infractions of the constitution or laws were impeachable offences. Only those violations that were grave enough from the constitutional standpoint deserved the extreme and unappealable judgment of dismissal from office.[45] This was particularly so in the case of presidential

43 Const. Ct. 2004 Hun-Na 1 (14 May 2004).

44 Const. Ct. 2016 Hun-Na 1 (10 March 2017).

45 For an analysis of this decision, particularly on the issue of whether it was strictly a legal decision, see Youngjae Lee, 'Law, politics, and impeachment: The impeachment of Roh Moo-hyun from a comparative constitutional perspective' (2005) 53 *American Journal of Comparative Law* 403–432.

impeachment, because the president's democratic mandate comes directly from the people through a nationwide election.

The court then tried to offer some guidelines for determining when an offence is grave enough to merit dismissal. Generally, it declared that the determination must be based on an analysis of the harm sustained by the constitutional order as a result of the offence weighed against the national loss likely to arise from dismissing a democratically elected president. Since impeachment is a means to protect the constitutional order, dismissal would be justified when deemed necessary to safeguard the constitution and to restore the damaged constitutional order.[46] Also, in view of the president's democratic legitimacy, which comes directly from the people, the court stated that dismissal would be warranted when the president, by committing the infractions, has betrayed the people's trust.[47] In the Roh Moo-hyun case, the court concluded that the harm to the constitutional order was slight because his actions did not reveal an affirmative intent to undermine the 'free and democratic basic order' of the constitution, nor did they amount to a sufficiently serious betrayal of the people's trust to merit dismissal.

In this case, the court also made some attempts to assert its supremacy in constitutional matters vis-à-vis other state agencies.[48] It chided Roh for his cavalier attitude towards the constitution and other coequal branches of the government. It stated that the president must be a role model for other public officials in his dedication to uphold the constitution and abide by the rule of law. Even if the president thought a given piece of legislation was unwise or outdated, he had a duty to observe it unless and until the Constitutional Court, as the sole institution with the authority to review the constitutionality of laws, decided to strike it down. It also declared that 'violations of the constitution' must be

[46] The court went on to explain that the constitutional order to be protected via impeachment meant the 'free and democratic basic order' of the constitution, which comprises the principles of rule of law (protection of basic human rights, separation of powers, judicial independence) and of democracy (parliamentary representation, multiparty system, electoral institutions).

[47] Examples of betraying the people's trust that were given by the court included abuse of power to engage in bribery and other forms of corruption, acts that clearly harm the national interest, encroaching upon the powers of the legislature and other state agencies, using state power to persecute citizens and actively seeking to manipulate election results. In such cases, the president could not be expected to protect the free and democratic basic order or faithfully execute the duties of the office.

[48] Hahm Chaihark and Sung Ho Kim, 'Constitutionalism on trial in South Korea' (2005) 16 *Journal of Democracy* 28–42, 37.

construed to include transgression of not only the constitution's textual provisions but also the principles of the constitution as expounded through the court's own jurisprudence.

In the 2017 decision on Park's impeachment, the Constitutional Court summed up her infractions into three categories. First was the violation of the president's duty to be impartial and pursue public interest. The court pointed to the abuse of presidential powers to benefit a personal friend via certain foundations created with funds extracted from the nation's major conglomerates, as well as the appointment of this friend's acquaintances to ministerial and other public offices. Her second infraction, according to the court, was infringement upon the conglomerates' rights to freely operate their businesses as well as their property rights by essentially coercing them to set up public interest foundations that benefitted only her friend. Park's third offence consisted of violation of the duty of public officials to maintain confidentiality. She had ordered or allowed many official documents containing state secrets, including her own schedule and texts of her speeches, to be leaked to her friend, a private individual, who could then use them to influence the conduct of state affairs and enrich herself.

Aside from these, the court rejected the other charges included in the National Assembly's impeachment resolution. It stated that there was insufficient evidence to support the claim that Park had abused her power by dismissing several public officials who had allegedly harmed her friend's interest. Similarly, the court found unsubstantiated the charge that Park had violated the freedom of the press by causing the layoff of the president of a daily newspaper which had reported on the possible existence of a 'secret line with real power' in the president's office. Lastly, the claim was held to be without merit that Park had violated the duty to protect the right to life of citizens by failing to respond in a timely and effective manner to the 2014 ferry-sinking disaster that took the lives of more than three hundred individuals.

Even without these offences, however, the court unanimously concluded that Park's infractions were serious enough to merit her removal from office. As for the standard to be applied in determining whether the violations were grave enough to merit dismissal, the court repeated almost verbatim the balancing test of the 2004 decision – the benefit to be derived from the president's dismissal should overwhelmingly outweigh the societal cost occasioned by such an extraordinary measure. It then went on to point out that allowing a personal friend to meddle in state affairs, abusing the powers entrusted by the people to help the pursuit of the friend's private interest and denying and covering up such facts, are 'acts that have damaged the principle of representative democracy and the spirit of rule of law', which amounted to a grave violation of the president's duty to pursue the public good. The court also declared that Park's apologies to the nation were insincere and that she failed to follow through with her promise to cooperate with the prosecutors' investigation and concluded that from such words and actions 'no will to uphold the constitution can be clearly discerned'. In sum, it stated that Park's violation of the constitution and laws were a betrayal of the people's trust which must be deemed a grave violation of the law that cannot be tolerated in order to defend the constitution.

Although the decision lacked specificity in terms of the actual weighing of the concrete harm to the constitutional order against the material benefit to be gained by the dismissal,[49] it is clear that it met the wishes of the millions of protesters who had assembled almost every weekend to demand Park's resignation and a thorough investigation. Many observers, both foreign and domestic, hailed it as a victory for Korean democracy and as evidence of a system that is able to manage a transfer of power in a peaceful and orderly manner.[50] In this regard, the court might be seen as having contributed once again to the consolidation of democracy. It remains to be seen, however, whether being involved in such a political and politicized controversy will help to advance the court's authority or the ideals of constitutionalism. On the one hand, it was unmistakable to the whole nation that the court could exert enormous influence on national politics by removing the president and forcing a snap election.[51] On the other hand, it was undeniable that the court faced a highly charged political environment that seemed to threaten the very independence needed to make a decision based solely on legal reasoning and not on political considerations.

[49] The court basically asserted, 'since the negative influence and ramifications of her violations of the law on the constitutional order are grave, we recognize that the benefit of defending the constitution to be derived from dismissing a president who derived democratic legitimacy directly from the people overwhelmingly outweighs the national loss occasioned by the president's dismissal.'

[50] E.g., Christian Caryl, 'South Korea shows the world how democracy is done' (10 March 2017) *Washington Post*; Kim Bo-eun, 'Candlelight revolution expels Park' (10 March 2017) *Korea Times*.

[51] Article 68(2) of the constitution provides that when the office of the presidency becomes vacant, a successor must be elected within sixty days.

Even if the judgment itself was not affected by pressure from politicians and the general public, this case revealed that the court could not escape having to make some strategic, if not explicitly political, choices in order to reach its decision. After it began hearing the case and before the justices finished their deliberations, the six-year term for the president of the court came to an end, leaving only eight justices on the bench. Six weeks thereafter, another justice (a designee of the chief justice of the Supreme Court) was due to step down. Faced with the prospect of having to decide such a momentous case with only seven justices, the court expedited the proceedings and issued the decision three days before it would be left with seven members. Under normal circumstances, it might have waited until the two were filled through nomination by the president, designation by the chief justice and confirmation by the legislature. Yet, with the passage of the National Assembly's impeachment resolution, all the president's powers had been suspended pursuant to Article 65(3) of the constitution. The prime minister was in charge of the government as the acting president, but it was unclear whether such a temporary caretaker had the authority to appoint new justices to the Constitutional Court. It was also unclear if the opposition-controlled National Assembly would even hold hearings for anyone who was nominated by the prime minister, himself one of Park's appointees.[52] Similarly, doubts were raised as to whether the chief justice, though not appointed by Park but known to be rather conservative, should designate a new member of the court in the middle of a presidential impeachment. If vacancies on the court could not be filled, however, the fate of a democratically elected president would be decided by less than the full nine-member bench.

Indeed, Park's attorneys argued that this would render the judgment illegitimate since the president's constitutional right to a fair and proper hearing would be impaired. The court rejected this argument by reasoning that the right to fair adjudication does not require the presence of all nine justices. At any rate, it stated that it could not afford to wait until the constitutional uncertainty regarding the appointment process was sorted out by the politicians. It is evident, however, that it wished to avoid making a decision with only seven members. Yet, in doing so, it had to take the risk of appearing to have unduly hurried through the

[52] Proposals had been made since the impeachment of Roh that legislation be adopted to define the precise extent of the powers that can be exercised by an acting president, but no action had been taken by the National Assembly by the time of Park's case.

proceedings. This was so because, at the time, a special prosecutor was still conducting an investigation into essentially the same wrongdoings as alleged by the National Assembly in its impeachment resolution. Indeed, by law, the court had the option of staying the proceedings until a parallel criminal investigation was concluded.[53] The fact that it chose not to exercise this option suggests that the court wished to avoid the other risk involved in issuing a decision with only seven justices.

5 *Transitional Justice*

The Constitutional Court has rendered a number of decisions regarding issues arising from efforts to address and rectify grievances and injustices sustained under past regimes. As is well known, transitional justice is still a live issue in Korea, where claims are often heard that the past has never been properly 'settled'. In 2013, the court had the occasion to deal with the notorious *Yushin* constitution of the Park Chung-hee era. Under that constitution, then-president Park was authorized to issue emergency decrees that could suspend the rights of citizens and which essentially operated as a supra-constitutional norm. Violations of some of the emergency decrees entailed trials by special court martial. The *Yushin* constitution also provided that those emergency decrees would not be subject to judicial review. As a result, when individuals whose rights had been affected filed claims at courts of law challenging the constitutionality of the emergency decrees, the courts at the time invariably dismissed the claims, citing the constitutional provision that precluded them from reviewing the decrees. In 2010, several citizens who had been convicted for violation of the emergency decrees and who were now seeking retrial filed a constitutional complaint claiming that the constitutionality of those emergency decrees had to be settled in order for the retrial to proceed.[54] Faced with the problem of having to decide whether the *Yushin* constitution's provision still precluded judicial review of emergency decrees, the Constitutional Court declared that the relevant constitutional criterion to be applied in this case was the current constitution, which does not have a provision precluding judicial review. Since there was no barrier to reviewing the constitutionality of the emergency decrees, the court proceeded to analyse the decrees and found them to be unconstitutional. Interestingly, complainants also charged that the

[53] CCA art. 51.
[54] Const. Ct. 2010 Hun-Ba 70 (21 March 2013).

said provision in the *Yushin* constitution was itself unconstitutional, but the court declined to entertain the theoretical puzzle of unconstitutional constitutional provisions.[55]

In another case, the Constitutional Court was involved in the issue of how to address the injustices that took place under colonial occupation by the Japanese empire during the first half of the last century. In a case involving property rights, it held that confiscation of property acquired in return for collaboration with the colonial authorities was constitutional.[56] Regarding the issue of retroactivity, it stated that even at the time the pro-Japanese collaborator acquired the property, it was foreseeable that such property would be confiscated upon national liberation. The collaborators (and their families) claimed that they were being singled out for discrimination, but the court reasoned that since the constitution does not particularly mandate equal protection for such people, the law that authorized the confiscation need only pass the rationality test. The court also rejected the argument that this was a violation of due process, by pointing out that avenues for contesting and appealing the confiscation are provided for by the law, and that an administrative appeals process and administrative adjudication are also available.

Perhaps the most controversial decision relating to issues of transitional justice may be the 2011 case involving the claims of the former 'comfort women' against the government of the Republic of Korea. For years, attempts by the victims of the wartime sex slavery to seek legal redress from the Japanese government had been unsuccessful. Turning now to the Korean government, they claimed that the government had a duty to actively assist them in the pursuit of justice against the Japanese government. In the case of a constitutional complaint filed against the Ministry of Foreign Affairs and Trade, the Constitutional Court held that their rights had, indeed, been violated by the inaction of the state.[57] It pointed out that there is a difference of viewpoints between Korea and Japan on the issue of whether the former comfort women's claims against the Japanese government had been extinguished as a result of the 1965 Agreement on the Settlement of Problems Concerning Property

[55] For more discussion on this case and a similar decision of the Supreme Court on the *Yushin* constitution, see Marie Seong-Hak Kim, 'Constitutional jurisprudence and the rule of law: Revisiting the courts in Yusin Korea (1972–1980)' (2013) 5 *The Hague Journal on the Rule of Law* 178–203.

[56] Const. Ct. 2008 Hun-Ba 141 (31 March 2011).

[57] Const. Ct. 2006 Hun-Ma 788 (30 August 2011).

and Claims and on Economic Cooperation between the Republic of Korea and Japan. The court then pointed out that Article 3 of that treaty deals with the courses of action (diplomatic routes and arbitration) that could be taken in case of a dispute over the interpretation of any of its provisions. The fact that the Ministry of Foreign Affairs and Trade was not taking any action under Article 3 to seek a resolution of the interpretative dispute was an unconstitutional violation of the complainants' rights.

This decision came at a time when the relationship between Korea and Japan was extremely strained. No dialogue had taken place between the two governments for years. Then, on 28 December 2015, just days before the end of the year that marked the fiftieth anniversary of the normalization of diplomatic relations between the two countries, an agreement was reached to settle the issue of comfort women. Shinzo Abe, prime minister of Japan, made an apology for having caused 'immeasurable pain and incurable physical and psychological wounds' to the comfort women, and the two governments agreed to set up a foundation to be funded with money from Japan's national budget to offer assistance to the surviving victims. While commentators disagree on whether this agreement satisfied the requirements of the court's decision in 2011,[58] its text stated that the issue had reached a 'final and irreversible resolution' and included a promise to refrain from mutual criticism in the future.

V Conclusion

As mentioned, the Korean Constitutional Court is an extremely busy institution. Over one thousand cases are filed at the court each year. It is, thus, difficult to discern a pattern from the myriad decisions made by the court. Whether it is becoming the guardian of the constitution or just acting upon the bidding of the government is a thorny question to answer. For some, the decision on the UPP is a prime example of the court acting as the mouthpiece of the regime. Despite the appearance of asserting the authority to set the parameters of the political process allowable under the constitution, to its critics, the court was merely

[58] Since it did not take the form of a treaty, the agreement's legal nature and binding force are still the subject of discussion. Politically, although Park Geun-hye's government touted it as a diplomatic success, it drew immediate criticism from comfort women's groups in Korea as a sell-out, for failing to make explicit the Japanese state's 'legal responsibility' for the sex slavery.

carrying out the wishes of the powers that be. Given that the UPP had very little power in the legislature, it was said that the whole case was really a means for the conservative President Park to carry out a personal vendetta against the leader of the party for hurtful comments made during the 2013 presidential campaign. By contrast, the impeachment case against Park might be viewed as an example of the court standing up to the government, for it actually removed from office the president, arguably the most powerful person in the nation. Similarly, in the case of the former comfort women's claim against Japan, the court did not shy away from putting the government in a very awkward and diplomatically tricky position. Likewise, the case on electoral districting schemes put legislators in a tight spot.

For an example of the Constitutional Court acting as an umpire presiding over the constitutional order, we might look to such cases as the one where the president turned to the court to settle a dispute between himself and another state agency. After his impeachment case was over, President Roh Moo-hyun filed a constitutional complaint claiming that his free speech rights had been infringed upon by the decision of the National Elections Commission to issue him a warning to stop taking sides and remain neutral about the upcoming general election.[59] While the court ruled that his rights had not been violated and that the provision in the election law requiring neutrality of public officials was not unconstitutional, the more interesting aspect of this case has to do with the fact that the court had been placed in the position of referee to oversee the proper balance and well-being of the entire government apparatus.

The court, however, is evidently not free to say whatever it wishes. It must be bound by the constitution and presumably follow its own interpretations thereof. Politically, as an institution commonly seen as suffering from democratic deficit, it has to be mindful of the fact that its decisions must ultimately be acceptable to the people. In a sense, the choice between guardian and mouthpiece may be premised upon a false dichotomy. Guardianship presupposes an image of an independent and overweening agency protecting a weak constitution by giving out orders to other government institutions. Mouthpiece suggests the opposite – a total lack of independence from other branches of the government. Yet, the two images are similar in that both presume that the court could

[59] Const. Ct. 2007 Hun-Ma 700 (17 January 2008).

choose to act freely, without regard to the requirements of the constitution or the will of the people. Perhaps the truth is much less dramatic. The Constitutional Court is just another agency operating under the constitution, trying to stake out its reputation and sphere of influence within a shifting political landscape and complex institutional framework mandated by the constitution. The only resource that it can draw on is the strength of its reasoning and the willingness of the people to accept its decisions.

Given the nature of the powers assigned to it by the constitution, the court sometimes attracts unwanted public attention and becomes embroiled in political controversies. It has thus far steered clear of overt politicization by issuing decisions based on constitutional principles and its reading of the will of the people. In cases such as those on presidential impeachment, dissolution of the UPP and the comfort women, all of which appeared to involve the court in megapolitical issues, it has sought to maintain its reputation and authority by rendering judgments that sided with, or at least did not stray too far from, the opinion of the general public.[60] As stated by the court's acting president in the impeachment case against Park, 'the constitution is the basis of existence for all state organs . . . and the people are the source of the power which creates that constitution'.[61] This strategy, of course, risks turning the court into a 'populist' institution. It may avoid that pitfall so long as it can show congruence between its interpretation of immutable constitutional principles and the admittedly transient will of the people. To the extent that the court can pull this off, it will not only ensure its own institutional survival but also contribute to the further consolidation of constitutional democracy in Korea.

[60] According to some scholars, this has been the case with the US Supreme Court since at least the early twentieth century. See Barry Friedman, *The Will of the People: How Public Opinion Has Influenced the Supreme Court and Shaped the Meaning of the Constitution* (New York: Farrar, Straus and Giroux, 2009); Neal Devins and Louis Fisher, *The Democratic Constitution* (New York: Oxford University Press, 2015).

[61] Interestingly, this passage appears in the summary of the decision read out by the acting president but is not found in the full text of the decision of the Court.

7

Avoiding Rights

The Constitutional Tsets of Mongolia

TOM GINSBURG AND CHIMID ENHBAATAR*

I Introduction

Now over twenty years old, the Constitutional *Tsets* (Court) of Mongolia has played a significant, if idiosyncratic, role in the country's democratic performance. Like many other constitutional courts around the world, it has assumed a role as the guardian of the Constitution and has become embroiled in a number of political conflicts. Unlike most other courts, however, it has made decisions that truly upended the structure of the political system, with a line of cases on government composition beginning in 1996. This has put it into direct conflict with the country's parliament. And it has also taken the unusual step of self-consciously limiting itself from hearing cases involving many constitutional rights. In this sense, it is an example of judicialization of politics without rights.

This chapter begins with a brief description of the *Tsets* and its jurisdiction, noting that it embodies a distinctive, relatively strong version of what is now known as dialogic or weak-form constitutional review. It then describes the history of the *Tsets*'s performance over the past decades. It focuses on the decisions on the political system and the novel interpretation of the *Tsets*'s jurisdiction as excluding rights. It characterizes the level of activism of the *Tsets* as being strong where it should have been weak, and weak where it should have been strong. The final section evaluates the *Tsets* from the perspective of comparative constitutional law, ultimately concluding that the lack of rights jurisdiction has not been fatal given the generally solid human rights record of the government.

* The authors would like to thank the members of the UNDP team with whom they collaborated on the report cited in note 14.

II The Constitutional *Tsets*: Structure and Jurisdiction

The Constitutional *Tsets* is a product of the country's democratization after the fall of the Soviet Union when the ruling Mongolian People's Revolutionary Party (MPRP) responded to public protests with a program of legal and political reform. After a brief transitional period, it adopted a constitution in late 1991, which took effect in early 1992. During the drafting process, the designers considered several models of constitutional review.

The Constitution as ultimately adopted included a new body to adjudicate constitutional disputes, named the *Tsets* after a kind of referee in traditional Mongolian wrestling. This body is the organ 'exercising Supreme supervision over the implementation of the Constitution, making judgment on the violation of its provisions, and resolving constitutional disputes'.[1] Judges are elected for six-year terms, renewable without limitation, and can be drawn from lawyers or from other professions, so long as they are forty years of age and have high levels of achievement. Three members are nominated from the country's unicameral parliament, known as the State Great Hural (SGH); three are nominated by the president and three from the Supreme Court. Details of the appointment process are contained in a law on the Constitutional *Tsets*, passed early in the constitution's history, while a 1997 law on Constitutional *Tsets* Procedure contains other details.

The *Tsets* does not fit squarely in any conventional model of constitutional review, and so is a distinctly Mongolian institution. The *Tsets*'s jurisdiction includes abstract review of legislation and other decisions of the SGH, as well as action by other government bodies. Claims can be brought by particular political institutions, such as the Supreme Court and parliament, as well as by individual citizens.[2] Requests from the parliament are brought by majority vote rather than the system found in many countries of minorities being allowed to send constitutional requests.

However, according to the laws on the *Tsets* and the *Tsets* Procedure, as interpreted, the *Tsets* has no jurisdiction to review ordinary judicial decisions. This intended, but idiosyncratic, part of the constitutional scheme is drawn from the interpretation of Article 50.2 of the Constitution which stipulates that the Supreme Court provides the 'final judicial decision'. This has been interpreted to mean that the *Tsets* has no

[1] Constitution of Mongolia, Art. 64.1.
[2] Constitution of Mongolia, Art. 66.

jurisdiction over Supreme Court cases. This means that citizens' rights might potentially be violated by the courts without redress. While the *Tsets* can hear petitions from citizens directed to constitutional rights violations, it cannot do so if the citizen has first gone to an ordinary court and obtained a judgment. While noted scholar (and later, minister of justice) Kh. Temujin filed complaints with the *Tsets* arguing that these statutes were unconstitutional, as interpreted, the petitions were rejected.[3] At the same, time, if an ordinary court refuses to take a case, the Constitutional *Tsets* can assign the case to a court.[4]

Because of the fact that the *Tsets* has interpreted its own organic law to limit jurisdiction to cases in which there is an abstract question of law, combined with the limitation on reviewing court cases, the *Tsets* has a very limited ability to protect rights. This has led some scholars, as well as the United Nations Human Rights Council, to recommend that the *Tsets* be given more explicit authority to hear human rights issues.[5] To be fair, political institutions can submit complaints on behalf of citizens who allege constitutional violations. The National Human Rights Commission is among these. Still, the jurisdiction of the *Tsets* does not match that of other constitutional courts around the world, which typically have the ability to redress basic rights in particular cases.[6]

One very distinctive feature of the procedure is the two-stage dialogic process described in Article 66 of the Constitution and elaborated in the law on the Constitutional *Tsets*. When the *Tsets* decides to hear a case, it begins with a five-member panel making an initial judgment. Any such decision that finds a law unconstitutional is sent to the parliament itself, which will review it and decide whether to accept it or not. Should the legislature disagree with the *Tsets*, it can reject the decision, which then goes before the full bench of nine justices. This bench can reaffirm the initial decision, in which case it will stand. Thus, the *Tsets* can have the last say, but the legislature has a say as well. This scheme fits in with the large political science literature on dialogic interpretation and weak-form review in which courts have a special role in constitutional

[3] Munksaikhan Odonkhuu, *Towards Better Protection of Fundamental Rights in Mongolia: Constitutional Review and Interpretation*, CALE Books vol. 4 (Nagoya, Japan: Centre for Asian Legal Exchange Books, 2014) at 95.

[4] Art. 14 of the law on Constitutional *Tsets* Procedure. See Munkhsaikhan, note 3 at 87.

[5] *United Nations Universal Periodic Review*, 2010.

[6] Ts. Sarantuya, 'Basic rights-courts-constitutional court', *Mongolian State and Law, #2* (2001) 1–10; Ts. Sarantuya, 'Basic rights and human rights: Comparison and theoretical thinking', *Law Theory, Practice, Methodology and Information Series, #1* (2000) 18–24.

interpretation but not the exclusive role.[7] However, the Mongolian procedure tends towards the stronger end of weak-form review in that the *Tsets* does have the final say, at least on paper.

III Performance

The *Tsets* has been quite active, receiving over 1,600 petitions in its first twenty years and issuing conclusions in 175 cases through 2016.[8] These have concerned a wide range of issues. Most of them were based on petitions from the public. The *Tsets* received nine requests: one from the general prosecutor, six from the Supreme Court and two from the president. During this time, the *Tsets* examined and resolved two major categories of disputes; the vast majority concerned whether a legal act breached the Constitution, while a small number concerned whether a high official breached the Constitution (ten disputes, or 7.5 per cent in data from 2013). Of disputes concerning whether a legal act was in breach of the Constitution, 101 disputes (or 76 per cent) concerned whether a provision of law was in breach of the Constitution, eight (or 6 per cent) were related to the provisions of resolutions of the SGH, ten (or 7.5 per cent) were about government regulations, two (or 1.5 per cent) were about decrees of the president and two (or 1.5 per cent) were whether the decisions of the High Election Commission were in breach of the Constitution.

Of the 175 conclusions, 100 (or 57 per cent) found a breach of the Constitution. The SGH accepted 45 of the 175 conclusions (both those finding and not finding a breach). Of the 100 in which a breach was found, the SGH rejected 56 and did not pass a resolution at all on several others.[9] Table 7.1 presents data by year, though readers should be aware that the SGH sometimes delays action on *Tsets* conclusions, and so the years may not correspond across columns. The *Tsets* made a final decision in 120 disputes (summing the third and fifth column of the table) and overrode the SGH in 63 disputes (column 7). Still, column 6 indicates that the SGH regularly declines to accept decisions of the *Tsets*. Sometimes, these

[7] Mark Tushnet, *Weak Courts, Strong Rights: Judicial Review and Social Welfare Rights in Comparative Constitutional Law* (Princeton: Princeton University Press, 2009); Stephen Gardbaum, *The New Commonwealth Model of Constitutionalism: Theory and Practice* (New York: Cambridge University Press, 2013).

[8] See Munkhsaikhan, note 3.

[9] Information on others was unavailable. Data adapted on an annual basis from *Mongol Ulsen 1992 Oni Undcen Xuuliin Xeregjiltiin Baidald Xiicen Dun Shinjulgee* (Ulaanbaatar: UNDP, 2016).

Table 7.1 Tsets' *decisions on constitutional violations*

	All conclusions	No violation of the Constitution (these conclusions are final)	Violation of the Constitution (these conclusions become final if accepted by the SGH)	Number of conclusions accepted by the SGH	Number of conclusions not accepted by the SGH	Number of resolutions of the *Tsets*
1992	1		1	–	–	–
1993	4	2	2	1	1	3
1994	9	2	7[a]	3	3	2
1995	7	5	2	–	1	2
1996	10	4	5	2	5	3
1997	6	3	4	3	2	3
1998	9	5	4	7	2	2
1999	1	1	–	1	–	–
2000	4	2	2	1	1	2[b]
2001	2	1	1	1	–	–
2002	4	–	4	–	3	3
2003	3	1	2	1	2	2
2004	3	2	1	–	–	–
2005	9	2	7	4	3	2
2006	13	5	8	4	3	4
2007	13	9	4	–	3	3
2008	10	4	6	3	2	3
2009	7	4	3	1	2	3
2010	8	3	5	2	3	2

2011	5	3	2	–	–	2
2012	5	4	1	–	3	3
2013	6	3	3	1	2	1
2014	8	3	5	2	3	2
2015	16	2	14	3	11	11
2016	12	5	7	5	1	5[c]
Total	175	75	100	45	56	63

[a] Three of the conclusions related to high officials; therefore, the SGH rather than the *Tsets* made the final decision.

[b] One resolution of the *Tsets* was its reaction to the amendments to the Constitution, so there was no reaction by the SGH.

[c] This number might look like a mistake. The explanation is that the SGH adopted the new law on *Tsets*, and the *Tsets* issued two resolutions rejecting several provisions of the law on the grounds of its incompatibility with the Constitution; in addition, two resolutions were adopted in relation to the SGH resolutions adopted the previous year.

Source: Adapted from United Nations Development Program, The Role of the Constitution of Mongolia in Consolidating Democracy: An Analysis (Ulaanbaatar: UNDP, 2015) at 15, available at www.mn.undp.org/content/dam/mongolia/Publications/DemGov/ConstReview_eng.pdf.

rejections seem to be motivated by political considerations rather than genuine concern about the integrity of the constitutional order. Furthermore, the SGH has frequently violated the legal time period allocated to decide on the conclusions of the *Tsets*, thus effectively stalling the procedure. While one might think that silence on the part of the SGH would mean that the *Tsets* conclusions would enter into force, the SGH has not adopted that interpretation and has taken the position that it is entitled to delay, through inaction, implementation of *Tsets* rulings. This was an unanticipated feature of the dialogic constitutional design and has meant that the *Tsets* has, in some cases, been ignored.

Some of the *Tsets* decisions have been very important, particularly with regard to the political system. For example, in 2007, in a case brought by D. Lamjav (described later), the *Tsets* held that the speaker of parliament had violated the constitution by editing versions of bills after passage.[10] The speaker, a very powerful MPRP politician named Ts. Nyamdorj, argued that he was simply making editorial changes that did not affect substance, but the *Tsets* was willing to stand up to him, and this led to his removal from office. In another case, the *Tsets* struck down a scheme which allowed members of parliament to spend state funds directly in their districts, in violation of all notions of separation of powers. This scheme was not renewed by the next government. Other cases involved the electoral system, the constitutional protection of Buddhism and many other matters.

In short, the *Tsets* is doing its job, for the most part, in a system with a very strong parliament that is explicitly empowered to question *Tsets* conclusions and which has arguably gone beyond the constitutional design in rejecting and ignoring final decisions. There are two grounds for criticism of the *Tsets*. Constitutions are schemes to resolve and channel political conflict. Yet the Mongolian *Tsets* has, through some of its more aggressive constitutional interpretations, found a way to exacerbate tensions within the political system. This is hardly ideal judicial behaviour, and indeed, the consequences have consumed a good deal of the political energy in Mongolia for nearly twenty years. Had these *Tsets* decisions been unimpeachable, this would hardly be a valid criticism, but in many cases, they rested on strained interpretations of the constitutional texts. Second, the *Tsets* has not found a way to develop a vigorous jurisprudence of fundamental rights, despite calls for it to do so.

[10] See discussion in Munkhsaikhan, note 3 at 167–170.

IV Exacerbating Political Conflict

For the past two decades, much of the political and constitutional debate in Mongolia has concerned the relationship between parliament and government, and, in particular, the issue of whether members of parliament could serve in the government. The main players were the MPRP (renamed the Mongolian People's Party since 2010), which has retained a good deal of popularity in the democratic era, and a set of other parties that have become known at various times as the Democratic Coalition or Alliance, now consolidated in the Democratic Party.

Mongolia's 1992 Constitution created a system of weak semi-presidentialism, combining a directly elected but non-partisan president with a very strong parliament (the SGH) and a government headed by a prime minister. Indeed, the parliament is considered to be one of the most powerful of such bodies in any democracy,[11] exercising what one might consider a kind of hyper-parliamentary power. It is explicitly declared the 'Supreme Organ of State Power',[12] with the explicit power to 'consider at its initiative any issue pertaining to domestic and foreign policies of the state'.[13] The president has the power of legislative initiative and veto as well as a symbolic role as head of state and commander-in-chief.

The Constitution was not exactly clear on the rules of government formation, and indeed, observers at the time the Constitution was being drafted commented on the relative weakness of the government vis-à-vis the other political institutions.[14] The Constitution did not specify what exact authority the president and Parliament exercise in appointing the prime minister and forming the cabinet, though it was clear that the cabinet is responsible to the Parliament while discharging its duty.[15]

Another ambiguity concerned who could serve in the government and whether MPs would have to resign their seats to do so. During the first phase of the transition to 1992, the MPRP included sitting MPs in its

[11] See M. Steven Fish and Mathew Kroenig, *The Handbook of National Legislatures: A Global Survey* (New York: Cambridge University Press, 2011); 'Comparative Constitution Rankings', Comparative Constitutions Project, http://comparativeconstitutionsproject.org/ccp-rankings/ (accessed 27 April 2018).

[12] Art. 20.

[13] Art. 25.

[14] United Nations Development Program, *The Role of the Constitution of Mongolia in Consolidating Democracy: An Analysis* (Ulaanbaatar: UNDP, 2015) at 15, available at www.mn.undp.org/content/dam/mongolia/Publications/DemGov/ConstReview_eng.pdf (accessed 6 October 2017).

[15] Art. 25.6.

cabinets but did not require that members of government be MPs. The issue was brought to the fore in 1996 in a suit by D. Lamjav, a prominent mathematician who has served in the country's transitional parliament but had not won a seat under the new Constitution. Lamjav became a kind of textualist enforcer of the Constitution, bringing repeated lawsuits on many issues before the Constitutional *Tsets*.

In 1996, for the first time, a coalition of parties opposed to the MPRP came to power. Before a government could be formed, however, Lamjav sought to prevent the coalition from filling the cabinet with members of the SGH, relying on Article 29, which states that 'members of parliament shall have no other employment'.[16] Answering this question required textual interpretation, of course, but also a sense of how political systems operate. Generally speaking, in presidential systems, the cabinet is separated from the parliament, and so members cannot become ministers. In pure parliamentary systems, however, the government is formed by the leading parties in parliament, and so it is common for at least some members to be ministers. Semi-presidential systems vary on this question: some emphasize the idea that the government is formed out of the parliament and forbid the simultaneous participation of members in government. Other systems allow simultaneous participation, leaning towards the more parliamentary model.[17]

Mongolian practice from 1992 to 1996 had allowed ministers to be members of parliament. When the *Tsets* was asked to resolve this issue, however, it adopted Lamjav's argument, and the initial panel found that members of parliament could not serve in the government. This decision was then sent to the newly elected parliament, where the majority Democratic Coalition members duly rejected the initial conclusion. After a second hearing before the entire *Tsets*, the *Tsets* issued a decision upholding its earlier judgment to the effect that MPs could not join the cabinet without resigning their seats. Under Article 66.3 of the Constitution, this decision was final.

Thus began a several-year process in which political forces sought to devise a workable system of legislative–executive relations that met with *Tsets* approval. The immediate aftermath was a crisis in the Democratic

16 See Tom Ginsburg and Gombosuren Ganzorig, 'When courts and politics collide: Mongolia's constitutional crisis' (Spring 2001) 14 *Columbia Journal of Asian Law* 309.

17 Countries in which the two are separated include Taiwan (Art. 75), France (Art. 23) and Portugal (Art. 154); countries in which it is allowed include Poland (Art. 103; 108), the Czech Republic (Art. 22), South Africa (Art. 47) and Romania (Art. 79).

Coalition. Although their candidate for prime minister had not run in parliamentary elections, many other leaders had done so. Resigning seats to serve in government would require by-elections. Because their majority was narrow, this was not an attractive option. Instead, the coalition put forward a cabinet composed of second-line leaders. This meant that the government was even weaker than usual relative to parliament. The next four years produced a series of weak, unstable governments, as the coalition was subject to factional rifts. Furthermore, the president exploited an ambiguity in the Constitution to reject several governments. Article 33(2) states that the president has the power 'to propose to the State Great Hural the name of a candidate for appointment to the post of Prime Minister' in consultation with the parliamentary majority. President Bagabandi interpreted this to mean that he could approve the majority's nominees.

To clarify matters and resolve the problem, parliament passed legislation in 1998 that would allow the members of parliament to serve in government. However, this law was rejected by the *Tsets*. In early 2000, the parliament passed (over the president's veto) a constitutional amendment to achieve the same goal. However, the amendment was challenged before the Constitutional *Tsets* and rejected.

According to the procedural law of the Constitutional *Tsets*, it was up to the SGH to accept or reject the *Tsets* decision within fifteen days after it received the *Tsets* opinion rejecting the constitutional amendments.[18] The SGH, however, chose to take no action at all. Without a rejection by the SGH, the *Tsets* could not hear the case again and issue a final decision en banc that would be permanent under Article 66.4. This state of limbo was precisely what the SGH desired, although it can be considered a perversion of the dialogic process as designed in the Constitution. On 5 April 2000, a group of lawyers sent a letter to the SGH urging the members to accept the ruling of the Constitutional *Tsets* which reflected the law and public opinion. Despite the public criticism and three formal requests by the Constitutional *Tsets*, the SGH delayed its consideration.

Elections in July 2000 led to an overwhelming victory over the Democrats by the MPRP, which took seventy-two out of seventy-six seats. Just

[18] This paragraph and the next are adapted from Tom Ginsburg and Gombosuren Ganzorig (note 16 earlier).

like the previous SGH majority, the MPRP parliamentarians wanted to allow MPs to serve in the cabinet. In the first session of the SGH meeting, the MPRP majority agreed to ignore the Constitutional *Tsets* ruling and allow the formation of a government that included members of the SGH, as if the controversial amendments to the Constitution had survived. On 28 July 2000, four months and twelve days after the *Tsets*'s decision and nearly four months after the expiration of the period required by law for consideration of such a decision, the SGH finally debated the Constitutional *Tsets* ruling but avoided a formal rejection. By a vote of sixty-two to two, it stated that the Constitutional *Tsets* had heard an issue outside its jurisdiction – namely, the constitutionality of a constitutional amendment. But it did not resolve the problem.

Instead of issuing a formal resolution reacting to the *Tsets* decision, as required by the law on the Parliament, the legislature decided to include a short note in its record indicating that it considered the issue finalized. The Constitutional *Tsets* expressed its dissatisfaction with the protocol, and on 1 August 2000, it sent a letter demanding an official resolution. The *Tsets* also asserted that the SGH had authorized itself to interpret the Constitution, which should be the exclusive job of the Constitutional *Tsets*. The SGH responded that the *Tsets* had no jurisdiction to hear questions of constitutionality of constitutional amendments passed with a supermajority.

On 29 October 2000, the *Tsets* reconsidered the constitutional amendment and again ruled that it was unconstitutional. It relied on procedural grounds, specifically Article 68.1, which states that amendments to the Constitution may be initiated by certain designated bodies. The *Tsets* read these as being exclusive, implying that a constitutional amendment initiated by SGH on its own was unconstitutional because the legislature failed to consult with the Constitutional *Tsets* and the president.

The SGH then passed another constitutional amendment with exactly the same text as had already been adopted – and rejected – the previous year, but this time, presented it to the *Tsets* and the president. It also made six other amendments to the Constitution, clarifying the rules of government formation and limiting the president's role in the process. Eventually, after extensive political consultations in 2001, these amendments were approved by the president and not rejected by the *Tsets*. A new equilibrium was established.

The *Tsets*'s performance in this long series of cases involving executive–legislative relations reflects a kind of formalist insistence on a particular reading of an ambiguous text. Through several elections won by both major political configurations in the country, the *Tsets* have continuously resisted demands from the political system for what was perceived to be a more workable system of legislative–executive relations. To what end?

Political debate over the functioning of the amendments continued. Some argued that the new system weakened the parliament, while others said it was the opposite. In one recent government, seventeen out of nineteen ministerships were held by concurrently serving MPs, meaning that there were only fifty-nine other members to shoulder much of the burden of the legislative and oversight work of parliament. Critics argue that laws are more poorly drafted after the amendments.[19]

Along with a set of Mongolian scholars, I recently recommended returning to greater separation between government and parliament. As we put it,

> Even if, as a formal matter, the government is still accountable to parliament, the latter does not have a strong incentive to threaten to end the government and so in practice there is less leverage for parliamentary oversight. Furthermore the small number of majority MPs who are not in the Government are left to take care of all purely legislative work. Having more people serving in both bodies will reduce the possibility that one faction can capture the governing apparatus, and will help to make sure that checks and balances operate effectively. Separating the two might encourage more technocratic participation in Government, which might bring policy benefits.[20]

At this writing, parliament is considering further legislation or constitutional amendments to re-establish a better balance between executive and legislature. One proposal stipulates that no more than one-third of the members of the cabinet (along with, or including, the prime minister) would be allowed to serve as MPs. This proposal is framed as allowing for greater accountability while also ensuring the institutional links between parliament and government.

Still, the entire saga could have been avoided had the *Tsets* had the good sense to listen to repeated political majorities, encompassing the entire political spectrum, seeking a workable system of executive–legislative relations. Constitutional systems require accommodation and pragmatic solutions to structural issues, and deference to political institutions on essentially political matters is often warranted. By adopting a

[19] *The Role of the Constitution of Mongolia in Consolidating Democracy*, note 14 at 24.
[20] Ibid., para. 65.

strict textualism and an interpretation shared by no other institution or political force in society, the *Tsets* created a constitutional crisis where none need have occurred. In this sense, it has been strong when it should have been weak.

Political conflict between the *Tsets* and the SGH has continued and recently intensified. In 2012, the Democratic Party won parliamentary elections and proceeded with a program of judicial reform to deal with the very poor reputation of the country's courts. When the *Tsets* rejected much of the legislation embodying the judicial reform package,[21] Minister of Justice Kh. Temuujin submitted a bill to introduce a mandatory retirement age of sixty-five and a limit on the number of reappointments into the law on the *Tsets*. After the SGH passed the bill in 2016, the chairman of the *Tsets*, noted jurist J. Amarsanaa, wrote a letter to SGH Chairman Z. Enkhbold telling him that the law was to be reviewed and that the SGH should not act until the *Tsets* had considered the constitutionality of the provisions in question. This letter infuriated the members of parliament, and they initiated a recall of Amarsanaa on the basis that he had violated a provision of the *Tsets* Procedure law that its members should not express opinions on pending matters or make recommendations to others in that respect.[22] After quick hearings, they removed Amarsanaa from office. The Supreme Court was asked its opinion and demurred, trying to stay out of the crisis. This itself created legal confusion. Although the law stated that removal of a *Tsets* member requires a judicial finding that he or she committed a crime or violated the law, the SGH amended the law to find that a 'competent authority' could make such a finding. By then acting to remove Mr. Amarsanaa without a prior judicial proceeding, the SGH implicitly set itself up as 'the competent authority'. This raises serious normative concerns about the parliament's overall level of power.

V Rights

Earlier, we argued that the *Tsets* has played too strong a role in an area in which it should have been deferential, namely, the structure of the political system. The inverse of this is the fact that the *Tsets* has been weak where, arguably, it should have been strong. The failure of the *Tsets* to develop a powerful rights jurisprudence has been criticized by scholars

[21] See cases presented in Altangerel, note 18 at 193–198.
[22] Law on *Tsets* Procedure, Art. 12, para. 4.

and activists.[23] It was even a topic raised by the country's Universal Periodic Review before the United Nations Human Rights Council in November 2010. That document advised Mongolia to provide a mandate to the Constitutional *Tsets* to act upon violations of the individual rights and freedoms guaranteed under the Constitution.

Yet, overall, the rights situation in Mongolia seems to be relatively stable. The protection of human rights has been a major impetus for reform since 1990, and the country has a vigorous civil society that monitors and criticizes government. Politicians regularly invoke human rights. The country has joined around thirty international human rights treaties, including the major multilateral treaties protecting human rights. Article 16 of the Constitution contains a long list of human rights, and the document includes social and economic rights along with civil and political rights. It has a National Human Rights Commission and a parliamentary subcommittee on human rights. The SGH adopted a National Human Rights Action Programme in 2003.

The recent UNDP assessment of the Mongolian Constitution looked at several rights, including freedom of religion and minority rights, which seem to be well protected.[24] There are no reports of discrimination on either religious or ethnic grounds, and the country's Kazakh minority seem to be well integrated. While Mongolia does have a strain of anti-foreign nationalism, particularly focused on Chinese, our own perception is that this is in decline. Ginsburg had rocks thrown at his head in 1993 with the epithet 'oros bish' (No Russians); such an experience is now unimaginable. The combination of markets and democracy has increased tolerance.[25] Freedom of assembly has been generally protected, and while one recent report of several non-governmental organizations noted some areas of concern with regard to the freedom of the press, this does not seem to be a severe problem in a dense media environment.[26] One issue of importance seems to be criminal libel laws that have been used to pressure journalists in some instances.[27]

[23] See discussion in Altangerel, note 18 at 172–179.

[24] *The Role of the Constitution of Mongolia in Consolidating Democracy*, note 14 at 77–80.

[25] Tom Ginsburg, 'Democracy, markets and doomsaying: Review essay on Amy Chua's *World on Fire*' (2004) 22 *Berkeley Journal of International Law* 310.

[26] Globe International Center, Press Institute, Mongolian Journalists Association, and Transparency Fund, *Assessment of Media Development in Mongolia* (based on UNESCO/IPDC'S Media Development Indicators) (Paris: UNESCO, 2016).

[27] *The Role of the Constitution of Mongolia in Consolidating Democracy*, note 14 at 79.

The violence around the 2008 parliamentary elections, during which five died and hundreds were injured in riots, led to the first and only state of emergency in Mongolian history.[28] Mutual recriminations followed, with some blaming the losing Democratic Party and others focusing on police overreaction. Yet, from a constitutional perspective, the system survived this major challenge. The state of emergency was declared in conformity with the constitution. The National Security Council was consulted. Constitutional rules were followed, and security officers involved in the violence were disciplined. A parliamentary investigation committee examined evidence and issued a report. And a national-unity government was created, even though the MPRP had enough seats to form a government on its own. The election of Ts. Elbegdorj as president the following year showed that the opposition was able to compete effectively in the aftermath of the emergency. In short, emergency powers were not abused in Mongolia.

Perhaps the major areas of concern for continued scrutiny are gender-based violence and other women's rights and the social and economic rights which have been pressured by the end of socialism and the rise of inequality. Mongolia faces high levels of urban poverty, as many people have moved from the rural areas to the outskirts of Ulaanbaatar. Living in yurts without basic services, their levels of unemployment are high, with associated social problems. Governments have responded with programs of cash transfers. This suggests that the major rights problems in Mongolia are being addressed, albeit imperfectly, by the political system. The social and economic rights which are the sources of the greatest challenge are not the rights most easily addressed by courts. Without minimizing the creative jurisprudence which has developed in South Africa and elsewhere on these rights, the *Tsets* as currently constituted does not seem to be in a position to make a major contribution here.[29]

In short, the country seems to have developed a strong culture of protecting at least some rights through the legislative and political processes. This leads one to wonder whether the recommendation to add a constitutional rights jurisdiction would be a major addition. One could imagine that a *Tsets* staffed with politicians may not be particularly active

[28] This paragraph and the next are adopted from *The Role of the Constitution*, ibid., paras. 261–262 at 81.

[29] Malcolm Langford (ed.), *Social Rights Jurisprudence: Emerging Trends in International and Comparative Law* (Cambridge: Cambridge University Press, 2009).

in supervising the ordinary courts. 'Weak courts, strong rights' seems to be a good way to characterize the Mongolian situation.

VI Conclusion

One of us has argued that the Mongolian *Tsets* is an example of a constitutional review institution set up as a form of political insurance.[30] While the MPRP knew it would be in a strong position in the new political order, it could not know that it would completely dominate post-transition elections. Smaller political parties, concerned with human rights, also wanted a system of constitutional review. Mongolia's parliamentary traditions, and the MPRP's strong position, meant that the drafters agreed to a system of dialogic review in which court and legislature would cooperate on constitutional interpretation.

The insurance policy paid off for the MPRP when it lost its first election ever in 1996. By weakening the opposition with its fateful decision to separate government and parliament, the *Tsets* set the stage for the return of the MPRP in 2000. Further conflict with parliament, however, weakened the *Tsets*'s authority. As parliament grew in power, it became willing to ignore the original dialogic scheme and to simply undercut the *Tsets* through inaction. The recent SGH effort to remove the chairman of the *Tsets* without any judicial finding of a violation of law shows that the original scheme has broken down. While the exercise of hyper-parliamentary power has not yet led to attacks on human rights, broadly construed, the lack of an effective check does not bode well for the *quality* of Mongolian democracy. Weak courts, strong rights works because of strong legislatures, but can a legislature be too strong? That is the question the Mongolian case poses.

30 Tom Ginsburg, *Judicial Review in New Democracies: Constitutional Courts in Asian Cases* (Cambridge: Cambridge University Press, 2003).

8

The Constitutional Court of Thailand

From Activism to Arbitrariness

KHEMTHONG TONSAKULRUNGRUANG*

Democracy is not only about holding elections. Freedom, transparency, and the rule of law are essential values that even the majority should not be able to undermine. The Constitutional Court of Thailand helps uphold these democratic values. However, over the past decade, Thailand has witnessed an expansion of the Constitutional Court's power that has weakened the concept of the rule of law. In addition to reviewing the constitutionality of statutes, the Court has the power to disqualify politicians and invalidate political processes. As a result, several cases have become critical turning points in Thai politics. Worryingly, the Court appears to be exploiting this power to impose its political viewpoint and is hostile toward elected politicians. Instead of promoting democracy and peace, the Court is now a part of Thailand's prolonged political conflict, and respect for it has been dwindling rapidly. This chapter begins with the general development of Thailand's Constitutional Court from 2005 onwards. It then examines shifts in the Court's structure and power and the ensuing alteration of its role under the changing political atmosphere. Finally, a few cases are selected to highlight the Court's contribution to the present crisis in Thai constitutionalism.

I Development of the Constitutional Court

The Constitutional Court is the product of the 1997 political reforms. Its two decades have seen both peace and turmoil during which its credibility has waxed and waned. Its conception was welcomed before the public grew sceptical of its performance. Later, it received both high praise and heavy criticism.

* Lecturer, Faculty of Law, Chulalongkorn University, Thailand, khemthong.t@chula.ac.th

1 1997–2005

Prior to the creation of the Constitutional Court, Thailand had tried several models of constitutional review. Thailand's first constitution, of 1932, vested in the Parliament the authority to interpret the constitution.[1] However, in 1946, the Supreme Court declared that the War Crime Act was unconstitutional because the act in dispute, which retroactively punished the Thai government for joining the Axis in World War II, was in opposition to the Constitution's guarantee of rights and liberties.[2] The decision alarmed the legislature, which saw it as the arbitrary expansion of judicial power. Parliament then responded by establishing the Constitutional Panel.

The War Crime decision resembled the American model of judicial review, while the Constitutional Panel reflected the French *Conseil Constitutionnel.* The Constitutional Panel was not a court. It was a tribunal comprised of *ex officio* members and experts: the president of Parliament, the speaker of the House of Representatives, the president of the Court of Justice, the attorney general and six legal or political science experts appointed by Parliament.[3]

However, the Constitutional Panel failed to create a strong sense of constitutionalism in Thai society – for two reasons. First, since 1947, Thailand witnessed a cycle of short-lived, shallowly democratic and also ruthlessly authoritarian regimes.[4] Once a coup happened, a constitution was abolished and so was the Constitutional Panel. Its short life undermined any attempt to deliver meaningful decisions that could impact society. The second setback was its status. While it performed a judicial function, the process was more political than judicial. The combination of politicians and political appointees on the bench led to concern over the nature of its expertise.

The breakthrough came with the 1997 political reforms. The reforms stemmed from the 1992 uprising against General Sujinda Kra-Pra-Yoon, the army commander and prime minister at the time. He had strong backing from the 1991 junta, but a violent crackdown forced him to

[1] Constitution B.E. 2475 (รัฐธรรมนูญแห่งราชอาณาจักรไทย พ.ศ. 2475) s. 62.

[2] Decision 1/2489 (1946) (War Crime Division of the Supreme Court).

[3] Constitution B.E. 2489 (รัฐธรรมนูญแห่งราชอาณาจักรไทย พ.ศ. 2489) s. 89.

[4] See Chris Baker and Pasuk Phongpaichit, *A History of Thailand*, 3rd edn. (Cambridge: Cambridge University Press 2014), chapters 4 and 9; Thongchai Winichakul, 'Toppling democracy' (2008) 38 *Journal of Contemporary Asia* 11–37, 15–17.

resign and the military to end its role in politics.[5] Thais then started demanding reform to permanently end the vicious cycle of elections and coups.[6] The final product of the reform was the 1997 Constitution.[7]

In order to successfully consolidate Thailand's democracy, the drafters of the 1997 Constitution aimed at protecting people's rights and liberties and introducing transparency into the government. The 1997 Constitution included independent watchdog agencies that would work together with specialized courts to implement the Constitution's goals. The judiciary was, as a result, split into three: the Court of Justice, the Constitutional Court and the Administrative Court. Despite early resistance from the Court of Justice, the Constitutional Court was formally established in 2001 and the first panel was installed.[8]

The first few years were promising. The Constitutional Court invalidated a few provisions of law to promote gender equality, the right of property and freedom of occupation, while deferring other matters in a delicate balance between protecting civil rights and respecting the separation of powers.[9] Even more rigorous was its pursuit of politicians. The Court convicted and imposed a five-year ban from politics on high-profile politicians who failed to disclose their assets.[10] The Court seemed to be directing Thailand toward a better democracy.

However, the Constitutional Court acquitted Thaksin Shinawatra in his asset disclosure case.[11] At the time, he was a popular businessman-turned-politician and candidate for prime minister. His aggressive populist social and economic policies earned him a decisive victory in the 2001 election. The acquittal was considered an error, but it cleared his path to power.[12] Thaksin proceeded to dominate the cabinet and the lower

[5] Baker and Phongpaichit, *A History of Thailand*, note 4, 250–251.

[6] Ibid., 253–254.

[7] Tom Ginsburg, 'Constitutional afterlife: The continuing impact of Thailand's postpolitical constitution' (2009) 7 *International Journal of Constitutional Law* 83–105, 90.

[8] Andrew Harding and Peter Leyland, *The Constitutional System of Thailand: A Contextual Analysis* (Oxford: Hart Publishing, 2011) 161–162.

[9] Decision 21/2546 (2003), 25/2547 (2004) and 30/2548 (2005) (CONST COURT).

[10] Harding and Leyland, *The Constitutional System of Thailand*, note 8, 180.

[11] Decision 20/2544 (2001) (CONST COURT). See Thitinan Pongsudhirak, 'The tragedy of the 1997 constitution', in John Funston (ed.), *Divided over Thaksin: Thailand's Coup and Problematic Transition* (Singapore: Institute of Southeast Asian Studies, 2009) 32–34.

[12] See James Klein, 'The battle for rule of law in Thailand: The Constitutional Court of Thailand', in Amara Raksasataya and James R. Klein (eds.), *The Constitutional Court of Thailand: The Provisions and the Working of the Court* (Bangkok: Constitution for the People Society 2003) 74–76.

house. At the same time, he was suspected of secretly influencing the Senate as well as watchdog agencies. He became blatantly corrupt,[13] and his regime was infamous for violations of human rights.[14] Although the judiciary appeared to be the only institution that Thaksin could not assert his power over, it was reluctant to intervene. The public grew more agitated by this deference, and the judiciary slowly lost public trust.[15] As a result, there was a call for 'judicial activism' and for judges to be more aggressive to balance Thaksin's abuses.[16]

2 2006–2007

The turning point came in April 2006. For the third time, Thaksin won a controversial election, but the public refused to accept his victory. The Constitutional Court invalidated the 2006 election, citing Thaksin's unnatural victory and the likelihood of fraud.[17] However, instead of solving the problem, the decision intensified the conflict. Thaksin was determined to arrange another election, but his enemy demanded the cabinet resign *en masse*; hence, there was political deadlock. With an interim government and no parliament, the military seized power on 19 September 2006.

Because of widespread public distrust, the junta, known as the Council of National Security (CNS), dismissed the Constitutional Court and installed the Constitutional Council, judges for which were chosen from the Supreme and the Administrative Courts.[18] The Council adopted a more aggressive stance and dissolved Thaksin's Thai Rak Thai (TRT) party, banning its executives for five years.[19] The Constitutional Court was revived under the 2007 Constitution, with the intention of assigning

[13] See Kevin Hewison, 'Thaksin Shinawatra and the reshaping of Thai politics' (2010) 16 *Contemporary Politics* 119–133.

[14] See Vitit Muntarbhorn, 'Human rights in the era of "Thailand Inc.', in Randall Peerenboom, Carole J. Petersen and Albert H. Y. Chen (eds.), *Human Rights in Asia: A Comparative Legal Study of Twelve Asian Jurisdictions, France and the USA*, (Abingdon: Routledge 2006) 320–345.

[15] Pongsudhirak, 'The tragedy of the 1997 Constitution', note 11 at 34.

[16] Björn Dressel, 'Judicialization of politics or politicization of the judiciary? Considerations from recent events in Thailand' (2011) 23 *Pacific Review* 671–691, 673.

[17] Baker and Phongpaichit, *A History of Thailand*, note 4, 269; Decision 9/2549 (2006) (CONST COURT).

[18] Interim Charter B.E. 2549 (รัฐธรรมนูญแห่งราชอาณาจักรไทย (ฉบับชั่วคราว) พ.ศ. 2549) s. 35 (2006 Interim Charter).

[19] Decision 3–5/2550 (2007) (CONST COURT).

it a greater role to guard the Constitution against politicians. For that reason, the 2007 Constitution isolated the Constitutional Court from political interference and expanded its jurisdiction to include the review of political questions.

3 *2008–2015*

After the coup, Thailand was deeply divided. The old conservative establishment formed the core of the yellow-shirts, who joined the People's Alliance for Democracy (PAD) and supported the 2006 coup.[20] Their opposition became known as the red-shirts.[21] The 2007 Constitution was the product of the yellow-shirts' attempts to undermine electoral politics while promoting moralistic politics.[22] The Constitution assigned the judiciary, the Senate and all watchdog agencies the task of constraining corrupt politicians and restoring ethics in government.[23] The Constitutional Court's claim to protect the rule of law thus fitted right into this mission. It has been the narrative of the Court's deliberation and reasoning since then. But the red-shirts were highly critical of the move.[24] They also feared that many appointees to the bench might be chosen for their critical anti-Thaksin attitude, not for expertise in constitutional law, transforming the Court into a tool to harass them.[25] While the Court gained back some support it had

[20] This old conservative establishment was described as a network of senior bureaucrats, academics and businessmen who long dominated governmental policies: Duncan McCargo, 'Network monarchy and legitimacy crises in Thailand' (2005) 18 *Pacific Review* 499–519, 501–510.

[21] It is easier to define the red-shirt negatively as non-yellow because they are loosely formed from various groups of grassroots people, Thaksin loyalists, liberals, those against the coup, anti-monarchists and some who do not even support Thaksin at all. See an explanation of the red–yellow identity in Marc Saxer, *In the Vertigo of Change: How to Resolve Thailand's Transformation Crisis* (Bangkok: Friedrich-Ebert-Stiftng Thailand, 2014) 17–29.

[22] See Winichakul, 'Toppling democracy', note 4.

[23] Vitit Muntarbhorn, 'Deconstructing the 2007 constitution', in John Funston (ed.), *Divided over Thaksin: Thailand's Coup and Problematic Transition* (Singapore: Institute of Southeast Asian Studies, 2009) 80–89; Ginsburg, 'Constitutional afterlife', note 7, 100–101.

[24] Baker and Phongpaichit, *A History of Thailand,* note 4, 273.

[25] Jaran Pakdeethanakul was the outstanding example. He had been publicly critical of Thaksin's regime before the 2006 coup. He was appointed to the Constitution Drafting Council, where he was actively supporting and defending the draft. He was then nominated into the Constitutional Court panel. Another example was Nakarin Mektrairat. See 'What they say on the draft 2007 constitution' Prachatai English, 20 August 2007, http://prachatai.org/english/node/156 (accessed 6 October 2017) and 'Old men and old ideas',

lost before the coup, it lost its politically neutral stance, making it unfit to be an arbiter for political disputes.

The Constitutional Court continued its activism through 2008 to 2014, the years under the 2007 Constitution. Its jurisdiction was arbitrarily expanded. Unforeseen constitutional tests were often added into the verdicts. In addition to controversial decisions, the Constitutional Court's reputation was tainted further by a series of scandals. Judges were secretly filmed discussing a dissolution case that ultimately resulted in an acquittal.[26] More scandals revealed conflicts of interest where a judge rigged an exam so his relative could get a job at the office of the Constitutional Court.[27] Another judge approved a scholarship for his son to study abroad.[28] But the Court always enjoyed independence, with little oversight. Neither serious investigation nor prosecution was made. Indeed, the Court actually threatened those who exposed these scandals with defamation and contempt of court charges.[29] It also asked the government to block all related video clips on the YouTube channel.[30] These scandals put the Court's professionalism and integrity in doubt.

After the Constitutional Court invalidated another general election[31] and later dismissed Thaksin's youngest sister, Yingluck Shinawatra, from her prime ministership,[32] the military seized power in May 2014. The Court was spared, and despite the fact that there are no cases to try and no constitution to guard,[33] the Court is still theoretically functioning and the judges' salaries are being paid.

Political Prisoners in Thailand, 19 September 2015, https://thaipoliticalprisoners.wordpress.com/2015/09/13/old-men-and-old-ideas/ (accessed 6 October 2017).

26 Bangkok Pundit (pseudonym), 'What are the five leaked videos about?' *Asian Correspondent*, 17 October 2010, http://asiancorrespondent.com/2010/10/what-are-the-five-leaked-videos-about/ (accessed 6 October 2017); 'Judges in the dock', *The Economist*, 11 November 2010, www.economist.com/node/17472738 (accessed 6 October 2017).

27 Saksith Saiyasombut, 'New leaked video dishes yet another scandal at Thailand's Constitution Court', *Asian Correspondent*, 10 November 2010, http://asiancorrespondent.com/2010/11/new-leaked-video-dishes-yet-another-scandal-at-thailands-constitution-court (accessed 6 October 2017).

28 Anuphan Chantana, 'Judge upbraided for letting son go on paid study leave', the Nation, 27 August 2013, www.nationmultimedia.com/breakingnews/Judge-upbraided-for-letting-son-go-on-paid-study-l-30213603.html (accessed 6 October 2017).

29 'Judges in the dock', note 26.

30 Ibid.

31 Decision 5/2557 (2014) (CONST COURT).

32 Ibid.

33 Interim Charter B.E. 2557 (รัฐธรรมนูญแห่งราชอาณาจักรไทย (ฉบับชั่วคราว) พ.ศ. 2557) ss. 44 and 47 (2014 Interim Charter).

II Structure and Power

Both the 1997 and 2007 Constitutions described the main structure and power of the Constitutional Court. Over the years, the body of the Court was streamlined, and its jurisdiction grew. Notwithstanding such changes, the Constitutional Court, overall, shows continuance. At the time of writing, Thailand has no permanent constitution. But provisions concerning structure, jurisdiction and procedure of the Constitutional Court from the 2007 Constitution are still applicable, as the 2014 Interim Charter provides.[34] In August 2016, the draft constitution was accepted by national referendum and is expected to come into effect in early 2017. The upcoming constitution would modify the structure of the Constitutional Court as well as authorize more involvement in politics.

1 Selection

While recruitment in other courts is made through entrance examination, the Constitutional Court judges are selected through a nomination system similar to that provided for independent watchdog agencies. Once fifteen in number, the Court was reduced to nine in 2007. The Council of the Supreme Court Judges nominated three of its members, while the Council of the Supreme Administrative Judges nominated two.[35] The nomination commission then chose two experts in law and two in political science. All nine judges were to be approved by the Senate and sworn in before the King.[36] Having judges who are not legally qualified on the bench is a unique characteristic indicating the need for broader wisdom in politics. However, the downside of this is the possibility that judges may rely less on law and more on politics.[37] The 2016 Draft Constitution would replace an expert in law and another in political science with two former senior civil servants.[38] The new composition surely raises further doubt as to the quality of the judges.

The nomination commission is an *ad hoc* body. In the 1997 Constitution, the nomination commission had comprised the president of the

[34] 2014 Interim Charter, ss. 5 and 45.

[35] Constitution B.E. 2550 (รัฐธรรมนูญแห่งราชอาณาจักรไทย พ.ศ. 2550) s. 204 (2007 Constitution).

[36] Ibid., s. 204.

[37] Dressel, 'Judicialization of Politics or Politicization of the Judiciary?', note 16, 684.

[38] Constitution Draft B.E. . . . (ร่างรัฐธรรมนูญแห่งราชอาณาจักรไทย พ.ศ. . . .) s. 200 (2016 draft Constitution).

Court of Justice, four deans of law schools in public universities, four deans of schools of political science in public universities, and four representatives from four political parties with seats in the House of Representatives.[39] This combination attempted to balance representation of the judiciary, civilian politicians and the lay public. The nomination commission prepared twice the number of nominees for the Senate to choose.[40] The 2007 Constitution streamlined the commission by reducing the body to five commissioners; the president of the Court of Justice, the president of the Supreme Administrative Court, the speaker of the House of Representatives, the leader of the opposition, and one member representing all watchdog agencies.[41] Moreover, the nomination commission could propose only the exact number of nominees so the Senate no longer had discretion to choose candidates.[42] If the Senate rejected the list, the nomination commission could supersede the rejection through a unanimous vote.[43] These changes reflected the increasing importance of courts and the reduced involvement of politicians and laypersons in the appointment process.[44] The 2016 Draft Constitution adopted that exact procedure.[45]

Nominees to the bench meet a long list of requirements.[46] They have to have acquired Thai nationality by birth and be aged forty-five or older. They must have been a minister; a nomination commissioner for a watchdog agency; a director-general, or the equivalent, of a government agency; a professor; or a practicing lawyer for at least three years prior to a nomination. Their record should be clean of imprisonment or impeachment. Most importantly, they must, for the three years prior to nomination, not have been a member of a political party. The final requirement reflects the fear of political influence over a candidate.

Once appointed, a judge is subject to strict prohibitions and requirements in order to maintain honesty and independence.[47] A judge cannot hold a position in a government agency or public enterprise. Nor can the judge be employed by a business entity. Judges must disclose the assets

39 Constitution B.E. 2540 (รัฐธรรมนูญแห่งราชอาณาจักรไทย พ.ศ. 2540) s. 257(1) (1997 Constitution).
40 Ibid., s. 257(2).
41 2007 Constitution, s. 206(1).
42 Ibid., s. 206(2).
43 Ibid.
44 Ginsburg, 'Constitutional afterlife', note 7, 93.
45 2016 Draft Constitution, s. 203 and 204.
46 2007 Constitution, s. 205.
47 Ibid., s. 207.

they hold, as well as those held by their spouses and immature children, to the National Counter-Corruption Commission (NCCC) every three years while in office.[48]

A term lasts nine years, and a judge cannot be renominated.[49] This is meant to prevent a judge from compromising his or her neutrality in exchange for arranging a second term. In addition, a few causes could result in a judge being removed before completion of the term. Retirement is mandatory at seventy, and a judge can be disqualified only if he or she holds a position prohibited by the Constitution, is impeached by the Senate with a three-fifths' vote, or if a court sentences the judge to a term of imprisonment.[50]

2 *Organization and Procedure*

The Constitution is the principal law that governs the Constitutional Court's structure and authority. The office of the Constitutional Court acts as its secretariat, the head of which is appointed by the president of the Constitutional Court.[51] The Office of the Constitutional Court enjoys autonomy to manage its personnel, budget and other administrative matters.

The 2007 Constitution provided basic procedural guidelines. It required that a quorum for hearing a case is no less than five out of nine judges. A simple majority is needed for reaching a verdict. Before a decision can be made, every judge has to prepare his or her personal decision to be presented verbally in the deliberation process. These, together with the Constitutional Court decision, are to be published in the Royal Gazette. A decision must contain the background of the allegations, a summary of facts, the reasoning and the relevant law. The decision is final, with no appeal available, and has a binding effect on Parliament, the Cabinet, other courts and other state agencies.[52]

Details of procedure were originally left to the Constitutional Court's internal regulation. The 1997 Constitution required only that the procedural rules had to guarantee an open trial, the right of a defendant to present a defence, the right to inspect evidence, the right to object to a

[48] Anti-Corruption Organic Act B.E. 2542 (พระราชบัญญัติประกอบรัฐธรรมนูญว่าด้วยการป้องกันและปราบปรามการทุจริต พ.ศ. 2542) s. 39.
[49] 2007 Constitution, s. 208.
[50] Ibid., s. 209.
[51] Ibid., s. 217.
[52] 2007 Constitution, s. 216.

judge and the giving of reasons for decisions.[53] The 2007 Constitution ordered that, in order to be more formal, procedural rules had to be in the form of an organic act.[54] But the National Assembly missed the deadline to legislate such law, so the Constitutional Court's internal regulation was still the only source of procedures.

3 *Jurisdiction*

The Constitutional Court serves both judicial and nonjudicial functions. The latter became increasingly important in the 2007 Constitution, where the president of the Constitutional Court joined the nomination commission for watchdog agencies.[55] Another nonjudicial function was in legislative affairs. The president of the Constitutional Court may directly propose to the House of Representatives a bill concerning his duties.[56] This direct channel bypassed the Cabinet's approval, so it had the effect of freeing the Constitutional Court from political oversight on this matter.

As the 1997 reforms redesigned the single-bodied judiciary into three, a conflict of jurisdiction was inevitable. Generally, the Constitutional Court and the Administrative Court are courts of specific jurisdiction, hearing only cases concerning the constitutionality of laws and administrative acts, respectively. The Court of Justice still retains general jurisdiction over all other disputes. However, if a jurisdictional dispute does arise, a *tribunal des conflits* shall decide the case. A *tribunal des conflits* consists of the president of the Supreme Court of Justice as the chairperson, the president of the Supreme Administrative Court, the chief of the Military Court, and not more than four legal experts.[57]

The name 'Constitutional Court' convinces many Thais, wrongly, that the Court can decide any dispute regarding the Constitution. Actually, its jurisdiction is limited to the following areas: reviewing laws and lawmaking, settling turf disputes, disqualifying public office holders and protecting the constitution and democratic values. Within these areas, its jurisdiction both expanded and shrank over the span of

53 1997 Constitution, s. 269(2).
54 2007 Constitution, s. 216 first paragraph.
55 Ginsburg, 'Constitutional afterlife', note 7, 93.
56 2007 Constitution, s. 143(3).
57 Ibid., s. 199.

two constitutions. The 2007 Constitution removed some areas but increased the scope of others.

4 *Reviewing Law and Lawmaking*

This is the primary function of the Constitutional Court's judicial review power. Should the Court find a provision of law unconstitutional, that law shall be invalidated. The term 'a provision of law' refers to a statute which is approved by the people's representatives, hence, an organic act and an ordinary parliamentary act. However, constitutional review of an organic act is compulsory, while review of an ordinary act is only optional. Before an organic law bill is presented to the King for his signature, it must be submitted to the Constitutional Court. For an ordinary act, there are several channels to submit it. As a bill, members of both Houses may ask the Constitutional Court to review its constitutionality. Once a bill becomes law, it can be submitted to the Constitutional Court through four channels. First, if a party or a court believes that a law which will be applied to a case is unconstitutional, a court may halt the reading of its decision and send that act for judicial review.[58] Secondly, an individual who believes that his or her rights were violated by an act may petition to the Constitutional Court. This is a novel idea of the 2007 Constitution. However, to avoid a huge flood of lawsuits, a petitioner must first exhaust other possible remedies before becoming eligible to file a petition.[59] Third, upon receiving a complaint, the ombudsman can send the law in question to the Constitutional Court.[60] The fourth channel is through the National Human Rights Commission.[61]

Before coming into effect, a review is based on both procedural and substantive grounds. As an example, the Court invalidated organic law bills because members of the National Legislative Assembly were absent at the time of voting.[62] But after an announcement in a government gazette, the Constitutional Court can no longer review the procedure. The Constitutional Court would also review a case where the government deprived a person of rights and liberties without due process. Deprivation of rights and liberties can only be by a provision of law. Such law must

[58] Ibid., s. 211.
[59] Ibid., s. 212.
[60] Ibid., s. 245(1).
[61] Ibid., s. 257(2).
[62] Decision 2/2551, 3/2551, 4/2551 (2008) (CONST COURT).

serve the purpose only as prescribed by the constitution to the extent of necessity and shall be applied without discrimination. Most importantly, it must not affect the essential substances of such rights and liberties.[63]

In addition to legislative acts, a few exceptions are allowed. An emergency decree is the cabinet's order in time when the national interest is at stake and urgency prevents normal legislative processes.[64] The Constitutional Court asks two questions.[65] First, does an emergency decree serve the purpose of protecting the national interest? Second, is the situation urgent? Previously, the Constitutional Court could examine only the first question. But since Thailand witnessed arbitrary promulgation of emergency decrees to avoid lengthy legislative processes, the 2007 Constitution broadened the scope of review.[66]

A treaty is another anomaly. Due to concern that the Cabinet had entered into international agreements that jeopardized the country's economy and society,[67] the 2007 Constitution imposed strict procedures for treaty-making, including disclosing information to the public and proposing relief to those who would be impacted. The Cabinet has to follow these procedures when it is entering into a treaty that changes the Thai territories or has vast impact on economic and social stability. A dispute whether a treaty falls into these categories is subject to the Constitutional Court's jurisdiction,[68] but the Court cannot invalidate the treaty, and thus, it would not affect Thailand's obligation to the other states in the treaty. The review of treaty-making is controversial. Previously, within the executive's discretion, the cabinet saw this change as the growth of judicial interference into

63 Ibid., s. 29.

64 Ibid., s. 184.

65 Ibid., s. 185.

66 The most notable example was the Decree on Public Administration in Emergency Situation B.E. 2548 (พระราชกำหนดการบริหารราชการในสถานการณ์ฉุกเฉิน พ.ศ. ๒๕๔๘) (2005), but there were also the Decree on Criminal Code Amendment B.E. 2546 (พระราชกำหนดแก้ไขเพิ่มเติมประมวลกฎหมายอาญา พ.ศ. ๒๕๔๖) (2003), which added terrorism as an offence under Thai law, and other decrees regarding tax and economic policies. See Andrew Harding, 'Emergency powers with a moustache: special powers, military rule and evolving constitutionalism in Thailand', in Victor V. Ramraj and Arun K. Thiruvengadam (eds.), *Emergency Powers in Asia: Exploring the Limits of Legality* (Cambridge: Cambridge University Press, 2010) 294–314, 303–305.

67 See Thitinan Pongsudhirak, 'The imperative of Thailand's trade policy', Bangkok Post, 23 October 2015, www.bangkokpost.com/print/740160/ (accessed 6 October 2017; 'Fighting FTAs: The experience in Thailand', FTA Watch, 15 March 2016 www.bilaterals.org/?fighting-ftas-the-experience-in (accessed 6 October 2017).

68 Ibid., s. 190, sixth paragraph.

foreign affairs. There was an attempt to amend this section, but the Constitutional Court prevented this change.[69]

5 *Settling Turf Disputes*

The 1997 Constitution created independent agencies that were under neither the legislative nor the executive branch. The Constitutional Court was then assigned the duty of helping interpret the Constitution regarding the power and duty of these independent agencies. Any dispute subject to the Constitutional Court's jurisdiction must involve two or more parties of the National Assembly, the Cabinet or independent agencies, but not courts.[70]

6 *Disqualifying Public Office Holders*

Both the 1997 and 2007 Constitutions emphasized the importance of eradicating corruption as a means to end Thailand's political problems. Politicians and other public office holders face a considerable amount of scrutiny. Failure to comply results in disqualification from their posts. The two primary measures for eradicating corruption are asset disclosure and conflict of interest.

Under the 1997 Constitution, the failure of a judge to disclose his or her assets, as well as those of a spouse or immature children, before assuming and leaving office triggered a dismissal and a five-year political ban by the Constitutional Court.[71] However, the 2007 Constitution reassigned this duty to the special criminal division in the Supreme Court[72] because the Constitutional Court had once acquitted Thaksin.[73]

The 2007 Constitution prohibited members of both Houses and ministers from getting into conflicts of interest, which were defined as follows:[74]

(1) Holding another position in any government agency;
(2) Receiving or interfering with any concession from the government or becoming a party to a state contract or even being a shareholder of such business entity;

[69] Decision 1/2557 (2014) (CONST COURT).
[70] 2007 Constitution, s. 214.
[71] 1997 Constitution, s. 295.
[72] 2007 Constitution, s. 263.
[73] Decision 20/2544 (2001) (CONST COURT). See discussion in Section 1, 1997–2005.
[74] Ibid., ss. 265–267.

(3) Receiving benefits from the government other than that normally given to the public;
(4) Owning or having a control over media;
(5) Interfering or intervening in the performance of an official's operation;
(6) Interfering or intervening in personnel administration of government agents other than political appointees; and
(7) Removing government agents other than political appointees from office.

For the prime minister and his cabinet members, the last three prohibitions are true obstructions of their positions as the head of the administrative branch. They were meant to protect the civil service from political oversight, but without oversight, there would be no nexus from the executive to the administrative bodies. As a result, exemptions were provided in two cases: when the cabinet was acting according to its statement of policies made before the National Assembly prior to assuming office, or when that act was permissible by law.[75]

Another restriction for the prime minister and other ministers was a prohibition from holding shares in a business entity that exceeded a legal threshold so that any excess shares had to be held in a special trust.[76]

7 *Protecting the Constitution and Democratic Values*

This is the most problematical power of the Constitutional Court. This duty reflects the ideal that democracy does not have to tolerate the exercise of freedom by those who do not believe in democratic values. According to Section 68 of the 2007 Constitution, the Constitutional Court acts as the guardian of democracy. Upon a request from the attorney general, it can order a person or a political party to end an attempt to overthrow a democratic government or acquire power through unconstitutional means. If such an act is carried out by a political party, the Court may order party dissolution.[77]

The problem began when the 2007 Constitution linked Section 68 with the innovative Section 237, which was a harsh tool meant for tackling electoral fraud. If a candidate was caught cheating in an election, and if

[75] Ibid., s. 268.
[76] Ibid., s. 269.
[77] Ibid., s. 68.

an executive of that political party knew or neglected to learn or failed to deter such fraud, the whole party was deemed to commit an act of acquiring power through undemocratic means.[78] Thus, a party could be dissolved and all party executives would be held collectively responsible. Their political rights would all be revoked for five years. This sweeping punishment was meant to encourage fair and honest elections,[79] but it turned out to be a tool used to weaken electoral politics. Most political parties were dissolved and key politicians were banned from politics.[80]

The Constitutional Court also expanded its safeguarding power. Claiming this duty to protect the Constitution, it began to review government actions that were not previously under its jurisdiction. The cases we discuss later reveal the Court's practice in this respect.

The 2015 and 2016 Constitution Drafting Committees tried to further expand the Constitutional Court's jurisdiction. They proposed various models of a crisis panel which, in a time of crisis, could override the government's control.[81] The Constitutional Court would determine if the crisis was legitimate to allow intervention.[82] The 2016 Draft Constitution finally translated the crisis panel idea into an *ad hoc* committee comprised of the leaders of both Houses and their opposition, the prime minister, the presidents of the three branches of the judiciary, and the presidents of every watchdog agency. This committee was to be convened by the president of the Constitutional Court to determine a proper solution when the constitutional text was absent in that case.[83] This could put the Constitutional Court into an even more awkward and anti-democratic position.[84] However, King Vajiralongkorn, upon his

[78] Ibid., s. 237, second paragraph.

[79] '"จรัญ" เชื่อ รธน.มาตรา 237 แก้ปัญหาซื้อเสียงได้' (Jaran believes Section 237 could solve vote-buying problem), *The Manager Online*, 9 June 2009, www.manager.co.th/Home/ViewNews.aspx?NewsID=9520000064995 (accessed 6 October 2017).

[80] In 2007, there were four major political parties: People's Power Party, Democrat Party, Chart Thai Party and Matchimathipatai Party. All except Democrat Party were dissolved in 2008, and the political rights of 109 party executives were suspended for five years. See Decision 18/2551, 19/2551, and 20/2551 (2008) (CONST COURT).

[81] Khemthong Tonskulrungruang, 'Coups and constitutions', *New Mandala*, 28 August 2015, http://asiapacific.anu.edu.au/newmandala/2015/08/28/coups-and-constitutions/ (accessed 6 October 2017).

[82] Ibid.

[83] 2016 Draft Constitution, s. 5.

[84] See Eugénie Mérieau, 'The constitutional court in the 2016 constitutional draft: A substitute king for Thailand in the post-Bhumibol era?' (2016) 18 *Kyoto Review of Southeast Asia* http://kyotoreview.org/yav/constitutional-court-2016-thailand-post-bhumibol/#note-9559–4 (accessed 6 October 2017).

ascension to the throne after the death of his father, King Bhumibol, made an unexpected request for a provision concerning this *ad hoc* committee to be removed.

III The Constitutional Court in Conflicts

Since its inception, the number of cases brought to the Constitutional Court has grown steadily.[85] Brief reductions in numbers came only after the 2006 and 2014 *coup d'etats* when democratic constitutions were absent. However, from 2005 to 2015, the Constitutional Court was seen more as the settler of Thailand's political crises than the protector of rights and liberties. Political controversies, unfortunately, clouded the Court's attempts to expand protection of rights and liberties. When the opponents of Thaksin Shinawatra could not stop him through the political process, they turned to the Constitutional Court to exercise its anti-majoritarian authority.[86] All of the cases presented later were key decisions that demonstrated the Constitutional Court's role in countering the popular voice as well as its expansive judicial review power to uphold the rule of law. All of them triggered abrupt changes in the political landscape, some of which were democratic, while others were not. These decisions form significant parts of Thai constitutional law jurisprudence.

Decisions of the Constitutional Court in the past decade tell the story of Thailand's political struggle. They revolved around Thaksin and the attempts to eradicate his presence. Thus, each case discussion will begin with the factual background from which the dispute was formulated. Then there will be a look at the Constitutional Court's decision and reasoning, followed by a recitation of the consequences.

1 *The First Election Invalidation Case (2006)*

The Constitutional Court in 2006 was already suffering from a legitimacy crisis. Earlier, it had acquitted Thaksin of charges he had failed to disclose his assets, a decision that paved the way to his premiership.[87] The Court was seen as being reluctant to scrutinize statutes backed by the TRT

85 'Cases statistics 1998–2015' (in Thai) (Constitutional Court of Thailand, July 2015) www.constitutionalcourt.or.th/index.php?option=com_content&view=article&id=468&Itemid=346&lang=thindex.php accessed 28 October 2015.

86 Hewison, 'Thaksin Shinwatra and the Reshaping of Thai Politics', note 13, 130.

87 See discussion earlier.

party,[88] and such deference upset the public, who were convinced that Thaksin was able to control the Constitutional Court.

In 2006, Thaksin called a snap election after the PAD conducted demonstrations following allegations of Thaksin's tax evasion. But the opposition parties refused to join the contest because Thaksin had chosen the election date too early for the opposition to campaign.[89] Thaksin refused to postpone the date, and the opposition urged voters to abstain from voting. As a result, the TRT party won a super-majority in the lower house. The rest were small unknown parties that willingly joined the TRT coalition; hence, the government was without opposition. The PAD rejected the election outcome and threatened to escalate its demonstrations. Thailand was then at the crossroads between anarchy and tyranny.

Shortly after the election, King Bhumibol delivered a speech to incoming judges during a swearing-in, urging the judiciary to help solve the country's problem after the other two branches had failed.[90] Taking that as a signal, the president of the Constitutional Court, together with the presidents of the Supreme Administrative Court and the Court of Justice, released a statement that they would abide by the royal advice.[91] PAD sympathizers then petitioned that the 2006 election was unconstitutional to the ombudsman, who referred the case to the Constitutional Court.

The petition rested on two grounds: first, the election date had been unlawfully and unfairly set to TRT's advantage, and second, the election commission (EC) changed its practice in arranging the voting booth so that bystanders could observe voters' choices more easily. But first and foremost, the Constitutional Court had to determine if an electoral dispute fell within its jurisdiction. The Constitutional Court was to review two objects: the Royal Decree setting an election date and the EC's regulations on the election.

As discussed above, the Constitutional Court may review only provisions of laws, namely statutes and organic acts, while the Administrative Court may review administrative acts, including a royal decree. But the Constitutional Court insisted it had jurisdiction over the Royal Decree setting an election date and the EC's regulations. Ambiguity helped justify the Constitutional Court's order because the language of the

[88] Dressel, 'Judicialization of Politics or Politicization of the Judiciary?', note 16, 673.
[89] Baker and Phongpaichit, *A History of Thailand,* note 4, 270.
[90] Dressel, 'Judicialization of Politics or Politicization of the Judiciary?', note 16, 680.
[91] Ibid.

1997 Constitution allowed the ombudsman to submit provisions of laws or regulations to either the Constitutional Court or the Administrative Court.[92]

On the first question, the Constitutional Court disagreed with the government that setting an election date was a political question and thus judicially non-reviewable. This election was held amidst growing public tension, so it served, according to long-standing constitutional custom, as an important venue for citizens to express their wishes. The Constitutional Court cited the fact that the number of invalid ballots and ballots that were voted as abstentions exceeded numbers of valid ballots. Moreover, the Court pointed out the outcome that TRT won a landslide victory, rendering checks-and-balances within the legislative system dysfunctional. These two irregularities indicated that this general election failed to serve its constitutional purpose. Since this failure stemmed from the early election date that triggered the opposition's boycott, the Royal Decree was declared unconstitutional. The government might have set the date within the constitutional time frame, but it did not lead to a fair election as mandated by the Constitution.[93] The Court also declared the EC's regulation unconstitutional due to the new practice that allowed bystanders to observe voters' choices easily.[94]

This decision marked the first in a series of aggressive constitutional review cases. Acting ostensibly within the scope of statutory provisions might be insufficient to satisfy the Court's stringent standard. The Court took the benefit of hindsight to accuse the government of failing to produce a fair election.[95] Meanwhile, it overlooked the government's argument that the opposition also did not act in good faith. It refused TRT's offer to discuss another possible election date.[96] Most importantly, the Court expanded its jurisdiction to cover a political question that used to be solely under the prime minister's discretion. This activism beyond the text of the law may indicate the Court's assertion of its personal choice into electoral politics.

Invalidation of the election was a surprise that sharpened the conflict. No one had even speculated it might happen since the 1997 Constitution apparently did not allow this, and the sixty-day time frame for a general election had passed. The PAD demanded Thaksin

[92] Decision 9/2549 (2006) (CONST COURT) 7–8.
[93] Ibid., 24–28.
[94] Ibid., 29–30.
[95] See Dressel, 'Judicialization of Politics or Politicization of the Judiciary?', note 16, 679.
[96] Decision 9/2549, 21.

resign from a caretaker prime minister position which he had earlier assumed, but Thaksin refused. Finally, by consensus, a new October election date was set. However, in September 2006, the military seized power. The junta justified its action as meant to prevent possible bloodshed between supporters and dissenters of Thaksin.[97] It promised to punish corrupt politicians and draft a better constitution. Unfortunately, it completely failed in both tasks.

From 2006 onward, Thai society would be irreconcilably divided over the Constitutional Court's performance. Invalidation of the election transformed the Constitutional Court from a passive umpire to an active game changer. It realized how powerful judicial review could be. On the one hand, it would be praised for relentlessly pursuing bad politicians. Its aggressive style of judicial review gave hope to instil transparency in Thai politics. On the other hand, it worried sceptics that the Court was tripping over checks-and-balances. The Court's over-intervention in politics would hurt its credibility in the long run.

2 *TRT Dissolution Case (2007)*

The 2006 election still haunted TRT after the coup. The 1997 Constitution required that, in cases where there was only one party in a constituency, a candidate needed 20 per cent approval. Thaksin circumvented this requirement by paying small unknown parties to superficially compete with TRT without the prospect of winning. The EC accused TRT of committing an unconstitutional attempt to acquire power and asked the Constitutional Court to dissolve it.

The case was filed with the Constitutional Court shortly before the coup happened. Although the CNS temporarily halted the Constitutional Court's operation, the membership of the new *ad hoc* Constitutional Council were drawn from the Court of Justice and the Administrative Court,[98] and the 2006 Interim Charter transferred all pending cases to the Constitutional Council.[99]

TRT challenged the Constitutional Council's competence and impartiality and argued that, once the 1997 Constitution was abolished, the case, which arose under that Constitution, was moot and the CNS's enactment

[97] The Council of National Security Announcement 1/2549 (แถลงการณ์คณะปฏิรูปการปกครอง ฉบับที่ 1 พ.ศ. 2549).
[98] 2006 Interim Charter, s. 35.
[99] Ibid.

of the 2006 Interim Charter did not revive it.[100] TRT raised the rule of law issue because it saw this Constitutional Council panel as a nonjudicial body specifically targeting them.[101] The setting would not make for a fair trial. The Constitutional Council rejected TRT's arguments, stating that the case was not moot because the CNS authorized the Constitutional Council to hear pending cases. The Constitutional Council followed the long-held precedent that the CNS had successfully seized power and became the actual sovereign of the state; therefore, its order was law. Moreover, the Council was rightly recruited according to the CNS's order and its internal regulation on procedures provided TRT with all the basic rights of a fair trial. Hence, the Council was not acting contrary to the rule of law as claimed by TRT.[102] It went on to find TRT guilty as charged.[103]

Facts were firmly established that TRT did hire small parties to superficially compete with it to circumvent the 20 per cent minimum vote rule. But what punishment did TRT deserve? According to the Election Organic Act, the party would be dissolved. But the CNS also issued an order that if a party was dissolved because of an unconstitutional attempt to acquire power, the party executives' right to vote should be revoked for five years.[104] Because the right to vote was a primary condition for political participation, its revocation would effectively ban those people from politics. The CNS did not elaborate its intention, so the Council had to figure out by itself whether it should be retroactively applied to TRT.

The Constitutional Council unanimously agreed that it was competent to try the case and that TRT was guilty and was, thus, dissolved. But opinions diverged on retroactive revocation of political rights. The minority three held firm that no law should be retroactively applied if it impinged upon rights and liberties of a person. The majority six cited that the criminal code was the only statute prohibiting retroactive application of law, and since the political ban was not a criminal punishment, all 111 TRT executives had their voting rights revoked for five years.[105]

The TRT dissolution marked the decline of Thailand's rule of law. The positivistic approach to uphold the junta's legality, reaffirm its

[100] Decision 3–5/2550, 17–18.
[101] Ibid., 18.
[102] Ibid., 38–39.
[103] Ibid., 91–92.
[104] The Council of National Security Declaration 27/2549 (ประกาศคณะปฏิรูปการปกครอง ฉบับที่ 27 พ.ศ. 2549).
[105] Decision 3–5/2550, 99–100.

jurisdiction and enforce an unjust *ex post facto* law was a great disappointment. While claiming itself the guardian of the Constitution, the Constitutional Council obediently surrendered itself to an authoritarian body that abolished the Constitution. By succumbing to the junta's wish, the Constitutional Council failed to stop the decade-long vicious circle of coups and elections.

Retroactive application of the law was clearly a mistake.[106] But the decision has never been revoked. The CNS order was later incorporated into the 2007 Constitution that made party dissolution and a five-year political ban compulsory in every case of electoral fraud.[107] The Constitutional Council also dissolved TRT's successor and other major parties.[108] These decisions significantly stunted the party system. The only survivor from the massive dissolution craze was the Democrat Party, which was the old ally of the anti-Thaksin faction.[109] It rose to power after the other parties were dissolved in late 2008. For Thaksin supporters, the TRT dissolution became the symbol of injustice that the judiciary deliberately imposed upon them.

3 *The Cooking Show Case (2008)*

To his enemy's dismay, Thaksin's new party, People's Power Party (PPP), won the first election after democracy resumed in 2008. Thaksin was in exile, but he ran PPP through his nominee, Samak Sundaraveja, the veteran right-wing politician. PAD regrouped, and the incoming Constitutional Court soon found itself with plenty of controversial cases.

In September, a group of senators petitioned the Constitutional Court alleging that then prime minister Samak had breached the conflict of interest prohibition that a cabinet member shall be disqualified if he was an employee of a business entity.[110] This prohibition aimed to prevent undue influence from the business sector on policymakers. Samak, known to be a gourmand and an able chef, ran a weekly cooking show that he continued until some time after he assumed office, and he was accused of being an employee of the television company.

The main debate was whether Samak truly was an employee. Samak argued that, relying on the definition in the Labor Protection Act, he was

106 Dressel, 'Judicialization of Politics or Politicization of the Judiciary?', note 16, 681–682.
107 2007 Constitution, s. 237.
108 Decision 18/25, 19/2551 and 20/2551 (2008) (CONST COURT).
109 Decision 15/2553 (2010) (CONST COURT).
110 2007 Constitution, s. 267.

not acting under the command of a television company because he retained freedom to design his show.[111] He did not receive a salary but received a fixed amount of reimbursement for his fuel costs for each episode. The Constitutional Court, however, viewed his status differently. Citing the standard Thai dictionary, the Court understood an employee to be a person who agreed to work in exchange for payment regardless of title. It was necessary, the Court concluded, that the definition of employee be broadly read because the Constitution purported to prevent all acts of conflict of interest.[112] The prime minister should be free from undue influence when making public decisions. As Samak did not stop hosting the show before coming into power, he was disqualified.

A dictionary was an unusual source of legal authority, especially against a more authoritative source as the Labor Protection Act.[113] According to the dictionary, the boundary of an employee was limitless. Any act in return for a favour constituted employment regardless of the actual relationship. Such reading imposed an impractically high moral standard upon politicians. It reflected an absolutist attitude that the Constitutional Court would not tolerate any mistake, even when it was committed in good faith.

The cooking show decision demonstrated how unstable Thai politics was in 2008. Only nine months after the first election, the prime minister was disqualified. PPP managed to select a new prime minister, but the Constitutional Court continued to pressure it. In December, PPP was dissolved for vote-buying.[114] The Democrat Party, PPP's archenemy, became the minority government under the brokerage of the military.[115]

4 *The First Constitution Amendment Case (2012)*

The Democrat government (2008–2011) was a relatively peaceful period for the Constitutional Court, as the battles were on the streets. The 2009 and 2010 deadly crackdowns hampered Thaksin's supporters.[116] Nonetheless, when Yingluck, Thaksin's youngest sister, was elected prime minister in 2011, cases began to pour into the Court's docket again. Her

[111] Decision 12–13/2551 (2008) (CONST COURT), 6–8.
[112] Ibid., 14–15.
[113] Dressel, 'Judicialization of Politics or Politicization of the Judiciary?', note 16, 682.
[114] Decision 20/2551 (2008) (CONST COURT).
[115] Pravit Rojanaphruk, 'Questions loom over new prime minister's legitimacy', *The Nation*, 17 December 2008, accessed 1 March 2016.
[116] Baker and Phongpaichit, *A History of Thailand*, note 4, 274–277.

Pheu Thai (PT) party tried to fulfil its promise by amending the 2007 Constitution, which her supporters saw as the product of the 2006 junta to ruin Thailand's electoral politics.

According to Section 291 of the 2007 Constitution, the House of Representatives and the Senate would jointly consider the proposal to amendment and vote with a super-majority. But any amendment would not change the form of government, the monarchy or the form of the state.[117] However, Yingluck wanted to amend Section 291 and create a Constitution Drafting Convention representing all the people, resembling the drafting of the 1997 Constitution.[118] Her opponents quickly filed a complaint with the Constitutional Court, claiming that Yingluck was jeopardizing Thailand's democracy.

The petitioners did not ask the Court to review a provision of law, which was obviously impermissible because the definition of a provision of law did not include the constitutional amendment.[119] It claimed, instead, that Yingluck's amendment of Section 291 was an unconstitutional attempt to acquire power, an accusation with far more serious consequences. However, the attorney general dismissed the allegation. The petitioners then submitted the complaint directly to the Court. The government argued that they did not exercise their rights according to Section 68 and the case should be dismissed.[120]

Section 68 had always been understood as prohibiting direct popular petitioning for fear of the Constitutional Court being flooded with frivolous lawsuits. The attorney general would filter out invalid claims. While the government's defence was in line with the Constitutional Court's precedents, in this case, the Court disagreed. It read Section 68 as providing two different tracks to petitioning: one via the attorney general, and one via a layperson. The first could not deprive the latter of the right to protect democracy. Moreover, the Court expressed concern that relying solely on the attorney general's investigation might not be sufficient in times of urgency. The petitioners, then, had lawfully submitted their complaint according to Section 68.[121] The Court stopped short of declaring the 'amendment to amend' unconstitutional.[122] But it recognized that the 2006 Interim Charter

[117] 2007 Constitution, s. 291(1).

[118] Harding and Leyland, *The Constitutional System of Thailand*, note 8, 22–23.

[119] See Part II.C (1).

[120] Decision 18–22/2555 (2012) (CONST COURT), 11–12.

[121] Ibid., 20–22.

[122] Ibid., 24–25.

required a referendum for the enactment of the 2007 Constitution.[123] It cited the concept of *pouvoir constituent* that because the Constitution created the Parliament, it was not plausible for the supreme law to be amended by normal legislative processes. The amendment should resemble the promulgation of that Constitution, and the government should hold another referendum first in order to inquire of the public if the government could propose amending section 291.[124]

The decision drew attack on three grounds. First, since Section 291 did not provide an explicit channel for judicial review of the motion for amendment, it should be assumed that the Constitution vested the duty to oversee the amendment in Parliament. By accepting a review of the amendment proposal, the judiciary unduly asserted its power over the people's representatives.

The second criticism was the Constitutional Court's arbitrary interpretation of Section 68. A sensible reading of the law could never result in the direct channel to petition. Its previous and subsequent cases also did not indicate such.[125] But the Court changed its interpretation without any clear justification. Outside the courtroom, while being questioned, the president of the Constitutional Court took it quite personally and referred to the English draft of the Constitution.[126] His reference was puzzling since there had never been such a draft, and it reflected his poor understanding of the history of the very constitution he was reading.

The last attack was on the Constitutional Court's suggestion of a public referendum. Although a referendum was compulsory for enacting the 2007 Constitution, it did not require public input regarding its amendment. It was obvious that the drafters of the 2007 Constitution did not consider this necessary. Moreover, the Court recommended, but did not order, a referendum before the drafting took place, not a referendum on the draft constitution. The Court was adding a new provision to the Constitution according to its personal preference, imposing a heavy burden on the government to comply with its wish.

The decision disrupted the fragile balance of power. The judiciary successfully encroached upon politicians' power to initiate a new social

[123] 2006 Interim Charter, s. 29.

[124] Decision 18–22/2555, 23.

[125] See Order 12/2556, 13/2556, 14/2556, and 15/2556 (2013) (CONST COURT).

[126] "“วสันต์” อ้างรธน.ฉบับภาษาอังกฤษ ยันทำถูกต้องสั่งสภาชะลอแก้รธน. -“เกษียร” จวกเล่นเกมไวยากรณ์" (Wasan urges a look at English draft), Khao Sod, 7 June 2012, tamanoon.biz/constitutionnews/132-tamanoon68.html (accessed 29 June 2018).

contract. The majority could no longer control their government since the minority had learned how to overpower them. Legal certainty was also at risk because the Constitutional Court rewrote the Constitution without warning or giving any clear reasons. At first, the government reacted to the judicial overreach by threatening to impeach the Constitutional Court judges.[127] But Prime Minister Yingluck was willing to compromise, and the attempt faded.

5 *The Second Constitutional Amendment Case (2013)*

After the first attempt was foiled, the PT government switched back to the more humble amendment by seeking to alter only an individual section. It proposed to change the selection of the Senate.

The 1997 Constitution created the powerful non-partisan Senate to scrutinize the lower house, and senators were barred from having affiliation with any political party.[128] However, the 1997 Constitution also designed the Senate to be elected. A Senate election nudged several candidates to seek implicit backing from political parties, and as a result, TRT was able to dominate the Senate.[129] The 2007 Constitution redesigned the Senate to be half-elected and half-nominated.[130] Nomination was from a special commission without prime ministerial intervention. This mixed approach was a compromise as the entirely nominated Senate was too unpopular among Thaksin's supporters. Yingluck proposed to change the Senate into an all-elected chamber, but opponents again accused her of destroying democracy.

The Constitutional Court tried to appear more reasonable by invoking the rule of law in accepting her case. The Court conceded that democracy was rule by the people, but an election was not the only feature of democracy. The Court cited the danger of tyranny by the majority to harass the minority and destroy basic democratic values. As the protector of the Constitution, it was required to scrutinize and balance the exercise of power.[131] It struck down the amendment on both procedural and substantive grounds. Camera footage had

[127] Keawmala (pseudonym), 'Thailand: How the meaning of "and" starts a constitutional crisis', *Asian Correspondent,* 7 June 2012, http://asiancorrespondent.com/2012/06/thailand-how-the-meaning-of-and-starts-a-constitutional-crisis/ (accessed 6 October 2017).

[128] Ginsburg, 'Constitutional afterlife', note 7, 91–92.

[129] Ibid., 96.

[130] 2007 Constitution, s. 111.

[131] Decision 15–18/2556 (2013) (CONST COURT), 19–22.

emerged that a few MPs had voted for the amendment on behalf of their peers who were absent.[132] But more importantly, the Court saw an election of the Senate as an unconstitutional attempt to acquire power. An election would move Thailand back to pre-coup politics when the whole Parliament was a family business – a reference to the notion of an MP's spouse sitting in the Senate. The practice would render the checks-and-balances intended by the 2007 Constitution meaningless. It could have led to another legitimacy crisis and another *coup d'etat*.[133]

The second attempt to amend the 2007 Constitution was, thus, aborted. The Constitutional Court spoke more clearly of its distrust in the majority's wisdom, especially in elections and emphasized its role as the protector of constitutional principles, which could not be terminated or altered. While the procedural flaw was rightly justified, its opinion on the senatorial election was questionable. There had never been a restriction for a relative of an MP being a senator. The House of Representatives was already full of MPs, regardless of parties, with familial ties to one another.[134] Finally, a senatorial election is actually a common practice in many democratic countries so it should not have been assumed to constitute an attempt to sabotage democracy.

The decision triggered an impeachment process of the 248 MPs from the PT party who had voted for the amendment. They were spared two years later when the National Reform Council could not reach the three-fifths parliamentary majority required to impeach the accused.[135]

Later, the Constitutional Court would find another amendment concerning Thailand's treaty-making procedure unconstitutional.[136] The government had tried to clarify the types of treaties that needed to undergo stringent constitutional procedure, but the Constitutional Court saw it as an attempt to evade public scrutiny.

[132] Ibid., 27–28.
[133] Ibid., 29–30.
[134] Satithorn Thananithichote, 'Political family in MP election 2011' (in Thai) *Thailand Political Database* www.tpd.in.th/content/details_1.php?ID=000197&type=000004#_ednref16 (accessed 6 October 2017).
[135] 'NLA rejects impeachment bid', *Bangkok Post*, 15 August 2015, www.bangkokpost.com/archive/nla-rejects-impeachment-bid/656484 (accessed 6 October 2017).
[136] Decision 1/2557 (2014) (CONST COURT).

6 *The Second Election Invalidation Case (2014)*

Political tension rose again when Prime Minister Yingluck introduced an amnesty law in late 2013. The law, which would have universally pardoned all those convicted in the decade-long conflict, was met with strong public condemnation because it would spare the military from murder charges as well as bring Thaksin back to Thailand. After a massive protest, the Senate voted down the bill. But the Democrat Party continued the demonstrations under the name People's Democracy Reform Council (PDRC), demanding the prime minister resign.[137] Yingluck eventually dissolved the house and called a snap election. Suddenly, Thailand was taken back to the situation in early 2006 when her brother Thaksin was fighting against the PAD.

Yingluck had learned well from her brother's mistake, so she set the election date as far out as possible within the sixty days that were allowed. But the Democrat Party still refused to join.[138] Its protesting wing, the PDRC, made a radical demand that the government postpone the election indefinitely and that a unity government be established to reform the country before the election could resume.[139] When Yingluck rejected this, the PDRC called its followers to boycott the election. In order to prevent the election from taking place, the PDRC raided venues where the application process was taking place, leaving many constituencies without candidates.[140] Also, on the election days, the PDRC blocked and assaulted voters.[141] As a result, voting did not occur in many constituencies, and the ombudsman asked the Constitutional Court to review the 2014 Election.

In 2006, the Constitutional Court had relied on ambiguous text to claim its authority to review the Royal Decree arranging the general

[137] Jeffrey Hays, '2013 political crisis after Yingluck government tries to pass amnesty bill that would allow Thaksin to return to Thailand', Factsanddetails.com http://factsanddetails.com/southeast-asia/Thailand/sub5_8a/entry-3201.html (accessed 6 October 2017).

[138] James Hookway and Wilawan Watcharasakwet, 'Thailand opposition Democrat Party to boycott election', *The Wall Street Journal*, 21 December 2013, at www.wsj.com/articles/SB10001424052702304866904579271862159417896 (accessed 6 October 2017).

[139] 'Like two countries', *The Economist*, 15 January 2014, www.economist.com/blogs/banyan/2014/01/thailands-political-crisis (accessed 6 October 2017).

[140] Ibid.

[141] Kocha Olarn, Pamela Boykoff and Holly Yan, 'Thailand elections marred by violence, delays', CNN, 2 February 2014, http://edition.cnn.com/2014/02/02/world/asia/thailand-election/ (accessed 6 October 2017).

election. The 2007 Constitution attempted to clarify that ambiguity by indicating that only a provision of law was to be reviewed by the Constitutional Court.[142] However, the Court still insisted on its jurisdiction over the matter. The Royal Decree arranging the general election was not an administrative rule, because a normal rule relied on a statutory mandate to be promulgated, and the power to promulgate a Royal Decree scheduling a general election derived directly from the Constitution, not a statute; hence, it holds a higher status as a provision of law similar to statutes.[143]

The government defended its decision not to postpone the election because the Constitution required a general election within sixty days. Unlike in 2006, no other parties raised an objection. The government blamed the EC for not successfully recruiting candidates and operating the voting.

The Constitutional Court dismissed the defence. When an election could not be set the same day across the country, it was contrary to the constitutional mandate. The government also did not take into account objections and concerns from relevant parties, including the Constitutional Court, to postpone the election. The government had to be fully aware that Thailand was then seriously divided so such disruption should have been expected.[144] Blaming the government's ignorance, the Court invalidated the 2014 election.

For the second time, the Constitutional Court had invalidated the majority's voice in order to protect asserted constitutional values. The Court asked the government to bear all the costs for holding a peaceful election without recognizing the fault of other parties. The nation was then split over the proposal to reform. While the PDRC was for it, the majority of voters disagreed. But the Court chose the option that was not in the Constitution. If the Cabinet agreed to postpone the election indefinitely, would it not be charged with acting outside of its constitutional limit? Should Section 68 lawsuits come up, would Yingluck be found guilty of trying to change the democratic regime? The Constitutional Court never answered these questions.

The invalidation produced another political deadlock. A few weeks later, the Constitutional Court disqualified Yingluck from her caretaker prime minister role on a charge of conflict of interest by finding that she

[142] 2007 Constitution, s. 245(1).
[143] Decision 5/2557 (2014) (CONST COURT), 4–5.
[144] Ibid., 13–19.

unlawfully transferred high-ranking government officers, including her relatives.[145] The military, under the auspices of the National Council of Peace and Order (NCPO), shortly seized power.

IV Conclusion

From deference to activism, the Constitutional Court of Thailand has stirred controversies and divided the society. The Court was right that democracy is not simply the rule by majority. The Court was thus created to protect essential democratic values from the majority's errors and abuse, and because Thaksin and other politicians will never stop seeking extra wealth and dominance of Thai politics, the Court has to guard the Constitution and welfare of Thais. But the Constitutional Court could not just dismiss the voice of the people, for both the results of elections and the rule of law must be upheld.

The nature of the Constitutional Court is anti-majoritarian as it relies not on popular consent. But the Constitutional Court must still be accountable to professional standards. The rule of law requires all state organs to appear predictable, transparent, and impartial,[146] but the Court's recent decisions showed that it easily changed its reading of the Constitution without giving adequate reasons. It added more tests to review the government's actions, but this aggressive review seemed to be felt only by Thaksin's supporters.[147] Absence of predictability, transparency and impartiality makes the Court unfit as an umpire, for it would not be able to deliver fairness to all parties in a conflict. That poses a difficult dilemma for Thailand. Democracy cannot survive without judicial review. However, democracy cannot survive under an arbitrary judiciary, either.

Once the Constitutional Court had been a much-revered institution tasked with the solemn duty of defending democracy. It has strayed. By being anti-Thaksin, the Court became anti-majoritarian and, ultimately, anti-democratic. Twice, the Constitutional Court invalidated elections, leading to *coup d'etats* and abolition of constitutions. The public was

[145] Decision 9/2557 (2014) (CONST COURT). See also 'Out of luck', *The Economist*, 10 May 2014, www.economist.com/news/asia/21601871-court-ousts-yingluck-shinawatra-pushing-country-further-towards-political-breakdown-out (accessed 6 October 2017).

[146] See Barry R. Weingast, 'Why developing countries prove so resistant to the rule-of-law' in James J. Heckman, Robert L. Nelson and Lee Cabatingan (eds.), *Global Perspectives on the Rule of Law* (Abingdon: Routledge, 2010), 28–53.

[147] Hewison, 'Thaksin Shinwatra and the reshaping of Thai politics', note 13, 130.

confused and frustrated. Unfortunately, one can do little to hold the Court to account, for it is insulated from political oversight. The only way to regain its deteriorating credibility is if the upcoming 2017 Constitution demands more accountability from the Court, restricting its arbitrariness. Sadly, given the current regime's negative attitude toward the rule by majority, it is unlikely that any meaningful measures will be introduced to correct the Court. The Constitutional Court is likely to continue to be a major source of conflicts in Thai politics for years to come.

9

Indonesia's Constitutional Court and Indonesia's Electoral Systems

SIMON BUTT

Indonesia's Constitutional Court was established in 2003.[1] It has nine judges, with the national parliament, the president and the judiciary selecting three each.[2] The Court has various constitutionally delineated powers, but its workload is dominated by constitutional reviews and electoral disputes. On the whole, the Court has been a model for judicial reform in Indonesia. It has generally exercised its powers professionally – that is, impartially, with a concern to issue consistent decisions that are justified by reference to the law. It has largely acted as an effective check on legislative power, making significant contributions to Indonesian law and democracy along the way.

After introducing the Court and discussing its establishment, institutional design and jurisdiction, this chapter analyses some of the Court's most important jurisprudence in constitutional review cases about Indonesia's electoral systems.[3] These cases, listed in Table 9.1 at the end of this chapter, provide examples of the Court at its most active: in them, the Court has made quite radical changes to those systems to, as the Court describes it, 'uphold the people's sovereignty' and ensure 'free and fair' elections.

1 By virtue of the enactment of Article 24C(3) of the Constitution.

2 Under Article 24C(3) of the Constitution.

3 Indonesian judicial decisions are referred to by case number rather than by the names of the parties. For readability, I have chosen to give most cases a name – usually the name of one of the applicants or the main issue raised by the case. I also include the year in which the case was lodged with the Court rather than the year in which the case was decided. Full references are provided in Table 9.1 at the end of this chapter.

Table 9.1 *Cases decided by the Indonesian Constitutional Court*

Affirmative action case (2013)	Constitutional Court Decision 20/PUU-XI/2013
Bali bombing case (2003)	Constitutional Court Decision 013/PUU-I/2003
Bibit and Chandra case (2009)	Constitutional Court Decision 133/PUU-VII/2009
Electoral roll case (2009)	Constitutional Court Decision 102/PUU-VII/2009
Electricity law case (2003)	Constitutional Court Decision 001–021–022/PUU-I/2003
Independent candidates case (2008)	Constitutional Court Decision 56/PUU-VI/2008
Independent candidates case (2012)	Constitutional Court Decision 38/PUU-X/2012
Independent candidates case (2013)	Constitutional Court Decision 17/PUU-XI/2013
Independent Pemilukada candidates case (2007)	Constitutional Court Decision 005/PUU-V/2007
Independent Pemilukada candidates case (2010)	Constitutional Court Decision 35/PUU-VIII/2010
Jumanto case (2015)	Constitutional Court Decision 42/PUU-XIII/2015
Open list case (2008)	Constitutional Court Decision 22–24/PUU-VI/2008
Papua DPD case (2009)	Constitutional Court Decision 47/PHPU.A-VII/2009
Papua gubernatorial election case (2013)	Constitutional Court Decision 4/PHPU.D-XI/2013
PKI case (2003)	Constitutional Court Decision 011–017/PUU-I/2003
Robertus case (2009)	Constitutional Court Decision 4/PUU-VII/2009
Simultaneous elections case (2013)	Constitutional Court Decision 14/PUU-XI/2013
Sisa suara case (2009)	Constitutional Court Decision 110–111–112–113/PUU-VII/2009
Tebing Tinggi mayoral election case (2010)	Constitutional Court Decision 12/PHPU.D-VIII/2010
Water resources law case (2005)	Constitutional Court Decision 8/PUU-III/2005
Wedlock case (2010)	Constitutional Court Decision 46/PUU-VIII/2010

I Background to the Establishment of the Indonesian Constitutional Court

The idea of having a constitutional court, or at least having a court exercising constitutional review, is hardly new for Indonesia. Both ideas had been discussed in constitutional debates in the Investigating Committee for the Preparation of Independence (*Badan Penyelidikan Usaha Persiapan Kemerdekaan*) in the lead-up to the declaration of Indonesia's independence on 17 August 1945[4] and again in the mid to late 1950s when Indonesia's *Konstituante* debated a new, permanent, constitution.[5] The ideas had also been discussed during parliamentary debates for a new judiciary law, which was enacted in 1970.[6] Each time, proponents of constitutional review were unsuccessful. (Some scholars, however, have argued that whether Indonesia should adopt constitutional review was never decided, because supervening events ended these debates before they were fully concluded.[7])

Nevertheless, the ideal of constitutional review did not end with these debates. Rather, they continued in reformist and some academic circles, even though such activities were undoubtedly subversive and therefore punishable for most of President Soeharto's authoritarian 'New Order' government (1966–1998). Under his rule, the government had manipulated the courts, primarily by controlling their administration and organization, including the salaries and career progression of judges. This left no scope for independent review of the legality of government action or laws.

By the time Soeharto left office in May 1998, the Indonesian judiciary was in a parlous state. Not only was it heavily dependent on government, it was also widely perceived to be largely corrupt and incompetent.[8] Judicial reform was, therefore, a high priority in the post-Soeharto

[4] H. Muhammad Yamin, *Naskah Persiapan Undang-Undang Dasar 1945*, 1 (Jakarta: Jajasan Prapantja, 1971) 410.

[5] Adnan Buyung Nasution, *The Aspiration for Constitutional Government in Indonesia: A Socio-Legal Study of the Indonesian Konstituante, 1956–1959* (Jakarta: Pustaka Sinar Harapan, 1992).

[6] Daniel S. Lev, 'Judicial authority and the struggle for an Indonesian Rechtsstaat' (1978) 13 *Law and Society Review* 37–71, 57.

[7] Jimly Asshiddiqie, *Menegakkan tiang konstitusi: memoar lima tahun kepemimpinan Prof. Dr. Jimly Asshiddiqie, S.H. di Mahkamah Konstitusi, 2003–2008* (Jakarta: Sekretariat Jenderal dan Kepaniteraan, Mahkamah Konstitusi, 2008) 3.

[8] Sebastiaan Pompe, *The Indonesian Supreme Court: A Study of Institutional Collapse* (Ithaca, N.Y: Southeast Asia Program, Cornell University, 2005).

Reformasi era, during which Indonesia transitioned from a highly centralized authoritarian state to a democratic polity in which power was dispersed amongst many institutions, both national and regional. The MPR (the People's Consultative Assembly, the only body with power to amend the Constitution) decided to introduce constitutional review in Indonesia by way of constitutional amendment. However, a matter of significant debate was whether it should be performed by the Supreme Court or by a new Constitutional Court.[9] Members of an expert team recruited by the MPR argued that giving the Supreme Court these additional functions was not a viable reformist option because of that Court's renowned decrepitude.[10] The MPR eventually agreed to establish a new Constitutional Court.[11]

The Constitutional Court struggled through humble beginnings, which suggests that the government viewed the Court with scepticism, fear or both. In the words of founding Chief Justice Jimly Asshiddiqie,[12] the Court *mulai dari nol* (started from scratch), with little more than the Constitution, and a copy of the 2003 Constitutional Court Law in hand to support it, and almost no budget.[13] Initially, the Court was housed in an office in the Supreme Court building, without administrative staff, before shifting to a Jakarta hotel.[14] After obtaining funding from the Finance Ministry, the Court then moved into an office complex, holding court sessions in the national parliamentary building and even in national police headquarters.[15] Only in January 2004 was the Court able to combine its offices and courtroom in a single building, owned by the

[9] Hendrianto, 'Institutional choice and the new Indonesian Constitutional Court', in Andrew Harding and Penelope Nicholson (eds.), *New Courts in Asia* (London: Routledge Law, 2010).

[10] Mahkamah Konstitusi, *Naskah komprehensif perubahan Undang-Undang Dasar Negara Republik Indonesia tahun 1945: latar belakang, proses, dan hasil pembahasan, 1999–2002, Buku VI: Kekuasaan Kehakiman* (Jakarta: Sekretariat Jenderal dan Kepaniteraan, Mahkamah Konstitusi, Revised edition, 2010) 461, 548.

[11] Incidentally, the MPR also decided to constitutionally entrench the institutional independence of Indonesia's preexisting courts (including the Supreme Court) as part of an overhaul of the Supreme Court and the courts below it.

[12] See note 6, 10.

[13] Purwadi, *Pendekar konstitusi Jimly Asshiddiqie: satria bijak bestari dari bumi Sriwijaya* (Jakarta: Hanan Pustaka, 2006) 168–169.

[14] Jimly Asshiddiqie, *Menjaga Denyut Konstitusi: Refleksi Satu Tahun Mahkamah Konstitusi* (Jakarta: Konstitusi Press, 2004) 14.

[15] Asshiddiqie, note 6, 109.

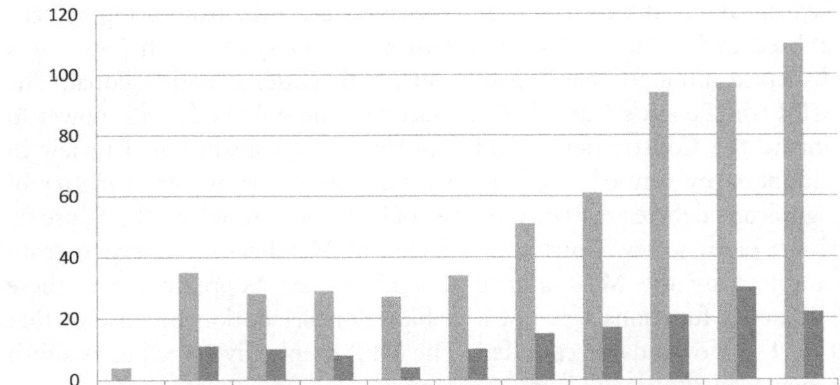

	2003	2004	2005	2006	2007	2008	2009	2010	2011	2012	2013
Cases	4	35	28	29	27	34	51	61	94	97	110
Granted	0	11	10	8	4	10	15	17	21	30	22

Figure 9.1 Judicial review cases[16]

Ministry for Communication and Information. In mid-2005, work began on a grand new Constitutional Court complex in central Jakarta, close to the Presidential Palace, the Supreme Court and government ministries. Two years later, the Court moved into this building and has occupied it since then.

II Jurisdiction of the Constitutional Court

The Constitution gives the Court several functions.

1 Constitutional Review

Applicants (primarily citizens and various legal entities) can challenge the constitutionality of national legislation. If the statute under review violates the Constitution, the Court can declare that statute to be no longer binding and then invalidate it. The Court has regularly exercised this power to strike down legislation that it deems to be unconstitutional, having decided many hundreds of review cases (see Figure 9.1).

[16] Statistics drawn from www.mahkamahkonstitusi.go.id (accessed 27 April 2018).

As mentioned, the Court has exercised its judicial review powers professionally. Particularly notable has been its continual refusal to shy away from cases that are highly political or are otherwise difficult, such as those involving significant vested interests of powerful political figures, including in the executive and the legislature. However, as we shall see, its decisions are also commonly criticized for lacking transparency and exhibiting inconsistent levels of deference to the legislature.

2 *Resolving Electoral Disputes*

The Court has handled thousands of electoral disputes, including those arising out of polls for the presidency; seats in national, provincial, city and county legislatures; and the national regional representative council (see Figure 9.2 for legislative election figures). Disputes arising from these elections, held every five years, swamp the Court, which must resolve the disputes within very short timelines.[17] For example, the Court heard over 900 disputes lodged by almost all political parties competing in the 2014 legislative elections.[18] As in previous legislative elections, the Court imposed tight time limits within which applications needed to be lodged. Applicants had to submit their claims within seventy-two hours of the General Election Commission announcing the election results – at 11:51 p.m. on 9 May.[19] The Court then gave applicants three days to remedy any errors in their applications.[20] The Court gave itself fourteen days to decide all 903 cases – a task it completed within this deadline, but which often required the Court to sit well into the night.[21]

More controversial has been the Court's handling of disputes arising out of elections for regional heads (*Pemilukada*). Case figures appear in Figure 9.3. (Regional heads [*kepala daerah*] are governors [*gubernur*] in provinces, regents [*bupati*] in counties and mayors [*walikota*] in

[17] Presidential elections were, in 2004, 2009 and 2014, held three months after the general legislative elections. However, in the *Simultaneous Elections* case (2014), the Constitutional Court ruled that, starting in 2019, general elections and presidential elections must be held together.

[18] Lulu Anjarsari, 'Tuntas Mengawal Suara Rakyat' (2014) 89 *Konstitusi*.

[19] Yusran Yunus, 'MK Resmi Buka Pengaduan, Ditutup Senin 12 Mei Pukul 23.51 WIB' (2014, May 10) *Bisnis Indonesia*.

[20] Veri Junaidi and Jim Della-Giacoma, 'Clock watching and election complaints in Indonesia's Constitutional Court' (2014, May 20) *New Mandala*.

[21] Ibid.

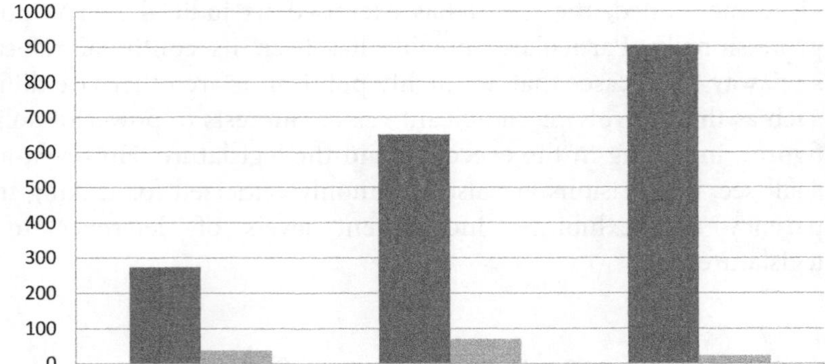

	2004	2009	2014
Applications	273	650	903
Granted	38	70	23

Figure 9.2 Legislative election disputes[22]

cities.) Direct *Pemilukada* elections commenced from June 2005,[23] and the results were initially challengeable before the Supreme Court.[24] However, after some questionable decisions, jurisdiction over these disputes was handed from the Supreme Court to the Constitutional Court in late 2008.[25]

3 *Resolving Jurisdictional Disputes between State Institutions*

On paper, this might appear to be a particularly important function, particularly in post-Soeharto Indonesia, where, as mentioned, power has been widely dispersed and jurisdictional overlaps are common. However, the Court hears very few of these disputes,[26] primarily, it seems, because the Court's authority is confined to resolving disputes between institutions that are established by the Constitution.

22 Statistics drawn from www.mahkamahkonstitusi.go.id (accessed 27 April 2018).

23 Stevie Emilia, 'Direct regional elections provide a taste of democracy' (2005, December 24) *Jakarta Post.*

24 Articles 106(1) and (2) of the 2004 Regional Government Law.

25 DPR, 'Risalah Rapat Kerja Dengan Menteri Hukum Dan Ham Dan Menteri PAN' (2010, September 30) *Jakarta.*

26 According to Court statistics, available at www.mahkamahkonstitusi.go.id (accessed 27 April 2018), the Court heard only twenty-four such cases between 2004 and 2014.

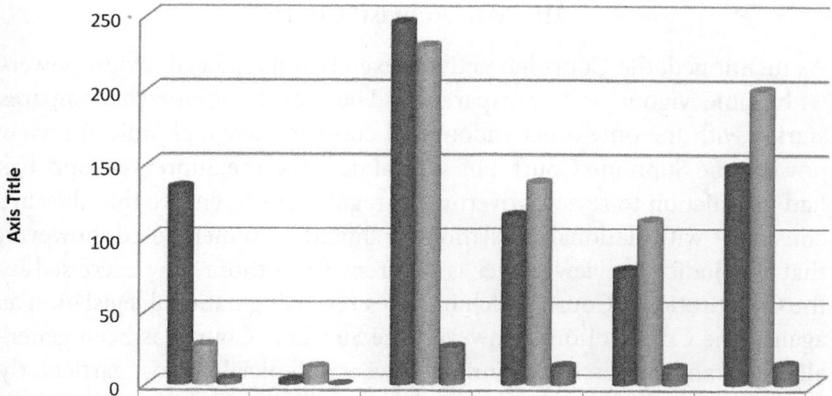

	2008	2009	2010	2011	2012	2013
Elections	135	3	246	116	79	149
Applications	27	12	230	138	112	200
Granted	4	0	26	13	12	14

Figure 9.3 Pemilukada disputes

4 *Dissolving Political Parties*

In these cases, the government applies to the Court to have a political party disbanded on grounds that the party has an 'ideology, basis, objective, program or activities' that violate the 1945 Constitution.[27] The Court has never been called upon to exercise this jurisdiction.

Impeachment proceedings

Under this power, the Court is to decide motions initiated by the DPR (the national parliament, or *Dewan Perwakilan Raykat*) to impeach the president or vice president. In such cases, the Court must 'provide a decision' if the DPR alleges that the president or vice president has committed treason or corruption, another serious crime or form of misconduct, or otherwise no longer fulfils the constitutional requirements to hold office. Even though some commentators argue that the Court was established primarily because of the constitutional crisis surrounding the impeachment of Indonesia's fourth president, Abdurrahman Wahid,[28] the Court has also never performed this function.

[27] Article 68 of the 2003 Constitutional Court Law.

[28] These accounts include Tim Lindsey, 'Indonesian constitutional reform: Muddling towards democracy' (2002) 6 *Singapore Journal of International and Comparative Law*

III An 'Activist' Court?

As mentioned, the Court has actively exercised its judicial review powers with some vigour and transparency. The Court's approach compares starkly with the only other Indonesian court to have had judicial review powers: the Supreme Court. For several decades, the Supreme Court has had jurisdiction to review government regulations to ensure that they are consistent with national legislation (it should be remembered, however, that this judicial review power is different from those now exercised by the Constitutional Court, which involves reviewing national legislation as against the Constitution). However, the Supreme Court has been generally reluctant to exercise its limited powers of judicial review, particularly during the Soeharto period.[29] Only recently has the Supreme Court begun actively hearing these cases,[30] probably because of pressure brought to bear by the Constitutional Court performing its constitutional review functions. The Constitutional Court is also the only Indonesian court to publish its decisions online almost immediately after they have been handed down in open court. Its decisions are also generally more discursive and better reasoned that those of Indonesia's other courts, and its judges regularly issue dissenting opinions.[31]

The Indonesian Constitutional Court is not only progressive by Indonesian standards; it has also been described as 'activist' by world standards[32] and could perhaps be categorized alongside the South Korean Constitutional Court[33] as amongst the most activist of the Asian constitutional courts. The Indonesian Constitutional Court's reputation

244–301, 244; B. Widjojanto, 'Mahkamah Konstitusi, Harapan Baru Pembangunan Negara Hukum?' in *Menjaga Denyut Konstitusi: Reflexi satu tahun Mahkamah Konstitusi* (Jakarta: Konstitusi Press, 2004) 211; Susi Harijanti and Tim Lindsey, 'Indonesia: General elections test the amended constitution and the new Constitutional Court' (2005) 4 *International Journal of Constitutional Law* 138–150, 147; Asshiddiqie, note 6, 28–43.

29 Pompe, note 7; Ni'matul Huda, *Problematika Pembatalan Peraturan Daerah* (Yogyakarta: FH UII Press, 2010).

30 Simon Butt and Nicholas Parsons, 'Judicial review and the Supreme Court in Indonesia: A new space for law?' (2014) 97 *Indonesia* 55–85.

31 Simon Butt, *Judicial Review in Indonesia: Between Civil Law and Accountability? A Study of Constitutional Court Decisions 2003–2005* (PhD Dissertation, Law Faculty, Melbourne University, 2007).

32 Björn Dressel (ed.), *The Judicialization of Politics in Asia* (New York: Routledge, 2012).

33 Chaihark Hahm, 'Beyond "law vs. politics" in constitutional adjudication: Lessons from South Korea' (2012) 10 *International Journal of Constitutional Law* 6–34; Tom Ginsburg, 'Confucian constitutionalism? The emergence of constitutional review in Korea and Taiwan' (2002) 27 *Law & Social Inquiry* 763–799; Tom Ginsburg, *Judicial Review in New Democracies: Constitutional Courts in Asian Cases* (Cambridge: Cambridge University Press, 2003).

is not without justification. For example, the Court has 'found' rights that are not expressly mentioned in the Constitution and then used those rights to invalidate statutory provisions. In particular, in several cases – the so-called implied rights cases – the Court has identified rights that flow from Indonesia being a 'law state' (*negara hukum*). These rights include the presumption of innocence (*Bibit and Chandra case* [2009]) and the right to a fair trial, which the Court has decided encompasses

> minimum [requirements] of procedural justice, including the presumption of innocence; equality of opportunity for the parties; announcement of the decision [which is] open to the public; ne bis in idem [the 'double jeopardy' rule]; the application of less serious laws for pending cases and the prohibition against retrospectivity (*Bali bombing case* [2003, 38]).

Other examples of activism – perhaps even overreach – include decisions in which the Court has invalidated statutes in their entirety. In these, the Court has held that the statute under review violates the spirit of the Constitution yet identifies only some of its provisions as unconstitutional (see, for example, the *Electricity Law case* [2003] and the *Water Resources Law* case [2015]). Much of this overreach appears to be unnecessary, with some observers arguing that instead of implying rights or invalidating entire statutes, the Court could simply have employed more conventional legal reasoning to reach the same result.[34]

Unsurprisingly, the Court has also pushed at the boundaries of its jurisdiction. Many courts around the world do this, but perhaps more gradually and incrementally than has the Indonesian Constitutional Court. For example, the statutes granting the Court power to resolve electoral disputes authorize it only to decide disputes about the vote counting and, if errors are identified, to stipulate the correct count. The Court has gone well beyond this, particularly in *Pemilukada* disputes, ordering revotes and recounts for some types of breaches of electoral laws that occur before counting even takes place.[35]

Perhaps the best examples of the Court expanding its jurisdiction in constitutional review cases are those in which it decides that the statute being challenged is conditionally constitutional. In these cases, the Court declares that the statute it has reviewed appears to be constitutionally defective, but does not just invalidate that statute, as the Court's own

34 Butt, note 31, 200.

35 Simon Butt, 'Indonesian Constitutional Court decisions in regional head electoral disputes', CDI Policy Papers on Political Governance (Canberra: Centre for Democratic Institutions, Australian National University, 2013).

governing law appears to require.[36] Rather, the Court decides that the statute under review can remain constitutional provided it is interpreted so that its effect is not unconstitutional.

The Court issued declarations of conditional constitutionality in its early decisions. For example, in one case,[37] the Court upheld the constitutionality of a statute allowing film censorship but said that it needed to be interpreted in line with the 'spirit of the times' – that is, the 'spirit of democracy' and 'respect for human rights'. Initially, these conditional constitutionality decisions appeared to indicate that the Court was being deferential to parliament because, in them, the Court gave parliament the benefit of the doubt by not invalidating the statute under review.[38] They also did not disrupt parliament, which was not forced to respond to the decision.

However, particularly under Chief Justice Mahfud, the way the Court employed these types of decisions changed in three important ways.[39] First, the Court has been issuing more of them. Under Asshiddiqie, around 35 per cent of successful challenges included declarations of conditional constitutionality. This increased to around 60 per cent under Mahfud. Preliminary indications point to subsequent chief justices issuing a similar proportion of these types of decisions. Second, the Court has consciously shifted towards declaring statutes conditionally unconstitutional – that is, unconstitutional unless interpreted in a particular way or given a particular meaning. This, the Court did in response to perceptions that the government was not heeding its conditionally constitutional decisions.[40]

Third, and perhaps most importantly, the Court's decisions in these types of cases have become more prescriptive and specific. If the conditions the Court imposed in its earlier days were perhaps vague and aspirational, now they resemble legislative amendments. This has prompted criticisms that the Court is making law and thus usurping the function of the legislature.

A clear example of the Court's current practices is provided by the *Wedlock case*, where the Court decided that a child born out of wedlock

[36] See Article 57 of Law 24 of 2003 on the Constitutional Court.

[37] Constitutional Court Decision 005/PUU-I/2003.

[38] Simon Butt, 'Indonesia's constitutional court: Conservative activist or strategic operator?' in Björn Dressel (ed.), *The Judicialization of Politics in Asia* (New York: Routledge, 2012) 98–117.

[39] Statistics drawn from Simon Butt, *The Constitutional Court and Democracy in Indonesia* (Boston: Brill Nijhoff, 2015).

[40] See, in particular, Constitutional Court Decision 54/PUU-VI/2008, para [3.2.2].

had a civil legal relationship not only with its mother as had previously been the case under Indonesia's Marriage Law, but also with its biological father. This *Wedlock* decision removes some of the legal roadblocks for so-called illegitimate children claiming maintenance from their fathers, and even to receiving an inheritance from them. This case involved a review of Article 43(1) of the Marriage Law,[41] which states,

> A child born out of marriage has a civil legal relationship with its mother and her family.

The Court's decision was to declare Article 43(1) conditionally unconstitutional – that is, unconstitutional unless interpreted to read

> A child born out of marriage has a civil legal relationship with its mother and her family, and its father and his family [provided that paternity] can be proven by science and technology and/or another form of legally recognised evidence that the father has a blood relationship with the child.[42]

Putting the obvious desirability of the decision to one side, the Court changed the words of Article 43(1) of the Marriage Law, granting rights to children, creating obligations for biological fathers and establishing how these rights and obligations arise. Are these not matters for the legislature? And, if the Court is usurping the function of the democratically elected legislature, has it undermined the separation of powers in this case and in the many other cases in which the Court has issued similarly prescriptive conditions upon the constitutionality of a statute? The Court's decisions in these cases appear to have the same effect as amending the legislation itself.

Yet declarations of conditional constitutionality are pragmatic responses to the highly realistic expectation that the legislature will respond to the Court's decisions slowly, if at all. (Quite apart from the fact that the DPR has rarely directly responded to Constitutional Court decisions, the DPR sometimes, for various reasons, usually political, goes for long periods enacting no legislation.) In this context, striking down legislation would probably result in a prolonged legal vacuum during which the invalidation might put the applicant in a worse position. Applied to the *Wedlock* case, for example, if the Court struck down Article 43(1) of the Marriage Law then children might have had no legal basis to claim from anyone, *including* their mothers.

41 Law 1 of 1974 on Marriage.
42 Constitutional Court Decision 46/PUU-VIII/2010, para [3.13].

IV The Power of Personality?

With some notable exceptions, the government has complied with the Court's decisions, even though the Court lacks formal enforcement powers.[43] This is a significant achievement in a political environment in which some politicians are still unaccustomed to having their legislative powers checked by an external body, and many remain openly hostile towards the Court. Similarly, in electoral disputes, the Court has, with some exceptions, handed down decisions widely regarded as impartial. These decisions have also been largely respected by electoral participants and citizens and have rarely resulted in unrest or further disputation. The Court appears, therefore, to have helped bolster the legitimacy of Indonesia's many elections.

Commentators have attributed the popularity of the Court and the willingness with which parties have complied with its decisions to the widespread respect held by the public and politicians for the Court leadership. The Court's first two chief justices, Jimly Asshiddiqie (2003–2008) and Mahfud (2008–2013), were respected legal scholars with strong personalities, political connections and institutional nous. Asshiddiqie, in particular, is often rightly credited with almost single-handedly securing a budget sufficient for the Court's operations to educate politicians and lawyers about the Court's functions and for popularizing the Court amongst the public. This, he did through artful use of media and strong advocacy skills. Under his leadership, the Court built a deserved reputation for independence from government and, as mentioned, for being more competent, reliable and impartial than other Indonesian judicial institutions. Mahfud, too, charismatically promoted the Court in the media and within government. While effectively maintaining the momentum built by Asshiddiqie, Mahfud's political aspirations appeared to affect some of the Court's decision-making practices, shifting its priorities to expeditiously solving political problems rather than developing constitutional jurisprudence (as had been one of Asshiddiqie's primary objectives).[44]

[43] Simon Butt and Tim Lindsey, 'Economic reform when the constitution matters: Indonesia's Constitutional Court and Article 33' (2008) 44 *Bulletin of Indonesian Economic Studies* 239–262.

[44] Butt, note 36. After much posturing, Mahfud eventually sought to become Prabowo Subianto's running mate for the 2014 presidential elections. Ultimately, he was unsuccessful and, instead, became head of Prabowo's election campaign team.

The danger of over-reliance on the personalities of chief justices for respect and credibility were brought into sharp relief when the Court's third chief justice, Akil Mochtar, was arrested in October 2013 by the anti-corruption commission for receiving bribes to fix electoral disputes.[45] In mid-2014, Mochtar was convicted of money laundering offences and sentenced to life imprisonment.[46] The Court's reputation nosedived, primarily because Mochtar was chief justice when arrested but also because he had served on the Court for several years, leading to suspicions that dozens of cases he had handled might also have been tainted by corruption and concerns that other judges might also be involved. As Mahfud put it in an interview with *Tempo* magazine, 'Rats don't work alone'.[47]

Many commentators feared that the Court might not recover given that much of its public and political support was based on its perceived integrity and impartiality, in addition to the personalities of its chief justices. To be sure, the Court's approaches to legal interpretation and judicial decision-making were far more sophisticated than those adopted by other courts, but in many cases, the Court jurisprudence was unclear, derived from undisclosed sources or inconsistently applied. However, as I have argued elsewhere, the Court's reputation might not have suffered to such a degree had it developed a stronger body of constitutional jurisprudence.[48] Consistent application of that jurisprudence would have lent its decisions a greater air of objectivity and legal justifiability. Without this, commentators and citizens naturally question what is really behind the Court's decision-making. Worse, when the professionalism of a *single* judge is brought into question, the conclusion can more readily be reached that the *entire* Court's professionalism is doubtful.

Fortunately, however, the Court appears to have regained much of the respect it lost from the Mochtar saga. It is said to have achieved this by handling the 2014 electoral disputes professionally and, in particular, by rejecting the challenge to the presidential election result brought by Prabowo Subianto and Hatta Rajasa, despite significant pressure being brought to bear on the Court. Mochtar's replacement, Hamdan Zoelva, was well regarded by some, but only served out the remainder of Mochtar's

[45] Mochtar was also investigated for narcotics offences after police found a small quantity of illicit substances in his chambers.

[46] Novrieza Rahmi, 'Divonis Seumur Hidup, Akil Akan Banding Sampai Ke Surga' (2014, July 1) *Hukumonline*.

[47] 'Mahfud MD: Rats don't work alone' (2013, October 17) *Tempo*. http://en.tempo.co/read/news/2013/10/17/241522255/Mahfud-Md-Rats-dont-Work-Alone (accessed 27 April 2018).

[48] Butt, note 39.

term (October 2013–January 2015), before being replaced by Arief Hidayat in early 2015. Both Zoelva and Hidayat lacked the personality or persuasiveness of Asshiddiqie or Mahfud. Zoelva in particular appeared concerned with continuing to build the standing of the Court and improving its decision-making. However, Hidayat drew criticism for breaching the Court's ethics code for meeting with members of the DPR, apparently to secure his continuing position on the Court.

V Selected Major Election System Challenges (2005–2015)

The Court has issued many important decisions that have shaped Indonesia's democratic processes, most notably its electoral systems. Indonesia's various electoral laws – whether concerning legislative, presidential, national or local elections – have, in fact, been amongst those most regularly challenged before the Court. Indonesia's Constitution contains only one provision dedicated solely to elections: Article 22E. The provision, added to the Constitution during the third amendment round in 2001, contains six paragraphs or subsections.

(1) General elections are to be direct, public, free, secret, honest and fair, and they are to be held every five years.
(2) General elections are held to elect members to the DPR, DPD (the Regional Representative Assembly, or *Dewan Perwakilan Daerah*) and DPRD (regional parliaments, *Dewan Perwakilan Raykat Daerah*), and to elect the president and vice president.
(3) Contestants of DPR and DPRD elections are political parties.
(4) Contestant of DPD elections are individuals.
(5) General elections are to be administered by a general election commission that is national, permanent and independent.
(6) Further provisions about general elections are to be regulated by statute.

Also fundamental is Article 1(2), which establishes the 'sovereignty of the people'. Article 18, amended during the second round in 2000, covers regional government and touches upon elections for regional representative institutions and regional heads in two of its paragraphs. Article 18(3) states that 'Provincial, county and city administrations have DPRDs whose members are chosen by general election'. Article 18(4) states that 'Governors, Regents and Mayors are heads of provincial, county and city governments, respectively, and are to be elected democratically'.

The Court has, in many decisions, emphasized that this constitutional framework gives lawmakers considerable scope to establish any of a variety of electoral systems. Lawmakers can choose, for example, whether to apply a proportional-representation system, a plurality/majority system or a mixed system, provided that the elections remain direct, public, free, secret, honest and fair and are held at least every five years. They can also choose various prerequisites for candidacy and thresholds for participation, provided that these systems fit within the above-mentioned constitutional provisions, including the various civil and political rights contained in Chapter 28 of the Constitution.[49] They can also choose how voting takes place, again, if the chosen mechanism does not contradict these provisions.[50]

I now turn to discussing some of the Court's key decisions in election legislation challenges, most of which have been issued in response to applications brought by citizens, prospective candidates wishing to stand for election, or political parties.

VI Candidacy Cases

The Constitutional Court has regularly been called upon to invalidate prohibitions on individuals standing for election on grounds such as political belief, criminal record or lack of affiliation with a political party. Indeed, in one of its earliest cases – the *PKI case* (2003) – a majority of the Court removed candidacy restrictions on former Indonesian communist party members and their families from standing for election, holding that those restrictions were discriminatory.[51]

Several candidacy cases have concerned local electoral commissions' application of Article 58(f) of the 2004 Regional Government Law. This provision prohibits people who have served a criminal sentence of five years or more from standing for election as the head or deputy head of a regional government. In a series of cases from 2007, the Court has progressively loosened this requirement, eventually holding, in the *Robertus* case (2009), that Article 58(f) could not prevent people found guilty of a crime from standing for election provided certain conditions were met. These were openly and honestly disclosing their previous

[49] *Parliamentary Threshold Case* (2009), cited in *Parliamentary Threshold and Party Verification Case* (2012, 96).

[50] The Constitutional Court has, for example, held that e-voting is a constitutionally valid method of voting, provided that the mechanism complies with Article 22E; is technologically sound, well-funded, and supported by software and staff; and the community is 'ready for it' (*E-voting case*, 2009, 41).

[51] Butt, note 35; Butt, note 31.

conviction to the public, five years having passed since the sentence had been served and the crime not being a repeat offence.

Article 58(f) was again at issue in the *Tebing Tinggi Mayoral election case* (2010). One of the pairs defeated in this election complained that Mohammad Syafri Chap, of the winning pair, had been ineligible to stand because he had been convicted of corruption and sentenced to one year's imprisonment. This was the minimum sentence for the crime, and it had been suspended for eighteen months, during which time Chap had stood for mayor.

The Court split five judges to four. The majority[52] found, following *Robertus*, that Chap fell foul of Article 58(f) because five years had not passed since his criminal punishment ended. He was, therefore, ineligible. Amidst claims from the Tebing Tinggi Electoral Commission that it could not afford to hold the revote and hundreds rallying in front of the commission's office,[53] the Court ordered a fresh election and disqualified Chap from standing in that election. The minority[54] appeared willing to not require strict enforcement of the conditions it had imposed in *Robertus*. Even though five years had not passed since completing his criminal punishment, Chap had not been incarcerated and had openly admitted his conviction. Also relevant for the minority was that other candidates had not objected to his candidacy when he formally registered his intention to stand with the local electoral commission.

The most recently issued law governing candidacy prerequisites is Law 8 of 2014 on Elections for Governor, Bupati and Mayors.[55] Article 7(g) of this law retains Article 58(f) in its original form – that is, it does not accommodate the Constitutional Court's decisions in the cases discussed in this section. This provision was challenged in the *Jumanto* case (2015). A majority of the Court declared Article 7(g) conditionally unconstitutional to the extent that they did not exclude former convicts who openly and honestly announced to the public that they had served prison sentences.[56]

[52] Justices Mahfud, Achmad Sodiki, Muhammad Alim, Arsyad Sanusi, and Ahmad Fadlil Sumadi.

[53] Apriadi Gunawan, 'Court orders re-elections as commission cries poor' (2010, August 15) *Jakarta Post*.

[54] Justices Akil Mochtar, Maria Farida, Hardjono, Hamdan Zoelva.

[55] This amends Presidential Emergency Law 1 of 2014, which the national parliament endorsed and 'upgraded' to a statue by enacting Law 1 of 2015.

[56] Incidentally, the Elucidation to Article 7(g) did appear to accommodate the Constitutional Court's decision in *Robertus*. It states, 'This pre-requisite does not apply to a

VII Independent Candidates

Prior to 2007, to stand for election, regional head candidates needed to be nominated by political parties or coalitions that had obtained 15 per cent of the votes or 15 per cent of the seats in the DPRD in the most recent election.[57] However, this changed when the Constitutional Court issued the *Independent Pemilukada candidates case* (2007). The applicant, Lalu Ranggalawe, was a local parliamentarian in Lombok who wanted to stand in regional head elections but suspected that the party with which he had been associated would not support him. He challenged the constitutionality of various provisions of the 2004 Regional Government Law that did not permit independent candidates standing for election as regional heads.

Ranggalawe pointed to the 2006 Aceh Government Law, which provided special autonomy to Aceh, allowing its lawmakers to pass laws on a wider variety of issues than provincial governments elsewhere in Indonesia. The Law also recognized that some exceptions to regional election practices were necessary in Aceh and allowed independent candidates to stand for regional head. In light of the 2006 Aceh Government Law, the applicant argued that the 2004 Local Government Law's prohibition on independent candidates was discriminatory and violated his right to legal equality under the Constitution.[58] The Court agreed, observing that Article 18(4) of the Constitution, which required that regional heads be democratically elected, was the constitutional foundation for contrary provisions: Articles 56 and 59 of the 2004 Regional Government Law, which required political party nomination, and Article 67(1)(d) of the 2006 Aceh Government Law, which permitted independent candidates. For the Court, the result was dualism because candidates could nominate themselves in Aceh but could not do so in other parts of Indonesia. The Court decided that, to resolve this inequality, independent candidates should be permitted to nominate themselves to stand as governors,

person who completed their sentence more than five years earlier, is an elected official, the person concerned announces honestly and openly to the public that he or she has been imprisoned, and is not a repeat offender. Persons convicted for political reasons are excluded from this provision.' The Court found that this Elucidation contradicted the provision it was intended to elucidate and, therefore, also declared it conditionally unconstitutional.

57 Article 59(2) of the 2008 Amendment to the 2004 Regional Government Law; Article 36 (2) of Government Regulation 6 of 2005 on the Election and Appointment of Regional Heads.

58 See Articles 27(1) and 28D(3) of the Constitution.

mayors or regents across Indonesia. The Court made various adjustments to the 2004 Regional Government Law to achieve this.

The Court's decision was unconvincing from a legal perspective. In particular, the Court did not explain why it did not invalidate Article 67 (1)(d) of the 2006 Aceh Government Law to extinguish this inequality. After all, Article 67(1)(d) was only ever intended as a temporary measure. Article 256 of the Aceh Government Law provided that Article 67(1)(d) would be 'valid and implemented only for the first elections held after this statute is enacted', on 1 August 2006. In subsequent elections, independent candidates would no longer be permitted. It is, therefore, strange that the Court intervened, given that by the time the Court had decided the case, almost one year later, on 23 July 2007, many of these first regional head elections had already taken place, presumably, under the 2006 Aceh Government Law.[59] In other words, it appeared that, by operation of Article 256, Article 67(1)(d) was no longer valid when the Court reviewed it.

Since the Court's establishment, dozens of applicants with presidential aspirations but no or insufficient support from political parties have also challenged the constitutionality of electoral laws that require them to be nominated by a political party or coalition. However, unlike in the cases involving *Pemilukada* elections, the Court has consistently held that presidential candidates can stand for election only if they have minimum standards of party support.

The leading case on this issue is the *Independent presidential candidates' case* (2008), which was brought by several citizens who appeared not to identify with or support any existing political party. One of them, Fadjroel Rachman, sought to exercise his right to participate in government by becoming a presidential candidate despite not being nominated by a party. Other applicants did not want, when electing a candidate pair, to be bound by the candidates chosen by a party or coalition. Instead, they wanted to be able to elect a president they trusted.

The applicants challenged Articles 1(4), 8, 9 and 13(1) of the 2008 Presidential Election Law. Together, these provisions imposed the political party nomination requirement and set the so-called 20/25 per cent threshold. Only those parties obtaining 25 per cent or more of the national vote in

[59] Elections for Aceh governor, for four city mayors and for fifteen county regents took place on 11 December 2006, with some requiring run-off elections in mid-March 2007. Kris Ann Riiber, 'Aceh, Indonesia: Governor and District Elections December 2006 – March 2007' (Norwegian Centre for Human Rights, 2007).

legislative elections or holding 20 per cent or more of seats in the DPR can nominate their preferred pair for president and vice president. Parties that do not meet this threshold must form a coalition with other parties so that they collectively meet the threshold if they wish to nominate a candidate.[60]

The applicants' main constitutional hurdle was convincing the Court that Article 6A(2) of the Constitution should not be given its plain textual meaning, but rather should be read alongside the political rights contained in Chapter XA of the Constitution, including Articles 27(1), 28C(2) and 28D(3) of the Constitution, which provide the rights to vote and stand for election, the 'same opportunity in government', 'collectively struggle for rights and to develop the nation', be free from discrimination and the like. Article 6A(2) states that candidate pairs 'are to be proposed by political parties or coalitions'. One of the applicants' contentions was that Article 6A(2) was not cast in mandatory terms – it did not contain the words 'must' or 'needs' – so that an individual 'could' stand for president without being nominated by the party and thereby fulfil their Chapter XA rights.

A majority of the Court rejected this argument, providing three primary reasons. First, the 'original intent' of drafters was that party nomination was mandatory, pointing to a transcript of constitutional amendment debates in the MPR.[61] Second, the majority distinguished between the right to vote and the right to stand for election. In various provisions of Chapter XA, the Constitution gave citizens the fundamental right to vote, themselves derived from Article 1(2) of the Constitution, which places sovereignty in the hands of the people. By contrast, the right to stand was subject to Article 6A(2), because Article 1(2) states that the people's sovereignty must be exercised in accordance with the Constitution (*Independent presidential candidates case*, 2009, para [3.17]). (In any event, the requirement for nomination by a political party did not prevent aspiring candidates from being nominated – they could establish their own party to nominate them (*Independent presidential candidates case*, 2009, para [3.15].) Third, the majority held that the law was not discriminatory because it did not require that a candidate be a member of a political party to be nominated by that party.

60 Article 9 of the 2008 Presidential Election Law. The 25/20 per cent threshold represents a significant increase from the 15/20 per cent threshold adopted in Article 5(4) of the 2003 Presidential Election Law.

61 The majority referred to constitutional debates in the MPR in very vague terms, later pointing to the Court's own compilation of those debates: Mahkamah Konstitusi, note 10, 165–360.

In subsequent cases, applicants have put forward similar arguments to convince the Court to invalidate provisions of the 2008 Presidential Election Law requiring party nomination for presidential candidates. In response, the Court has referred to the *Independent candidates case* (2008), often extracting long passages from it, and held that the constitutionality of the party nomination requirement has already been decided. The Court has, therefore, consistently rejected these applications, declaring them *ne bis in idem.*[62]

VIII Electoral Systems

The Court has issued several foundational decisions concerning the constitutionality of important aspects of Indonesia's electoral systems. Of particular importance was the *Electoral roll case* (2009), where the Court held that citizens can vote even if not registered to vote, provided that they present a valid form of identification, such as their identity card or passport, to polling officials on election day. For the Court, the right to vote, to stand for election and to participate in government were fundamental and could not, therefore, be limited or diverged from, including by imposing rules or procedures that made exercising them more difficult (*Electoral roll case*, 2009, para [3.18]).

Also significant was the *Sisa suara case* (2009), where the Court determined how votes would be 'converted' into seats. The Court decided that once a party had reached the number of votes required to obtain one or more seats, it could not then claim any remaining seats on the basis of its overall proportional share of the votes. The votes already used to obtain seats were extinguished. This gave smaller parties a greater opportunity to obtain seats. In a much more questionable decision, the Court even held that holding presidential and legislative elections three months apart is unconstitutional.[63] From 2019, it is expected that legislative and presidential elections will be held together.

The Court has also issued decisions concerning the constitutionality of the semi-open list system that have had far-reaching implications. During the 2004 legislative elections, parties obtaining sufficient votes to obtain seats could allocate seats to their preferred candidates formally registered with the electoral commission on a candidate list even if those preferred candidates had received fewer votes than other candidates from

[62] See, for example, *Independent candidates* cases (2012) and (2013).
[63] Constitutional Court Decision 14/PUU-XI/2013.

the same party. These rules were changed for the 2009 elections so that if an individual candidate received 30 per cent of the number of votes required for a seat in a given electoral district, the party had to allocate any seats they obtained to that candidate. If none of a party's candidates met this reduced quota, then the choice of the party would prevail – that is, seats would be allocated to candidates based on their positions on the party candidate list.[64]

In the *Open list case* (2008), the Court made party lists obsolete, requiring parties to allocate seats to their candidates receiving the most votes 'in the name of democracy'. While the Court accepted that political parties played a significant role in the democratic process, primarily by identifying and then nominating candidates, they could not 'breach the principle of people's sovereignty' established by Article 1(2) of the Constitution. For the majority, this was a fundamental and absolute principle.

> It is not merely a basic norm. It is more than that. It constitutes the morality of the Constitution for the entire life of the state and nation in politics, social affairs, economics and law. This principle must exist side by side with – and not undermine but rather uphold – human rights, the basis of human dignity (*Open list case*, 2008, 102).

Candidates must, therefore, be elected based on the number of votes they receive, not their position on the party list (*Open list case*, 2008, 105). To maintain the list system also ignored the political legitimacy obtained by the candidates receiving the most votes.

While this decision was widely praised, it was problematic, not least for foiling attempts to increase the proportion of females in parliament. One of the applicants in the *Open list case* (2008), DPRD candidate Muhammad Sholeh, objected to 2008 General Election Law provisions on affirmative action which required at least one in every three candidates on every party's candidate list to be female. Sholeh argued that these provisions discriminated against male candidates and were, hence, unconstitutional, pointing to Articles 27(1), 28D(1) and 28I(2) of the Constitution.[65] An eight-judge-to-one majority rejected this argument,

[64] Stephen Sherlock, 'Indonesia's 2009 Elections: The New Electoral System and the Competing Parties' (2009/01, Canberra: Centre for Democratic Institutions, Australian National University, 2009) 14.

[65] Article 27(1): 'All citizens have an equal status in the law and government and must uphold the law and government without exception'; Article 28D(1): 'All people have the right to recognition, guarantees, protection, legal certainty which is just and equal treatment before the law'; Article 28I(2): 'Everyone has the right to be free from discrimination'.

holding that even if affirmative action breached the constitutional rights of male candidates as alleged by the applicant, this would be a permissible limitation under Article 28J(2) of the Constitution (*Open list case*, 2008, pp. 98–99).[66] Article 28H(2) of the Constitution gives every person the right to facilitation or special measures (*perlakuan khusus*) to ensure that they have the same opportunities and benefits as others to obtain equality and justice. This right prevailed over anti-discrimination rights. In any event, however, the section of the Court's judgment about the list system had made the relative position of candidates on the list meaningless. Even though parties still needed to ensure that 30 per cent of their candidates were women, there was no absolute requirement that women occupy 30 per cent of the seats in parliament.[67] The proportion of women sitting in parliament was a matter for voters to determine.

IX Customary Voting Processes

Customary voting systems, primarily practised in parts of Papua, deserve brief mention.[68] Some – commonly referred to as *noken* – are said to have been employed since the 1971 general elections and are apparently still used for all types of elections across many, but not all, electoral districts in Papua.[69]

Noken literally means a traditional bag made from bark.[70] However, the term is also used to refer to a variety of voting practices. Panggabean[71] describes two of them. The first is called '*noken gantung*' or 'hanging bag'. This involves the customary chief, usually the village head, instructing constituents to vote for one candidate by putting their votes in a bag rather than voting by secret ballot. The main objective is for votes to be distributed either to a single candidate or amongst candidates in a proportion determined by the chief or agreed upon by the community.[72]

[66] Article 28J(2): 'In exercising their rights and freedoms, every person must submit to limitations stipulated by statute with the sole intent of protecting the rights and freedoms of others and which accords with moral considerations, religious values, security and public order in a democratic society'.

[67] The Court made this observation in the *Affirmative action case* (2013).

[68] Similar practices – called 'represented voting' (*pemilihan diwakilkan*) – are also used in parts of Bali: Cillian Ihsanuddin, 'MK: Suara Yang Bisa Diwakilkan Pada Pilkada Bali Bersifat Spesifik' (2013, November 26) *Kompas*.

[69] 'Ahli: Penggunaan Sistem Noken Harus Dihargai' (2014, August 13) *Hukumonline*.

[70] Cillian Nolan, 'Votes in the bag' (2012, September 11) *Crisis Group*.

[71] 'Sistem Noken Dan 'Bigman' (2014, August 18) *Kompas*.

[72] *Hukumonline*, note 69.

The second type of *noken* is the so-called Bigman process, under which citizens in a particular area allow their customary chief, such as their village head, to vote on their behalf. Under this process, voters might not even need to attend polling stations, with community leaders deciding how many votes each candidate should get, either marking ballot papers themselves or noting the final result on tally forms and sending them on to election officials in their regional area.[73]

Applicants who claim to have lost seats in various elections held in Papua in which these practices were employed have challenged the results in the Constitutional Court. For example, in the *Papua gubernatorial election case* (2013, para [3.24.4.4]), the applicant described the *noken* process as a 'conspiracy' between the regional electoral commission and his electoral competitors to ensure his defeat. Even the unsuccessful Prabowo-Hatta presidential candidates complained about these practices in their challenge to the results in 2014.

However, the Court has consistently held that these practices are legitimate expressions of local custom and are, therefore, protected under Article 18B(2) of the Constitution, which states,

> The State recognises and respects *adat* [customary] law communities and their traditional rights, provided that they remain in existence and accord with community developments and the principle of the Unitary State of the Republic of Indonesia, as regulated by statute.

In the *Papua DPD election case* (2009, para [3.24]), for example, the Court said,

> The Court can understand and value the cultural values alive in the unique Papua community in running the election by 'community agreement' or 'acclamation'. The Court accepts the method of collective voting ... which has been accepted in Yahukimo [county] because if forced to have an election that accords with the applicable law, there are concerns that conflict will emerge in the local community. The Court believes that it is best that they are not involved/carried to a system of competition/division within and between groups that could disturb the harmony with which they have been instilled.

Though these decisions have drawn praise from those seeking greater recognition for customary law and practices within the Indonesian legal system, these voting processes are highly problematic from a democratic perspective. In particular, in these cases, the Court appears to have

[73] Cillian Nolan, 'How Papua voted' (2014, April 7) *New Mandala*.

underemphasized or ignored Article 22E(1) of the Constitution, which requires that general elections be 'direct, public, free, secret, honest and just'. Of course, when citizens' voting preferences are determined by another, or when citizens cast their votes by placing them, in full public view, into a bag representing a political party, elections are neither free nor secret. Yet the Court has not sought to openly reconcile Article 22E (1) with recognizing these customary voting processes via Article 18B(2).

Worse, when 'accepting' these practices, the Court does not appear to have considered their other shortcomings. These traditional voting methods are highly susceptible to fraud and conspiracy, particularly between candidates and customary chiefs, to fix outcomes. And, even if fraud is not present and customary law chiefs genuinely prefer one candidate over another for policy reasons, *noken* voting can lead to skewed results. In particular, many *noken* processes result in 100 per cent participation rates, with 100 per cent of votes cast for a particular candidate.[74] One would never expect such results in an electoral system that is free and fair and in which voting is not mandatory. Indeed, Indonesia's participation rate for the 2014 legislative and presidential elections was around 70 per cent.[75]

X Conclusions

As the cases discussed in this paper demonstrate, Indonesia's Constitutional Court has significantly changed Indonesia's electoral systems and their operation. Though established within a highly dysfunctional legal system with almost no history of judicial professionalism, the Indonesian Constitutional Court has become an institution widely respected by government and citizens. In particular, it appears to have largely restored the trust it lost after the Akil Mochtar scandal. Through this respect and trust, the Court has lent weight to its decisions, pushing the government, political parties and individual applicants towards compliance with those decisions.

However, while the Court genuinely tried to legally justify many of its decisions, this paper has highlighted the problematic reasoning in many of them. This does not, however, appear to have seriously undermined or otherwise affected the Court's legitimacy or credibility. It seems that the

[74] *Hukumonline*, note 66; Nolan, note 70.

[75] For voter turnout data for Indonesia, see www.idea.int/data-tools/question-countries-view/521/142/ctr.

Constitutional Court's decisions are, legally speaking, 'good enough' to satisfy the generally low legal appreciation held by Indonesian politicians and citizens alike. Although its decisions often raise controversy, this controversy is rarely, if ever, legal. In other words, the Court's decisions are rarely criticized for being poorly reasoned, but rather on the basis of their outcome. This is perhaps to be expected in a country whose Constitution has for most of its independent history been a rather nebulous document not previously applied or otherwise used as a check on government power. However, in my view, the Court must pay greater attention to developing a more robust body of jurisprudence and then apply it consistently. If it does this, then when the Court becomes embroiled in scandal once more, the Court, as an institution, will be better able to withstand attacks on its professionalism.

10

Constitutional Council of Cambodia at the Age of Majority

A History of Weathering the Rule of Law Storms in Peacetime

TEILEE KUONG

I Introduction

A mechanism for judicial review is guaranteed under the 1993 Constitution by the establishment of the Constitutional Council. However, the controversial context in which the relevant law was adopted and the Council established has led to general allegations of a lack of credibility of the body.[1] There have been a number of important rulings by this Council on the question of constitutionality of legislation adopted by the National Assembly and interpretation of constitutional and legal provisions. Some of them were not without controversies, but the Council continues to be seized frequently by questions of constitutionality and other important legal interpretations. Although, arguably, there is still room for technical improvement to enhance popular trust in its work, the nature of this Constitutional Council as a constitutional and apolitical body to guarantee development of post-conflict constitutionalism in Cambodia needs to be properly understood in the context of constitution-making and political development of the country in the last eighteen years. The political environment continues to pose a serious challenge for the Council itself and for the development of a political and judicial system based on constitutional principles.

[1] Eric Pape and Samreth Sopha, 'Bar president challenges constitutional counselors' (1998, June 19) *The Phnom Penh Post*; Chris Fontaine 'Say Bory complains to King over "Council of Six"' (1998, September 4) *The Phnom Penh Post*; Elizabeth Moorthy and Pok Sokundara, 'Son Soubert becomes second critic to sit on council' (1998, August 21) *The Phnom Penh Post*.

In addition to the mandate to review constitutionality questions, the Council is also given the exclusive power to adjudicate electoral disputes. During the electoral seasons, the Council has been mostly occupied by electoral cases. This was particularly remarkable in the latest election of 2013, when the opposition party managed to gain quantitatively and made efforts to challenge the fairness of the electoral process and neutrality of the National Election Committee (NEC). Much attention has been given to the Council's role in examining electoral disputes and, on that basis, its capacity to settle political conflicts in the newly established and evolving electoral system of the country.

This chapter will review the development and work of this Council and see how far it has gone since its establishment in 1998 in upholding post-conflict and post-socialist Cambodian constitutionalism, democracy, peace and political order. Section II briefly introduces the history of the establishment of the Council and gives a general overview of its roles and functions. Subsequent sections will examine some theoretical and practical issues characterizing the development of the Council over the last eighteen years. Finally, Section VI concludes.

II The System in a Nutshell

The 1993 Constitution provides for establishment of the Constitutional Council to safeguard the Constitution and to decide electoral disputes.[2] The Constitutional Council consists of nine members. Three of the members are appointed by the King, three are elected by the National Assembly and three others are elected by the Supreme Council of Magistracy.[3]

[2] The 1993 Constitution of the Kingdom of Cambodia and subsequent amendments up to 2016, (hereinafter the Constitution), Chapter XII.

[3] The Constitution, Art. 136 (new). The Supreme Council of Magistracy is constitutionally charged with supervising the judicial and prosecutorial institutions. Appointment of and disciplinary actions against judges and prosecutors belong to the exclusive power of this council. Pursuant to the latest legislation, in 2014, regarding its organization and functioning, the Supreme Council of Magistracy now consists of twelve members, presided over by the King. The minister of justice is *ex officio* a member. Six other members come from the courts and prosecutors' offices at all levels, whereas another four are appointees from the National Assembly, the Senate, the Constitutional Council and the Ministry of Justice. Art. 4 of the Law on Organization and Functioning of the Supreme Council of Magistracy, the new law promulgated on 23 May 2014. See also Kuch Naren, 'New Supreme Council rules aim to ensure impartiality', (2015, January 31) *The Cambodia Daily*.

The King, the prime minister, the president of the National Assembly, one-tenth of the members of the National Assembly, the president of the Senate, or one-quarter of the senators may send laws adopted by the National Assembly, and voted in approval by the Senate, to the Constitutional Council for review before promulgation.[4] The Constitutional Council may also conduct *a posteriori* review of laws. The new Article 141[5] provides that, after promulgation of any law, the King, the president of the Senate, the president of the National Assembly, the prime minister, one-fourth of the senators, one-tenth of the members of the National Assembly, or the courts may request the Constitutional Council to review the constitutionality of that law.[6] The courts may refer any constitutionality issues raised in ongoing litigation to the Council for interpretation and ruling. Citizens may also use any of the above channels to indirectly submit their queries regarding the constitutionality of laws or legal provisions to the Council.

Historically, the 1972 Constitution of the Khmer Republic also contained one section on the establishment of a constitutional court to handle constitutional interpretation, constitutionality review and regulations and disputes related to presidential and parliamentary elections.[7] However, due to the period of intensifying civil war in the 1970s, the constitutional court was never established. As such, the Constitutional Council established by the 1993 Constitution is the first-ever constitutional body to practise constitutional review in more than half a century of constitutional history of the country. Although the 1972 Constitution envisaged the establishment of a constitutional court, the said court was, in fact, structurally and functionally more similar to the French Constitutional Council than, say, the Federal Constitutional Court of the Republic of Germany of that time. Six members of the court were to be appointed; two each by the president of the Republic, the National Assembly and the Senate. Constitutional review concerned only *a priori* examination of legislation adopted by the National Assembly before its promulgation. In contrast, the current Constitutional Council is made up of nine members. It is manned by people entrusted by three different institutions, i.e., the King as the symbolic

[4] The Constitution, Art. 140 (new).

[5] The 'new' articles hereinafter refer to articles of the Constitution and laws which have been amended up to October 2016. Some of these articles were simply renumbered as a result of the several constitutional amendments.

[6] The Constitution, Art. 141 (new).

[7] Section 1 and Art. 95 of Chapter Four of the 1972 Constitution.

constitutional institution, the democratically elected National Assembly and the Supreme Council of Magistracy, which oversees the judicial branch. Each of the three members appointed and selected by the three institutions is subjected to replacement every three years after he or she has served the full mandate of nine years.[8] The Council is given a more liberal mandate to conduct *a posteriori* review of constitutionality questions than what was projected in 1972.[9]

1 *The Council and the Judiciary*

The Constitutional Council is by no means meant to be a court, even though one-third of its members are elected by the Supreme Council of Magistracy, which represents the judicial branch and has the power to nominate judges and prosecutors.[10] The Constitutional Council members are not considered judges but are instead regarded as public

[8] This was made possible by inserting an exception to the mandate of some first-batch members. The King, the National Assembly and the Supreme Council of Magistracy each appointed three first-batch members to the Constitutional Council to serve the first periods of three, six and nine years, respectively. Subsequent batches of members have since been appointed for the full mandate of nine years. The Council is now guaranteed uninterrupted operation with election and appointment of three new members every three years. This makes sure that, normally, a minimum number of six members will be sitting at any point in time. See the Constitution, Art. 137 (new) and the Law on the Organization and the Functioning of the Constitutional Council and its amendment in 2007 (hereinafter the Law on the Constitutional Council), Art. 3 (new).

[9] Despite the possible argument that the 1993 Constitution adopted the French model of constitutionality review mechanism, it may be worth noting that Cambodia attempted a more liberal approach in the 1993 constitution-making by including the Supreme Council of Magistracy, which sits at the top of the judicial branch, in the appointing institutions of the Council members and by taking a quicker step than the French Constitutional Council in introducing the *a posteriori* procedure into the review function of the Council. For a brief review of the French reform in 2008, see Pasquale Pasquino, 'The new constitutional adjudication in France: The reform of the referral to the French Constitutional Council in light of the Italian model', (2009) 3 *Indian Journal of Constitutional Law* 105–117.

[10] The new Law on the Supreme Council of Magistracy was promulgated in 2014 to allow for four of the twelve members to come from a nonjudicial institution. This is a change from the previous law adopted in 1994, whereby only the minister of justice was from a nonjudicial institution. The King has, since 1994, been made to preside over the Council. This organizational change, however, does not change the fact that this Council remains the only institution to exercise supervisory functions over the judicial branch, independently from the other branches.

officials having the highest ranking in the state institution.[11] In the Constitution, the Constitutional Council is stipulated in a separate chapter from the judiciary. Members are chosen from among dignitaries holding a higher education level diploma in law, public administration, diplomacy or economics and having extensive professional experience.[12] During one's time of service as a member of the Council, one is not allowed to be a member of the Royal Government, a deputy in the National Assembly or a senator, an incumbent magistrate, a person holding public function, a president or vice president of a political party or a president or vice president of a trade union.[13]

Despite the provision on separation of powers, the Constitution does not envisage the Council to be one of the three branches. It stands out as a constitutional body made up of members elected and appointed by three separate institutions, involving particularly legislative and judicial powers,[14] and entrusted to work out a majority-based solution to questions of constitutionality or electoral fairness and freedom. There has been no allegation of political interference in the decisions of the Council, despite the initial lack of confidence of some critics in the dominant roles played by the ruling party in selecting the members at the conception of the Council in 1998. However, the fact that the ruling party has managed to keep firm control over the two legislative houses and allegedly has many sympathizers among the members of the Supreme Council of Magistracy and inside the leadership of the judicial structure has made it difficult to refute the general perception of the natural tie between most of the Constitutional Council members and the incumbent establishment and, for that reason, the conceivable tendency of the Constitutional

[11] The president of the Council has the rank equivalent to, and enjoys all the same privileges as, the president of the National Assembly, whereas members hold the same rank and privileges as the vice presidents of the National Assembly. See Art. 4 of the Law on the Constitutional Council.

[12] The 1993 constitutional requirements are in many ways similar to the stipulation of the 1972 Constitution except for the addition of 'diplomacy' as an admissible area of specialization for potential members and the requirement of a graduation diploma instead of simply 'being well-known for profound knowledge' and the provision on 'professional experience' as an additional condition but not alternative to the educational requirement, whereas the 1972 Constitution regarded the factor of extensive 'experience in State affairs' as a qualification in its own right.

[13] The Constitution, Art. 139 (new).

[14] The King is the symbolic head of state who reigns but does not rule and, therefore, does not represent the executive branch. In appointing the members, the King is not required to act on any advice from the government.

Council to rule in favour of maintaining the *status quo*. Without being able to show evidence of external influences, critics have mainly attributed the trend of favouring the *status quo* to the result of historical, political and social ties between individuals as a result of the lack of political balance in the appointment process.[15] In fact, there were expectations after the promulgation of the 1993 Constitution that the coalition government created by the UN-sponsored elections would be able to secure a significant level of political balance in the appointment of members of the Supreme Council of Magistracy and, thereby, the Constitutional Council.[16] The late King Norodom Sihanouk, without waiting for the birth of the Law on the Organization and Functioning of the Constitutional Council, hastily appointed the three Council members as stipulated by the Constitution.[17] But the National Assembly did not vote for the other three members, whereas the Supreme Council of Magistracy, which also had the duty to appoint three members, had not been established until the relevant legislation was promulgated, and the Supreme Council reportedly convened its first meeting only in December 1997.[18] Technically, despite the hasty appointments made by the King, the Constitutional Council could not function without the enabling law to provide for some essential details. The Law on the Organization and the Functioning of the Constitutional Council was only adopted in April 1998, after the coalition government was substantially dismantled by internal fighting between the forces loyal to the two co-prime ministers in July 1997.[19]

2 *Decision-Making and Case Patterns*

Decisions issued by the Council are based on majority voting. Unlike litigation in court, adjudications by the Council may proceed with a

[15] See, further, Chapter 3 by Björn Dressel.

[16] Tricia Fitzgerald, 'King Sihanouk pushes for council formation', (1995, November 17) *The Phnom Penh Post*.

[17] 'Key constitution council in limbo' (1995, October 6) *The Phnom Penh Post*; Eric Pape, 'Council "too busy" for details' (1998, January 16) *The Phnom Penh Post*.

[18] *Kingdom of Cambodia: Law and Order – Without the Law*, (AI Index: ASA 23/01/00, March 2000) Amnesty International.

[19] Sorpong Peou, 'The Cambodian elections of 1998 and beyond: Democracy in the making?' (1998, December) 20 *Contemporary Southeast Asia* 279–297.

quorum of five at the Council's deliberations.[20] In the case of a tie, the president's vote is decisive.[21] There is no public hearing for constitutional review. But in some election-related litigation, the Council may decide to hold a public hearing.[22] If it is necessary, the Council may summon individuals to submit relevant clarifications or documents.[23] Decisions of the Council are not subjected to appeal.[24] However, the same issue or the same piece of legislation may be sent to the Constitutional Council for review again if justifiably new elements emerge.[25]

Among the former and current members of the Constitutional Council, those appointed by the King have normally been members of the Royal family or dignitaries who used to be with the opposition party in different capacities or active in various civil society movements,[26] whereas members elected by the Supreme Council of Magistracy or the National Assembly were mostly dignitaries from the ruling party, i.e., the Cambodian People's Party (CPP), either as former parliamentarians or

[20] Art. 12 of the Internal Rules of the Constitutional Council, as amended on 7 August 2007. The amendment reduced to five the original quorum of seven members adopted by the first Council on 22 June 1998.

[21] Art. 22 (new) of the Law on the Constitutional Council.

[22] Art. 12 of the Internal Rules on the Proceedings in Front of the Constitutional Council, adopted on 8 July 1998 and amended on 21 May 1999 to change the auxiliary verb from 'shall' to 'may'.

[23] Art. 21 of the Law on the Constitutional Council.

[24] Art. 142 (new) of the Constitution.

[25] In its decision no. 118/006/2011 (14 July 2011) related to its second review of the constitutionality of the revised pre-promulgation Anti-Corruption Law, the Constitutional Council declared it constitutional after citing the consideration that 'there is no new issue that deserves the provision of opinions for a second time'. By implication, one may interpret it as suggesting that emergence of a new relevant issue would justify the second review of a legislative piece.

[26] For example, His Excellency Seng Chum Kosal, an old-time prime minister under the Sihanouk government in the 1960s who stayed in exile until the early 1990s; His Excellency Say Bory, who was a member of parliament from the Liberal Democratic Party in the early 1990s, then the first president of the Bar Association of the Kingdom of Cambodia after its re-establishment in 1995; and His Excellency Son Soubert, who was the son of the founder of the Buddhist Liberal Democratic Party and a parliamentarian from the same party during the mid-1990s. Currently, Prince Norodom Sirivuth, who used to be the minister of foreign affairs in the mid-1990s, from the FUNCINPEC Party, is serving as a member appointed by the King. A brief biography of members on the official website of the Council reflecting membership changes every three years is available at www.ccc.gov.kh/ccc_member_composition_kh.php (accessed 27 April 2018).

senior government officials.[27] Former judges or justices from the Supreme Court or the Appeal Court constituted a minority on the Council.[28]

A rough review of the statistics of cases handled by the Constitutional Council[29] since its establishment in 1998 shows frequent use of the institution by political parties and the legislative institutions. Cases directly or indirectly brought by private organizations and individuals occupied only a small portion of the total. A great majority related to electoral disputes, particularly in 1998, 2003, 2008 and 2013, when national elections for a new legislature, and therefore a new government, took place. Cases involving review of constitutionality of laws included those automatically referred to the Council as required by the Constitution[30] and others brought against laws adopted by the legislative body and promulgated by the King.

The case statistics from 1998 to the first half of 2016 also show a pattern of disputes that went through the Council during different periods. In the years when national elections took place, election-related cases dominated the agenda of the Council. But in 1999, 2004, 2006 and 2014–2015, one to two years immediately following general national elections, there were remarkable increases in the number of constitutionality reviews. Numbers of submissions for constitutional or legal interpretation remain quite low, ranging from one to five cases per annum throughout the eighteen-year history of the Council.[31] Most of the election-related cases were brought by opposition party members who

[27] They include His Excellency Chuor Leang Huot, His Excellency Thor Peng Leath, His Excellency Pin Chhin, His Excellency Ek Sam Ol and the current president, His Excellency Im Chhun Lim. *Ibid.*

[28] Among the current nine members, only one member, a woman, was formerly a judge. Throughout the eighteen-year period, only three former judges have been appointed or elected to serve as members, including Her Excellency Chem Veyrith, just mentioned. *Ibid.*

[29] The statistics are based on information made available by the secretariat on the Council's website and the Council's official bulletins on decisions and notifications from 1998 to 2003 (hereinafter the Bulletin).

[30] Art. 140 states, 'Internal rules of the National Assembly, internal rules of the Senate and other organizational laws shall be sent to the Constitutional Council for review before their promulgation. The Constitutional Council shall decide within thirty days (30) at the latest whether the above laws and internal rules of the National Assembly or the Senate are constitutional.'

[31] The data is based on the Bulletin and the statistics made public on the Council's website as of December 2016. Some inconsistencies have been detected, partly suggesting that case classifications are yet to be better defined and kept consistent throughout the years.

intended to challenge the results of an election pronounced by the NEC or to challenge some particular incidents that had allegedly happened before or during election day in order to raise doubts over the regularity of the electoral process at specific locations. Most of the constitutionality reviews have related to submissions by the chair of the National Assembly to the Constitutional Council, requesting a review of legislation adopted by the National Assembly and approved by the Senate. They were constitutionally mandated submissions related to institutional laws, also called 'organic laws' in the unofficial English translation of the Constitution.[32] These include laws that were intended to pave the way for establishment or reorganization of an institution or internal rules of state organs as a direct result of post-election political negotiations between the winning and losing political parties to conclude a politically acceptable power-sharing formula in order to form a new government. Earlier examples included constitutional review of the internal rules of the Senate established by the constitutional amendment after the elections of 1998 as the result of a new power-sharing formula between the two major political parties of the time, namely the CPP and the FUNCINPEC Party.[33] One of the recent cases was that of the overhaul of the Law on Organization and Functioning of the National Election Committee following prolonged negotiations between the ruling and opposition parties after the general elections in 2013.[34]

Nonetheless, there have also been cases of constitutionality raised by civil society and groups of politicians, requesting the Council to review some laws or legal provisions which they alleged violate fundamental constitutional principles. It is important to note here that, whatever the motives and the results, constitutional cases have so far revealed the vigorous political struggles in Cambodia that have gradually been entrusted to the Constitutional Council instead of resorting to violence.[35]

However, the inconsistencies do not seem significant enough to enable a reversal of the observations made in this paragraph.

32 The Constitution, Art. 140 (new). The unofficial translation supervised by the Constitutional Council is available among the basic texts posted on the Council's website at www.ccc.gov.kh/index_en.php (accessed 27 April 2018).

33 Yan Vandeluxe, 'The senate of the Kingdom of Cambodia', in Hor Peng, Kong Phallack and Jörg Menzel (eds.), *Cambodian Constitutional Law*, (Phnom Penh: Konrad-Adenauer-Stiftung, 2016) 137–156, at 143–144.

34 Decision no. 153/001/2015 CC.D of the Constitutional Council, 24 March 2015. See also Meas Sokchea, 'Trust the NEC, Rainsy says' (2015, April 22), *The Phnom Penh Post*.

35 Unfortunately, incidents of violence also took place quite frequently after some of the elections. However, in most of these incidents, both the winning and the losing parties

So far, parties in these disputes have also shown their willingness to accept the rulings of the Council despite their dissatisfaction. The rulings sometimes seem to have been a facilitating factor in promoting the conclusion of political compromises that would, in all four of the last elections, happen a few months after the litigation.

III Some Theoretical Issues

1 An Election Dispute Settlement Body

The main reason for the establishment of the Council in 1998 was to prepare for the national elections in July of that same year. After the July 1997 fighting between the forces of the two prime ministers, the international support for and internal legitimacy of the coalition government fell to its lowest level since 1993.[36] It was imperative that the new elections be organized freely and fairly, or at least be seen as free and fair. This would have been politically difficult and legally disastrous had the Constitutional Council not been established at that time.[37] As a result of the establishment of the Council, many electoral disputes were handled in public hearings in 1998, 2003, 2008 and 2013.[38] Issues brought to the attention of the Council included protests against decisions of the NEC in registration of political parties competing in the elections,[39] alleged irregularity in voter registration,[40] alleged irregularity

would choose to distance themselves, despite pointing fingers at each other. 'Deadly post-election violence erupts in Phnom Penh', (2013, September 15) *Radio Free Asia*, Khmer Service, available at www.rfa.org/english/news/cambodia/violence-09152013170126.html (accessed 27 April 2018).

[36] Sorpong Peou, 'Cambodia in 1997: Back to square one?' (January 1998) 38 *Asian Survey* 69–74.

[37] For some details of the situation between the two elections in 1993 and 1998, see Jeffrey Gallup, 'Cambodia's electoral system: A window of opportunity for reform', in Aurel Croissant (ed.) *Electoral Politics in Southeast and East Asia* (Singapore: Friedrich-Ebert-Stiftung, 2002) 25–73, at 32–35.

[38] Art. 117 (new) of the Law on General Elections makes it obligatory that the Constitutional Council hold public hearings to decide on appeals against the decisions made or election results pronounced by the NEC. For an example regarding the 2013 election, see Khan Sophirom, 'Constitutional Council to open public hearing on post-election complaints' (2013, August 29) *Agence Kampuchea Press*.

[39] Decision of the Constitutional Council in case no. 1, 13 July 1998. See the Bulletin 1998–1999.

[40] Decision of the Constitutional Council in cases no. 2 and 3, 17 July 1998. See the Bulletin 1998–1999.

at the polling stations,[41] alleged impartiality of the NEC[42] and so on. The mechanism undoubtedly facilitated the opportunity to have doubts and disputes solved by peaceful and legal means before political negotiations and trade-offs finally removed the political deadlocks.[43]

2 *Judicial Functions*

Although the Constitutional Council is not a court and does not fully fall into the category of a judicial institution, it nonetheless exercises a few extremely important parts of the judicial power, both by adjudicating election-related disputes and pronouncing the final word on the question of constitutionality and constitutional interpretation. In the constitutional framework of the separation of powers, it must be conceded that the Council in fact exercises judicial power alongside the courts in resolving disputes and preventing the legislative power from abusing its conceived democratic mandate in legislating regarding constitutional issues. This function was delegated to the Council by the 1993 Constitution. However, the judicial nature of the function does not allow the Council to initiate a review on its own, but only to respond to questions or disputes directly brought to its attention. At least in theory, some petitions submitted to the Council have significant political merit. The abstract *a posteriori* review of a promulgated law is an example, particularly with regard to an organic law, which is constitutionally designated to be subject to constitutionality review by the Constitutional Council before promulgation. If a group of parliamentarians from the opposition party or a certain interest group who have a problem with an organic law that has been promulgated by the King decide to bring their concerns to the attention of the Constitutional Council after the promulgated law has been implemented, the Council will not be able to refuse to conduct the review. The Council may either reconfirm its original ruling on the constitutionality of the said law or decide to reverse its earlier decision

[41] Decision of the Constitutional Council in case no. 8, 26 August 1998. See the Bulletin 1998–1999.

[42] Decision no. 055/006/2003 of the Constitutional Council, 25 August 2003.

[43] For details on the politics of the 1998 elections and its aftermath, see David W. Roberts, *Political Transition in Cambodia – Power, Elitism and Democracy* (Great Britain: Curzon Press 2001) at 181–201. On the aftermath of the 2003 elections, see Tom Fawthrop and Vong Sokheng, 'Coalition deal close to completion' (2004, March 26) *The Phnom Penh Post*, and Luke Hunt and Michael Hayes, 'New government formed after Chea Sim leaves the country' (2004, July 16) *The Phnom Penh Post.*

and rule that the law, or a part thereof, is unconstitutional, based on a new analysis of the details. But even in the case of a reversal, the new ruling will not directly lead to resolution of any dispute but may only result in revision of the said law, as the complaint is not based on any concrete case of litigation. But for the group of parliamentarians or the interest group concerned, this will be a significant political victory for their fight against the potential application of that law or a part thereof. Despite it being a seemingly hypothetical scenario, this may potentially occur at least in one of the following circumstances: (1) emergence of new evidence to show that the law resulted, or as further implemented will result, in an alleged situation of unconstitutionality, as theoretically, this may happen in the aftermath of a constitutional amendment giving rise to a new petition against a previous decision of the Council; (2) changes in social or other contexts, or simply changes in the general perception of the reality underlying the original legislative rationale of the law or part thereof; (3) dramatic changes in the way the opposition or interest groups manage to present their concerns and legal arguments to convince the Council members that the said law or part thereof is, indeed, constitutionally problematic; or (4) radical changes in the Council membership resulting in a significant share of voices against the views held by the parliamentary ruling party or the previous Council members at the time the law was reviewed in its pre-promulgation period.

Another scenario may also happen in case of a concrete review subsequent to the promulgation of a law. Theoretically, it is possible to imagine that a law that was considered constitutionally valid by the previous Constitutional Council ruling at the time of its enactment may be challenged by a party in a legal dispute against its constitutionality when applied in the context of a concrete legal dispute. However, since the court does not have the authority to decide on constitutionality of laws, it has to refer the question to the Constitutional Council. The submission has to go through the Supreme Court. Neither the Constitution nor the Law on the Organization and Functioning of the Constitutional Council clarifies whether this is a symbolic or a substantive process. If it is meant to be substantive, the Supreme Court may then have to decide whether or not this constitutionality question is valid for a referral to the Constitutional Council for review. The Supreme Court will function as a filter, but whether this is only a procedural filter or a substantive one also remains technically unanswered. Should it be purely a procedural filter, the Supreme Court would not have the authority to deny the referral on any substantive ground. If there is any technical procedural mistake in the submission, the request for referral may have to be submitted again by the lower court to the Supreme Court following the corrective instruction by the Supreme Court.

However, should the Supreme Court exercise substantive screening and refuse to forward the question to the Constitutional Council, the Supreme Court would at least have to pass its own judgment or present its own argument that the said law or legal provision does not concern a constitutional question and therefore does not merit a referral to the Constitutional Council for review. This may, in some cases, result in a conflict of competence between the Supreme Court and the Constitutional Council. However, should the Supreme Court choose to stop the referral by arguing that the question is not constitutional but only legal, on which the Supreme Court has the competence to decide, this will help avoid the problem of conflict of jurisdictions but may still put into serious question the independence of the lower courts because of possibly undue interference by the Supreme Court in changing the nature of questions submitted by the lower court to the Constitutional Council. The result may also have very significant impacts on the ruling by the lower court which has yet to settle the dispute relating to the law caught in the constitutionality question. The entrustment of this aspect of judicial function to the Constitutional Council within the current legal framework indeed makes the separation of powers in the Cambodian Constitution theoretically unique and peculiar.

3 *The Independence and Impartiality Elements*

As noted above, at the inception, there were serious debates about the independence, impartiality and competence of the Constitutional Council members against the political background in which the majority of the members were appointed and elected. However, so far, there has not been evidence of political interference in the decision-making of any individual member. Neither has it been made known that there were in the last two decades any controversies in the professional relationship among the members of the Council. If all these observations hold true, the Council may be one of the very few constitutional institutions where members from different political backgrounds and tendencies are able to keep a stable and professional working relationship, notwithstanding the occasional political turmoil and frequently fierce confrontation between the ruling and opposition parties as often witnessed in the National Assembly and, at least during most of the 1990s and early 2000s, in the administration, or sometimes even in some non-constitutional organizations such as non-governmental organizations.[44]

However, these collegial relations may be possibly partly due to the strict rules of confidentiality and collectivity stipulated by the Internal Rules of the Council. The collectivist nature of the Council may technically limit the visibility of the independence of each individual member in dissenting from the majority. This is attributable to the following factors: (1) the apparently restrictive rule to prevent an individual member from speaking or writing in any publication;[45] (2) the non-existence of individual or dissenting opinions in decisions made by the Council; and (3) the lack of public revelation of the pattern of votes at each ruling, which gives a potentially false impression that the rulings have all been based on consensus, inclusive of members appointed and elected by the three constitutional institutions, thus giving the decisions unquestioned legitimacy. It is possible to argue that, not being a judicial institution, the independence of the Council members may have its own definition and standard of independence not necessarily similar to that expected of a judge at the ordinary court. Perhaps that justifies the need in the first place to establish a Constitutional Council to carry out constitutional review separately from the Supreme Court and other lower courts. However, such argument does not seem to do enough justice to the very important constitutional requirement for the Council to be composed of members appointed and elected by three different institutions and against the background of its duty to realize a significant portion of judicial functions in the context of constitutional guarantee for separation of the three powers in a democratic system.

With regard to the question of impartiality, the initial question to ask should be whether the Council members who are working under the current standard of independence tend to vote in favour of the *status quo* or in favour of the challenges. Since the decision is based on majority votes, it is not too difficult to foresee the outcome of the deliberations if one knows the tendencies of all Council members involved in these deliberations and if the information is made public and transparent

[44] Political rift in addition to breakdown of the weak institutionalization process reportedly happened in other governmental and non-governmental institutions. Sorpong Peou, 'Toward democratic consolidation in Cambodia? Problems and prospects', in Mely Caballero-Anthony (ed.), *Political Change, Democratic Transitions and Security in Southeast Asia* (New York: Routledge, 2010), 77–96.

[45] Art. 4 of the Internal Rules of the Constitutional Council adopted on 26 June 1998.

enough for public perusal. But what may be even more relevant is the level of reasoning to be made to support the ruling of the Council as a collective. Any doubt as to impartiality may be best addressed if the reasoning is made with such great detail and logic that even the most sceptical observers will feel it was difficult for the Council to decide otherwise. Unfortunately, as far as the assessment of the selected decisions in this chapter suggest, impartiality of the Council as a whole has yet to be proven in many of the important constitutional controversies. The reasoning has often been short of detail and does not seem to present the issues in their entireties.

Given the fact that the Council is not made up of career judges but may include politicians, albeit not holding any public position at the time of service, and people of potentially strong ideological stances, some level of political tendency in each member's choice of votes should not be excluded. Perhaps this is also theoretically the strength of a constitutional council as opposed to a constitutional court in helping to conciliate conflicting interests involved in a constitutional question. But there has to be an acceptable limit in the use of this strength. Ultimately, impartiality is an important factor in securing the legitimacy of the decisions.

IV Selected Surveys of Cases Brought to the Council

This section will examine some selected sample cases reviewed by the Council over the last eighteen years. The selection will contain cases of electoral disputes and constitutionality reviews, which will further be classified into *a priori* and *a posteriori* reviews and review of administrative actions.

1 Settlement of Electoral Disputes

The Constitution and the Law on Organization and Functioning of the Constitutional Council limit the competence of the Council to addressing only national-level election of members of the National Assembly and Senators. It has no direct role in adjudicating disputes related to results of local elections at the subnational level, except for complaints related to registration of voters and political parties which may be subjected to reviews by the Constitutional Council in any elections. The NEC is the first body to respond to electoral disputes, both at the national and local levels. The Constitutional Council can be seized to look into a complaint that is filed against measures taken, decisions made or election results pronounced by the NEC. As both of them had their debut in 1998 to deal with the first general elections organized exclusively by the Royal Government of Cambodia, they were, in some cases, confused over what their duties were vis-à-vis each other in dealing with a concrete dispute.[46]

The two institutions continued to settle electoral disputes in 2003, 2008 and, most recently, in 2013. There have been no major changes in the organization and functioning of the Constitutional Council except for some procedural revisions to enable a smaller quorum for convening of members and expansion of the secretariat's functions. In 2013, the Constitutional Council received the most number of electoral complaints in its eighteen years of practice.[47] Many of them were complaints against the process of vote counting conducted by the NEC and its local offices. The Council ordered recounting of ballots in some locations but rejected the merits of most of the complaints. The opposition party claimed that there were more cases that deserved a recounting. But the Council insisted that the cases had been properly reviewed and reminded the public that the decisions of the Council bound every individual and institution. Article 36 of the Law on Organization and Functioning of the Constitutional Council makes it a criminal offence not to abide by the decisions of the Council. In one incident, legal critics argued that the spokesman of the Council referred to these penal provisions for the purpose of warning the public about the legal consequence of defiance,

[46] One example was the handling of complaints filed by the FUNCINPEC Party in 1998 against the seat allocation formula under the then election law and the preliminary electoral results in Kampong Thom Province pronounced by the NEC. It was not clear in whose court the ball was and how the review could start when a complaint against the legitimacy of the seat allocation formula suddenly propped up pending the announcement of the election results and whether the NEC defaulted by not promptly issuing a notice of rejection or acceptance of a filed complaint. Samreth Sopha and Chris Fontaine, 'Opposition left in the cold by legal loophole' (1998, September 4) *The Phnom Penh Post*. For more detailed descriptions, see Jeffrey Gallup, 'Cambodia's electoral system' in Aurel Croissant (ed.), note 37 at 41–45.

[47] The total number was reportedly 42, including three filed during the voters registration period, 12 filed during the campaign period, 12 filed on the day of the elections, and 15 filed in protest of the NEC's preliminary announcement of the vote-counting results. The Council ordered recounting of votes in four out of the 15 postal-voting complaints. The four complaints were filed against the polling stations in Kratia, Siem Reap, Battambang and Kandal provinces: speech by Her Excellency Chem Veyrith on the summary contents of the Constitution and the competency of the Constitutional Council, made at the Regional Pedagogic Center in Battambang in 2015, available in Khmer only at www.ccc.gov.kh/whatisccc_en.php (accessed 30 June 2018).

allegedly responding to a statement made earlier by the lawyer of the Cambodian National Rescue Party that there had been sufficient evidence of the NEC falsifying some public documents in favour of the ruling party and that the opposition party would file a complaint against the leaders of the Committee in the Phnom Penh court.[48] However, there has not been any reported case of someone being criminally charged for defiance of the said decisions, although the opposition party and their supporters continued to challenge the official election results pronounced by the NEC for many more months.

The Constitutional Council also found that some disputes had substantive merits as they had resulted from mistakes committed by election officials. In one case, the Constitutional Council ordered the NEC to punish the polling station officers and ballot counting officers at eight polling stations in Svay Chreah commune of Kratie Province due to their mistakes in having left unsealed eight secured packets of cast ballot papers. But the Council rejected the opposition party's demand for a recount.[49] Some electoral monitors representing the civil society and the opposition party criticized this decision for its failure to punish the NEC as the institution ultimately responsible for the conduct of the election. The decision was seen as targeting only the lowest-level officials while not trying to censure those in charge.[50] Critics also argued that an order to further investigate the incident would be more effective in calming down many of the suspicions and allegations.[51] Although its efforts to settle electoral disputes deserved positive appraisal and had assisted in facilitating the final conclusion of political negotiations, the essential role of the Council as an institution to ensure apolitical peaceful resolution of electoral disputes based on law and justice need to be improved in sophistication.

2 *Constitutional Review*

Regarding responses to questions of constitutionality of laws, the Council has sometimes been asked to solve politically sensitive issues. This subsection will be organized into two parts. The first one will look into

[48] Meas Sokchea and Abby Seiff 'Dissent denied: Council', (2013, September 13) *The Phnom Penh Post*.

[49] Meas Sokchea, 'Poll workers to be "lightly" punished' (2013, September 2) *The Phnom Penh Post*.

[50] *Ibid.*

[51] *Ibid.*

the Council's *a priori* examination of adopted laws, whereas the second section will focus on its *a posteriori* review of unconstitutionality allegations.

A Priori Examination of Adopted Legislation

1 The 2003 Case of the Additional Constitutional Law After the 2003 general election of National Assembly members, the opposition parties refused to accept the results pronounced by the NEC and asked for concessions from the CPP. Even though the latter won more than half of the seats in the National Assembly, it could not meet the constitutional requirement of two-thirds majority to form the new government.[52] At the end of a long process of political negotiations, the CPP was able to convince the FUNCINPEC Party, which came out second in the election, into accepting a new coalition formula to allow for inauguration of the new legislature. The bipartisan agreement provided for parliamentary votes in favour of the composition of the cabinet proposed by the CPP in exchange for the support of some parliamentarians from the FUNCINPEC Party to gain the chairmanship in a number of important parliamentary committees.[53] However, to keep the FUNCINPEC Party from refusing to honour its promises, the CPP managed to secure further mutual agreement on a constitutional law called the Additional Constitutional Law to Guarantee the Regular Functioning of the National Institutions, which requires a package voting to combine approval for the formation of the new cabinet with appointment of parliamentary committee chairs.[54] The Additional Constitutional Law also requires all parliamentary members

[52] This constitutional hurdle was later lowered to a simple absolute majority of 50% plus 1 in the 2006 constitutional amendment forged jointly between the Sam Rainsy Party and the CPP. Anthony Tsekpo and Alan Hudson, '*Parliamentary strengthening and the Paris principles – Cambodia case study*' (Working and Discussion Papers, 2009, January 1) Overseas Development Institute at para. 26.

[53] *Annual Report on National Assembly Performance, October 2003–September 2004*, COMFREL Report No. 1.3, Cambodia.

[54] Arts. 3 and 4 of the Additional Constitutional Law make this possible by requiring the parties in the would-be coalition government to collaborate and submit together a single list naming the proposed members of the government and the nominated president and vice presidents of the National Assembly, as well as chairs and vice chairs of the specialized committees of the National Assembly, for vote casting by the first plenary session of the newly elected National Assembly.

to vote by a show of hands in approving or disapproving the package voting.[55] This may theoretically frighten some members from voting in accordance to their preferred choice. The Sam Rainsy Party, that was not part of the deal, argued that the Additional Constitutional Law itself was unconstitutional. A group of twenty-one members of the National Assembly submitted a petition to the Constitutional Council and asked for an unconstitutionality ruling.

In response, the Council issued a decision stating its lack of competence to review this law, on the grounds that neither the 1993 Constitution nor the Law on the Organization and Functioning of the Constitutional Council gave it the mandate to review the constitutionality of an Additional Constitutional Law which had the same status as a constitution. The relevant paragraphs in the reasoning part state as follows:

> Whereas the paragraph 1 of the Article 136 (new) of the Constitution stated that '*the Constitutional Council shall have the duty to safeguard the respect of the Constitution, interpret the Constitution and the laws adopted by the National Assembly and entirely reviewed by the Senate.*' This paragraph does not stipulate the competence of the Constitutional Council in examining the constitutionality of the Additional Constitutional Law;
>
> . . .
>
> Whereas the request of the 21 MPs on 9 August 2004 'for examining the constitutionality of the Additional Constitutional Law . . .' is not within the framework of the Article 136 (new) of the Constitution and does not come under the competence of the Constitutional Council, provided for in the Article 15 of the Law on the Organization and the Functioning of the Constitutional Council;
>
> Whereas the Constitutional Council has examined the constitutionality of many laws, but has never examined the constitutionality of a law having the quality of a constitution such as this Additional Constitutional Law. Furthermore, the Additional Constitutional Law is a supreme law stipulating the objectives of the law containing separate articles, and having a hierarchy equal to that of the 1993 Constitution; therefore, this Additional Constitutional Law is the Constitution of which the constitutionality cannot be examined.

[55] Art. 5 of the Additional Constitutional Law. This Article also requires no debates before and no explanations after the voting of approval or disapproval of the single vote taking.

2 The NGO Law In 2015, the Government proposed a law to regulate the activities of non-governmental organizations in Cambodia. This was in response to the constitutional provision that 'Khmer citizens have the right to create associations and political parties but this right shall be determined by law'.[56] However, the civil society, including national and international groups, considered this a repressive effort of the Government to rein in some outspoken organizations.[57] A group of thirteen National Assembly members from the National Rescue Party submitted the Law before its promulgation to the Council for constitutional review, particularly with regard to its potential infringement on the right of association due to the new red tape created thereby to make formation of associations more burdensome than it had been.[58] The Constitutional Council met with the petitioners to hear about the issue and issued a decision on 12 August 2015 to declare the Law constitutional.[59] Instead of responding specifically to the 30 July petition of the thirteen members of the National Assembly, the Council combined this petition with a 28 July submission by the president of the National Assembly and delivered a single decision on the issue.[60] The reason for the Council to do this seems a bit obscure. Although the petition and the submission were about one single piece of legislation, they were submissions of a very different nature. Perhaps as a result of this combination, the decision of the Council took the form of a general review of the Law chapter by chapter but not a more specific review of issues raised as matters of concern by the unconstitutionality petition. For example, Article 24 of the Law provides that 'domestic non-governmental organisations, foreign non-governmental organisations, or foreign associations shall maintain

[56] Art. 42 of the *Constitution*.

[57] Some key arguments can be found in the open Joint Statement 'ADHOC and LICADHO urge Cambodian Constitutional Council to reject unconstitutional LANGO', available in English at www.licadho-cambodia.org/press/files/390jul302015(eng).pdf (accessed 27 April 2018), and the urgent appeal made by the Worldwide Movement for Human Rights, *Cambodia: Constitutional Council must reject problematic provisions of the Law on Associations and NGO*, published on 28 July 2015, available at www.fidh.org/en/region/asia/cambodia/cambodia-constitutional-council-must-reject-problematic-provisions-of (accessed 27 April 2018).

[58] Hul Reaksmey, 'Lawmakers urge Constitutional Council to amend NGO law' (2015, July 30) *VOA Khmer*; and Hul Reaksmey, 'Constitutional Council, rescue party to meet over draft NGO law' (2015, August 11) *VOA Khmer*.

[59] *Cambodia's Draconian NGO Law Receives Final Approval*, available at http://old.civilrightsdefenders.org/news/cambodias-draconian-ngo-law-receives-final-approval/ 13 August 2015 (accessed 27 April 2018).

[60] Decision no. 156/004/2015 of the Constitutional Council, 12 August 2015.

their neutrality towards political parties in the Kingdom of Cambodia'. These are among the many Articles which the civil society organizations and the United Nations experts argued to be potentially violating the protection of freedom of expression and peaceful assembly in Cambodia under Article 42 of the Constitution and Article 19 of the International Covenant on Civil and Political Rights.[61] However, instead of specifically addressing the detailed concerns surrounding Article 24, the Council only reviewed Chapter Five of the Law, which consists of Articles 20 to 25, in a very general way and considered that no provisions of this Chapter appeared to violate the Constitution. The relevant paragraph of the decision reads as follows:

> Considering that Chapter 5 on Rights, Benefits and Obligations of Associations or Non-Governmental Organisations consists of six articles, from Article 20 to Article 25, stipulating about associations or non-governmental organisations which have been registered or have concluded the MoU shall be subject to the existing general fiscal law and receive various incentives and exemptions in conformity with existing laws and regulations. They shall also bear a number of obligations (*sic*), such as the right to enter into cooperation contracts with partners to implement their projects, and the right to recruit staff or workers to fulfill their tasks. Foreign staff are not entitled to immunities and privileges of diplomats as defined by the Vienna Convention of 1961. Domestic non-governmental organizations, foreign non-governmental organizations or foreign associations shall be neutral towards all political parties in the Kingdom of Cambodia. Domestic associations or non-governmental organizations shall submit annual activities and financial reports to the Ministry of Interior. Foreign non-governmental organizations shall submit summary report of activities and annual financial report to the Ministry of Foreign Affairs and International Cooperation and the Ministry of Economics and Finance. In case it is necessary, the Ministry of Economics and Finance and the National Auditing Agency may monitor and conduct auditing at the associations and non-governmental organizations. There is no provision which is inconsistent with the Constitution.[62]

In the normal practices of the Council, a chapter-by-chapter method of review is adopted for examining in a general way the constitutionality questions raised with regard to a pre-promulgation law. But to examine constitutionality questions related to specific articles, the Council would

[61] *Joint Statement*, note 54; 'A human rights analysis of the Law on Associations and Non-Governmental Organizations' (2015, August 5) prepared by the Office of the United Nations High Commissioner for Human Rights in Cambodia, at 6.

[62] Decision no. 156/004/2015 of the Constitutional Council, 12 August 2015.

often resort to a different method of review focusing specifically on the individual articles raised in the petition. An illustrative example of this targeted review of specific articles is the case of Article 8 of the Law on Aggravating Circumstances for Felonies, to be elaborated in the next section.

A Posteriori Reviews of Unconstitutionality Allegations

There have been relatively few petitions for *a posteriori* review of the unconstitutionality of promulgated legislation. Referrals by the court have never taken place. Most of the cases were brought by members of parliament from the opposition party, the civil society through the National Assembly or the King requesting the Council to conduct abstract review of some laws or specific provisions thereof. Since there were no specific disputes or damages emerging directly in connection with the said legal questions, these were, in fact, reviews in abstract.

One of the most cited cases is the review of the promulgated Law on Aggravating Circumstances for Felonies. This case has been cited as the first official legal pronouncement about the relationship between an international treaty and the national law.[63]

Until the current Criminal Code was promulgated in 2009, Cambodia had applied transitional criminal provisions adopted in 1992 and other subsequent special criminal laws for specific categories of crimes.[64] To facilitate consistent application of aggravating circumstances in considering application of harsher punishments for serious felonies, Cambodia adopted the Law on Aggravating Circumstances for Felonies in 2007. A group of civil society organizations saw the risks that the 2007 Law might impose on juveniles and, thus, negatively affect the legal protection which they were entitled to under the provisions of the Convention on the Rights of the Child. The group sent a petition through the King to the Constitutional Council for a review of this question.[65] In its decision of

[63] Decision no. 092/003/2007, 10 July 2007. See also '*The Declaration of Human Rights in the Cambodian Constitution*', (Cambodia: Office of the United Nations High Commissioner for Human Rights, July 2008) at 37; Daniel Heilmann 'Fundamental rights protection: A comparative and international law perspective', in Hor Peng, Kong Phallack and Jörg Menzel (eds.), *Cambodian Constitutional Law*, (Phnom Penh: Konrad-Adenauer-Stiftung, 2016) 339–356, at 353–355.

[64] Provisions Relating to the Judiciary and Criminal Law and Procedure Applicable in Cambodia During the Transitional Period (10 September 1992), generally referred to as the UNTAC (Criminal) Law.

[65] Legal Aid of Cambodia (LAC), *Progress Report*, Oxfam Novib Project #KAM-505184–0005480 (Project name: Legal Aid of Cambodia – Core Project January

12 February 2007, the Council stated that the Law in question did not violate the Constitution. The decision was based on the consideration that international law, including the Convention on the Right of the Child, to which Cambodia is a party, is one part of the national law to be applied by the judges and that, by implication, the provisions of this 2007 Law do not prohibit judges to do so. The relevant paragraphs stated,

> Considering that Article 8 modifies only article 70 of UNTAC law, it does not affect the rights and interests of children. The provision of Article 8 of the law on the aggravating circumstances above is not unconstitutional.
>
> Considering that at trials, in principle, a judge shall not only rely on Article 8 of the Law on the Aggravating Circumstances to punish an offender, but also relies on law. The term law here refers to the national law including the Constitution, which is the supreme law, and other applicable laws as well as the international laws that the Kingdom of Cambodia has recognized, especially the Convention on the Rights of the Child.

Reviews of Administrative Decisions and Actions

This has been a little-established area of intervention by the Council. It has not been made clear how the Council would deal with allegedly unconstitutional administrative decisions or actions, although Article 19 of the Law on Organization and Operation of the Constitutional Council enables an 'individual engaged in a court proceeding' to bring to the attention of the Council any law or 'decision made by any institution' that he/she considers violates his/her fundamental rights and freedom. There has not been any case of such referral.

In a related context, when a petition was filed by a non-governmental organization in 1999 requesting the Council's intervention in the government's extrajudicial measure to re-arrest a group of inmates who were earlier released on court orders,[66] the Council dismissed the case on the

2007–December 2007; submitted on 31 March 2008), available at http://lac.org.kh/wp-content/uploads/2011/11/LAC-Annual-Report-2007.pdf, at 15–16 (accessed 27 April 2018). It is not clear why the petition was submitted through the King rather than the other individuals or institutions having the legal standing to submit petitions to the council under Art. 141 of the Constitution. However, the King is surely the least politicized institution, as His Majesty only reigns but does not rule and is, therefore, most ready to submit constitutional review petitions to the Council whenever there is a technical need to do so.

66 Sorpong Peou, *International Democracy Assistance for Peace Building: Cambodia and Beyond*, (New York: Palgrave Macmillan, 2007) at 95–96.

grounds that the questions raised by the petitioner were not within the jurisdiction of the Council.[67]

This phenomenon was noticeable due to the indication of a preference by the civil society and the opposition political force at that time to have recourse to the constitutional institution in settling differences with the executive branch. However, the Council did not make enough attempts to elaborate its views more convincingly. Rather, it merely expressed its strong regret that it could not address this case because it did not have the competence to do so. This broadly stated justification did not point to the issue of legal standing, which the petitioner apparently did not have under Article 19 of the Law on Organization and Functioning of the Constitutional Council, and appeared quite ambiguous as to what exactly was the 'competency' that the Council said it did not have in order to address this particular petition.

As the only institution to utter final voice in judging these sensitive and highly controversial constitutional questions, a simple declaration of lack of competence without making necessary analysis and well-reasoned justification did not do enough good to the cause of public trust in the resolve of the Council to uphold the spirit of the Constitution. It was not even clear whether the Council had held any deliberations before it issued the rejection.

V Light and Darkness in the Eighteen Years of Experience

The above reviews of selected cases indicate some initial trends of the Council in exercising its constitutional mandate. The following are some observations over five key issues relevant to the functions of a constitutional council as the superior organ in dealing with constitutional and legal interpretation and adjudications.

1 *Sensitivity to Political Questions*

This was made explicit in the Council's advisory opinion to King Sihanouk in 2003, when the latter asked the Council for opinion on whether the King had the obligation to be present at the inauguration ceremony of the newly elected National Assembly, when the King did not want to preside over the new legislature due to the political controversies about

[67] Letter of the Constitutional Council, no. 019/002/2000, 19 July 2000.

its legitimacy raised by Prince Norodom Ranariddh, who was then the president of the FUNCINPEC Party, which had come out second in the election. The FUNCINPEC and Sam Rainsy parties boycotted the National Assembly on the grounds of alleged electoral irregularities, asking for recounting of votes.[68] In responding to the question raised by the King, the Council started the opinion by stating:

> After having received the above-mentioned message of Your Majesty, the Constitutional Council met on September 22, 2003 and has the honor to bring to the high information of Your Majesty that the Constitutional Council has no competence to interpret the political aspects raised in the letter of Samdech Krom Preah NORODOM RANARIDDH, President of FUNCIPEC Party. But we would like to clarify some legal aspects as follows.[69]

In making this communication to the King, the Council decided that it would not respond to questions related to political aspects of the issue even though they were alleged to be relevant by one of the interveners. Despite the fact that the Constitutional Council was not meant to be a judicial institution but a constitutional institution consisting of experts in a number of specialized fields, namely law, economics, diplomacy and public administration, its position seems to be that it only takes into consideration the narrower legalistic aspect of disputes. It is, however, unfortunate that nowhere did the Council elaborate in more detail where an appropriate line should be drawn between the purely legal aspect as opposed to other peripheral questions in a dispute. It is not clear whether the Council was declaring a preference for adopting a plain text based legal formalism[70] as the appropriate method for constitutional and legal interpretation, or if it was only trying to avoid the political arguments. If a strictly plain text based legal-formalist approach is preferred, what would be the Council's position with regard to other non-political considerations, such as social changes, economic realities or cultural

[68] More details about this case can be found in Taing Ratana, 'Constitutional Council: Election, structure, procedure, and competencies', in Hor Peng, Kong Phallack and Jörg Menzel (eds.), *Cambodian Constitutional Law*, (Phnom Penh: Konrad-Adenauer-Stiftung, 2016) 189–218.

[69] The Constitutional Council's communication to His Majesty King Norodom Sihanouk no. 20/2003 CC.I, 22 September 2003.

[70] Frederick Schauer, 'Formalism: Legal, constitutional, judicial', in Keith E. Whittington, R. Daniel Kelemen and Gregory A. Caldeira (eds.), *The Oxford Handbook of Law and Politics* (Oxford: Oxford University Press, 2008) 428–436.

sensitivities? Should they, too, not be subjected to consideration when conducting constitutional and legal interpretations requested by a petitioner who refers to these circumstantial factors as the basis for a constitutional challenge?

2 *Applicability of International Law in Domestic Courts*

Although the decision of the Council in the case of Article 8 of the Law on Aggravating Circumstances of Felonies did not elaborate in clearer terms how international law is supposed to be applied by the Cambodian courts, which had never had the experience of applying international law, it was epochal for the Council to state at least in principle that international law, particularly human rights law, in this context, forms a part of national law and that judges need to make sure that interpretation and application of national laws should not result in conflict with international law. The Council did not reveal the analytical basis for it to decide this way, but it clearly paved the way for future challenges against any institutional decision which may appear to be in breach of Cambodia's international obligations. However, it is uncertain whether this decision would open up the opportunity for challenging any court judgment which is deemed to have applied the Law on Aggravating Circumstances of Felonies in breach of Cambodia's obligations under the Convention on the Rights of the Child.[71]

3 *An Emerging Constitutional Avoidance Doctrine in Cambodia?*

This may seem to be not quite in line with the plain text based approach to reasoning indicated above, but this position was rather obvious in the case of the Council's interpretation of the Law on Aggravating Circumstances for Felonies. The Council indicated that, in the absence of an explicit provision of the Law to incur violation of the right of the child under international law, Cambodian courts should be presumed to be upholding the law in their legal interpretation and ensuring consistency with Cambodia's international legal obligations. The Council did not try to examine the standard approach, if any, for a Cambodian court to interpret a national law consistently with international law and whether there is any

[71] This should be theoretically possible by arguing that a court decision or judgment is an institutional decision referred to by Article 19 of the Law on Organization and Functioning of the Constitutional Council.

safeguard against intrusive application of the contended law that could keep the courts away from violating Cambodia's international legal obligations. The reasoning also did not give the least analysis of the hierarchical relationship between national law and international law under the Constitution.[72] The decision seemed to suggest the existence of a strong presumption that courts would take a rather liberalist approach to statutory interpretation in favour of respect of international obligations. The Council seemed to believe that there was a common unwritten principle that all courts in Cambodia would surely abide by when interpreting a national law that could have impacts on the country's obligations derived from international law to such an extent that any pre-emptive review of the potential unconstitutionality became unnecessary.

4 *Self-Restraint in Dubious Circumstances?*

The Council seemed to apply the plain text based approach to interpretation one more time when asked to review the constitutionality of the Additional Constitutional Law. It did not bother to consider whether the making of the Additional Constitutional Law was itself constitutional as the Additional Constitutional Law was nowhere mentioned in the 1993 Constitution, nor did it consider how different this Additional Constitutional Law was from the constitutional amendment stipulated in Article 151 (new) of the Constitution.[73] Article 151 (new) allows the National

[72] This is important given the fact that international treaties of any sort were not required to be automatically vetted for their constitutionality at the time of ratification or concession by the legislative branch.

[73] One slight difference might have been the Council's view that the Additional Constitutional Law was not a constitutional amendment, but a separate constitutional law in its own right, as stated in the Q&A compiled by the Secretariat of the Constitutional Council in 2011 (available in Khmer only at www.ccc.gov.kh/khmer/he_speech/Answer%20Question.pdf (accessed 1 December 2016). The Q&A compilation is not a Council decision and not binding for anybody. However, the contents were approved by the president of the Council for public reference. See the preface (19 August 2011) to the Q&A by Chan Rasy, secretary-general of the Constitutional Council.

But this *prima facie* difference may seem more formalistic than real since the Additional Constitutional Law did, in fact, change the mode of voting by members of the parliament and resulted in a substantive change in the way the National Assembly conducts its business in forming a new government after the general elections, albeit it is being applied during special circumstances. See Art. 3 of the Additional Constitutional Law. Moreover, a constituent assembly was not set up to draft and adopt the Additional Constitutional Law, but the ordinary National Assembly did that. This could have given rise to some procedural questions.

Assembly to adopt a constitutional law to amend the Constitution based on a two-thirds' majority vote. But then Article 143 mandates the King to seek the advice of the Constitutional Council on any proposed constitutional amendment. The Council is, therefore, given the mandate to technically review the constitutionality of a proposed ordinary law, if not the 'additional constitutional law' as well. The Council could have chosen to deliberate on the legitimacy – not the contents – of the Additional Constitutional Law, as it might be necessary to find out what is permissible for the legislators to do in conformity with the 1993 Constitution due to the absence of an explicit constitutional provision on this issue. Instead, however, the Council chose to shy away from taking this challenge and declare that the Council was not mandated by the Constitution, nor by the Law on the Organization and Functioning of the Constitutional Council, to review the constitutionality of the Additional Constitutional Law. Politically and strategically, the approach the Council took to shun the constitutional question involving the Additional Constitutional Law seems to be quite obviously the wisest way for the Council to avoid the tension or even a technical headlock with the legislative branch.[74]

5 *Authoritativeness in Different Dimensions*

The Constitutional Council has the constitutional and legal mandate to make authoritative interpretation of the Constitution and laws. Over the years, it has tried to carry out this task as faithfully as possible to the letter of the law by sticking to legal formalism and self-restraint in case of a potential political conflict with the legislative branch. It has gained significant legitimacy from the letters of the law and stability from its cautious pragmatism in making crucial decisions. However, the interpretation has been short and lacking in detailed analysis. The termination of disputes by means of an authoritative decision is very different from attempts to conciliate conflicting trends or views regarding the fundamental legal issues. From a long-term perspective, it may also be necessary to earn popular legitimacy[75] in its work by sharing with the citizens,

[74] Politically, the Additional Constitutional Law was justified as a necessary legislative action to break the post-election deadlock of 2003. This is mentioned in the general Q&A. *Ibid.*

[75] The Constitutional Council seems to have taken popular legitimacy seriously by launching different publicity activities such as initiating public lectures throughout the country, publishing its decisions and notifications on the website and compiling a long list of Q&A's about the mandate, the work and the thoughts of the Council as a public

in a transparent and unhidden manner, the debates and different views that may exist among the members of the Council. Strong popular legitimacy should theoretically be more helpful for the Council in fulfilling its constitutional roles. Popular legitimacy may make up for the allegedly weak 'democratic legitimacy'[76] faced by the Council since its inauguration. It will serve as pressure for politicians to be more willing to compromise in a way relatively more acceptable to the population in general. The absence of dissenting views in the published decision[77] also compromised the role of the Council in facilitating and conciliating important constitutional and legal debates, which are necessary in forming the future of constitutional and legal thought relevant to the legal development of the country.

VI Concluding Remarks

While it is a positive sign for Cambodia to increasingly rely on a professional body to deliver constitutional opinions and to solve constitutionality questions, politicians and a large part of the public are yet to have full trust in the neutrality and professionalism of this body, particularly because of its conception at a time when political stability in Cambodia reached its lowest level as the result of internal fighting between supporters of the two prime ministers, leading to the end of the 1993 co-premiership system. However, the birth defect of the Constitutional Council is not necessarily incurable. Institutionally, there should be unambiguous mandates for the Council to intervene in a broader spectrum of issues involving constitutionality and electoral disputes. Professionally, the Council should pay more attention to the issue of transparency in passing its judgments. Dismissal of complaints or other submissions on the ground of weakly reasoned proclamation of jurisdictional limits can sometimes be frustrating for those who believe that the

document. See the Council website in Khmer, www.ccc.gov.kh/index.php (accessed 27 April 2018).

[76] Victor Ferreres Comella, 'The rise of specialized constitutional courts', in Tom Ginsburg and Rosalind Dixon (eds.) *Comparative Constitutional Law* (Cheltenham, UK: Edward Elgar, 2011) 265–278, at 270–271.

[77] Secrecy of deliberation requires that members of the Council keep deliberations and votes secret. This is reported in a description prepared by the Constitutional Council for the 3rd Congress of the World Conference on Constitutional Justice on the topic of *Constitutional Justice and Social Integration* in Seoul, Republic of Korea, 28 September–1 October 2014, 5.

Council could do much more to resolve constitutional questions. In the post-1993 institutional history of Cambodia, the Council appears to be the only institution to survive two decades of ordeals without serious interruption in collaboration among people of different political and professional trends. This spirit of promoting peaceful settlement of electoral, constitutional and legal disputes in a highly volatile political environment, where political parties are struggling vigorously for political dominance in a yet-to-develop culture of the rule of law, is worthy of appraisal. However, without a broad-based legitimacy recognized by different sectors and stakeholders in society, the Council may also risk losing its relevance in the long process of the legal, social and political development of the country.

11

The Short but Turbulent History of Myanmar's Constitutional Tribunal

ANDREW HARDING

The Constitutional Tribunal of Myanmar (CT) owes its existence to the 2008 Constitution (CM2008, otherwise, 'the Constitution'[1]), which effectively provided the framework for transition from military to civilian, democratic government during 2010–2016. CM2008 was the outcome of a lengthy and controversial process of constitution-making which was almost universally condemned outside of Myanmar, but which has also provided a framework for the transition. It is the first plausibly democratic constitution since that of 1948, which was revoked following the military coup of 1962. CM2008 instituted the CT, an innovation in Myanmar, to provide authoritative interpretations of this new Constitution.[2]

The Constitution was dismissed too readily by international commentators as a self-serving piece of cosmetic reform enacted by the *Tatmadaw* (Myanmar military) to disguise an intention to remain in control of Myanmar's government by maintaining a façade of civilian government.[3] Nine years further down the road to democracy (six since the coming into effect of the Constitution), this view needs radical revision. Few

[1] *Constitution of the Union of Myanmar 2008* (Naypyithaw, Printing and Publishing Enterprise, Ministry of Information).

[2] See CM2008, s.46, set out in full below, for the purposes of the CT.

[3] See, e.g., Yash Ghai, 'The 2008 Myanmar Constitution: Analysis and assessment' (2008): www.burmalibrary.org/docs6/2008_Myanmar_constitution-analysis_and_assessment-Yash_Ghai.pdf (accessed 6 October 2017); David Williams, 'Lessons of experience in the enterprise of constitutional design: Constitutionalism before constitutions: Burma's struggle to build a new order' (2009) 87 *Texas Law Review* 1657; David Williams, 'What's so bad about Burma's 2008 Constitution? A guide for the perplexed', in Melissa Crouch and Tim Lindsey (eds.), *Law, Society and Transition in Myanmar* (Oxford: Hart Publishing, 2014) 117–139; David Williams, 'A second Panglong agreement: Burmese federalism for the twenty-first century', in Andrew Harding (ed.), *Constitutionalism and Legal Change in Myanmar* (Oxford: Hart/Bloomsbury, 2017) 47–70.

would have thought it possible that such a restrictive, partial and rigid constitution[4] could lead to a transition to a National League for Democracy (NLD) government in office by March 2016, as well as many other remarkable changes. It is true that the Constitution contains a number of extraordinary features that render it, for all these unanticipated positive developments, potentially a basis for lack of accountability of the military; for military control over the government and the process of constitutional change; and possibly even, in an extreme case, for a return to the military rule that prevailed from 1962 to 2010.[5] These considerations made the claim that the Constitution was a façade for military rule all too compelling at the time it was brought into force. However, these problems all now seem remote in contemplation compared to the situation in 2011: the *Tatmadaw* did not stand in the way of the NLD taking power, nor of Daw Aung San Suu Kyi becoming the *de facto*, if not *de jure*, head of government in March 2016 despite a provision (the controversial Section 59(f)) apparently making this impossible via disqualifications for presidential office.[6] Nonetheless, the fact remains that Myanmar has an unusually rigid constitution that is, as a result, hardly well adapted to the need for rapid transition to democracy.[7] Many changes currently deemed desirable are confronted with a Constitution no longer facilitating but rather blocking the process of democratic development.

As of this writing, it is difficult to see how the process of constitutional change will proceed, let alone to say what part in this process might be played by the CT; but it is commonplace in comparative constitutionalism that constitutional change can occur other than via formal constitutional amendment, and one principal way this happens is through the

[4] This rigidity has been the basis of standing criticism of CM2008 with regard to many issues, and the provisions on constitutional amendment themselves (ss.436–439) were the object of the greatest number of criticisms during the debates on amending the Constitution in 2013. See, further, Andrew Harding, 'Irresistible forces and immovable objects: Constitutional change in Myanmar', in Andrew Harding (ed.), *Constitutionalism and Legal Change in Myanmar* (Oxford: Hart/Bloomsbury, 2017) 71–82.

[5] Janelle Saffin, 'Seeking constitutional settlement in Myanmar', in Andrew Harding (ed.), *Constitutionalism and Legal Change in Myanmar* (Oxford: Hart/Bloomsbury, 2017) 1–24.

[6] Andrew Harding, 'Editorial note: The debate concerning Section 59(f) of Myanmar's Constitution: A Gordian knot of rule of law, democracy, and the application of problematical constitutional provisions', in Andrew Harding (ed.), *Constitutionalism and Legal Change in Myanmar* (Oxford: Hart/Bloomsbury, 2017) 253–260; see, further, the Law on the State Counsellor 2016, and CM2008, ss. 217–218.

[7] Dominic Nardi, 'Will democracy and constitutionalism mix in Myanmar?' (2012, October 24) I-CONnect Blog, available at www.iconnectblog.com/2012/10/will-democracy-and-constitutionalism-mix-in-myanmar/ (accessed 6 October 2017).

exercise of judicial power in interpreting the constitution. Another way is via political practice, which can also add flesh to the bare bones of legal text. In this sense – and despite a number of difficulties discussed in the course of this chapter and the rough ride the CT has endured over the brief span of its existence – the creation of the CT nonetheless presents the possibility for future constitutional development via constitutional interpretation.[8] Of course, in turn, this raises the issue of what is expected of the CT and how it might proceed with regard to interpretation of Myanmar's problematical constitution.[9]

The story of Myanmar's CT is confined entirely within the last decade (on which this book offers a special focus) and, indeed, is a fairly short narrative, albeit a dramatic one in several respects. The entire CT was compelled to resign after a decision in 2012 to which parliamentarians objected strenuously. This constitutional-review crisis[10] will be discussed in more detail in Section IV. In 2016, following some changes in the law governing the CT (discussed in Section III) and a change in government, the CT was established with new membership.[11] At this juncture, we do not know whether the CT Mark II will make a real difference to constitutionalism in Myanmar, but the potential obviously exists that it could do so decisively over the next few years if a number of uncertainties and variables concerning the institution fall into line to enable this to occur. Alternatively, there are arguments suggesting that the CT may have already withered on the vine; added to this is an argument that constitutional review should be carried out not by the CT but in the Supreme Court, which already exercises prerogative writ jurisdiction over administrative acts and decisions.[12] Currently, no cases have yet been decided

[8] Gabriela Marti, 'The role of the Constitutional Tribunal in Myanmar's reform process' (2015) 10 *Asian Journal of Comparative Law* 153–184.

[9] Dominic Nardi, 'Finding Justice Scalia in Burma: Constitutional interpretation and the impeachment of Myanmar's Constitutional Tribunal'(2014) 23 *Pacific Rim Law and Policy Journal* 660–669.

[10] See further, Nardi, ibid.; Dominic Nardi, 'How the Constitutional Tribunal's jurisprudence sparked a crisis', in Andrew Harding (ed.), *Constitutionalism and Legal Change in Myanmar* (Oxford: Hart/Bloomsbury, 2017) 173–192. For another example of legislature-judiciary conflict arising from the exercise of jurisdiction by a constitutional court, see Ginsburg and Enhbaatar, Chapter 7 in this volume.

[11] 'Membership approved: Parliament approves election commission, Constitutional Tribunal' (2016, March 29) Global New Light of Myanmar.

[12] Melissa Crouch, 'The common law and constitutional writs: Prospects for accountability in Myanmar', in Melissa Crouch and Tim Lindsey (eds.), *Law, Society and Transition in Myanmar* (Oxford: Hart Publishing, 2014) 141–157.

by the CT Mark II. The rigidity of the Constitution makes it inevitable, one supposes, that the CT will continue, at least for the foreseeable future. It may well be that, given the CT's recent history and the fact that the CT Mark II comprises figures acceptable to an NLD parliament and president, there is likely to be some reluctance to challenge executive actions or legislation via the CT. Unlike other similar institutions across Asia, the CT does not have jurisdiction over electoral disputes or political parties, and it, therefore, lacks an inevitable docket of cases.[13]

The case of Myanmar's CT offers us insights on constitutional courts in Asia and beyond for three reasons. One is that it is a case where constitutional review was instituted as part of a rapid transition from military to democratic government. A second is that Myanmar's CT is unusual in exercising, in a common law country,[14] the specialized, centralized, constitutional review that one normally finds in civilian jurisdictions, inspired as they are by the Kelsenian model first established in 1920s Austria. The only other comparable experience is that of South Africa,[15] which has a mixed common law and civil law heritage. A third reason is that Myanmar's CT raises the issue of how to best provide for constitutional review. In this volume, there appear chapters on Japan, China and Vietnam, which also have debates concerning the appropriate body for the exercise of constitutional review.[16] This conundrum seems to be endemic to many of the Asian states discussed in this book. Malaysia is another state (not discussed in this book) where a debate continues on this question.[17]

In this chapter, we will see how and why the CT was established, the issues that have arisen in relation to its establishment, including those arising from the crisis over the CT in 2012, and we will also look at the

[13] See, e.g., Chapter 9 by Simon Butt.

[14] Myanmar is usually classified as common law in the sense that its private law and legal institutions conform broadly to the common law system. It is certainly closer to common law than to civil law. See, further, Tun Shin, 'As Myanmar belongs to the common law legal system family, Myanmar judicial system is deeply rooted with legal maxims, judicial customs and precedents' [short title], (2013, February 10) New Light of Myanmar.

[15] Heinz Klug, 'South Africa's Constitutional Court: Enabling democracy and promoting law in the transition from apartheid', in Andrew Harding and Peter Leyland (eds.), *Constitutional Courts: A Comparative Study* (London, Wildy, Simmonds and Hill, 2009).

[16] See Chapters 12, 13 and 14.

[17] Andrew Harding, 'The constitution and Malaysia's bifurcated legal system' (2017) 1 *Perak Letters* 1.

case law that has emanated from the CT for some guidance as to the crisis and what to expect in the future.

I Origins of the Tribunal

The independence Constitution of 1947 contained provision for constitutional review by the Supreme Court via writ jurisdiction.[18] In practice, during 1948–1962, the Supreme Court exercised careful review of administrative actions using this jurisdiction but did not go so far as to strike down legislation.[19] As we will see, this is in contrast to the CT during 2011–2012. The Supreme Court's writ jurisdiction has survived in CM2008.[20] The 1947 Constitution was effectively revoked following the military coup of 1962,[21] and independent constitutional review did not feature again in Myanmar law until CM2008 came into effect on 31 January 2011, following which the CT was established. During the period 1974–1988, under the 1974 one-party Constitution, constitutional interpretation, so far as it was salient, was reserved to the legislature.[22]

The proposal to create a CT was contained in the statement of 'The Fundamental Principles and Detailed Basic Principles', which were adopted by the National Convention as early as 1993 and created the basis for, and much of the detail in, CM2008. However, although it would not be quite correct to call the CT a constitutional afterthought, it is, significantly, not mentioned in CM2008's Chapter I (Fundamental State Principles, which notably *does* mention every other major institution) but only at the very end of this 101-page document, in Chapter XV (General Provisions).[23] The terms for establishing the CT were finally set at the

[18] Nick Cheesman, 'How an authoritarian regime in Burma used special courts to defeat judicial independence' (2011) 45 *Law and Society Review* 801–830; Nick Cheesman, 'The incongruous return of *habeas corpus* to Myanmar', in Nick Cheesman, Monique Skidmore and Trevor Wilson (eds.), *Ruling Myanmar: From Cyclone Nargis to National Elections* (Singapore: ISEAS/ Yusoff Ishak Institute, 2010) 90–114; Nardi, note 10, at 643–653.

[19] Nardi, *ibid.*, at 645.

[20] CM2008, s.296; Judiciary Law, No 20/2010. See, further, Crouch, note 13.

[21] Nang Mo Kham Hom, '"Revolutionary legality": The coup d'état of 1962 and the Burmese military regime' (2000) 4 *Southern Cross University Law Review* 60–106.

[22] 1974 Constitution, ss. 200–201. This is, of course, typical of socialist constitutional systems; see, e.g., Chapter 14 by Ngoc Son Bui.

[23] The functions allocated to the CT at para. 20 are reflected in CM2008, ss. 320–336: see Section II.

Convention's meeting on 2 August 2007. The CT was duly established on 31 March 2011 under Section 46 of the Constitution.

Section 46 reads:

> A Constitutional Tribunal shall be set up to interpret the provisions of the Constitution, to scrutinize whether or not laws enacted by the *Pyidaungsu Hluttaw* [Union Parliament], the Region Hluttaws and the State Hluttaws [Region and state assemblies] and functions of executive authorities of *Pyidaungsu*, Regions, States and Self-Administered Areas are in conformity with the Constitution, to decide on disputes relating to the Constitution between Pyidaungsu and Regions, between *Pyidaungsu* and States, among Regions, among States, and between Regions or States and Self-Administered Areas and among Self-Administered Areas themselves, and to perform other duties prescribed in this Constitution.

The Constitution Drafting Committee inserted into CM2008, at Sections 320–336, the terms agreed on in 2007.[24] Dominic Nardi, in his study of the debates, points out that delegates to the National Convention appeared to justify the CT's creation on the basis of its role in resolving inter-elite disagreements rather than in limiting government as such or protecting human rights.[25] This is supported by the terms of Section 46 itself. Nothing is said explicitly there about the CT as an enforcer or protector of constitutional law or principle, nor of the imposition of limits on the executive, nor of the protection of human rights.[26] Of course, it may be argued that such objectives are implicit, but their absence may present an obstacle in the future in that decisions pursuing such objects might appear to be ambitious or activist in nature.

However that may be, one representative to the National Convention in 2006 described the CT as 'a must for perpetual existence of the constitution and in discharging responsibilities in accordance with the constitution'.[27] It is far from obvious, however, that the CT is a 'must' in this sense. Given the history and nature of the common law system in Myanmar and the fact that the CT members, like ordinary judges, must

[24] Nardi, note 11, at 174ff.

[25] Ibid., at 184.

[26] Catherine Renshaw, 'Human rights under the new regime', in Andrew Harding (ed.), *Constitutionalism and Legal Change in Myanmar* (Oxford: Hart/Bloomsbury, 2017) 215–234.

[27] 'Proposal on "general provisions" to be included in the Constitution', a proposal of the Delegate Group of Workers, presented to the Constitutional Convention, 28 December 2006, reported at *New Light of Myanmar*, Yangon, 1 January 2007.

be legally qualified,[28] one might plausibly ask, as indeed some are doing, why the Supreme Court could not adequately carry out the function of constitutional review instead of the CT, much as it had exercised writ jurisdiction in the past (and presumably will in the future, too).[29] Indeed, it is the position of the NLD itself that the power of constitutional review should be returned to the Supreme Court that exercised it (at least in theory) before the coup of 1962.[30] One learned writer on this issue from Myanmar considers the CT to be the best locus for constitutional review, subject to some changes designed to bolster its independence.[31] Perhaps the constitution-makers did feel that a strong enforcer, independent of *all three* branches, was required. Yet, the language of the Constitution is ambiguous on the issue of judicial independence.[32] Or perhaps the military simply wanted to ensure that its vested rights and interests would not be easily overturned by a parliamentary majority. An even more likely motive is that of avoiding serious splits amongst elites as powers became divided in various ways with the implementation of the Constitution. What is clear is that understanding of the CT and its constitutional role was and still is lacking, as there was no wide debate about it during or after the National Convention, and it was not thought to be of great significance even before the crisis occurred in 2012.

The reference to civil law countries is odd in that Myanmar is the only common law country apart from South Africa (which has a hybrid system) to have specialized constitutional review. The formation of the CT is stated on its website to be 'in accord with the principle of the Supremacy of the Constitution adopted in *civil law countries*'.[33] From the discussions of the CT's role, it seems that the transplanting of this essentially civil law institution into a common law framework and a

[28] This is not a given; in Thailand (see Chapter 8), it has been normal to include political or social scientists on the Constitutional Court's bench.

[29] Crouch, note 13.

[30] Dominic Nardi, 'Is constitutional review moving to a new home in Myanmar?' (2014, June 11) I-CONnect Blog, available at www.iconnectblog.com/2014/06/is-constitutional-review-moving-to-a-new-home-in-myanmar/ (accessed 6 October 2017). One practical argument here might be that, given the paucity of cases coming before the CT (the reasons for which are discussed later), would the spare capacity of such highly qualified individuals not be better used in deciding ordinary civil or criminal cases?

[31] Khin Khin Oo, 'Judicial power and the Constitutional Tribunal: Some suggestions for better legislation relating to the tribunal and its role', in Andrew Harding (ed.), *Constitutionalism and Legal Change in Myanmar* (Oxford: Hart/Bloomsbury, 2017) 193–214.

[32] CM2008, ss.11, 18.

[33] Emphasis added.

constitutional history owing much to the Westminster model, or at least Anglo-Indian ideas about government, is a potential legal irritant, in Teubner's sense.[34] The adoption of this mechanism for constitutional review is, at the least, far from being an obvious step. We will see that in 2012, the CT was shown to be an actual rather than merely potential irritant. The debate as to the proper locus (but not the salience as such) of constitutional review continues, but major change in the near future is, in effect, prohibited by the rigidity of Myanmar's Constitution. Interestingly enough, given the paucity of cases before the CT, it could be that this 'irritant' has provoked disdain rather than outright rejection.[35]

II Powers and Their Invocation

According to the Constitution, the CT has, as we have seen, general powers of interpretation of the Constitution, scrutiny of laws and resolution of disputes between state organs.[36] However, the ability to invoke these powers is given only to a court of law;[37] the president; the speakers of the *Pyidaungsu Hluttaw*, the *Pyithu Hluttaw* and the *Amyotha Hluttaw* (the National Assembly and its lower house and upper house, respectively); the chief justice; the chairman of the Union Election Commission; a region or state chief minister; a speaker of a region or state Hluttaw; a chairman of the leading body of a self-administered area; and at a group of at least 10 per cent of the members of the *Pyithu Hluttaw* or the *Amyotha Hluttaw*.[38] Under this dispensation, neither an individual citizen nor a civil society organization, nor even a sole member of Parliament, would be able to bring a case before the CT. It is hardly surprising, then, that the civil society and the citizenry generally did not react to the 2012 crisis in such a way as to defend the CT, an institution

[34] Teubner describes legal transplants as irritants that ultimately create change as laws and institutions adjust to the presence of the newcomer. This may well accurately describe the trajectory of the CT in Myanmar: Gunther Teubner, 'Legal irritants: Good faith in British law or how unifying law ends up in new divergences' (1998) 61 *Modern Law Review*, 11–32.

[35] One interesting 'dog that didn't bark' is that the USDP's (military party) constitutional objections in Parliament to the law creating the state counsellor in 2016 (discussed earlier) have not been brought to the CT, even though there are presumably some telling arguments that could be made against this law; see, however, CM2008, s. 217.

[36] CM 2008, ss. 46, 322.

[37] CM2008, s. 323, apparently not used as yet.

[38] CM2008, ss. 325–326.

in which they were able to play no direct role and whose purpose was essentially unclear. The literature on constitutional courts tends to emphasize the need for these bodies to project an image to the public and to have widespread support for their function.[39]

Highly relevant is the fact that the CT's jurisdiction, although potentially broad, does not cover electoral disputes, on which the Union Election Commission has the final say.[40] In some Asian jurisdictions, it may be seen that electoral jurisdiction is very prominent (see especially the chapters on Taiwan, South Korea and, especially, Indonesia) and has tended to cement the role of constitutional courts. The adoption of *ex ante* jurisdiction, in which laws can be scrutinized before they are passed (a feature of many constitutional courts), was also suggested by the Speaker of the *Amothya Hluttaw* in 2011, but this was defeated.[41]

III Appointment of the Constitutional Tribunal

The 2011 Law on the Constitutional Tribunal came into effect on the same day as the Constitution, and rules under this law were passed by the CT itself.[42]

Under the Constitution, the CT is composed of nine members, including a chairperson, who hold office for five years. Three members are chosen by the president and three each by the speaker of each house of Parliament; these are subject to confirmation by the whole parliament.[43] This system replicates, but only in part, the one adopted in South Korea (see Chapter 6) and Indonesia (see Chapter 9). In those cases, too, three bodies each nominate a third of the judges, but the bodies reflect the separation of powers between the legislature, the executive and the judiciary; in Myanmar's case, the judiciary does not have this power (contrast Thailand, where the judiciary plays a very important part in the process of selection, but the selection is given to an independent

[39] Tom Ginsburg, *Judicial Review in New Democracies: Constitutional Courts in Asian Cases* (Cambridge: Cambridge University Press, 2003); Theunis Roux and Fritz Siregar, 'Trajectories of curial power: The rise, fall and partial rehabilitation of the Indonesian Constitutional Court' (2015) 2015-30 *UNSW Research Paper*. https://papers.ssrn.com/sol3/papers.cfm?abstract_id=2605664 (accessed 6 October 2017).

[40] CM2008, s.402.

[41] Nardi, note 11, at 185.

[42] CTU Rules Notification No 30/2011, 28 June 2011.

[43] CM2008, s.321, 327.

commission: see Chapter 8). The Myanmar system is notable in this comparison not only for not enabling the ordinary courts to embark on constitutional review, but also for not enabling them to partake of the process of appointments. This, in turn, betokens a signal lack of trust in the ordinary judiciary to fulfil a role of real constitutional significance.

Those nominated must be at least fifty years of age and must have a legal background (that is, have served five years as a judge, ten years as a judicial officer, twenty years as an advocate or otherwise be an 'eminent jurist, in the opinion of the President'). They must also be loyal to the union and have a 'political, administrative, economic and security outlook'.[44] It is not clear what this latter requirement means. Clearly, it does not require career experience of all four varieties listed, as nobody would be able to fulfil such a requirement. As Nardi points out,[45] most previous and current members of the Tribunal had no military experience.

Regarding the 2016 appointments,[46] two nominations were contested by military MPs, who appeared to challenge the legal credentials of the two nominees. The issue is instructive concerning the process of appointment. One nominee, in particular, was controversial. Daw Khin Htay Kywe was the only female nominee and the only nominee from the NLD (in fact, a party executive committee member), having a record as a human rights lawyer and as Daw Aung San Suu Kyi's own lawyer. Military MPs argued that the papers filed with Parliament did not show her as having sufficient legal expertise. Parliament voted not to discuss the matter, the speaker arguing that the onus was on those opposed to the appointments to bring evidence rather than simply relying on a request for more information, and both nominees were appointed.[47]

[44] CM2008, s.333.

[45] Nardi, note 11, at 175.

[46] The presidential order for the appointment of the new CT appears at www.president-office.gov.mm/en/?q=briefing-room/orders/2016/03/31/id-6172; for information on the new members, see www.elevenmyanmar.com/politics/constitutional-tribunal-nominated (both accessed 6 October 2017).

[47] The Speaker relied on CM2008, s.328, which places the burden of proof on those who object to a nomination. The controversies were related to the qualifications of two nominees: Daw Khin Htay Kywe and U Twar Kyin Paung. See Swan Ye Htut, 'NLD silences military concerns on Tribunal', (2016, March 29) *MyanmarTimes*, at www.mmtimes.com/national-news/nay-pyi-taw/19684-nld-silences-military-concerns-on-tribunal.html; 'Aung San Suu Kyi Preps NLD lawmakers for handover of power in Myanmar', (2016, March 28) Radio Free Asia, at www.rfa.org/english/news/myanmar/aung-san-suu-kyi-preps-nld-lawmakers-for-handover-of-power-in-myanmar-03282016163123.html; and 'Arakan MPs oppose Tribunal appointment', (2016, October 20) Eleven Myanmar, at www.elevenmyanmar.com/politics/6272 (all websites accessed 6 October 2017).

The appointments of these two nominees were, nonetheless, challenged in the CT in a case to secure an interpretation of the relevant provision, but in January 2017, the CT ruled that it had no jurisdiction to rule on this matter as it was within the purview of the legislature.[48] The CT, as reconstituted in 2016, is therefore likely to consider as its first case the qualifications of two of its own members. Given Parliament's role in the appointment process, it is hard to see why MPs should not be allowed to raise questions concerning nominees or even the information that has been adduced concerning their qualifications. In the instant case, there might well also have been an argument, if the matter had been debated, that the nominee might show bias towards NLD legislation or executive actions. That debate might well also have been instructive. Despite the constitutional provision giving the legislature the power of approval of nominees, the membership of the legislature has not in the event been involved to any great extent in the nomination process, as we can see from the process for the most recent appointments.

CT members are appointed after each presidential election, and their terms are coterminous with that of Parliament.[49] This means not only that their terms are very short by international standards, but also that their jurisdiction is only ever exercised in relation to one parliament. This position is counter-intuitive: surely, the CT would be strengthened if its terms overlapped those of parliaments and presidents, creating a firmer impression of impartiality?

Under a 2013 statutory amendment to the 2011 Law on the Constitutional Tribunal, the CT members are required to report to the person or body nominating them.[50] This provision is likely to be unconstitutional, as it tends to interfere with the independence of the CT.[51] It also, oddly, rather implies that the members should be guided by the interests or expectations of their nominators rather than their view of the legal arguments presented to them. Neither of these issues is reassuring with regards to maintaining the CT's independence from the legislature and the executive.

[48] Htet Naing Zaw, 'Constitutional Tribunal members remain despite USDP objections' (2017, January 20) The Irrawaddy, at www.irrawaddy.com/news/burma/constitutional-tribunal-members-remain-despite-usdp-objections.html (accessed 6 October 2017 2017); see also 'Arakan MPs oppose Tribunal appointment', note 47. A full report of the CT case was not available at the time of writing.

[49] CM2008, s.335.

[50] Law Amending the Constitutional Tribunal Law 2013, s.12.

[51] Khin Khin Oo, note 31, at 206.

More generally, on the appointment process, it has been argued that the requirement that nominees should be at least fifty years old closes off some potentially excellent appointees as well as being inconsistent with other offices under the Constitution.[52]

IV The Crisis of 2012

We now turn to the critical juncture, the crisis of 2012.[53]

The CT began well enough with a decision defending judicial independence.[54] In *Chief Justice* v. *Ministry of Home Affairs*, it struck down an attempt by the ministry to enable sub-township officials to deal with criminal cases. This was held to be a breach of the principle of judicial independence.[55] In fact, the Constitution, at Section 11(a), requires the separation of powers 'to the extent possible' and for the powers to 'exert reciprocal checks and balances among themselves'. This provision is worryingly vague, but in adopting a restrictive view of the latter phrase and a broad view of the guarantee of judicial independence, the CT has effectively imposed a requirement that the government show why failing to adopt a particular limitation on judicial independence is impossible. This sets a high bar for future attempts to interfere with judicial power.

In the second case, *Dr Aye Maung* v. *Myanmar*, the CT struck down statutory provisions concerning ministerial emoluments, holding that ministers for 'national races affairs' [sic] were ministers within the meaning of the Constitution and could not be discriminated against in terms of their salaries. What is most interesting about this case is that the

[52] Ibid., at 203.

[53] For extensive comment on this crisis, see the literature cited notes 10 and 11; see also Dominic Nardi, 'Why did it happen?' (2012, September 7) Rule By Hukum Blog, at rulebyhukum.blogspot.ch/2012/09/why-did-it-happen-myanmarburma.html); Dominic Nardi, 'The Constitutional Tribunal strikes back' (2012, September 5) Rule by Hukum Blog, at rulebyhukum.blogspot.ch/2012/09/the-constitutional-tribunal-strikes.html); Dominic Nardi, 'After impeachment, a balancing act', (2012, October 1) *MyanmarTimes*, at www.mmtimes.com/index.php/opinion/2013-after-impeachment-a-balancing-act.html (all websites accessed 6 October 2017).

[54] For judicial independence more generally, see Myint Zan, 'Judicial independence in Burma: No march backwards towards the past' (2000) 1 *Asia-Pacific Law and Policy Journal*, 1; Myint Zan, 'Judicial independence in Burma: Constitutional history, actual practice and future prospects' 4 *Southern Cross University Law Review*, 17; John Southalan, 'Impunity and judicial independence' (2004) 17 *Legal Issues on Burma Journal*, 40; Nick Cheesman, note 18.

[55] For the reasoning in this and the other pre-impeachment cases, and detailed anlaysis and comment, see Nardi, note 11.

president petitioned the CT to reconsider its decision: not surprisingly, the CT ruled that its decision was final under the Constitution.[56]

However, in its decision in March 2012 in *President* v. *Pyidaungsu Hluttaw*, the CT decided that parliamentary committees were not 'union-level' institutions. This had the effect of reducing Parliament's capacity to call the executive to account by, for example, issuing subpoenas to ministers. This proved highly controversial, in this case, and highly damaging for the prospects of constitutional review.[57] As a matter of strict interpretation, the CT did appear to be correct in drawing a distinction between parliamentary committees, which are provided for by the Constitution, and union-level organizations such as Parliament itself, but the effect of the interpretation was to deprive these committees of oversight powers, which was not helpful in terms of the separation of powers. In terms of interpretive technique, the case also raised the question of what should be taken into account when interpreting the Constitution.

Whereas the earlier decisions had been accepted – albeit with the grumbled dissent that tends to accompany such rulings everywhere – Parliamentarians were enraged by this last decision, despite what might well be seen as a plausible if rather wooden interpretation of the Constitution. In August and September 2012, the crisis played out. More than two-thirds of the members of the lower house voted for an initial motion to impeach the CT members. A similar majority of the upper house signed a petition to impeach the CT members.[58] The lower house formed an investigatory body in order to investigate charges of unconstitutional action.[59] It was, therefore, inevitable that the final outcome would be a vote in favour of impeachment. Accordingly, all nine CT members 'voluntarily' resigned. Interestingly enough, the military members voted against impeachment, but the military-supporting USDP, President Thein Sein's own party, voted in favour of impeachment, as did the NLD and Aung San Suu Kyi. The president himself, however, was against impeachment.

[56] Khin Khin Oo, note 31, at 219 describes this as Myanmar's '*Marbury* v. *Madison* moment'.

[57] It decided one other case, *Mon State* v. *Myanmar* (for which see Nardi, note 11, at 180) which supports the notion that the pre-existing legislation CM2008 remains in force until repealed; this places a considerable restriction on the CT's jurisdiction.

[58] Fifty-three out of 224 members of the *Amyotha Hluttaw* voted against impeachment. See Nardi, 'Will democracy and constitutionalism mix in Myanmar', note 3, at 2.

[59] CM2008, s.334.

The constitutional provisions of relevance to this episode are contained in CM2008, Section 334, which allows the president or a quarter of MPs of either house to initiate proceedings against a member of the CT on grounds of 'high treason', 'breach of the Constitution', 'misconduct', or 'inefficient discharge of duties'. In this case, the charges were breach of the Constitution and inefficient discharge of duties. Presumably, the former charge is not to be read as equivalent to 'adopted an improper interpretation of the Constitution', as that would make the CT's interpretation equivalent to anyone else's, whereas the Constitution is quite clear at Section 324 (as is the case law referred to earlier) that the CT's interpretation is final and conclusive. 'Inefficient discharge of duties' implies institutional dysfunction (for example, a failure to decide), of which there does not appear to be any evidence. The basis for the impeachment remains somewhat incoherent legally, as it is unclear in what way the CT members were supposed to have breached the Constitution or been inefficient.[60] Essentially, the report issued by Parliament merely stated that the CT was in error, indicating its disagreement with the CT rather than a violation, as such, of constitutional norms or procedures. Arguably, therefore, if anyone breached the Constitution in this episode, it was actually Parliament rather than the CT. The real issue appears not to be the merits of this decision (or the CT's decisions generally) from a technical viewpoint: the CT adopted a perfectly reasonable and plausible interpretation of the Constitution's text, employing some convincing arguments in reaching its decision.[61] Indeed, the CT had also, as we have seen, decided cases against the president: it can scarcely be argued on the case law that the CT had shown favour to the military or to a president who, as a former general, hailed from that same quarter. Rather, the issue appears to be that the first tranche of members appointed to the CT had been, in effect, selected by the military, which was still dominant in 2011. This adds evidence in support of the notion that the real purpose of creating the CT was for it to act as a brake on the independence of Parliament. That appears to be how it was seen by MPs, who viewed the CT as undemocratic. Seen in these broader terms, the impeachment becomes a scene of battle not between Parliament and the CT, but between the military and Parliament. One commentator sees the impeachment crisis in the following light:

[60] See s.334 a ii and iv.
[61] See, further, Nardi, note 11.

> it seems that the impeachment proceedings against the Tribunal members were seen to be a solution for a more profound problem – namely, the perceived lack of legitimacy of the members of the Constitutional Tribunal, which may suggest that the impeachment was viewed as a singular, cathartic remedy.[62]

Thus, the impact of the crisis on the separation of powers under CM2008 was, in fact, more nuanced than might appear from the foregoing. On one hand, Parliament, as part of a trend,[63] established its independence of the other branches, standing against the president on this matter as well as against the CT. On the other hand, the impeachment did not promise a bright future for judicial independence, given that the CT's purposes include (or should be seen as including) acting as a check on the legislature as well as on the executive. For all that, the parliamentarians voting for impeachment did not impugn the *concept* of constitutional jurisdiction as such: it was not suggested that the CT be abolished, and judicial independence as such appears to be supported by the current NLD leadership. Rather, they were opposed to the membership of the CT. Of course, as stated above, given the rigidity of the Constitution, it would, in fact, have availed them nothing to demand abolition of the CT itself. In any event, the CT has, as we have seen, survived this challenge to its authority and has been reconstituted. The fate of CT Mark I suggests that a bold approach by the CT towards the exercise of its jurisdiction is likely to create an adverse reaction. On the other hand, one might ask, would a low-profile response be more likely to result in retention of the CT and its fulfillment of an important purpose?

Constitutional courts are faced with a dilemma at the outset of their work. Should they act strongly to lay down clear lines and clearly mark out their place in the polity? Or should they proceed carefully to avoid creating enemies in a fluid situation? These questions assume (although much of the literature appears to consider it irrelevant) that a reasonable understanding of the law gives them such options in the first place; the issue is, after all, one of correct and consistent interpretation, not minute calculation of political advantage, which surely would undermine the notion of judicial independence, not to mention the rule of law. Yet even

62 Marti, note 8.

63 Michael Lidauer and Gilles Saphy, 'Elections and the reform agenda', in Melissa Crouch and Tim Lindsey (eds.), *Law, Society and Transition in Myanmar* (Oxford: Hart Publishing, 2014) 201–224, at 214–215.

where the law is very clear, there are, nonetheless, when it comes to remedies, options that can be strategically deployed.[64] In the case of *Mon State* v. *Myanmar*, for example, the CT employed some flexibility in prescribing a process for dealing with unconstitutional laws.[65] In the case of Myanmar, it seems as though CT Mark I had adopted the first position indicated above in using its jurisdiction actively and, indeed, also impartially. However, debate and understanding concerning the CT, unlike in Indonesia and South Africa, for example, had been thin on the ground. The National Convention was lacking in transparency, and the relatively marginal attention given to the CT during the drafting process ensured that its position was not generally seen as critically important. When the crisis erupted, the CT had decided only three cases and was short of defenders or admirers, and in the end, appeared to give up its position rather meekly.

What is critical to understanding both the CT's situation and its potential is the type of reasoning they have adopted. Interpretation lies on a scale on which, to different extents, material apart from the text itself may be employed to decide the case. In the chief justice case, the CT intelligently construed the Constitution as embracing judicial independence, adopting a narrow interpretation of permissible restrictions thereon and denying the relevance of previous judicial practice. Here, one can see the Constitution being endowed with a capacity for conceptual growth beyond the actual text. In the parliamentary committees' case, careful textual analysis would probably (although this is clearly arguable) produce a result along the lines of the CT's actual decision. A more imaginative decision might have seen the necessity of a broad construction of the Constitution to allow these committees to exercise legislative oversight. At the same time, this 'living tree' approach, if applied consistently, might have ultimately led to the very type of concern that exercised MPs – namely that the CT was erecting itself as a power over Parliament and, thereby, disabling Parliament's power to supervise the government in a democratic manner.[66]

[64] Nardi, note 11, at 678ff.

[65] For discussion of this case, decided in 2012, but after the impeachment process began, see Nardi, note 9, at 667ff.

[66] I remain uncertain whether the usual dichotomy between the 'originalism' and 'living tree' approaches is really applicable in Myanmar, where the Constitution is both recent and enjoys limited legitimacy; see, however, Nardi, note 9, at 635ff.

One further case requires mention, decided in early 2015, after the CT was reconstituted. In what is known as the White Card case, the CT struck down a law allowing those holding white cards (that is, non-citizens who nonetheless have a right to remain in Myanmar) to vote in a referendum.[67] This had the effect of depriving 750,000 people of the vote, these being mainly Rohingya or Muslims living in Rakhine state. This decision was politically popular (it was, in any case, anticipated by the president cancelling white card status prospectively) despite ostensibly limiting Parliament's power.

V Issues and Changes Regarding the Framework of the Constitutional Tribunal

Given the rigidity of the Constitution, the law concerning the CT is changeable by Parliament only to a certain extent. In 2013, the Constitutional Tribunal Law 2010 was amended to increase the role of the legislature in appointing CT members and to secure their greater accountability. The law now (as was mentioned earlier) requires the CT members to report to the body/person nominating them (the president or the speaker of one of the two houses of Parliament), and the legislature rather than the president now selects the chairperson of the CT. Very arguably, these provisions are both unconstitutional,[68] but the CT has not had an opportunity to consider them. In the case of the selection of the CT's chair, the constitutional provision is less than clear.[69] An attempt in 2014 to amend the law to enable the president to select the chair 'in whatever way he thinks fit' was rejected by Parliament. As it stands, the law on the CT requires that one of the nine nominees be assigned as the chairperson, nominated by the president in consultation with the speakers of the two houses of Parliament. The point is that this rather vague provision might be used to overturn the president's nomination of the CT's chairperson in a future instance, increasing the possibility of political interference.

[67] Wendy Zeldin, 'Burma: Temporary citizens will be allowed to vote in constitutional referendum' (2015, February 6) *Global Legal Monitor*, at www.loc.gov/law/foreign-news/article/burma-temporary-citizens-will-be-allowed-to-vote-in-constitutional-referendum/ (accessed 6 October 2017).

[68] Khin Khin Oo, note 31, at 200ff.

[69] CM2008, s.321.

VI Analysis of the Myanmar Case

Looking at the CT in light of general ideas about constitutional review, one would expect that there would be a military interest in creating and retaining the CT as insurance against constitutional change.[70] That would assume a secured role for the CT as a conservative force, blocking implicit or gradual change short of constitutional amendment. If so, one would wonder why the CT members were given relatively short terms of office (five years), which could be ended relatively easily (as was proved) by an impeachment process in Parliament. On the other hand, parliamentarians, rightly or wrongly, viewed the CT as a hostile force serving the military, or at least advanced this image of the CT to support their case, and the military members voted consistently against impeachment.[71] This theory must, however, deal with the fact that it implies a conservative or 'originalist' mode of constitutional interpretation, whereas it is far from clear from the decisions that such mode was, in fact, adopted by the CT. Indeed, the cases tend to support the notion that the CT was trying to put flesh on the bone of the Constitution, or – to change the metaphor – view the Constitution as a living tree. The case that led to the crisis could be viewed analytically either way: as a decision enforcing the separation of powers, or as one tied to the Constitution's text. There is really not enough evidence, nor is there enough reasoning in the decisions, to decide this either way, but the political reality is that it was simply viewed by the legislature as a hostile act.

There is a point of view advanced by well-known scholars working on constitutional transition that in its early years, a constitutional court should tread carefully, eschewing activism.[72] The Myanmar case would appear, as we have seen, to support this position. The alternative view is that a constitutional court needs to make an early and assertive mark. The latter position may be true only where there is both a constitution enjoying legitimacy and a clear expectation that constitutional review will enforce it with rigour. Both of these conditions, I suggest, are missing in Myanmar's case.

70 For this type of analysis, see Ginsburg, note 18.

71 Nardi, note 13, at 669ff.

72 Nuno Garoupa and Tom Ginsburg, 'Building reputation in constitutional courts: Political and judicial audiences' (2011) 28 *Arizona Journal of International and Comparative Law* 539–568; Ran Hirschl, 'The political origins of judicial empowerment through constitutionalisation: Lessons from four constitutional revolutions' (2000) 25 *Law and Social Inquiry* 91–149.

We are left with a double conundrum. Is constitutional review essentially dead or capable of being successfully revived (as occurred in Taiwan and South Korea: see Chapters 5 and 6, respectively)? In either case, is it to be, and should it be, vested in the CT or the Supreme Court? The answer to these questions depends, first, on whether the limited range of potential litigants is willing to bring cases; this depends on whether the CT's decisions may be regarded as legitimate and enforceable. Secondly, it depends on how, if it gets opportunities, the CT handles the cases. In view of the 2012 crisis, the outcome probably depends not on the technical quality of the decisions but on what we might call the politics of the separation of powers. Given the support of Parliament for the current membership of the CT, these considerations meld into the question whether the CT will be supported on all sides as an institution. There is no shortage of constitutional controversy capable of being resolved through the CT. Parliamentarians argued before, but will not be able to argue again, that the membership of the CT is objectionable; after all, it was they who, in essence, chose the members. Accordingly, they will have to accept its decisions. The matter thus rests with Myanmar political society: will the CT be put to use, or will it become, to use Bagehot's terms, a dignified (perhaps not very dignified) rather than efficient element[73] in Myanmar's evolving constitutionalism?

[73] Walter Bagehot, *The English Constitution*, 1st edn. (London: Chapman and Hall, 1867), 4–5.

12

The Supreme Court of Japan

A Judicial Court, Not Necessarily a Constitutional Court

YASUO HASEBE

Although Japanese courts have not been very active in exercising their power of constitutional review,[1] their rulings on constitutionality have had significant impacts on various areas of Japanese legal thinking. This chapter first describes the organization of the Supreme Court of Japan and then summarizes some of its prominent constitutional decisions.

I Organization of the Court

After World War II, under the 1946 Constitution of Japan, which was largely based on the draft prepared by the American occupying forces, Japan adopted an American-style judicial review system. Within this system, the Supreme Court (*Saikō-Saibansho*) is the highest judicial court of the country, and, according to Article 81 of the Constitution, it is also the 'court of last resort with power to determine the constitutionality of any law, order, regulation or official act'. Hence, the Court's constitutional review authority inheres in its judicial power; it exercises constitutional review to the extent necessary to resolve legal disputes. In one of its early rulings, the Court declared that even without Article 81, its review authority is entailed from the fact that all judicial courts should obey and uphold the supreme law of the land, that is, the Constitution.[2] The reasoning is reminiscent of that of *Marbury* v. *Madison*, 5 U.S. 137 (1803), which argues for the power of judicial review without explicit textual authority in the US Constitution.

The Supreme Court is composed of the chief justice and fourteen associate justices. The chief justice is appointed by the Emperor as

[1] Since its establishment, the Court has held statutes enacted by Parliament unconstitutional in only ten cases.

[2] The Grand Bench decision of 8 July 1948, 2 KEISHû 801.

recommended by the Cabinet,[3] and other justices are formally appointed by the Cabinet,[4] subject to the process described below. Since the 1960s, a convention has been established that of the fifteen justices, six are appointed from among the judges of the lower courts, four from among attorneys at large, four from among bureaucrats (including public prosecutors) and one from among academic lawyers. As for justices appointed from the population of attorneys at large, when a vacancy occurs, a committee within the Japan Federation of Bar Associations recommends several candidates to the Supreme Court. The chief justice selects some of them and makes recommendations to the Cabinet. As for justices appointed from judges and public prosecutors, the Supreme Court itself prepares the list of candidates. With regard to justices appointed from bureaucrats, the Cabinet decides on the candidates based on the advice of the Court.

Strictly speaking, the Cabinet has the final veto on the appointment of justices. But in practice, the Cabinet always takes into consideration the Court's recommendations when it makes appointments to the Supreme Court. Usually, the chief justice acts on behalf of the Court in making the recommendations.[5] Almost every justice is appointed when he or she is around sixty-four years old and retires when he or she reaches the age of seventy.[6]

Hearings and adjudications of the Supreme Court are carried out either by the Grand Bench composed of all fifteen justices or by one of the Petty Benches, each composed of five justices. A constitutional question that reaches the Court for the first time is decided by the Grand Bench, and a statute, regulation, order or other official act can be held to be unconstitutional only by the Grand Bench. When a majority of justices at one Petty Bench reaches the conclusion that they should decide on a novel constitutional question or hold any official action to be unconstitutional, the case is referred to the Grand Bench. The doctrine of constitutional avoidance, imported from the United States in the 1960s, has often been used to avoid referring cases to the Grand Bench, as hearings and adjudications involving all the justices are

3 Article 6(2) of the Constitution.

4 Article 79(1) of the Constitution.

5 Masao Ohno, *Bengoshi kara Saibankan he (An attorney turned a justice)* (Tokyo: Iwanami Shoten, 2000) 66–67. Mr Ohno was formerly a practicing attorney and served as a justice of the Court from 1993 to 1997.

6 Article 50 of the Judicial Courts Act requires that justices retire at seventy.

cumbersome.[7] About forty research officials, selected from among lower court judges, assist the justices in their work. They are not assigned to individual justices, but belong to the entire Court. The Court decides approximately 9,000 cases per year.[8]

II Adjudication by the Supreme Court: Prominent Constitutional Cases

1 *Equality*

Article 14(1) of the Constitution stipulates that '[a]ll of the people are equal under the law and there shall be no discrimination in political, economic or social relations because of race, creed, sex, social status or family origin.' According to the case law of the Supreme Court, differential treatment of people is constitutional as long as it has a 'reasonable' basis.[9] To be reasonable, the treatment should have a legitimate purpose, and the content of the differential treatment should be proportionally related to the purpose. While the dominant academic view argues that under the influence of American jurisprudence, classifications based on 'race, creed, sex, social status or family origin' are inherently suspect, and strict scrutiny should be applied to them, case law has not clearly adopted such a view.

In its ruling on 4 April 1973, 27 KEISHÛ 265, the Grand Bench held that Article 200 of the Criminal Code, which stipulated that patricide and matricide should be punished with the death penalty or imprisonment for life, was unconstitutional and void. While the legislative purpose upholding the traditional moral of respecting parents was legitimate, the Court reasoned that the punishment was disproportionately severe

7 Masami Ito, *Saibankan to Gakusha no Aida (A Life between a justice and an academic)* (Tokyo: Yūhikaku, 1993) 118–119. Mr. Ito was formerly a professor at the University of Tokyo and served as a justice of the Court from 1980 to 1989. According to the doctrine of constitutional avoidance, judicial courts should construe ambiguous statutes in a manner that avoids raising serious constitutional doubts. See, for example, *NLRB* v. *Catholic Bishops*, 440 U.S. 490, 507 (1979).

8 According to a former justice of the Court, around 95% of the cases are trivial ones. See Tokiyasu Fujita, *Saikōsai-Kaisōroku (Memoirs of a supreme court justice)* (Tokyo: Yūhikaku, 2012) 42. Mr Fujita, an administrative law professor, served as a justice from 2002 to 2010.

9 The Grand Bench decision of 27 May 1964, 18 MINSHÛ 676, in which temporarily laying off a local civil servant in light of his old age and mediocre performance was held to be not contrary to the equality clause.

and against the principle of equality under the law, since a patricide or matricide could be committed under mitigating circumstances.[10] Some academics argue that the Court's holding implies that Article 200 is unconstitutional on the grounds that it inflicts cruel punishment prohibited by Article 36 of the Constitution.

In a decision of 4 July 2008, 62 MINSHÛ 1367, the Grand Bench struck down the treatment of an illegitimate child born of a foreign mother and acknowledged by a Japanese father after the birth.[11] According to the then Nationality Act, such a child could have Japanese nationality only when his or her parents were married. Taking into account the fact that the Japanese nationality is a necessary condition for a child to obtain basic social services like education in Japan, as well as the fact that a child is not accountable for whether her parents get married, the Court held that the constitutionality of such a differential treatment should be 'carefully scrutinized'. While the law has a legitimate purpose in according nationality only to a child who is closely related to Japanese society, the Court reasoned that the marriage of parents is not a necessary condition for a child to acquire a close relationship to Japanese society in light of changing social perceptions about marriage and family and recent trends in foreign laws.

Article 24 (1) of the Constitution stipulates that 'marriage shall be based only on the mutual consent of both sexes, and it shall be maintained through mutual cooperation with equal rights of husband and wife as a basis.' This clause can be traced back to the draft Constitution prepared by General MacArthur's staff at General Headquarters (GHQ),[12] who intended to raise the social status of women and, more

[10] In this case, the accused had been sexually abused by her father since her childhood and killed him as he tried to forcibly confine her to obstruct her marriage to her boyfriend. As to the constitutionality of capital punishment, see Section IV.

[11] See Norikazu Kawagishi, 'Japanese supreme court: An introduction' (2013) 8 *National Taiwan University Law Review* 240–243.

[12] Kenzō Takayanagi, Ichiro Ōtomo and Hideo Tanaka, *Nihonkoku Kenpō Seitei no Katei* (The making of the constitution of Japan), Vol. 2 Comments (Tokyo: Yūhikaku, 1972) 169–170. The 1946 Constitution of Japan was imposed by the Allied occupying forces after World War II. Immediately after the war, the Japanese government had been preparing a more conservative, lukewarm proposal to amend the then-current Constitution of the Empire of Japan 1889. However, after learning of this proposal, General Douglas MacArthur, supreme commander for the Allied Powers (SCAP), decided to propose his own version of a draft constitution prepared by his staff in the government section at the GHQ of the Occupation, which he pressed the government to adopt as the basis of an amended constitution.

specifically, to reform traditionally accepted ideas regarding the subservient relationship of wife to husband. Article 24(2) stipulates that 'with regard to choice of spouse, property rights, inheritance, choice of domicile, divorce and other matters pertaining to marriage and family, laws shall be enacted from the standpoint of individual dignity and the essential equality of the sexes.'[13] After the enactment of the Constitution, in 1947, clauses of the Civil Code relating to family and inheritance were fundamentally rewritten from the standpoint of these two constitutional clauses. This newly enacted part of the Code is generally referred to as the New Civil Code.

Some scholars, however, maintained that certain pre-modern ideas persisted in the laws pertaining to family matters. For example, according to Article 900 of the Civil Code, an illegitimate child (born out of lawful wedlock) could inherit by intestate succession from his or her parent's estate only half of the portion inherited by a legitimate child. In its decision of 5 July 1995, 49 MINSHŪ 1789, the Grand Bench upheld this clause on the grounds that this apportionment protects not only the interests of legitimate family members but also, to some extent, those of illegitimate children as well. If desired, the majority reasoned, the parents of illegitimate children could either adopt them (turning them into legitimate children) or specify a larger bequest to them in a will. A minority opinion supported by five justices argued that this unequal treatment of illegitimate children unreasonably punishes and stigmatizes them on grounds for which they are not themselves accountable.

In a decision of 4 September 2013, 67 MINSHŪ 1320, the Grand Bench completely changed its former doctrine, holding the unequal treatment of illegitimate heirs under Article 900 to be unconstitutional. Taking into consideration changing social perceptions about marriage and family and recent trends in foreign laws, as well as the recent amendment of relevant statutes, the Court held that the notion that every child should be respected as an equal individual had become firmly established in Japanese society. Moreover, the Court held that the concept of inflicting disadvantages upon an illegitimate child on the grounds that his parents were not formally married, for which fact the child himself is totally unaccountable, is without reasonable basis and

[13] Apparently, this text does not recognize the possibility of same-sex marriages, though this does not necessarily mean that the legalization of same-sex marriage would be unconstitutional under the current constitution.

unjustifiable, despite the broad discretion of the Legislature. The Court concluded that the relevant clause became unconstitutional at the latest in July 2001, when the inheritance in dispute commenced.[14]

On 16 December 2015, the Grand Bench delivered two decisions regarding the constitutionality of marital institutions.[15] While Article 733 of the Civil Code stipulated that females had to wait for six months after their divorces before they could remarry, the Grand Bench held that since the purpose of this clause is to avoid the overlap of presumptions of legitimacy of children from two consecutive marriages, the waiting period should be reduced to 100 days. According to Article 772 of the Civil Code, children born 200 days after the time of a marriage, as well as those born within 300 days of the dissolution of a marriage, are presumed to be legitimate children born from the legal marriage. The Court, therefore, held that a waiting period exceeding 100 days is an excessive and unconstitutional limitation of the liberty to marry, which is guaranteed under Article 24(1) of the Constitution.

On the other hand, as to Article 750 of the Civil Code, which stipulates that the surnames of a husband and wife should both be either his or her former surname, the Grand Bench held it constitutional. While the Court admitted that this clause may incidentally impede the marriages of some couples who both want to retain their surnames, it reasoned that the rule that a husband and wife share the same surname shows clearly their marital status and sustains the interests of their children.

2 *Electoral Systems*

The Principle of 'One Person, One Vote'

The Court has tried vigilantly to guarantee the equality of voting rights in malapportionment cases. Indeed, the Court has proclaimed that the

[14] Although the Court affirmed in 1995 that the relevant clause was constitutional, strictly speaking, this decision did not overrule its precedent. Still, this ruling means a colossal policy change on the part of the Court. To avoid overturning established legal situations that retroactive effects of this ruling might bring about, the Court added that legal decisions and arrangements already settled would remain valid and effective after July 2001. We might say that the Court made recourse to the device of prospective overruling to avoid destabilizing earlier inheritances.

[15] 69 MINSHÛ 2427 and 69 MINSHÛ 2586.

protection of the democratic process, including free communication of ideas and information,[16] is among its most important roles.

The Equal Protection Clause in Article 14 of the Constitution of Japan provides that 'all of the people are equal under the law', and Article 43(2) specifically prohibits 'discrimination because of race, creed, sex, social status, family origin, education, property or income' where the right to vote is concerned. A disputed question was whether equal value must be given to each vote so that a gross malapportionment of seats between constituencies would be unconstitutional. When the districts for the election of members of the Lower House were first drawn in 1947 under the current Constitution, the maximum difference between the numbers of voters per seat was 1:1.5. The difference widened subsequently, however, mainly because people moved with increasing frequency from rural to urban areas.

In 1976, the Supreme Court faced a case where the maximum difference in the weights of votes amounted to 1:5; that is, in the most populated district, an MP represented five times the number of voters of the least populated one. The Grand Bench held that the Constitution required that each vote must be given equal value, and while the Parliament could take into account various factors, such as administrative boundaries, residents' composition, traffic convenience and geographical features, in drawing up constituencies, a gross difference of 1:5 was unconstitutional since no mitigating rationale for it was conceivable.[17]

However, the Court indicated no clear standard of constitutionality for deciding whether a particular difference in the weights of votes is permissible. In any event, the Court did not demand stringent mathematical equality here. According to the Court, a difference is unconstitutional only when 'no mitigating rationale is conceivable' and 'a reasonable grace period for redrawing districts has elapsed' after such a gross difference had been identified. The Court has never indicated any numerical standard.

[16] For example, see the Grand Bench decision of 26 November 1969, 23 KEISHÛ 1490 (wherein the press was accorded qualified privileges against seizure of its unpublished materials by investigative authorities) and the Grand Bench decision of 11 June 1986, 40 MINSHÛ 872 (holding that a judicial injunction against publishing a journal conveying information about candidates in an election is permitted only in the most exceptional circumstances, for example, when the information is untrue or the publication manifestly lacks any intention to realize public interests).

[17] The decision of 4 April 1976, 30 MINSHÛ 223. See Norman Dorsen, Michel Rosenfeld, Andras Sajó and Susanne Baer (eds.), *Comparative Constitutionalism: Cases and Materials*, 2nd edn. (St. Paul, MN: West 2010) 1477–1478.

Until the 1994 electoral reform, members of the Lower House were elected by the single non-transferable vote system.[18] Constitutional law scholars read the somewhat murky case law of the time as implying that a 1:3 deviation in the weights of votes was acceptable for the House of Representatives.[19] On the other hand, the dominant academic view has been that a deviation beyond 1:2 should be unconstitutional in the light of the 'one person, one vote' principle. However, this 1:2 standard does not seem much superior to 1:3 because the only tenable principle is that the value of each vote should be equal or almost equal.[20]

Since the reform of 1994, 300 members of the Lower House are elected from single-member constituencies.[21] The Act Establishing the Boundary Commission provides that the Boundary Commission established under the Cabinet Office (*Naikakufu*) will make recommendations every ten years about how to redraw the boundaries of constituencies. Seven members of the Commission are appointed by the prime minister, with the assent of both houses of Parliament, for a term of five years. Their recommendations are submitted to the prime minister, who must then report them to Parliament. Parliament is expected to amend the boundaries in accordance with the recommendations. In drawing up recommendations, the Commission shall see to it that in principle, the maximum difference of the weights of votes between constituencies should be within 1:2.[22] While the

[18] A voter could cast just one vote in a multi-member constituency under this system. See David Farrell, *Electoral Systems: A Comparative Introduction* (New York: Palgrave, 2001) 46.

[19] Hidenori Tomatsu, 'Equal protection of the law', in Percy R. Luney, Jr., and Kazuyuki Takahashi (eds.), *Japanese Constitutional Law*, (Tokyo: University of Tokyo Press, 1993) 196; Masami Koshiji, 'Constitutional Issues concerning the Franchise', in Yōichi Higuchi (ed.), *Five Decades of Constitutionalism in Japanese Society* (Tokyo: University of Tokyo Press, 2001) 142.

[20] This is not to deny that the 1:2 standard is better than the 1:3 standard in light of the principle of equal value for each vote. However, neither standard follows *logically* from that principle.

[21] The number of MPs was 500 when the new electoral system was introduced in 1994. At the time of writing, the number of MPs is 475, among whom 180 are elected by the proportional representation system, and the remaining 295 are elected by the first-past-the-post system.

[22] The Act Establishing the Boundary Commission, Article 3 (1). However, this Article included a peculiar seat allocation system called *Hitori-Betsuwaku-Hōshiki*, under which, among the 300 seats of the Lower House that are elected by the first-past-the-post system, one seat is first allocated to each of forty-seven prefectures, and after that, the remaining 253 seats are allocated in proportion to the population of each prefecture. On the constitutionality of this system, see the text accompanying note 27.

text of the Act does not require Parliament to follow the recommendations of the Commission, Parliament has respected them to date.

When the first general elections after the reform took place in 1995, the maximum difference was 1:2.309. The Supreme Court, in a 1999 ruling, applied the same standard as before, holding that the difference was within the Legislature's discretion.[23]

In elections for the House of Councillors, the Court apparently uses the same standard of constitutionality,[24] but applies it more leniently, partly because, according to the Court, Parliament is allowed to take into account the fact that councillors elected from local districts or prefectures function as *de facto* representatives of their prefectures. In a 1983 ruling,[25] the Court held that a deviation of 1:5.26 was within the Legislature's discretion. However, in 1996, the Court ruled that a difference amounting to 1:6.59 was unconstitutional because no mitigating rationale was conceivable for such a gross difference.[26]

The Court's attitude in malapportionment cases has become more stringent in recent years. In a decision of 23 March 2011, 65 MINSHÛ 755, the Grand Bench held that the one-seat special allocation system (*Hitori-Betsuwaku-Hōshiki*)[27] was unconstitutional, since this peculiar seat allocation system, bringing about significant deviation from the one person, one vote principle, lacked a rational basis. While the purported rationale was that this system was necessary to effectively reflect the opinions of people residing in less populated districts, the Court reasoned that since MPs should be 'representatives of the whole nation',[28] this rationale could not constitute sufficient justification to deviate from the equal value principle. In compliance with this decision, Parliament abolished the one-seat special allocation system in November 2012.

23 The Grand Bench decision of 10 November 1999, 53 MINSHÛ 1441.

24 That is, a difference is unconstitutional only when no mitigating rationale is conceivable and a reasonable grace period for redrawing districts has elapsed after such a gross difference has been recognized.

25 The Grand Bench decision of 27 April 1983, 37 MINSHÛ 345. Prefectures are administrative units similar to French *departements*. About half of the councillors are elected from the same geographical areas as prefectures.

26 The Grand Bench decision of 11 September 1996, 50 MINSHÛ 2283. However, the Court held that a reasonable grace period for redrawing districts had not elapsed.

27 See note 22.

28 See Article 43(1) of the Constitution.

In addition, in its ruling in 2012 on an election for the House of Councillors,[29] the Court clearly held that to realize the equal value principle, the basic architecture allocating seats based on prefectural boundaries should be re-examined. The Court now seems to indicate that the essential function of councillors is not representing prefectures where they are elected but representing the nation as a whole.

Access to the Ballot: Postal Voting

In 1948, Parliament introduced a system that enabled severely handicapped voters to cast votes by mail. However, in 1951, on the grounds that this system was often abused, Parliament abolished it. A physically handicapped person who was denied access to the ballot since the abolition sued the government, contending that he was discriminated against on the basis of his disability.

In 1974, the Sapporo District Court held that the abolition and inaction afterwards on the part of Parliament was unconstitutional and awarded damages to the plaintiff. The court said that the Constitution required Parliament to ensure that every voter could actually cast a vote. Parliament was absolved from this duty only when there was a legitimate interest to protect and Parliament had no less restrictive means to vindicate the interest. The court found that although preventing abuses of the postal voting system was a legitimate purpose, Parliament should use less drastic means to realize it than totally abolishing the system.

On appeal, the Sapporo High Court ruled in 1978 that the abolition of the system was unconstitutional, but in a 1985 ruling, the Supreme Court dismissed the plaintiff's claim by drastically limiting the scope of responsibility Parliament owed in compensation litigation.[30] Referring to the parliamentary immunity stipulated in Article 51 of the Constitution, the Court held that Parliament is not legally liable for legislative action or inaction unless Parliament commits 'gross errors', such as making laws that are literally in contradiction to the Constitution. In principle, the Legislature is only politically responsible to the entire nation, not legally responsible to any individual in its legislative activities.

[29] The Grand Bench decision of 17 October 2012, 66 MINSHÛ 3357.

[30] The First Petty Bench decision of 21 November 1985, 39 MINSHÛ 1512.

In 1974, after the Sapporo District Court decided the case against it, Parliament amended the Public Offices Election Act and resurrected the postal voting system.[31] In other words, though the government conceded that abolishing the postal voting system was politically imprudent, it still defended its position up to the Supreme Court, to save face.

Access to the Ballot: Japanese Nationals Living Abroad

In 1998, the Parliament amended the Public Offices Election Act to make it possible for Japanese nationals living overseas to participate in elections for members of both houses of Parliament. The Act stipulated, however, that voters living abroad could vote only for members elected by proportional representation.[32]

In a ruling on 14 September 2005,[33] the Supreme Court held that this limitation of access to the ballot was unconstitutional. A restriction on the right to vote is not allowed unless there is compelling reason to do so, and it is compelling only when the fair execution of an election becomes extremely difficult without the restriction.[34] The government asserted that it could not inform voters abroad of information necessary for them to participate effectively in elections of single-member constituencies for the Lower House and prefectural constituencies for the Upper House. The Court held, however, that such an assertion was implausible in this age of global information. The Court also held that Parliament negligently failed to make it possible for Japanese living abroad to participate in national elections until 1998 and that this denial of access to the ballot was a 'gross error' entitling plaintiffs to compensation from the state.

[31] Article 49(2) of the Public Offices Election Act. The decisions explained in the text are in response to the government's failure to resurrect and implement the postal voting system at elections from 1951–1974.

[32] Supplementary Provision, Article 8. That is, nationals overseas could not vote for single-member elections for the House of Representatives, nor for councillors elected from prefectures.

[33] The Grand Bench decision of 14 September 2005, 59 MINSHÛ 2087.

[34] Following this doctrine, the Tokyo District Court, in its decision of 14 March 2013, held that Article 11(1) of the Public Offices Election Act, which denied people under guardianship the right to vote, was unconstitutional because there was no compelling reason to restrict the right for them. In May 2013, Parliament abolished the clause and reinstated the right to vote of every person under guardianship.

Political Contributions by Corporations[35]

Under the Political Funds Control Act, corporations may contribute money to political parties.[36] Since a corporation is composed of individuals who may not share a common political view, there was dispute over whether corporations may make contributions to political parties.

In March 1960, Yahata Steel Corporation, the largest steel corporation in Japan at the time, contributed JPY3.5 million to the Liberal Democratic Party, the party in power. The plaintiff, a shareholder of the corporation, brought an action against the directors seeking compensation for the money, claiming that contributing to a political party was not authorized by the statutes of the company.

The Tokyo district court held for the plaintiff on the grounds that contributing to a specific party was unlikely to receive the unanimous approval of stockholders. The Tokyo High Court reversed the decision, and the Supreme Court affirmed the high court ruling.[37] According to the Court, corporations are not entitled to political rights (including the right to vote), but since corporations are obliged to pay taxes, there is no reason to prohibit them from expressing opinions regarding national or local government policies. Besides, the Court went on, since the articles on fundamental rights in the Constitution should be applied to corporations as far as their characteristics allow it, corporations should enjoy the same liberty as natural persons to carry out political activities, such as supporting, endorsing or objecting to specific policies of the government or political parties. The Court, therefore, held that the corporations' right to contribute money to political parties was guaranteed under the Constitution. This rather peculiar image of the democratic process is reasonably in congruence with the conception of pluralist democracy that the Court appears to embrace.[38]

However, the Court has treated contributions from certain corporations differently. In March 1996, it held that an association of licensed tax accountants could not contribute money to political organizations on the grounds that tax accountants in practice were legally required to be

[35] See Yasuo Hasebe, 'Rights of corporations, rights of individuals: Judicial precedents', in Yōichi Higuchi (ed.), *Five Decades of Constitutionalism in Japanese Society* (Tokyo: University of Tokyo Press, 2001) 79–85.

[36] Articles 21–21.3 of the Political Funds Control Act. While this law was first enacted in 1995, the legal situation regarding contributions by corporations has not changed much since the 1960s.

[37] The Grand Bench decision of 24 June 1970, 24 MINSHŪ 625.

[38] See part 3 of Section II below.

members of their local associations.[39] From the Court's perspective, since contributions to political parties were closely related to individual freedom of speech and creed, such 'involuntary' associations should not by a majority vote coerce their members to contribute to specific political organizations. According to this line of reasoning, the *Yahata Steel Corporation* decision may be distinguished, because stockholders of *Yahata* can sell off their shares whenever they think political views of management conflicts with theirs.

3 *Economic Freedoms and the Conception of Democracy*

The precedents pertaining to the electoral system and related issues show that the Court should not be viewed as excessively deferential to the political branches. Its decisions have had an undeniable impact in favour of an open and transparent political system based on the principle of equality of citizens. The question remains: What kind of democracy does the Court endeavour to protect? Given that the Court has repeatedly declared its main task to be the preservation of democratic process, we need to ask how the Court understands its own mission. It is possible to conclude that the Court is attempting to preserve a pluralist democracy,[40] and this self-definition of the Court's role makes its attitude appear deferential to the political branches. This may be explained as follows.

In a pluralist democracy, numerous parties seek to advance their own goals. The parties compete with each other and make alliances to achieve these goals as effectively as possible. This process of competition and compromise eventually produces legislative acts that are implemented by judges and administrators.[41]

In general, these laws reflect not genuine public interests but, rather, various private interests of particular groups or corporations. From the perspective of a pluralist democracy, if a proposed legislative bill genuinely serves some wider public interest, its benefits will be spread too thinly throughout the populace for individual citizens to have an

[39] The Third Petty Bench decision of 19 March 1996, 50 MINSHŪ 615.

[40] Yasuo Hasebe, 'Constitutional borrowing and political theory' (2003) 1 *International Journal of Constitutional Law* 224–243, at 236.

[41] John Hart Ely, *Democracy and Distrust: A Theory of Judicial Review* (Cambridge, MA: Harvard University Press, 1980); see also Paul P. Craig, *Public Law and Democracy in the United Kingdom and the United States of America* (Clarendon Press, 1990) chs. 3 & 4.

incentive to fight for its enactment. Since it is more rational to free-ride on the altruistic initiatives of others to promote bills in the public interest than to risk one's own initiatives, no rational person is likely to undertake such initiatives. By contrast, if a proposed bill is likely to advance the private interests of particular groups or corporations, then those interests are likely to devote substantial resources and energy to promoting its enactment. Thus, more often than not, legislative initiatives and results reflect particular, rather than general, interests.[42]

In the realm of economic freedoms,[43] the Supreme Court has adopted a doctrine that differentiates between legislation that is passivist (*Shō-kyokuteki*) and legislation that is activist (*Sekkyokuteki*) in purpose. In legislation that is passivist, which purports merely to maintain the public order or protect public health and safety, the Court requires a strict correlation between the legislative purpose and the measures adopted.[44] On the other hand, if Parliament proclaims an activist purpose of intervening to protect particular industries or social groups, the Court requires only a theoretical rationale for the adopted legislative measures.[45] Consequently, whereas passivist legislation is closely scrutinized and, in some cases, found unconstitutional, activist legislation is almost invariably upheld as constitutional.[46]

Constitutional scholars in Japan are widely sceptical of the wisdom of this judicial doctrine, which apparently makes it more difficult for Parliament to pursue passivist legislation benefiting the general interests of society than it is to pursue activist legislation benefiting particular narrow interests. However, many of the same academics naïvely assume that members of Parliament are usually forthright in expressing their

[42] See Mancur Olson, *The Logic of Collective Action* (Cambridge, MA: Harvard University Press, 1965) 44, 64.

[43] Article 22(1) of the Constitution of Japan guarantees 'every person' the freedom of choosing his occupation.

[44] The Grand Bench decision of 30 April 1975, 29 MINSHÛ 572 (wherein regulation prohibiting a new drugstore near existing stores of the same trade was struck down as insufficiently related to its purpose of protecting public health).

[45] The Grand Bench decision of 22 November 1972, 26 KEISHû 586 (wherein regulation against setting up a new marketplace for small retailers was upheld as rationally related to its purpose of protecting retailers from excessive competition).

[46] Cf. Mutsuo Nakamura, 'Freedom of economic activities and the right to property', in Percy R. Luney, Jr., and Kazuyuki Takahashi (eds.), *Japanese Constitutional Law*, (Tokyo: University of Tokyo Press, 1993) 255–267.

purposes and motivations in the course of the legislative process. Actually, lawmakers may often disguise their genuine purposes.[47]

According to the so-called pluralistic view of democracy, competing parties in the legislative process are likely to pursue their own narrow interests rather than the general interests of society. From this perspective, the role of the Supreme Court is restricted to assuring fairness and transparency of the legislative process.

By this logic, when a passivist legislative bill purports to promote general public interests, its expressed purpose is usually a smokescreen concealing some purpose that serves special interests.[48] The Court must, therefore, ensure that Parliament has, indeed, promoted the public interest in such legislation by including measures to realize its publicly asserted purpose. If there is no close correlation between the alleged purpose and the adopted measures restricting economic freedoms, it is the responsibility of the Court to send it back to Parliament. Through this process of constitutional review, the real purposes of legislation are brought to light, and fairer competition will ensue. On the other hand, activist legislative bills endorse particular interests openly and have been approved by a majority of Parliament; hence, the Court sees no need to intervene. Therefore, under this curious judicial doctrine, we may say that the Court has performed its proper function.

If the Court applies more stringent constitutional tests to activist pieces of legislation and strikes them down, this would merely bring us back to the previous regulatory situation before the invalidated regulation was enacted, and this earlier legislative regime could be similarly contaminated with the particular private interests that existed at that time. If every regulation is thrown away, no economic activity is practicable. Since there would be no neutral baseline that everyone would regard as fair and unobjectionable, most basic rules coordinating economic transactions would be invalidated.

47 In other words, lawmakers are likely to perform the 'strategic speech in law-making', which is analysed in Andrei Marmor, 'Can the law imply more than it says? On some pragmatic aspects of strategic speech', in Andrei Marmor and Scott Soames (eds.), *Philosophical Foundations of Language in the Law* (Oxford: Oxford University Press, 2011) 83–104.

48 Yasuhiro Okudaira points out that the entry regulation of drugstore, struck down by the decision of 30 April 1975, in fact was actually introduced in response to the demand to protect the interest of existing drugstores. See his *Kenpō Saiban no Kanōsei (Potential of Constitutional Adjudication)* (Tokyo: Iwanami Shoten, 1994) 103–104.

While *Comparative Constitutionalism* by Dorsen et al. takes the view that the Supreme Court has followed the lead of the German Constitutional Court decision,[49] which differentiates between the regulation of subjective conditions of admission to a trade, such as requiring proper qualification, and the objective conditions of admission that are out of the individual's control, the current author does not share this view. The Grand Bench decision of 30 April 1975 involved a case of a general drugstore, not of a pharmacy in the strict sense, which is a store managed by a qualified pharmacist. Moreover, the Court does not strictly review every objective restriction of entry into a market, as the Grand Bench decision of 22 November 1972 shows. This view of Dorsen et al. cannot coherently explain the series of relevant precedents in this area.

4 *The Right to Life*

In its second sentence, Article 13 of the Constitution states that the 'right to life . . . shall, to the extent that it does not interfere with the public welfare, be the supreme consideration in legislation and in other governmental affairs'. As the qualification concerning the public welfare indicates, this right is not considered absolute. Article 31 provides that a person may be deprived of life as a criminal penalty. The Supreme Court has held that capital punishment is not a cruel punishment prohibited by Article 36 if it is executed by hanging.[50]

One judicial precedent[51] indicates that the right to autonomy derived from Article 13 of the Constitution may override the obligation to respect life. The plaintiff, a Jehovah's Witness suffering from liver cancer, asked her doctor not to conduct any blood transfusions during her operation. Although the doctor accepted the patient's request, he actually conducted a blood transfusion when he thought it absolutely necessary to save the patient's life. The Tokyo High Court held that the doctor infringed the patient's religious autonomy and awarded her consolatory compensation.

[49] Dorsen et al., *Constitutional Constitutionalism*, note 17, p. 1348. The German case law holds that objective conditions of admission to a trade are permissible only when they are necessary for the prevention of demonstrable or highly probable danger to community, while subjective conditions are permissible if they bear a reasonable relationship to the end pursued.

[50] The Grand Bench decision of 12 March 1948, 2 Keishû 191. Article 51 of the Juvenile Delinquency Act *(Shōnen Hō)* stipulates that no person should be executed for crimes which he committed before he reached eighteen years of age.

[51] The Tokyo High Court decision of 9 October 1998, 1629 HANREI JIHÔ 34.

The Supreme Court rejected the defendant's appeal, confirming that the plaintiff's right to autonomy must be respected under tort law.[52] This line of reasoning seems to imply that if the doctor had not made a blood transfusion and the patient had died, the doctor would not have been legally responsible for her death. Moreover, it also seems to imply that what must be respected is not life itself or the state of being alive, but the value of autonomous life, which may be violated when others rewrite an agent's life plan.

The legality of abortion is not as controversial an issue in Japan as it is in some Western countries. According to Article 14 of the Maternity Protection Act, officially designated doctors may artificially terminate pregnancy when continuing pregnancy is 'unusually harmful to the mother for physical or *economical* reasons' (emphasis added).

5 *Religion and the State*

Article 20 of the Constitution provides that 'no religious organization shall receive any privileges from the state' and 'the state and its organs shall refrain from religious education or any other religious activity'. Moreover, Article 89 stipulates that 'no public money or other property shall be expended or appropriated for the use, benefit or maintenance of any religious institution or association'. Under the Meiji Constitution, Shinto was regarded as a *de facto* established religion, and other denominations were often suppressed or persecuted. Articles 20 and 89 were enacted in light of these hard experiences. As to the test of constitutionality of state action with regard to these disestablishment clauses, the Supreme Court has adopted the so-called purpose-effect standard (*Mokuteki-Kōka-Kijun*), which is modelled roughly on the *Lemon* test in the United States.[53]

In one case, a governor of Ehime prefecture donated public money to the Yasukuni and Gokoku shrines on the occasions of customary Shinto fetes. Both are Shinto shrines dedicated mainly to soldiers of the Imperial Army killed in action, mostly during World

[52] The Third Petty Bench decision of 29 February 2000, 54 MINSHÛ 582 [Blood Transfusion Case].

[53] *Lemon* v. *Kurtzman*, 403 U.S. 602 (1971). The *Lemon* test is composed of three elements: first, the government action must have a secular, legitimate purpose; second, the primary effect of the government action must neither advance nor inhibit religion; third, the government action must not cause an excessive governmental entanglement with religion.

War II.[54] Donated money from 1981 until 1986 amounted to JPY166,000 in all. The plaintiffs, residents of Ehime prefecture, brought an 'inhabitants' suit' under Article 242-2 of the Local Government Act (*Chihō-Jichi-Hō*) challenging the constitutionality of the donations.[55]

The Supreme Court found the donations to be unconstitutional in light of the purpose-effect standard.[56] According to the Court, 'the principle of the separation of religion and the state enshrined in Articles 20 and 89 does not ban every governmental involvement with religion but prohibits merely such involvement that exceeds the appropriate limit in light of the social and cultural circumstances in Japan'. Moreover, the 'religious activities' the state should refrain from under Article 20 are 'such activities as their purposes have religious significance and their effects advance or inhibit religion'. In this case, 'it is unthinkable that ordinary people regard the donations as mere gestures of social courtesy. Then the donors themselves cannot but recognize more or less that the donations have religious significance. ... It is undeniable that these activities have provoked the impression that the prefecture advances these particular religious bodies ... and that they have raised concerns about these particular religions'. Therefore, the Court concluded, as the purpose of the donations 'had inevitably religious significance, and their effects advance particular religions', they are unconstitutional under Articles 20 and 89 of the Constitution.

In another case, Sunakawa City in Hokkaido Prefecture leased its land for no charge to one of its neighbourhood associations for decades. Residents built a Shinto shrine on the land, where they periodically held religious fetes. Citizens of the city brought an inhabitants' suit asserting that letting the property of the city be used for the shrine was against Articles 20 and 89 of the Constitution. In its decision of 20 January 2010, the Supreme Court agreed,[57] pointing out that there was no legitimate

[54] Gokoku shrines of local prefectures are regarded as branches of Yasukuni shrine, which is situated in Kudan, Tokyo. Both *Gokoku* and *Yasukuni* mean securing peace of the country.

[55] This suit is comparable to the taxpayers' suit in the United States. In an inhabitants' suit, the plaintiff need not show that he or she is a taxpayer of the relevant local government. The plaintiff only needs to show that he or she resides there.

[56] The Grand Bench decision of 2 April 1997, 51 MINSHÛ 1673. See Yasuo Hasebe, 'Japan', in Cheryl Saunders and Graham Hassall (eds.), *Asia-Pacific Constitutional Yearbook 1997* (Melbourne: Centre for Comparative Constitutional Studies, University of Melbourne, 1999) 125–131.

[57] The Grand Bench decision of 20 January 2010, 64 MINSHÛ 1.

secular purpose for the city to lease the land, and this gratuitous leasing provoked the impression that the city advanced this particular shrine. However, the Court added that retrieving the land and having the shrine destroyed was not the only way to correct the illegal administration of the public property. The city could reconcile the constitutional principle of anti-establishment with the residents' free exercise of religion by, for example, leasing the land for an appropriate charge or transferring it to the neighbourhood association outright, the Court argued.

It is noteworthy that the Court did not use the purpose-effect standard in this case. Instead, it used a more obscure and lenient standard of 'whether the government's involvement with religion exceeds the appropriate limit in light of the basic end of Articles 20 and 89: that is, securing freedom of religion'. It is possible that the Court thought that the accommodating options like transferring the land to the neighbourhood association would be unconstitutional if the purpose-effect standard were adopted, which would mean there was no way out but to destroy the shrine. In order to deliver an appropriate solution for this case that would uphold both the anti-establishment principle and freedom of religion, therefore, the Court seemed to conclude that the purpose-effect standard should not be used here.

Eventually, Sunakawa City decided to rent out to a representative of the residents a portion of the land to maintain the shrine. The Court concluded that the city's action did not contravene the anti-establishment principle since renting the land for an appropriate price did not provoke the impression that the city advanced a particular religion.[58]

6 *Horizontal Effects*

Both the dominant academic view and case law recognize that constitutional rights have so-called horizontal effects. In the *Mitsubishi Resin* case, the Court held that 'while provisions of the Constitution were not intended to regulate directly the relations between private parties ... where actual or feared damage to an individual's basic equality or freedom inflicted by other private parties exceeds socially permissible limits in mode and extent, through appropriate interpretation and/or application of various general clauses like Article 90 and 709 of the Civil

[58] The First Petty Bench decision of 16 February 2012, 66 MINSHŪ 673.

Code, proper accommodation of conflicting interests would be achieved.'[59] According to this case law doctrine, these general clauses of the Civil Code should be interpreted in conformity with the import of the principles of the Constitution.[60]

For example, in the well-known *Nissan Motors* case, the Supreme Court voided an employment regulation of a major corporation that stipulated different retirement ages for male and female employees.[61] Moreover, to offer a different example, when the privacy of an individual is infringed by a media company, the constitutional right to privacy is understood to apply indirectly through the tort clause in the Civil Code.[62] The Court has seen to it that through its horizontal effects control, the dignity and autonomy of each citizen are duly protected.

III Conclusion

With regard to the role of judicial review in protecting freedoms of speech, conscience and religion, the predominant academic view is that the Court has not been sufficiently activist in upholding its commitment to the 'preferred position' of these freedoms.[63]

59 The Grand Bench decision of 12 December 1973, 27 MINSHÛ 1536. Article 90 of the Civil Code states that contracts against the public order and good morals are void. Article 709 states that damage caused by torts should be compensated.

60 This is called the 'indirect horizontal effects' doctrine in Japan. While several scholars assert that the Supreme Court has recognized no horizontal effect, this view is not widely shared. Justice Masami Ito points out in his constitutional law textbook that the *Nissan Motors* decision (see note 61) holds that Article 90 of the Civil Code should be interpreted in conformity with the equality principle of the Constitution. He joined the Court's opinion in this decision. See his *Kenpō*, 3rd edn. (Tokyo: Kōbundō, 1995) 35.

61 The Third Petty Bench decision of 24 March 1981, 35 MINSHÛ 300.

62 See, for example, the Third Petty Bench decision of 8 February 1994, 48 MINSHÛ 149, and the Second Petty Bench decision of 13 March 2003, 57 MINSHÛ 229.

63 The Court has repeatedly declared that these freedoms are basic components of the democratic political process which judicial review should sustain. See, for example, the decisions of 11 June 1986, 40 MINSHÛ 872 (note 16) and 8 March 1989, 43 MINSHÛ 89. That the Court has not been very active in upholding its commitment to the preferred freedoms does not mean that the Court has always been passive. Frank Upham points out that the Court has been quite active in protecting labourers' economic interests or promoting the status of women in the workplace and the family. See Frank Upham, 'Nihon ni okeru Seiji to Shihou no Kinô (The Functions of the Political and Judicial Branches in US and Japan)', in Masakazu Doi (ed.), *Iwanami-Koza Kenpo (Iwanami Lectures on Constitutional Law)*, vol. 4 (Tokyo: Iwanami Shoten, 2007). I basically agree with Upham's analysis.

Several explanations have been offered for the apparent reluctance of the Court to use its review powers. One explanation is that the constitutionality of most laws enacted by Parliament is meticulously scrutinized in advance by the Cabinet Legislation Bureau, which was set up in 1875, modelled on the French *Conseil d'Etat*.[64] Members of the bureau are recruited from the judiciary or bureaucrats with equivalent abilities in law. Therefore, the Court is assured that it does not need to examine carefully the constitutionality of most statutes. In other words, the constitutional review system in Japan is composed of two parts: *a priori* review by the Cabinet Legislation Bureau, and *a posteriori* review by the Supreme Court.

Second, some scholars argue from an external point of view that the conservative orientation of the Court is only to be expected given the fact that it has long been immersed in a conservative political environment.[65] It seems that a similar *esprit de corps* has been internalized by justices to some extent. A former justice confesses that because of the lack of democratic accountability, justices often hesitate to give decisive answers to questions that have grave political implications.[66]

Third, the conception of 'pluralist democracy' as discussed above, which the Court seems to embrace, may explain why, in the eyes of constitutional law scholars, the Court is not sufficiently vigilant in policing the democratic process.[67]

It should be noted that these explanations are not incompatible with one another. Nor are they incompatible with a fourth approach, which is to suggest that the main reason why the Court is reluctant to strike down state actions may reside in its primary self-image as a judicial body.

[64] Mutsuo Nakamura and Teruki Tsunemoto, 'The legislative process: Outline and actors', in Yōichi Higuchi (ed.), *Five Decades of Constitutionalism in Japanese Society* (Tokyo: University of Tokyo Press, 2001) 197–219, at 195, 199 and 200.

[65] David Law, 'The anatomy of a conservative court: Judicial Review in Japan' (2008–2009) 87 *Texas Law Review* 1545. Law describes how the ruling LDP has delegated political control of the judiciary to ideologically reliable chief justices and the general secretariat of the Court.

[66] A remark by Tokuji Izumi, cited in Tsukasa Mihira, *Ikenshinsasei o meguru Politics (Politics surrounding Constitutional Review Systems)* (Tokyo: Seibundō, 2012) 204. Before his appointment as a Supreme Court Justice in 2002, Mr Izumi was a career judge.

[67] See part 3 of Section II above. For other possible explanations, see Tom Ginsburg and Tokujin Matsudaira, 'The judicialization of Japanese politics?', in *The Japanese Legal System: An Era of Transition* (Berkeley, CA: The Robbins Collection, 2012) 33–43; see also, Yasuo Hasebe, 'The Supreme Court of Japan: Its adjudication on electoral systems and economic freedoms' (2007) 5 *International Journal of Constitutional Law* 296–307.

One prominent former justice says that the primary task of the Court is not to wield the power of constitutional review or constructing coherent jurisprudential doctrines, but rather, it is to give an appropriate solution to each case at hand. It strikes down a statute only when it is absolutely necessary to give concrete justice to the case.[68]

From this viewpoint, constitutional review is just a contingent power for the Court to perform its duty as a judicial body. The Court has preferred having recourse to restrictive (saving) construction of the relevant statutes in order to avoid raising serious constitutional questions, than declaring state actions to be unconstitutional, for which the Court has to convene its Grand Bench.[69] If the Court can resolve a case appropriately by some restrictive construction and without striking down a state action, the Court is more than willing to do so.[70] For the Court, its constitutional review power is just one of its toolkits to use in delivering concrete justice to cases at hand.

The movement in Japan for setting up a new Kelsenian-style, centralized constitutional court has been not strong to date. While the *Yomiuri Shimbun* newspaper has proposed the establishment of a constitutional court on the grounds that such an institution would perform its role more aggressively and swiftly resolve constitutional questions,[71] constitutional scholars are generally sceptical of the wisdom of the proposal. Critics point out that no one knows how an institution newly grafted to the old cultural soil would function.[72] The judiciary is, naturally, hesitant to hand over its constitutional review power, and politicians are not inclined to construct an organ that would aggressively examine the constitutionality of their activities.

[68] Tokiyasu Fujita, note 8, at 136, 138, 145. This self-image as a judicial body is closely correlated with the recognition that the essential capacity for justices is *phronēsis*, or the capacity of concrete judgment that is not itself rule-governed (ibid., 122). See also his 'The Supreme Court of Japan: Commentary on the recent work of scholars in the United States' (2011) 88 *Washington University Law Review* 1507–1526, at 1508, 1521–1522.

[69] See note 7 and the accompanying text.

[70] A recent example of such an attitude is the Second Petty Bench decision of 7 December 2012, 66 KEISHÛ 1337, where the statutes prohibiting public servants from engaging in political activities were restrictively interpreted to protect freedom of speech, and a public servant who distributed communist newspapers while he was off-duty was held not guilty.

[71] *Yomiuri Shimbun*, 3 November 1994.

[72] Okudaira, note 48, at 3–6.

13

Establishing Judicial Review in China

Impediments and Prospects

QIANFAN ZHANG

Judicial review is commonly seen as a necessary ingredient for constitutionalism, without which the constitution can hardly be put to effective use in real life. Judicial review of the constitutionality of legislative acts is also seen as a necessary mechanism, providing a check on the majoritarian abuse of legislative power. However, for China, a country governed neither by democracy nor by rule of law for millennia, the absence of judicial review is not surprising. And it is not alone among states in the 'socialist camp' in rejecting judicial review. Leftist ideology in socialist countries typically hyperbolizes popular sovereignty in opposition to any institutional control, particularly control exercised by a judiciary commonly viewed as part of an undemocratic 'elite' minority. Thus, the current Constitution, enacted in 1982, is completely silent on the issue of judicial review. It neither authorizes ordinary courts nor establishes any special institution to engage in judicial review. As a result, there has not been a single constitutional case, so to speak, since the establishment of the Communist regime in 1949,[1] despite the fact that numerous issues of constitutional significance occur on a daily basis.

The long constitutional dormancy was briefly interrupted in 2001, when the Supreme People's Court (SPC), in a historical act, cited a constitutional provision in its reply to a provincial high court. In retrospect, this was a somewhat extraordinary event, viewed in the context of an ambitious judicial reform initiated two years before, which aimed to

[1] The same can be said about the Republican regime that was defeated by the Communists and retreated to Taiwan in 1949. In 1946, it enacted the Constitution of the Republic of China (ROC), which is still effective in Taiwan. The ROC Constitution does authorize the grand justices of the Judicial Yuan to engage in constitutional interpretation and review, but the mechanism never had the chance to operate in mainland China during the barely two years when the Constitution was in force on the mainland. See Chapter 5 of this book.

fundamentally transform the status and role of judges. But that precedent for the judicial application of the Constitution was never followed and was repealed by the SPC itself without providing a reason in 2008, when the judicial reform suffered a setback with the judiciary coming under the control of Zhou Yongkang, the Party leader in charge of political and judicial affairs in the Politburo, and the new SPC president, Wang Shengjun. While Zhou was subsequently convicted of corruption and Wang retired from the SPC presidency in 2013, the judicial application of the Constitution has not found new hope.

Divided into five sections, this chapter analyses China's existing mechanism of reviewing the constitutionality and legality of legislation and its deficiencies. The first section describes the *Qi Yuling* case and the failure to develop a judicial review mechanism. The second section discusses some of the constitutional cases, mostly on equality, that have been dealt with without reference to the Constitution. The third and fourth sections explore the political and legal context for the existing review mechanism, in which the role of the judiciary is minimized, and the limitations that inhere in the mechanism of legislative review. The fifth section examines China's court system and its 'judicial syndrome'. The final section discusses the theoretical and practical impediments to establishing judicial review in China and proposes several reforms aimed at improving the mechanism for ensuring conformity to China's Constitution and laws.

I Establishing Judicial Review?

1 The Qi Yuling Case of 2001

The case of *Qi Yuling* v. *Chen Xiaoqi et al.* is now a desolate milestone in the constitutional history of contemporary China.[2] In 1990, Qi Yuling passed the entrance examination for specialized secondary professions (*zhongzhuan*) and was admitted by Jining Commercial School (Shandong province). Yet her admission letter was stolen by her classmate, Chen Xiaoqi, who then studied under her name and went on to take a good job in a bank upon graduation. Qi found out about the whole affair only a decade later, during which time she had sought to find a good job but was unsuccessful owing to her lack of technical education. After she

[2] 'Right to education is not to be violated: The topic introduced by the first case on violation of right to education', *Guangming Daily* (4 September 2001) (in Chinese).

initiated litigation, the middle-level court of Tengzhou (Shangdong province) ordered the defendants to pay RMB35,000 for the emotional damage caused by the infringement of Qi's right to her name, which is protected by civil law, but the court declined to provide a remedy for the alleged violation of her right to education, which is protected in Article 46 of the 1982 Constitution.

During appeal, in an extremely succinct reply to the request of the Shandong High Court for judicial interpretation, the SPC held that the plaintiff's 'basic right to education as provided by the Constitution' was violated.[3] This was the first case in which the SPC explicitly cited a constitutional provision as the legal grounds for a judicial decision or interpretation. The Shandong High Court went on to order the defendants to pay RMB100,000 for the loss that Qi suffered from the infringement of her constitutional right to education. The decision, often hailed as China's 'first constitutional case', since it formally judicializes the Constitution,[4] took the legal community by surprise and generated a large body of academic literature debating the propriety of 'constitutional judicialization'.[5]

Despite minor technical problems, the first constitutional case did offer some bright hope not only for the right to education, specifically, but also for the promotion of constitutionalism as a whole. Western experience almost unanimously suggests that the words of a constitution do not count unless it is somehow judicialized – in the United States by ordinary courts, in France by the special Constitutional Council and in Germany by federal and state constitutional courts. Had it been allowed to develop under its own momentum, China's constitutionalism could have travelled along a similar path, and the *Qi Yuling* case might now be known as China's *Marbury* v. *Madison*.[6]

[3] 'Reply regarding whether one who violated the constitutionally protected basic right to education of the citizen should bear civil liability' (2001) *Sifa jieshi* (*Judicial Interpretation*) 25.

[4] To be precise, this was not the 'first case' in which the Constitution was cited as grounds for a judicial decision, since several local civil courts had previously done so in their judgments, but it was the first time the SPC explicitly affirmed that constitutional provisions could be cited as independent grounds for judgment.

[5] 'The admission theft event triggered the first case of constitutional judicialisation', *Nanfang zhoumo* (*Southern Weekend*), 16 August 2001.

[6] 137 US 5 (1803).

2 *The Failure of Constitutional Judicialization*

Unfortunately, subsequent developments quashed the prospect of developing constitutionally enforceable rights. Chinese judges have not taken any steps to consolidate their power in the aftermath of the *Qi Yuling* case; on the contrary, they have chosen to avoid invoking the Constitution. Since 2001, there has not been a single constitutional case to speak of. This is not to say that the People's Republic has not made any progress on constitutional issues. Indeed, in recent years, there have been several cases on equality in which the plaintiffs won, either in court or outside the courts by settlement or otherwise, but none were decided on constitutional grounds.

More fundamentally, judicial application of the Constitution has been viewed as potentially threatening to the leadership of the Chinese Communist Party (CCP). It was rumoured that the SPC circulated an internal directive forbidding following the *Qi Yuling* decision, which might have explained the *de facto* demise of the potential precedent. In any case, the new SPC president, who assumed the post in 2008, seemed to be dissatisfied with even *Qi Yuling*'s dysfunctional existence and moved to explicitly delete the *Qi Yuling* case from the casebook. In December 2008, the SPC published a document that officially voided the legal effect of several outdated judicial explanations, among which the *Qi Yuling* case was the only one so voided without even a brief explanation.[7] In retrospect, the demise of the *Qi Yuling* case came as no surprise. It was the product of Huang Songyou, the then progressive chief judge of the civil division of the SPC; he was under investigation for corruption by 2008,[8] and the constitutional progress he helped to initiate came to an end along with his judicial career.

The failure of the judicial experiment with constitutional review vividly illustrates the powerless and dependent status of China's judiciary and particularly of individual judges. While rank-and-file judges are obliged to follow the directions of their court presidents, lower courts are obliged to follow the directions of higher courts, and the SPC is

[7] 'The Seventh Decision of the Supreme People's Court to Repeal Relevant Judicial Interpretations Released before 2007', 18 December 2008. Most of these judicial interpretations were voided either because their effective period had expired or because the circumstances in which they were enacted had changed.

[8] He was convicted of corruption and sentenced to life imprisonment: Zhu Yan, 'Disagreeing with the trial sentence, Huang Songyou will appeal', *Xinjingbao* (*New Beijing Daily*), 29 January 2010.

dominated by its president. The SPC president is himself but a leader of middle rank in the power echelons of the Party and is under the leadership of the Central Politics and Law Commission (PLC), the secretary of which used to be a member (among nine members) of the Politburo Standing Committee (PSC) headed by the general secretary of the CCP, the most powerful decision-making institution in China today. Such practice was *not* followed by the Xi Jinping regime, under which the number of PSC members was reduced to seven in 2012, and the secretary of the Central PLC was no longer one of them. However, General Secretary Xi Jinping has established numerous groups (*xiaozu*) within the ruling party, most of which are directly headed by himself. Judicial reform in the Xi regime has been orchestrated by a group in charge of 'deepening reform' and the Central PLC.

In any case, the courts in China remain dependent on the political will of the ruling party, which apparently opposes the idea that the courts should have anything to do with the Constitution. The SPC president, who is in charge of drafting and implementing plans for judicial reform, merely follows and executes the directives of the ruling party's leadership. And when the president changes during a shift in the political leadership, so does the direction of judicial and constitutional reform. The Decision issued at the end of the Third Plenum of the 18th Central Committee of the CCP in November 2013 opened a new era for judicial reform and rehabilitated the professionalization of the judiciary – as one of the goals of judicial reform – initiated in 1999.[9] Indeed, the Decision expressly referred to the importance of improving the procedure of constitutional application so as to strengthen the legal effect of the Constitution. But the Decision says nothing about the judicial role in implementing the Constitution, and it seems unlikely that the first constitutional case will be rehabilitated in the foreseeable future. The lack of institutional independence thus preordained the premature death of the judicially initiated experiment with constitutional review.

II Protecting Rights in Spite of the Constitution? Taking Equality as an Example

Despite its failure, the first constitutional case mentioned above illustrates that the courts can be crucially important to the future of Chinese

[9] The CCP Decision on Several Important Issues Concerning Comprehensively Deepening the Reform.

constitutional law. If the Constitution is judicialized through right to education, the judicialization may, in turn, bring the realization of this right as well as of other rights stipulated in the Constitution to a new height. Most significantly, Article 33 of the Constitution explicitly dictates that 'all citizens are equal before law', and presumably also before the education laws. If this provision is directly enforceable, the Chinese courts *can* become the most effective organ for combating the now ubiquitous inequality and discrimination that are officially sanctioned, as clearly demonstrated in the practices in education.[10] One can even hope that Article 33 (or similar provisions in future constitutions) might play a role as important as the Fourteenth Amendment in the United States.

Indeed, since the *Qi Yuling* case, there have been several cases specifically based on the equality clause of Article 33. In the *Bank Employment Advertisement* case (2002),[11] the Chengdu Branch of the People's Bank of China put up an employment advertisement that limited applicants to certain majors and educational qualifications. In addition to those, however, the bank also required the heights of male and female applicants to be above 168 centimetres and 155 centimetres, respectively. Jiang Tao, one of the male applicants and a law student at Sichuan University at that time, fell short of the height requirement. He alleged that the bank infringed his constitutionally guaranteed equal right to public employment. The court of the Wuhou district, Chengdu, decided that the employment practice was not an administrative act (*xingzheng xingwei*) in the sense of an exercise of its administrative management functions as defined by law. Furthermore, the defendant bank had already revised its advertisement and deleted the height restrictions after the litigation was initiated and before the effective date of application. Thus, the court declined to decide the case against the bank. It should be pointed out that, unlike the *Qi Yuling* case, where the Constitution could not directly be applied against the private defendants, this case was litigated against the proper defendant – a state-owned bank, which had the 'colour' of the state and was thus legally obliged to observe the constitutional provisions

[10] To just give one example, students who are residents in the major cities, especially Beijing and Shanghai, can be admitted by the best colleges located in these cities at grades that are significantly lower than those of students from other places.

[11] *Jiang Tao* v. *People's Bank of China, Chengdu Branch*, see Zhang Qianfan, *Xianfaxue daolun (Introduction to Studies of Constitutional Law)* (Beijing: Law Press, 2004) 503–504.

and principles.[12] The rationale given by the court with respect to the nature of the act was quite suspicious, since there is little reason to exclude the bank employment process from the purview of its administrative acts.

Employment of civil servants in China is subject to a variety of discriminatory limitations. Frequent complaints were made against the criterion for excluding non-infectious hepatitis B virus carriers, giving rise to a tragic case in which an applicant rejected on that ground committed manslaughter out of sheer fury.[13] In the *Hepatitis B Virus* case (2004), the government of Anhui province was sued for maintaining such a restriction in the employment of civil servants. The victim argued that such health criterion constituted discrimination in violation of Article 33 of the Constitution and his constitutionally protected interest in applying to become a civil servant. The court of Wuhu city (Anhui) held the concrete decision of rejecting the application invalid on the grounds of insufficient evidence, but eschewed the constitutional grounds. In fact, the chief judge of the administrative section of Anhui High Court believed that the constitutional guarantee of equality was limited only to the application of relevant laws in the administrative process and was not applicable to the legal classifications themselves.[14] Such a limited understanding, which used to be taken for granted in the legal community and is still not uncommon among Chinese officials, obviously constitutes an impediment to the general application of the equality clause.

More recently, women have become active in vindicating their equal rights in employment practice. After the Communists took over power, gender equality was a priority in policy agenda, and women were given earlier retirements out of consideration for their health conditions. Yet the implications of such gender policy changed over the years,

[12] An earlier case encountered the same defendant standing problem as the *Qi Yuling* case did. In the *Restaurant Advertisement* case (2000), a private restaurant in Chengdu advertised that state servants could enjoy a deduction from the normal food price. Several law students at Sichuan University challenged such practice on the grounds of Article 33. The court in that case quite properly declined jurisdiction as civil law activities were governed by the General Principles of Civil Law (*Minfa tongze*), not the Constitution.

[13] Shen Ying, 'Zhou Yichao kill for hepatitis-B discrimination', *Nanfang zhoumo* (*Southern Weekend*), 7 August 2004.

[14] Zhou Wei, *Xianfa jiben quanli sifa jiuji yanjiu (Study of Judicial Remedies Relating to Fundamental Constitutional Rights)* (Beijing: China People's Public Security University Press, 2004) 100.

and what used to be considered a privilege may now become a disadvantage. Nowadays it is a settled practice for female employees in state-owned enterprises to retire at the age of fifty-five and their male counterparts at sixty, but earlier retirement means, to women, loss of job opportunities and income. A woman employee who just reached the retirement age challenged the employment policy of China Construction Bank (Mount Pingding Branch), which was based on the State Council's Provisional Method for Settling (*anzhi*) Old, Weak, Sick and Handicapped Cadres, which had been in force since 1978. She argued that she was in excellent health condition and could perform her professional functions competently and that the retirement policy violated both Article 33 of the Constitution and relevant provisions in the Labour Law regarding gender equality. The dispute was brought before the labour arbitration board of Mount Pingding city, but the plaintiff failed to win her claim.

Since China lacks a mechanism for constitutional adjudication, cases involving constitutional issues have been dealt with *not* by constitutional litigation but by administrative litigation or other means. This is the most obvious and most fundamental limitation for the Chinese constitutional cause. At this stage, we can only hope that constitutional rights can find some protection in the administrative law divisions of the Chinese courts through continuing improvements in the processes of administrative justice, which can, hopefully, provide a springboard for establishing a formal mechanism for constitutional adjudication in the future. However, it does not seem optimistic that the Chinese judiciary will live up to that hope.

III Ensuring Uniformity of Laws: The Law on Legislation and Its Limitations

The above discussion does not mean, however, that a procedure for constitutional review is completely absent in China. Rather, it only means that the review is not to be conducted by the courts, but rather by other institutions. Article 67 of the 1982 Constitution provides that the Standing Committee of the National People's Congress (NPCSC) has the authority to 'interpret the Constitution and supervise its implementation'. Thus, the Constitution provides for a legislative rather than judicial review. Unfortunately, the NPCSC has been woefully deficient in fulfilling its constitutional mandate. Since the enactment of the 1982 Constitution, the NPCSC has interpreted many laws, including the Basic Law of the Hong Kong Special Administrative Region and the Criminal Code, but it has never interpreted a single provision of the Constitution, despite the fact that a number of laws and regulations were suspected to be in serious violation of the Constitution. In the landmark event that caused the death of Sun Zhigang in 2003, for example, the notorious Detention and Repatriation Measures was publicly challenged for violating the Constitution (Article 37 protecting personal freedom) and the Law on Legislation (LL) (Article 8 requiring the compulsory restriction of personal freedom to be authorized by law), but the NPCSC failed, once again, to take any action. The Measures were promptly repealed by the State Council itself to reduce the mounting public pressure caused by Sun's abnormal death.[15] Failure to interpret and implement the Constitution not only leaves the constitutional rights unenforced but also reduces the uniformity of the entire legal system since the Constitution, according to its own preamble, 'is the fundamental law of the state and has supreme legal authority'. In fact, due to judicial inaction and the lack of an alternative effective mechanism for interpreting and applying laws, laws enacted by the NPC and the NPCSC are often left helpless before the encroachments of local regulations and practices, producing pervasive local protectionism. During the last three decades of reform, local authorities have gained freedom to provide for local interests, and conflicts between local and central legislation have become inevitable. The problem is especially acute for a giant country like China, where central and local legislative competences are not constitutionally delimited. Article 3 of the 1982 Constitution merely states a vague principle of 'giving full scope to the initiative and enthusiasm of the local authorities under the unified leadership of the central authorities', which provides little guidance for dividing the central and local functions. As a result, China's central–local relationship has been trapped in a rather lawless state in which conflict between legal norms at different levels, commonly known as 'legislation fighting', has been both pervasive and perennial.

In 2000, the LL was enacted precisely to curb legislation fighting by specifying the hierarchy of legal norms and their lawmaking procedures as well as the mechanisms for resolving legislative conflict. In this sense,

[15] See Qianfan Zhang, *The Constitution of China: A Contextual Analysis* (Oxford: Hart Publishing, 2012) 75–80.

the LL is the 'law of laws', with a prominent status next to the Constitution.[16] Unlike the Constitution of the United States, the LL does not provide an absolute principle of national supremacy but employs a complex *ex post facto* review procedure to resolve the conflicts between local regulations and rules and national legal norms that are below the level of administrative regulations. If a discrepancy occurs between a local rule enacted by a local people's government (LPG) and a national administrative rule enacted by a ministry or commission under the State Council, or between different administrative rules concerning the same matter, a ruling shall be made by the State Council (Article 95(3) of the LL, as amended in 2015). If a discrepancy occurs between a local regulation enacted by a local people's congress (LPC) and an administrative rule concerning the same matter, then the process becomes more cumbersome, and the 2015 amendment does nothing to ameliorate the cumbersome procedure:

> The State Council shall give its opinion; where the State Council deems that the local regulation should apply, then in the local jurisdiction the local regulation shall be applied; where the State Council deems that the administrative rule should apply, it shall request the Standing Committee of the National People's Congress to make a ruling on the issue.[17]

Since China lacks a centralized mechanism for reviewing the legality of legislation, the LL is at pains to define a complex hierarchy of reviewing authorities. Generally, a state institution has the authority to review legislation enacted by another that is situated at one level below in the constitutional hierarchy, and an enabling agency has the authority to directly invalidate delegated legislation beyond the scope of authorization or inconsistent with the objective of the enabling decision (Article 97(7)). For example, while the NPC has the power to 'amend or withdraw any inappropriate law enacted by its Standing Committee' (Article 97(1)) and to 'amend or withdraw any inappropriate administrative rule or local rule' (Article 97(3)), the NPCSC has the power to invalidate, among other things, any administrative regulation that contravenes the Constitution or any law, and any local regulation that contravenes the Constitution or any law or administrative regulation (Article 97(2)). Likewise, while the State Council has the authority to amend or invalidate an

[16] For a concise explanation of the Chinese legal structure, see Albert H. Y. Chen, *An Introduction to Legal System of the People's Republic of China*, 4th edn. (Hong Kong: LexisNexis, 2011) chs. 1 and 2.

[17] LL Art 95(2).

inappropriate departmental or provincial rule (Article 97(2)), a provincial LPG has the power to amend or withdraw any inappropriate local rule enacted by the LPG at the next lower level (Article 97(6)). To facilitate legislative review, an inferior agency is obliged to report its legislation within thirty days of its promulgation to its superior (Articles 97 and 98). This complex setup of cascading review aims to ensure the legality of legislation at all levels.

Finally, the LL grants to state institutions, social organizations and individual citizens the right to request review of legislative conflict. Unlike judicial review, which usually requires personal standing to initiate review procedures, China's legislative review process may be initiated by almost anyone. First, Article 99 provides that certain state institutions can request and initiate the review process by right, even though such request has never been put forward since the promulgation of the LL in 2000. The State Council, the Central Military Commission, the SPC, the Supreme People's Procuratorate, a special committee of the NPCSC or a standing committee of a provincial LPC may all make written requests to the NPCSC for review if they consider that an administrative regulation or local regulation contravenes the Constitution or any law. The working office of the NPCSC, known as the Legal Affairs Commission (LAC), distributes such requests to the relevant special committees of the NPC for review and comment, a process that may eventually lead to the NPCSC deliberating on and deciding the matter.

Second, a private citizen or social group may also make written proposals to the NPCSC for review if any of the above kinds of legislation are deemed to contravene the Constitution or any law, but their proposals will be 'studied' by the LAC and distributed to a relevant special committee for review and comment only 'where necessary' (LL, Article 99(2)). So far, although hundreds and perhaps even thousands of such private requests have been made, none of them has been deemed necessary enough to initiate the formal review process; even the request made by legal scholars to invalidate the egregious Detention and Repatriation Measures, which were repealed shortly afterwards by the State Council itself, failed to initiate the review process under the LL in the aftermath of the Sun Zhigang incident. In fact, although a special office was created under the LAC for 'regulatory review and record' in 2005, it has never even published the list of requests received, making it impossible to assess the number or nature of such requests. Despite the minimal standing requirement, private individuals have never been able to trigger the seemingly well-designed, albeit convoluted, review process provided for by the LL, and no public institution has ever even bothered to try.

IV Limitations of the Law on Legislation

As the 'law of laws', yet seldom, if ever, used since its promulgation in China, the LL suffers from several serious limitations. First, although its original purpose was to curb legislation fighting, it has done little to strengthen the uniform application of national legislation and to resolve conflicts among different norms below the level of administrative regulations. In contrast to a federal system such as that of the United States, where federal powers are limited to those granted in the Constitution but have supremacy vis-à-vis state and local legislation,[18] China's centrally made legislation needs no constitutional grant. However, neither is it supreme over local legislation in the complete sense – a State Council departmental rule is not necessarily superior to a local regulation or rule, even if the former is entirely consistent with national laws and regulations that, in turn, comply with the Constitution. Far from curbing legislation fighting, then, the LL runs the serious risk of encouraging conflict between legislative acts that sit below the level of administration regulations. While it may accommodate local diversity and avoid the disadvantages of 'cutting across the board with one knife' (*yidaoqie* in Chinese) by departmental rules or decisions, it undermines legal uniformity as a basic requirement of the rule of law.

Second, it is not only impossible to decide *a priori* the rank of a departmental rule vis-à-vis a local regulation or rule, it is also extremely difficult to apply the review mechanism in practice. If a conflict between a departmental rule and provincial regulation or rule occurs, a request for review will have to be submitted to the State Council, an extremely busy bureaucratic centre that has only one legal affairs office (LAO) (*fazhi bangongshi*) to handle issues of legislative conflict, and this results in long delays in conflict resolution. Adding to that agony, if the State Council decides in favour of its department and against a provincial regulation, the matter will have to be appealed further to the NPCSC, which is preoccupied with its own legislative agenda.[19] This process is meant to both temper the natural inclination of the State Council to side with its own departments, which would disqualify it as a neutral arbitrator in

[18] Art. 6, Constitution of the United States.
[19] See Zhang, *The Constitution of China* (note 14 earlier), 84–96.

dispute resolution, and make up for any democratic deficit inherent in a process where the national administration imposes its decisions on locally elected People's Congresses. In reality, however, it simply prolongs an already lengthy process and creates further delays.

On the whole, both the State Council and the NPCSC are preoccupied with their own administrative and legislative work and, thus, can hardly devote significant time to resolving pervasive legislation fighting in such a massive state as China or to processing the massive number of individual complaints that are made possible by the lack of a standing requirement. Timely resolution of legal conflicts requires a far more decentralized process whereby impartial judicial institutions across the country are able to take up and speedily dispose of the local complaints.

This leads to the third and most important point: the conspicuous absence of courts in the entire review process. Indeed, the LL completely leaves out the courts. This is consistent with the old version of Administration Litigation Law (ALL), which limits the scope of judicial review to 'concrete administrative acts' and does not extend to 'abstract administrative acts' such as laws, regulations (*fagui*), rules (*guizhang*) or any normative documents of a general nature.[20] In fact, the courts are obliged to take laws and regulations as legal grounds and rules as references (*canzhao*) in adjudications.[21] Although the new version of ALL, revised in 2014, does not explicitly limit the scope of review to concrete as opposed to abstract administrative acts, it does exclude the jurisdiction over 'administrative regulations and rules or decisions and orders with general binding force developed and issued by administrative agencies' (Article 13(2)).

A small breakthrough was made in Article 53 of the ALL (as amended in 2014), which now allows citizens to challenge the legality of a normative document below the level of rules (*guizhang*) in litigation against a concrete administrative act. If the court finds a norm in such a document to be legally groundless, the norm should not be used as grounds for holding the administrative act legal, and the court shall recommend a solution to the agency that enacted the norm (Article 64). Such a small step does not, however, change the overall characterization of China's courts as an inadequate institution for resolving the conflicts of laws.

That the courts play little role in resolving legislation conflicts merely reinforces the impression that the review provided for in the LL is purely

[20] Ibid., 160–168.

[21] Arts. 52–53, ALL (as enacted in 1989), Art. 63, ALL (as amended in 2014).

legislative – or more accurately, political rather than judicial in nature. Not only is the review of legislation directed to purely abstract norms with no requirements about personal standing – and thus able to avoid the concrete cases and controversies normally associated with judicial review – but when review is conducted by a nonjudicial institution without the guidance of any higher legal principles such as the supremacy of national legislation, legal criteria are completely absent. When the State Council or the NPCSC confronts a conflict between a departmental rule and a provincial regulation deemed to be of the same rank, what can possibly be the legal ground that predictably governs its ruling except *ad hoc* policy considerations? As a result, the legislative review contemplated in Article 99 of the LL is nothing but *ad hoc* lawmaking by the reviewing agency, which does so, at best, with a vague idea of the relevant situation at the time of review. In other legal systems in which the hierarchy of legal norms is well defined, such clear violations of higher norms as found in the Detention and Repatriation Measures in China may meaningfully be reviewed even without a concrete case, but such review is best conducted by an impartial institution of a judicial nature since, as Chief Justice Marshall pointed out in *Marbury* v. *Madison*, 'It is emphatically the province and duty of the judicial department to say what the law is'.[22] Unfortunately, the courts in China are excluded from this task, leaving the basic objective of curbing legislation fights unfulfilled.

Precisely two centuries after the *Marbury* decision, a similar case appeared in Luoyang, Henan province of China, but the very opposite result was reached. The case itself was simple enough: a seed company agreed with the plaintiff to provide an amount of corn seeds but defaulted by selling the seeds to other parties at market price. The dispute came to the Luoyang City Court in 2003, focusing on the amount of damages to be awarded to the plaintiff. While the plaintiff insisted on the calculation of damages on the basis of the market price in accordance with the Seed Law enacted by the NPCSC, which would amount to damages of CNY700,000, the defendant, citing Article 36 of the Henan Provincial Regulations on Crop Seeds enacted by the standing committee of the provincial people's congress (PCSC), claimed that the 'government guidance price' should be the standard for calculating the damages, which would amount to CNY20,000. The assistant judge presiding over the case, Li Huijuan, found for the plaintiff, interpreting the Seed Law as

[22] *Marbury* v. *Madison*, 5 US 137 (1803).

having established the principle of applying a market price standard. Since the Henan Regulations are local legislation, which is below the level of national law in the legal hierarchy, the relevant provision in the Regulations that conflicted with the Seed Law were held null and void.[23]

The case did not even implicate any constitutional provisions, as *Marbury* did, although the nature of the question was similar: does the court have *any* power in reviewing abstract norms, if only to safeguard the supremacy of the Constitution and national laws? And the answer provided by the Luoyang court was commonsensical enough in any jurisdiction committed to rule of law: of course, the court, through the pivotal role of judicial review, is obliged to maintain a rational legal order, and reason dictates that a higher law be given effect, notwithstanding lower-level laws to the contrary. But the Henan provincial PCSC reacted strongly against the decision and forced the City Court to renounce the judgment.[24] When the courts are unable to defend the law, local protectionism necessarily runs amuck, fatally damaging the uniformity of the entire legal system.

V China's Judicial Syndrome

Although it might be desirable to entrust China's constitutional review to the courts, the courts as they stand now are institutionally incapable of conducting independent judicial review. As China recovered from the lawless destruction of the Cultural Revolution and began to recognize the importance of law, the 1982 Constitution reaffirmed the courts as 'judicial organs of the state' (Art. 123), composed of the SPC, local courts at various levels, military courts and other special courts. Inheriting the Chinese revolutionary tradition, however, the courts are not independent, but subject to the supervision of the People's Congresses at the same (national or local) levels as the courts (Art. 128). Article 126 of the Constitution does provide that 'the people's courts exercise judicial power independently, in accordance with the provisions of the law, and are not subject to interference by any administrative organ, public organization or individual'. But the significance of this provision has been questioned on at least two grounds.

[23] See Guo Guosong, 'The judge struck down a local regulation: Is she violating the law or vindicating the law?' *Nanfang zhoumo (Southern Weekend)*, 20 November 2003.

[24] See Zhang, *The Constitution of China* (note 14 earlier), 84–96.

First, although it excludes interferences by the government, individuals, organizations and possibly political parties, if they are interpreted to be a form of public organization, it is silent on the People's Congresses and the Procuratorates, both of which are in charge of supervising the courts – the former through the appointment of judges and supervision of the courts' performance as a whole, and the latter through the procedure of 'protest' (which is a kind of appeal) against individual court judgments they consider to be wrong. It was once debated whether the People's Congresses could supervise courts' adjudication of individual cases (*ge'an jiandu*), and this question has been answered in the negative. Deputies to People's Congresses may, according to the Constitution and laws, investigate or remove judges who improperly perform their functions, but such power does not authorize them to inquire into cases they suspect to have been wrongfully decided.[25]

Second, and more importantly, Article 126 provides for the 'independence of the court' rather than independence of individual judges. Literally understood, a court enjoys institutional protection against interferences from other institutions or individuals, but individual judges do not enjoy the same protection in daily judicial practice; in other words, they may be subject to the direction and supervision of the court leaders, and in fact, they are. The Organic Law of the People's Courts establishes the so-called president responsibility system (*yuanzhang fuzezhi*) by which the court's president, assisted by the judicial committee (*shenpan weiyuanhui*) of the court, is held responsible for all the judgments made by the court. If the president finds 'definite error in the determination of facts or application of law' in a judgment of his court, he is obliged to submit the judgment to the judicial committee for review (Art. 13). Presided over by the court president and staffed by the vice presidents, the party secretary (usually one of the vice presidents), the chief judges of divisions and senior judges, the judicial committee is a court within the court whose major task is to practise democratic centralism by 'summing up judicial experience and discussing important or difficult cases' (Art. 10). In fact, it can directly decide a case in a way contrary to the judgment of the presiding judge who originally tried the case even though none of the committee members may have been directly involved in trying the case originally.

[25] Cai Dingjian, 'The current status and the reform of the people's Congress's individual case supervision', in Cai Dingjian (ed.), *Jjiandu yu sifa gongzheng: Yanjiu yu anli baogao [Supervision and Judicial Fairness: A Study and Case Report]* (Beijing, Law Press, 2005) 69.

Against this background, Article 8 of the Judges Law, which lists a number of *judges'* rights, among which is 'to brook no interference from administrative organs, public organizations or individuals in trying cases according to law' (Art. 8(2)), must be understood as a heedless slip of the pen. In fact, the same law establishes a more rigorous assessment and reward-and-punishment scheme for the judges whose performance is evaluated by a 'commission of examination and assessment' headed by the court president (Arts. 48, 49). The judges are divided into twelve 'grades', to be 'determined on the basis of their posts, their actual working ability and political integrity, their professional competence, their achievements in judicial work and their seniority' (Art. 19). In such a tightly regulated scheme, an individual judge can hardly find space for any independent judgment based on his or her own conscience and free from interference of the court. And judges with enough courage to insist on independent judgment will sooner or later get into trouble. For example, Wang Guangya, a judge at Fuping county court (Shan'xi province), was officially denounced and removed for arguing with the judicial committee and 'adamantly refusing to admit his errors'.[26] Jia Tingrun, the former president of the Lulong county court (Henan province), was also removed for refusing to follow the direction of the superiors and suffered reductions in rank and salary.[27] These painful lessons serve as sufficient deterrent to independent judges, making judges' independence impossible.

Nor is the constitutional provision for the institutional independence of the courts implemented in practice. The *Luoyang Seed* case clearly illustrates how the court is controlled (or 'supervised') by the LPC and the superior courts, which are ultimately all controlled by the ruling party. Once the independence of individual judges within the court is compromised, so is the institutional independence of the court from external interference by the ruling party and administration since the latter can easily put pressure on the president of the court and virtually influence any judgment via the president responsibility system.

As a result, China's courts suffer from the judicial syndrome, an interlocking combination of dysfunctional symptoms: (1) local protectionism that seriously undermines the uniformity of law; (2) low

[26] 'It's no crime to decide cases according to law', *Renmin ribao* (*People's Daily*), 22 February 2001; Huang Guangming, 'A judge's cost for "disobeying the superior"', *Nanfang zhoumo* (*Southern Weekend*), 22 March 2001.

[27] Guo Guosong, 'How difficult is it for judge to abide by his conscience', *Nanfang zhoumo* (*Southern Weekend*), 5 December 2002.

professional and moral quality of some judges, making them prone to corruption and unfit for impartial administration of justice; (3) primacy of bureaucratic management of the courts and political control of the judges, which is at odds with the generally recognized principle of judicial independence and impartiality and (4) the lack of adequate material provisions (income, funding and working conditions) that are necessary for the effective functioning of the courts.[28]

In order to cure the judicial syndrome, in October 1999, the SPC launched the first Outline of Five-Year Reform of the People's Courts (Outline). In response to academic criticism and local experimentation over the years, the Outline vowed to improve the existing judicial structure in China, to enhance the power and autonomy of the individual judges and to guarantee judicial efficiency and fairness. Undertaking to make China's judges 'real judges',[29] this ambitious reform aimed to professionalize the hitherto politicized courts and did manage to change the judicial outlook from that of 'army uniform and starred epaulets' to 'gavel and black robe'. Judges would be more carefully selected from the existing stock of judicial tribunals and lawyers who have established records of good performance.[30] In the meantime, those judges who were unable to meet the professional standard would be laid off.

These objectives are yet to be achieved, though China's judiciary has made observable progress in the course of the implementation of the three successive outlines of five-year reform published since the first judicial reform outline of 1999. The measures adopted by the most recent reform laid the foundations for establishing a more professional judiciary and were directed against the judicial syndrome that has plagued China's courts for decades. The centralization of judicial power, a conspicuous aspect of the current reform, is expected to reduce, if not eliminate, judicial interference from the party and government at the same level. Such interference has dogged the uniform application of national laws and regulations. The centralization reform is coupled with a reduction in political and administrative control inside the courtroom and the enhancement of the role of individual judges in deciding cases. It remains

[28] Qianfan Zhang, 'The People's Court in transition: The prospects of the Chinese judicial reform' (2003) 12 *Journal of Contemporary China* 69.

[29] Words used by the former SPC president, Xiao Yang, who was instrumental in hammering out the first five-year plan for judicial reform. See *Xinhua Daily*, 25 October 1999 (in Chinese).

[30] *Xinhua Daily*, 25 October 1999, B1 (in Chinese).

to be seen whether these measures can effectively transform China's courts and improve the judges' independence.

VI Impediments and Prospects

Both the *Qi Yuling* case and the *Corn Seed* case illustrate the necessity for establishing some form of judicial review in China. While the *Qi Yuling* case proves positively the importance of courts for protecting constitutional rights, the *Corn Seed* case shows negatively that the legal system will fall into disorder if courts are prevented from playing an effective role in enforcing the Constitution and national laws. Repealing the legal effect of the SPC reply in the *Qu Yuling* case, thus foreclosing the judicial remedy for constitutional violations, merely leaves the Constitution unenforced. When the courts cannot apply the Constitution in adjudicating cases, constitutional issues cannot be adequately dealt with. As the equality cases amply illustrate, the principle of administrative legality is no substitute for constitutionality, not to mention that the Chinese courts are severely handicapped in reviewing the legality of administrative acts.

At the theoretical level, some argue that judicial review is impeded in China by a parliamentary system akin to that of the Westminster system.[31] According to A. V. Dicey, the British do not accept judicial review of legislation because Parliament is thought to be the supreme legislator, whose legislative enactments cannot be invalidated by judges.[32] They further argue, citing populist critics of constitutional judicial review in the United States, that judicial review is undemocratic in the sense that it allows a few judges unaccountable to the populace to strike down, in the interest of elite minorities, legislation enacted by popularly elected representatives, hence, the counter-majoritarian difficulty.[33] These arguments seem to make a point, but only superficially. To begin with, no matter whether Dicey's argument still holds true today, the British case differs fundamentally from China because Britain does *not* have a written constitution as the higher law in its legal system, so that British judges have nothing against which to review parliamentary legislation. As soon as the

[31] See e.g., Fei Shancheng, 'On the choice of constitutional review models in China' (1999) 2 *Zhengfa luntan (Tribune of Political Science and Law)* 5–6.

[32] A. V. Dicey, *Introduction to the Study of the Law of the Constitution*, 8th edn. (London: Macmillan, 1915) 39.

[33] For a critique, see Zhang Qianfan, 'Judicial review and democracy: A community of contraries?'(2009) 1 *Huanqiu falü pinglun (Global Law Review)* 58–66.

United Kingdom changes this feature of its legal system and enacts a law higher than ordinary legislation, its judges will immediately confront the same question raised by Chief Justice Marshall over two centuries ago: If a law 'be in opposition to the constitution; if both the law and the constitution apply to a particular case, . . . the court must determine which of these conflicting rules governs the case', and of course, the only reasonable answer is that 'an act of the legislature, repugnant to the constitution, is void'.[34] Since the task of statutory interpretation and conflict resolution is traditionally relegated to the courts, judicial review will immediately come into being as a natural consequence of resolving any legal conflicts that might arise between the higher law and ordinary laws. Indeed, the British situation has already been changed in 1998, when the Human Rights Act incorporated the European Convention on Human Rights and empowered British judges to review legislation and make declarations of incompatibility with the Act. Although Parliament may choose to ignore such a declaration, it has, in fact, respected every judicial declaration the court has made so far so that the declaratory scheme has already been categorized as a weak form of judicial review.[35]

Although China's NPC enjoys a supremacy similar to that of the British Parliament; is the supreme body which elects the key positions in the Chinese state, including the leading judges; and is a body to which all these positions are held accountable, China differs from the United Kingdom in one key respect, which is that China does have a written constitution, which defines itself in the preamble as 'the fundamental law of the state', with 'supreme legal authority'. It further commands that 'all state organs . . . must take the constitution as the fundamental standard of conduct'. Article 5 of the Constitution dictates explicitly that

> No laws or administrative or local regulations shall contravene the Constitution.
>
> All state organs . . . shall abide by the Constitution and the laws. All acts in violation of the Constitution or the laws must be investigated.
>
> No organization or individual is privileged to be beyond the Constitution or the laws.

Here, 'all state organs' obviously includes the NPC itself and the NPCSC. It is certainly possible that the NPC or the NPCSC enacts a law that

[34] *Marbury* v. *Madison*, 5 U.S. 137, 178 (1803).

[35] See Rivka Weill, 'The new commonwealth model of constitutionalism notwithstanding: On judicial review and constitution-making' (2014) 62 *American Journal of Comparative Law* 127.

contravenes the Constitution so that it is necessary to establish a mechanism that reviews the constitutionality of laws. Neither the NPC nor the NPCSC is suitable for such a vocation since they would violate the basic principle of impartiality by judging their own cases – the constitutionality of legislation they make. Unfortunately, Article 67 of the Constitution does just that by authorizing the NPCSC to 'interpret the Constitution and supervise its enforcement' (Clause 1 of Article 67). For reasons just explained, however, this clause should not be interpreted as authorizing the NPCSC to be the *sole* body capable of interpreting the Constitution. At least, the Constitution never prohibits other state institutions from interpreting the Constitution. Indeed, they are required, just as the NPC or the NPCSC is, to 'take the constitution as the fundamental standard of conduct'. How do they take the Constitution as their 'fundamental standard of conduct' without even understanding and interpreting it, particularly on occasions where the NPCSC fails to provide any interpretive guidance? And the NPCSC has failed to do that ever since the Constitution was enacted in 1982. Thus far, it has never produced a single constitutional interpretation, a crucial task that Article 67 of the Constitution entrusts to it. Does that mean that the enforcement of the Constitution is entirely at the mercy of the NPCSC, and should be left unenforced when it has failed to any take action? Is it not much more reasonable to interpret Article 67 as conferring only the interpretive power of last resort on the NPCSC, while allowing other state institutions to make their own constitutional interpretations, as long as theirs do not contradict the NPCSC interpretation, if there is one?

Since the Constitution characterizes itself as 'the fundamental law', and since the court is in charge of the daily application and interpretation of laws, it seems only natural that the courts should have the authority to interpret the Constitution. Moreover, judicial interpretation of the Constitution should bind all state institutions other than the NPC and the NPCSC. In other words, the judicial constitutional interpretation should be inferior only to that of the NPCSC (and occasionally, to the NPC, if it takes the initiative to apply the Constitution, a highly unlikely event). Indeed, this is precisely the way in which the normal interpretive business is conducted in China. In areas such as civil, criminal and procedural laws, the NPCSC often issues official interpretations, which bind the courts and other state institutions in interpreting and applying these laws. The same Article 67 authorizes the NPCSC to interpret the laws (Clause 4 of Article 67), and this clause has never been interpreted as prohibiting the courts from interpreting laws, which would be contrary to common sense. What is the rationale to interpret two clauses of the same Article 67 to mean the opposite?[36] True, the courts are not authorized to review the legality of, say, an administrative regulation made by the State Council in implementing a law, but if the court finds that regulation to be inconsistent with either the NPCSC's interpretation or its own interpretation of a relevant law, then good policy counsels against applying the regulation, just as Judge Li Huijuan declined to apply the Henan provincial regulation in the *Corn Seed* case. Anyway, there is nothing in sound jurisprudence that prevents courts from interpreting and applying the Constitution as the fundamental law in adjudicating cases. Quite to the contrary, the Constitution binds courts, just as any law does, and imposes upon them the duty to properly interpret and apply the fundamental law of the state to concrete cases tried by them.

Nor is the counter-majoritarian difficulty anything serious to worry about once the courts begin to apply the Constitution in China. The difficulty is felt acutely in the United States, primarily because it has, in James Bryce's term, a 'rigid constitution'. Since the text of the US Constitution is difficult to amend, the Supreme Court has become the *de facto* supreme interpreter of the Constitution. In Chief Justice Hughes's perhaps exaggerated expression in his 1907 speech, 'We are under a Constitution, but the Constitution is what the judges say it is'.[37] During the New Deal, the Supreme Court even obviated the need for the state democratic process to discharge the heavy burden of constitutional amendment by changing its own constitutional interpretation. As a result, the American constitutional dialogue is dominated by the Supreme Court, which in effect, has the final say on what the Constitution means. Even if there are objections to this in the United States, given its constitutional process, such objections are irrelevant to China since the 1982 Constitution is rather flexible, requiring only a two-thirds majority of the NPC to amend the text, and it has since been amended five times, adding such new principles as rule of law and respect for human rights and private property to the Constitution.[38] Thus even if the court errs in a constitutional interpretation, it

[36] Art. 67 authorizes the NPCSC to interpret the Constitution and the laws. It is generally accepted that clause 4 of Art. 67 does not exclude the judicial interpretation of laws. Yet, clause 1 of Art. 67 is apparently interpreted to exclude the judicial application of the Constitution.

[37] Quoted in Craig R. Ducat, *Constitutional Interpretation: Rights of Individual*, vol. 2 (Belmont, CA: Wadsworth Publishing, 2012) xvi.

[38] There are exceptions, of course. The Liberal Democratic Party that has dominated the Japanese parliament since 1955, for example, attempted to amend the 1946 Constitution several times, but it has not been able to muster the two-thirds majority required to

can be overturned by the NPC amending the constitutional text. In most cases, however, it need not go that far, since the judicial interpretation can easily be overridden by an NPCSC interpretation, if it chooses to act. If the court is authorized to interpret the Constitution in China, it is expected to engage itself in a healthy dialogue with the NPC and the NPCSC, among other state institutions, rather than dominating the constitutional interpretation, as in the United States. And, even in the United States, hardly anyone seriously challenges the legitimacy of judicial review *per se* and proposes its total abolition; rather, the debates focus on the proper functions of judicial review so as to make it fit congenially with democracy. As this chapter has shown, prohibiting judicial review raises the serious question of whether the Constitution has any meaning at all.

The alternative, which is the legislative review mechanism, as laid out in the LL, has proven to be ineffective in ensuring the supremacy of the Constitution and the laws in China. To make the words of the Constitution and the laws count, then, serious institutional reforms are called for. A proposal often put forward by China's legal community is to establish a constitutional committee to oversee the interpretation and implementation of the Constitution. It will be best, of course, if such committee can maintain an independent status, much like a court. Under the current dominant understanding, however, such an independent institution seems to be incompatible with the supremacy of the NPC, which supposedly represents the will of the nation through its legislation. An alternative arrangement would be to place the constitutional committee as a special committee within the NPC or the NPCSC. As an initial step, for example, the constitutional committee can be a working agency on behalf and under the direction of the NPCSC. In such a situation, the mechanism of constitutional review can be established even without amending the Constitution. The reviewing committee can simply deal with ordinary constitutional claims on a daily basis, with the NPCSC acting as a rubber stamp and intervening only in politically important cases. The constitutional committee may become more formally independent when it gains more experience and reputation. So far, however, there has been no sign that even such modest constitutional design is within the purview of the ruling party.

Despite the setback suffered by the *Qi Yuling* case as an experiment in judicializing the Constitution, the role of courts cannot simply be cast aside. Even if constitutional issues are politically too sensitive to be handled

initiate the constitutional amendment. Hence, the Constitution has never been amended in the past seventy years.

by courts, at least they should be sufficiently empowered to decide cases like the *Corn Seed* case, i.e., to review the legality of abstract norms and resolve the conflicts among legal norms at different levels of the hierarchy. Otherwise, the unitary socialist state will be reduced by local protectionism of various sorts into feudal fiefdoms within a fragmented legal system. No matter whether any special institution is established for ensuring the constitutionality of legal acts, the existing mechanism of legal interpretation needs fundamental reform. Either courts should be authorized to review the legality of regulations and rules of an administrative nature, thus becoming a regular institution for resolving the conflict of legal norms, or a specialized judicial mechanism should be established for the review of legal norms.[39] It is apparently more consistent with the order of things that the principle of legality in the ordinary sense be observed before introducing a mechanism to ensure the constitutionality of all laws.

Up till now, however, the same force that has handicapped China's rule of law has handicapped its constitutionalism. The lack of judicial review is far from a purely theoretical question; I have shown that nothing in the Chinese constitutional jurisprudence prevents courts from taking the Constitution seriously. Nor is the total absence of the NPCSC's constitutional interpretation, in spite of the constitutional mandate in Article 67, a pure accident. The NPC, the NPCSC and the courts all depend on the ruling Communist Party, which has yet to make up its mind to bind itself by the Constitution and laws, despite its high-pitch commitment to 'build a socialist state of rule of law' avowed in Article 5 of the Constitution. It is particularly difficult for a socialist state to establish rule of law and constitutionalism when the ruling party, with its totalitarian legacy, is above all limitations and refuses to be bound by the limits of law. In 2003, the same year that the *Corn Seed* case was decided, I wrote that China's rule of law is 'limited by the ultimate political bottom line: a party that is essentially above the law'.[40] Very much the same can be said today about China's prospect of constitutionalism and judicial review.

The October 2017 Report of the 19th CCP Congress did promise to "promote constitutional review", for the first time in the history of the ruling party, and the Constitution was amended for that purpose in March 2018, replacing the "Law Committee" in the National People's Congress (NPC) with the "Constitution and Law Committee". But such "constitutional review" will remain legislative (within the NPC committee), *not* judicial.

[39] For details, see Zhang Qianfan, 'Establishing review of legal norms in China: A theory of constitutional revision' (2004) 2 *Zhanlue yu guanli (Strategies and Management)* 61–69.

[40] Zhang, 'The People's Court in transition', 100–101 (note 28 earlier).

14

Why Do Countries Decide Not to Adopt Constitutional Review?

The Case of Vietnam

NGOC SON BUI

I Introduction

Professors Tom Ginsburg and Mila Versteeg co-authored a seminal piece entitled 'Why Do Countries Adopt Constitutional Review?' which explains the logic of the global movement towards the adoption of constitutional review in the last few decades.[1] In this context, constitutional review is understood as '*the formal power of a local court or court-like body to set aside or strike legislation for incompatibility with the national constitution*'.[2] The quantitative empirical account by these scholars indicates that by 2011, 83 per cent of the world's constitutions have provisions for constitutional review.[3] What about the other 17 per cent? Within Asia, four socialist constitutions in China, Laos, North Korea and Vietnam do not allow courts to determine constitutional meaning or set aside arguably unconstitutional legislation. The constitution of another socialist nation in the Western hemisphere, Cuba, also does not provide for constitutional review. The rejection of constitutional review is not distinctive to the socialist world. In Western Europe, the Constitution of Netherlands explicitly prohibits judicial review of constitutionality of legislation and treaties.[4] This chapter asks a negative question which has been underexplored in the existing comparative constitutional law scholarship: Why do countries decide not to adopt constitutional review?

[1] Tom Ginsburg and Mila Versteeg, 'Why do countries adopt constitutional review?' (2013) 3 *The Journal of Law, Economics, and Organizations* 587–622.

[2] Ibid., 589 (original italics).

[3] Ibid., 590.

[4] The Constitution of the Kingdom of the Netherlands (2002), Article 120.

I will focus on the case of Vietnam. After almost a decade of vibrant deliberation, Vietnam eventually rejected constitutional review in its new Constitution adopted in late 2013. The Vietnamese case stands as the paradigmatic example of rejection of constitutional review during a constitutional design process that has occurred recently and deserves scholarly attention. Elsewhere, on the positive side, I have extensively examined the rise of the discussions supporting the creation of constitutional review in Vietnam.[5] In this study, I turn to a negative approach to understand the reasons behind its rejection.

This study is epistemologically connected to the comparative constitutional law scholarship on negative responses to transnational or international constitutional influence. In terms of methodology, this study adopts an empirical rather than normative approach to the issue of constitutional review in Vietnam.[6] This empirical approach is qualitative rather than quantitative. The quantitative approach is useful to conduct large-N comparative analysis of gigantic data, but to comprehend the actual intention of constitutional designers, it is important to qualitatively consider their discourse and the surrounding context through small-N comparative studies.[7] Therefore, to understand the rejection of constitutional review in Vietnam, I look at the actual constitutional debates during the constitution-making process and consider how opponents of constitutional review articulate their dissenting arguments. To examine these debates, I rely on original sources available in Vietnamese, including documents produced by Vietnamese constitution-makers and journalistic materials. The qualitative empirical approach is supported by my engagement in debates on constitutional review in Vietnam. This has allowed me to interact with some constitution-makers, legislators, constitutional intellectuals, lawyers and officials.

I argue that there is a resistance model in constitutional review design. The institution of constitutional review is resisted not merely because it is unsuitable or there are better alternatives but because there is a weighty consideration of constitutional review as a threat to the political elite's

[5] Ngoc Son Bui, 'The discourse of constitutional review in Vietnam' (2014) 9 *Journal of Comparative Law* 191–221.

[6] For a normative approach to the issue of constitutional review in Vietnam, see Huong Nguyen, *Anticipating Constitutional Politics: Designing a Constitutional Review Mechanism for Transitional Vietnam* (PhD Dissertation, Indiana University, 2014).

[7] For different methods of casual inference in comparative constitutional studies, see Ran Hirschl, *Comparative Matters: The Renaissance of Comparative Constitutional Law* (Oxford: Oxford University Press, 2014) 244.

preferences. As the case of Vietnam illustrates, some influential political elites, drawing from past and contemporary experiences, intentionally construct a negative image in which constitutional review presents dangers to their own preferences for the sake of which they resist it. This resistance model is not hegemonic in the Vietnamese discourse on constitutional review but is consequential in that this negative imagination practically induces an uncertainty among constitutional decision-makers about the future effects of constitutional review in Vietnam, which effectively results in its rejection.

An understanding of the rejection of constitutional review has important implications. The study of both adoption and rejection of constitutional review deserves a more balanced and fuller picture of the fate of constitutional review in various systems. Moreover, the account of the rejection of constitutional review has general implications for comparative constitutional law in the global age. The emerging scholarship on global constitutionalism tends to focus on the global factors that lead to global constitutional convergence. Equally important, however, are local factors that engender constitutional resistance. The rejection of constitutional review, for example, illustrates that local preferences resist the global impact of constitutional review. Another general implication is for comparative law's perennial concern for legal 'transplantation', 'borrowing' or 'unification'. The rejection of constitutional review casts doubts on the assumption that 'all good things always go together'.

I will briefly introduce constitutional review rejection in the socialist world, then describe the specific Vietnamese story, articulate the theoretical model of resistance in constitutional review design, analyse the working of this model in Vietnam and conclude with some thoughts about the more general implications.

II Constitutional Review Rejection in the Socialist World

Although the rejection of constitutional review is not distinctive to the socialist constitutions, I focus here on the socialist cases. The Soviet bloc basically rejected constitutional review for its conflict with the fundamental principles and assumptions of socialist constitutional law.[8] In the socialist world, legislation was traditionally conceived as expressive of the people's will beyond the review of judicial bodies. Moreover, the principle

8 Rhett Ludwikowski, 'Judicial review in the socialist legal system: Current developments' (1988) 37 *The International and Comparative Law Quarterly* 89–108.

of unity of power elevated the legislature to the supreme position, which denied judicial evaluation of its actions. In contrast, the legislature was in charge of constitutional supervision. Some socialist constitutions of the Soviet bloc provided for parliamentary committees with advisory functions designed to uphold the principle of parliamentary supremacy, such as the Constitutional Committee in Romania, created in 1965, or the Council of Constitutional Law in Hungary, established in 1984.[9] Judicial review was also inconsistent with the socialist understanding of the constitution. Socialist constitutions were not merely legal documents which included only judicially enforced rules. They were, in many ways, programmatic and aspirational documents which served as a framework for the implementation of socialism. Programmatic and aspirational provisions concerning fundamental social and economic policies are not judicially reviewable. Finally, although provisions not relevant to political economy might be reviewed in theory, socialist constitutional culture regarded constitutional litigation as individualist enterprise. Consequently, socialist theorists looked down at 'the institution of bourgeois judicial review' as a 'reactionary institution'.[10]

Yet, some socialist countries did consider constitutional review. For example, Yugoslavia established a Federal Constitutional Court and special constitutional courts in 1963.[11] Czechoslovakia also attempted to introduce some form of judicial review, but this development was hampered by the Russian intervention in 1968.[12] Poland also created the Constitutional Tribunal in 1982. But, if this body found legislation to be inconsistent with the Constitution, it could only submit that finding to the legislature for consideration.[13] The legislature had the final word on the constitutionality of its legislation, and therefore, the principle of legislative supremacy was guaranteed.

The fall of the Soviet bloc engendered the spread of the third wave of democratization in the late twentieth century.[14] This democratization process was accompanied by the creation of constitutional review (with the centralized model as the dominant model) in the former Soviet Union itself, its former members in Eastern Europe and Asia (e.g.,

[9] Ibid., 94.
[10] Ibid., 90–91.
[11] Ibid., 91.
[12] Ibid.
[13] Ibid., 101.
[14] See generally, Samuel P. Huntington, *The Third Wave: Democratization in the Late Twentieth Century* (Norman: University of Oklahoma Press, 1991).

Mongolia).[15] In a different line, five socialist countries, namely China, Cuba, Laos, North Korea and Vietnam, survived the collapse of the Soviet bloc and rejected the third wave of democratization as well as constitutional review. Core socialist constitutional principles, such as unity of power, legislative supremacy and single leadership of the Communist Party, have still defined these socialist systems, which are hostile to constitutional review. Instead, the function of constitutional supervision is vested in the legislature.

Among the five socialist countries, China and Vietnam tend to be more active in economic, legal and constitutional reforms. Adaptive reforms open the door for discussion of the possibility of introducing constitutional review in the socialist system. For several decades, Chinese scholars have discussed the potential creation of a special constitutional review body.[16] But the possibility of a centralized constitutional review body has not yet been considered in any national forum. In addition, the abortive movement towards 'judicialization of the Constitution' in China triggered by the *Qi Yuling* case, which attempted to vest the ordinary courts with a constitutional review function, was soon quelled by the communist government, and since then, courts have been prohibited from citing the Constitution.[17] The story in Vietnam is even more striking in the sense that the institution of constitutional review was discussed in the national platforms for constitutional design but was eventually rejected. This story is described in detail in Section III.

III The Rejection of Constitutional Review in Vietnam

Vietnam has had five constitutions enacted under the leadership of the Communist Party – in 1946, 1959, 1980, 1992 and 2013. The post-soviet 1992 Constitution focused on economic reform and left the socialist constitutional system virtually intact, defined by the single leadership of the Communist Party and the unity of power. The system of constitutional supervision by the legislature was also confirmed. However, since the turn of the twenty-first century, local constitutional scholars have actively discussed the potential creation of constitutional review.

[15] Samuel Issacharoff, 'Constitutional courts and democratic hedging' (2011) 99 *The Georgetown Law Journal* 962–1012, at 996. For Mongolia, see Chapter 7.

[16] Guobin Zhu, 'Constitutional review in China: An unaccomplished project or a mirage?' (2010) 43 *Suffolk University Law Review* 650–679. See also Chapter 13.

[17] Ibid., 644–647.

The dominant trend was advocacy for the establishment of a centralized constitutional court to realize the nation's new commitments to building the rule of law state, 'controlling the state power' and protecting human rights.[18] The Communist Party of Vietnam has also issued several documents supporting reform of the constitutional supervision system, but the Party did not provide clear guidance towards judicial constitutional review. In 2011, the party-state introduced a plan to comprehensively amend the national Constitution, and constitutional supervision reform was one of the central concerns of the constitution-makers. In early 2013, a draft of the new Constitution was released for public debate after its deliberation in the National Assembly. Among other things, the constitutional draft introduced a constitutional council which was institutionally independent from the legislature but could only have advisory power, like Poland's Constitutional Tribunal of 1982. In different popular official and unofficial forums debating constitutional issues, this institution was strongly criticized for its weak powers. Alternatively, the public called for a stronger adjudicative institution, like a constitutional court or a constitutional council with review powers. The institution also caused considerable division among the National Assembly members and constitution-makers. Some opposed the proposal of the constitutional council, while others agreed with its establishment with stronger review power. Eventually, the new Constitution adopted by the National Assembly in late 2013 rejected the proposal of the constitutional council and any proposals for judicial constitutional review.[19]

I will consider the figures, forums and arguments rejecting constitutional review during the 2013 constitutional debate. To begin with, who opposed constitutional review? The Party provided general guidance on the reform of the constitutional supervision system and opened the door for discussions of different options. There was virtually a consensus among legal scholars and public intellectuals in advocating for constitutional review. The strong support for constitutional review was also evident in most forums of public constitutional consultation. Among political elites, there was a considerable division regarding the question. Yet, constitutional debates among political elites were confidential. However, access to internal resources and conversations with local

[18] For more details, see Bui, 'The discourse of constitutional review in Vietnam', note 5, at 203.

[19] For more details, see Bui, 'The discourse of constitutional review in Vietnam', note 5.

constitutional scholars can help identify several opponents of constitutional review among the political elites.

While there are political leaders like the president of the National Assembly and of the Constitutional Amendment Committee who supported the creation of a constitutional review,[20] other political elites strongly opposed this institution. The opponents held key positions in state institutions and party institutions (such as the Politburo or the Party's Central Committee) which play a key role in decision-making in the Vietnamese authoritarian structure. They were concurrently National Assembly deputies and members of the Constitutional Amendment Committee. A Word document of the draft of the revised constitution, with tracked changes remaining, was circulated among the participants of a conference commenting on the draft held by an organ of the National Assembly.[21] The tracked changes indicated the specific views of key politicians on different provisions in the constitutional draft. Concerning Article 117 in the draft on the constitutional council, the tracked changes dated 17 July 2013 listed the names of four leaders who believed that 'the current mechanism of constitutional supervision is sufficient; it is necessary to fortify the leadership of the Party; it is not necessary to create a new mechanism'.[22] They were the Minister of Public Security, the Minister of National Defence, the Vice President of the State, and the President of the Supreme People's Court.[23] Among them, the Minister of Public Security's view may have had significant weight. He is an influential member of the Politburo, the highest institution within the party structure. By the time of this writing, he had become president of the State. A report by the Editorial Board of Constitutional Amendment also indicates that the Ministry of Public Security disagreed with the creation of a constitutional council.[24] So, it seems that

[20] This is evident in a workshop he convened in Hanoi where constitutional scholars were invited along with constitution-makers to discuss the possible creation of a constitutional council with review power. See Thu Trà, 'Hội đồng Hiến pháp trong Dự thảo sửa đổi Hiến pháp năm 1992 [The Constitutional Council in the draft amendments to the 1992 Constitution]' (2013, 17 August) VTV, http://vtv.vn/trong-nuoc/hoi-dong-hien-phap-trong-du-thao-sua-doi-hien-phap-nam-1992-95779.htm (accessed 6 October 2017, in Vietnamese; workshop attended by the author).

[21] On file with the author, who received the document and attended this conference.

[22] Ibid. (emphasis added).

[23] Ibid.

[24] Constitutional Amendment Committee, 'Báo cáo Tổng hợp ý kiến nhân dân về Dự thảo sửa đổi Hiến pháp năm 1992 (từ ngày 02/01/2013 đến ngày 30/4/2013) [Synthesis report on people's opinions on the draft amendments to the 1992 Constitution (From 2 January

there is an agreement among the public security community on the rejection of constitutional review.

Another political figure who opposed constitutional review was the President of the Supreme People's Procuracy. In a meeting of the National Assembly deputies debating constitutional revision issues, he explicitly opposed the creation of any constitutional review body.[25] A report of the People's Supreme Procuracy regarding a collection of opinions of members of the procuracies on the draft revised constitution indicates that 130 out of 201 opinions concerning the proposal of the constitutional council held a negative view.[26]

In addition to some political leaders, the opponents of constitutional review also included many Assembly deputies. Before the adoption of the new Constitution, the National Assembly conducted a trial vote on the specific issue of constitutional review, which indicated that 216 out of 357 deputies believed that the creation of a new institution of constitutional review was not necessary.[27] Some deputies expressly spoke out at the National Assembly meetings opposing the constitutional council or court.[28]

What are the platforms for disputing constitutional review? The Assembly deputies were willing to publicly express their dissenting views expressed in National Assembly meetings. Their speeches at the National Assembly meetings on constitutional revision were televised, recorded,

2013 to 30 April 2013)]', 692, available at http://duthaoonline.quochoi.vn/DuThao/Lists/DT_DUTHAO_NGHIQUYET/View_Detail.aspx?ItemID=32&TabIndex=2&TaiLieuID=1066 (accessed 6 October 2017, in Vietnamese).

25 Minh Thắng, 'Hội đồng Hiến pháp Và Nỗi Lo 'Phình' Biên Chế [The Constitutional Council and the worry of 'distention' of personnel]' (2013, 27 May) *Báo điện tử Quân đội nhân dân* [*People's Military Online Newspaper*], www.qdnd.vn/thoi-su-quoc-te/binh-luan/hoi-dong-hien-phap-va-noi-lo-phinh-bien-che-446613 (accessed 6 October 2017, in Vietnamese).

26 Supreme People's Procuracy, 'Báo Cáo Tổng Hợp Ý Kiến Của Ngành Kiểm Sát Nhân Dân Góp Ý Dự Thảo Sửa Đổi Hiến Pháp Năm 1992 [Report on The People's Procuracy's opinions on the draft amendments to the 1992 Constitution]', available at http://duthaoonline.quochoi.vn/DuThao/Lists/DT_DUTHAO_NGHIQUYET/View_Detail.aspx?ItemID=32&TabIndex=2&TaiLieuID=1016 (accessed 6 October 2017, in Vietnamese).

27 Constitutional Amendment Committee, 'Synthesis report on people's opinions', note 24, 20.

28 See, for example, Bích Lan, 'Chưa nên thành lập Hội đồng Hiến pháp [The Constitutional Council should not be established]' (2013, 4 June) *VOV Online*, http://vov.vn/chinh-tri/quoc-hoi/chua-nen-thanh-lap-hoi-dong-hien-phap-264914.vov (accessed 6 October 2017, in Vietnamese).

transcribed and published on the website of the National Assembly.[29] The platform for political elites presents some complexity. They debated the issue of constitutional review in the meetings of party bodies like the Politburo or the Party's Central Committee or in the meetings of the Constitutional Amendment Committee. Yet, these debates were not publicized, and the competing views in these debates were kept confidential. Except for the president of the People's Supreme Procuracy, political elites who opposed constitutional review did not attend to present their views in public. But their views were able to be expressed indirectly through the media under their control. For example, the popular media controlled by the public security authorities, particularly *Báo Công An nhân Dân* (*People's Public Security Newspaper*) and *Báo An Ninh Thủ Đô* (*Capital's Security Newspaper*), are the most active in disseminating articles (mostly written with pseudonyms) repudiating the creation of constitutional review. The *People's Public Security Newspaper* published twelve articles rejecting constitutional review, while the *Capital's Security Newspaper* published six similar articles.

Let us now consider the ideological tool for rejecting constitutional review. Opponents of constitutional review relied on Marxist 'historical materialism' to articulate their arguments. Accordingly, constitutional review is considered a foreign institution unsuitable to the Vietnamese context. One typical example is an article published in *Capital's Security Newspaper* advocating for 'choosing the model of constitutional supervision suitable to the political system'.[30] This article reviewed the different models of constitutional review (the centralized model, the decentralized model and the model of constitutional council) and the socialist model of constitutional supervision practised in Vietnam, China, Laos and Cuba. It then explained that '[c]ountries in the world employ different models of constitutional supervision because, according to the Marxist–Leninist theory on economic and social mode, each economic-social mode is corresponding to its economic system, and have [a] certain model of state, constitution, and law'.[31] The article eventually concluded that 'We

[29] See http://duthaoonline.quochoi.vn/DuThao/Lists/DT_DUTHAO_NGHIQUYET/View_Detail.aspx?ItemID=32&TabIndex=4 (accessed 6 October 2017, in Vietnamese).

[30] D. C. N., 'Lựa Chọn Mô Hình Bảo Hiến Phù Hợp Với Thể Chế Chính Trị [Choosing the model of constitutional supervision suitable to the political system]' (2013, 7 September) *Báo An Ninh Thủ Đô [Capital Security Newspaper]*, http://anninhthudo.vn/chinh-tri-xa-hoi/lua-chon-mo-hinh-bao-hien-phu-hop-voi-the-che-chinh-tri/514699.antd (accessed 6 October 2017, in Vietnamese).

[31] Ibid.

cannot simply take the theory and practice of constitutional supervision in the above [capitalist] countries and apply in Vietnam, because those countries have historical, political, economic, cultural, and social conditions different from those in Vietnam'.[32]

In a similar vein, the *Capital Security Newspaper* published another article particularly focusing on rejecting the argument put forward by Dr Đinh Xuân Thảo, an active Assembly delegate and the director of the Institute of Legislative Studies under the National Assembly, who argued that the French model of Constitutional Council is suitable for Vietnam. The article rejected this position, stating that

> The Constitution shall reflect the nature of the State which has given birth to it. Each political system has a corresponding constitution. The French Republic has the historical, political, economic, cultural, and social conditions different from those in our country. The fact that the French Republic chooses the model of Constitutional Council stems from the concrete condition of this country.[33]

On that Marxist historical-materialist ground, the opponents articulated arguments against constitutional review. These included institutional, functional, and political arguments. To begin with, constitutional review is conceived as unsuitable for the institutional structure featuring parliamentary supremacy in Vietnam. For example, a delegate argued that as the National Assembly is established in the Constitution as the supreme body of state power, a constitutional review body cannot be created.[34] Similarly, another delegate worried about the uncertain and ambiguous position of a potential constitutional review body within the Vietnamese institutional framework. He said,

> It is proper to consider the constitutional council, but if we comparatively consider the entire structure of the state machinery, it is unclear where to locate this institution. In Western countries, the constitutional councils operate independently. In our country, if a constitutional council is created with just advisory and assistant power, the independence cannot be guaranteed. Meanwhile, the National Assembly is the supreme organ

[32] Ibid.

[33] Nguyễn Văn Đức, 'Không thành lập hội đồng Hiến pháp [The Constitutional Council should not be established]' (2013, 5 September) *Báo An Ninh Thủ Đô [Capital Security Newspaper*], http://anninhthudo.vn/thoi-su/khong-thanh-lap-hoi-dong-hien-phap/514322.antd (accessed 6 October 2017, in Vietnamese).

[34] Minh Thắng, ['The Constitutional Council and the worry of "distention" of personnel'], note 25.

> of state power, which has the supreme power in supervision, and the power to handle unconstitutional actions.[35]

The second type of functional argument tries to persuade that the Vietnamese system of constitutional supervision has been functioning effectively, and therefore, the creation of a new judicial institution of constitutional review is unnecessary.[36] One functional argument focused on the conviction that the process of lawmaking is stringent enough to avoid the enactment of laws inconsistent with the Constitution. Moreover, it was argued that the multilevel system of constitutional supervision in Vietnam, in which different state institutions (the National Assembly, president of State, government and local government) are vested with constitutional supervision powers, has functioned well to prevent and handle constitutional violations. Other functional arguments underlined the overlapping functions between the party's bodies and the potential constitutional review body:

> In our nation, the law-making program, sensitive issues relating to politics and international relations, and other significant issues which engender different opinions among the Government, the National Assembly's Standing Committee, and other bodies must be presented to the Politburo for discussion and decision. If there is a constitutional council, this will be very overlapping.[37]

The functional arguments led to the conclusion that Vietnam should perfect the existing constitutional supervision system rather than adopt a new institution of constitutional review.[38]

Perhaps the most powerful method that has been employed to counter constitutional review is to invoke political reasons. Accordingly,

[35] Ibid.

[36] See several articles published in the *Capital Security Newspaper*, Lê Minh, 'Một số vấn đề về Hội đồng Hiến pháp [Some problems on the Constitutional Council]' (2013, 26 August) *Báo An Ninh Thủ Đô [Capital's Security Newspaper]*, http://anninhthudo.vn/chinh-tri-xa-hoi/mot-so-van-de-ve-hoi-dong-hien-phap/513106.antd (accessed 6 October 2017, in Vietnamese).; Lê Kiên Định, 'Một số vấn đề lý luận và thực tiễn về việc không thành lập Hội đồng Hiến pháp ở Việt Nam [Some theoretical and practical issues on not to create the constitutional council in Vietnam]', (2013, 30 September) *Báo An Ninh Thủ Đô [Capital Security Newspaper]*, http://anninhthudo.vn/chinh-tri-xa-hoi/mot-so-van-de-ly-luan-va-thuc-tien-ve-viec-khong-thanh-lap-hoi-dong-hien-phap-o-viet-nam/517937.antd (accessed 6 October 2017, in Vietnamese).

[37] Minh Thắng, ['The Constitutional Council and the worry of "distention" of personnel'], note 25.

[38] Ibid.

constitutional review is conceived of as the result of pluralist and divided politics and is, therefore, not suitable for the Vietnamese monist and unitary politics. This political argument is put forward strongly in an article published in the *Capital's Security Newspaper*. The article argued that

> Countries following the developmental path of capitalism which all employ the decentralised or central models of constitutional review are all countries possessing pluralist political systems with multi-parties. In these countries, the constitution and the political system was constructed according to the principle of political pluralism, the separation of power, which results in contentious and forceful struggles for power among political parties, such as appeals in election fallacies, refusal of failure [in elections], deployment of extremist methods to create political pressures, carrying out coup d'état, etc. Therefore, these countries have to use 'arbitrator', namely constitutional court or constitutional council to adjudicate and resolve conflicts between the governing party and opposition parties, and create the mechanism of 'check and balance'.[39]

Such kinds of political arguments were adopted by some Assembly delegates. One delegate, for example, forcefully refused constitutional review along these lines:

> When the separation of legislative, executive, and judicial powers becomes extreme, a constitutional council or constitutional court will be developed and perfected to make sure that the struggle for power among different political parties and even the conflicts among the three powers will not significantly undermine the public interest, national interest, and people's interest. It is virtually the place to handle conflicts of political parties and to separate powers. It is not relevant to what we have traditionally thought, namely issues concerning the citizens.[40]

Looking at Vietnam on that basis, he suggested that

> Our country places the entire society and state under the comprehensive and absolute leadership of the [Communist] Party, and practices solidarity of the entire people. We also have a political system with many socio-political organizations, social organizations, and we are practising democratization . . . Do we need a body to separate state power when

[39] D.C.N, ['Choosing the model of constitutional supervision suitable to the political system'], note 30.

[40] Tuệ Khanh, 'Vì sao Việt Nam không cần Tòa án Hiến pháp? [Why doesn't Vietnam need a constitutional court?]' (2013, 27 May) *Việt Báo*, http://vietbao.vn/Xa-hoi/Vi-sao-Viet-Nam-khong-can-Toa-an-Hien-phap/66205554/157/ (accessed 6 October 2017, in Vietnamese).

> state power in our country is unified and belonged to the people? Pursuant to this principle, I believe that our country does not need a constitutional court or constitutional council.[41]

In response, supporters of constitutional review argued that this institution is more relevant to the rule of law and human rights protection than to political struggle. For example, the popular media of the National Assembly, called *Báo Đại Biểu Nhân Dân* (*People's Representative Newspaper*) published several articles along these lines. Immediately, the popular media under the control of the Ministry of Public Security published an article with counterarguments.[42] Moreover, that article referred to critical moments when a constitutional court or tribunal was created in former socialist nations to argue against its potential creation in contemporary Vietnam:

> Concerning Czechoslovakia, the year of 1968 was the moment of a coup d'état in which the opposition force opposed the revolutionary government; and the year of 1982 was the moment when in People's Republic of Poland, the Solidarity after two months of its creation has become the force opposed to the *Polish* United Workers' Party [the communist party] and later came to power in 1989. These historic lessons suggest that a constitutional council is not suitable to the political system of our country.[43]

Another contentious debate on the politics of constitutional review should be mentioned. An article was published in the *People's Public Security Newspaper* as a response to a junior constitutional law scholar at Vietnam National University-Hanoi, Đặng Minh Tuấn, who supported the institution of constitutional review in his speech in the *Voice of Vietnam*, the national radio broadcaster.[44] The article restated Đặng Minh Tuấn's argument that constitutional review is irrelevant to political

[41] Ibid.

[42] Nguyễn Sinh Sự, 'Về bài báo 'về những điều chưa hiểu đúng về hội đồng hiến pháp' của Tác giả Bùi Ngọc Sơn [On the Article "Misunderstandings about The Constitutional Council" by author Bùi Ngọc Sơn]' (2013, 27 September) *Báo An Ninh Thủ Đô [Capital Security Newspaper]*, http://anninhthudo.vn/chinh-tri-xa-hoi/ve-bai-bao-ve-nhung-dieu-chua-hieu-dung-ve-hoi-dong-hien-phap-cua-tac-gia-bui-ngoc-son/517531.antd (accessed 6 October 2017, in Vietnamese).

[43] Ibid.

[44] P.N. 'Một kiểu lập luận ngụy biện về Hội đồng Hiến pháp [A Sophism on the Constitutional Council]' (2013, 11 October) *Báo Công an nhân dân điện tử [People's Public Security Online Newspaper]*, http://cand.com.vn/Su-kien-Binh-luan-thoi-su/Mot-kieu-lap-luan-nguy-bien-ve-Hoi-dong-Hien-phap-240557/ (accessed 6 October 2017, in Vietnamese).

parties but is designed to implement the rule of law and protect human rights.[45] The article then castigated this argument as a sophism.[46]

Eventually, the opponents of constitutional review won. On 22 October 2013 the Constitutional Amendment Committee presented to the National Assembly the rationales of several changes in a new version of draft constitution, one of which was the removal of the provision on the constitutional council. The Committee explained that

> The Constitutional Amendment Committee contends that the creation of the Constitutional Council is a new issue, and there are different opinions on this. Therefore, in the current situation, our country needs to continue to perfect the current mechanism of constitutional supervision. It is appropriate to strengthen the responsibility of the National Assembly, the National Assembly's organs, especially the Legal Committee of the National Assembly, and other state organs, in protecting the Constitution. Therefore, the Constitutional Amendment Committee suggests that the National Assembly should not supplement the provision on the constitutional council in the [constitutional] Draft.[47]

After some discussions, the National Assembly passed the new Constitution on 28 November 2013. The new Constitution rejected constitutional review, reconfirmed the legislative mechanism of constitutional supervision and stipulated that a statute will provide for the details of this mechanism. Since the passage of the new Constitution, the discussion on constitutional review in Vietnam has virtually disappeared. Law journals and popular media in Vietnam ceased publication of writings on constitutional review. The promised statute has not been enacted.

IV The Resistance Model in Constitutional Review Design

How can we explain the rejection of constitutional review in Vietnam? To explain this question, I locate the Vietnamese story of constitutional review rejection within the comparative constitutional law scholarship on negative responses to transnational or international constitutional influence. Comparative constitutional inquiry into the cross-national

45 Ibid.
46 Ibid.
47 'Không thành lập Hội đồng Hiến pháp [Not to create The Constitutional Council]' (2013, 23 September) *Tuổi Trẻ Online*, http://tuoitre.vn/tin/chinh-tri-xa-hoi/20131023/khong-thanh-lap-hoi-dong-hien-phap/576015.html

constitutional influence has been dominated by the propensity towards positive convergence.[48] The accounts of globalization of constitutional review follow this positive trend.[49] This trend, however, failed to provide for a complete picture of multidimensional responses to constitutional globalization. Global constitutional values are not merely adopted but also resisted by local actors. Leading constitutional comparativists such as Vicki C. Jackson, Mark Tushnet, Kim Lane Scheppele and Sujit Choundry[50] are more balanced in their approaches, discussing both positive and negative responses to transnational constitutional influence. Yet, none of these scholars has substantively accounted for the negative response to global influence in constitutional review design, although their scholarship includes relevant ideas.

Jackson, for example, focusing on constitutional adjudication, identifies three models in responding to transitional constitutional influences, namely the convergence, resistance and engagement models. Given the negative story in this study, the resistance model is most relevant. Jackson demonstrates several sources for resistance to citing transnational or international sources in national constitutional interpretation. These include the understanding of a constitution as self-constituting and self-expressive, the understanding of law as autochthonous identity, several interpretative theories (such as originalism, contractarianism, popular sovereignty and majoritarianism) and political resistance (nation-building, Western dominance and cultural exceptionalism).[51] However, Jackson limits her study to the working of

[48] See, for example, David S. Law and Mila Versteeg, 'The evolution and ideology of global constitutionalism' (2011) 99 *California Law Review* 1163–1257; Benedikt Goderis and Mila Versteeg, 'The diffusion of constitutional rights' (2014) 39 *International Review of Law and Economics* 1–19.

[49] Ginsburg and Versteeg, 'Why do countries adopt constitutional review?' note 1; Ran Hirschl, *Towards Juristocracy* (Cambridge, MA: Harvard University Press, 2004); C. Neal Tate and Torbjörn Vallinder (eds.), *The Global Expansion of Judicial Power* (New York: New York University Press, 1995).

[50] Vicki C. Jackson, *Constitutional Engagement in a Transnational Era* (New York: Oxford University Press, 2010); Mark Tushnet, 'The inevitable globalization of constitutional law' (2009) 50 *Virginia Journal of International Law* 985–1006; Kim Lane Scheppele, 'Aspirational and aversive constitutionalism: The case For studying cross-constitutional influence through negative models' (2003) 1 *International Journal of Constitutional Law* 296–324; Sujit Choundry, 'The Lochner era and comparative constitutionalism' (2004) 2 *International Journal of Constitutional Law* 1–55.

[51] For more details, see Jackson, *Constitutional Engagement*, note 50, at 19–30. For Asian cases, see Li-ann Thio, 'Reception and resistance: Globalisation, international law and the Singapore Constitution' (2009) 4 *National Taiwan University Law Review* 335–386;

constitutional review (constitutional adjudication). Moreover, although she proposes the resistance model, she focuses more on normative justifications for the engagement model.

I submit that the resistance model can be extended to constitutional design, including the design of mechanisms of constitutional oversight. Constitution-makers, like constitutional judges, also resist transnational influence. The sources of resistance may also involve the construction of understanding about the nature of the constitution and the law and political reasons for resistance. For example, the understanding of the constitution as expressive of national identity, or as a social contract, or as the embodiment of popular sovereignty will reasonably result in the rejection of foreign influence in constitutional design. Also, the fear of Western dominance can engender political resistance to Western constitutional influence in constitution-making in developing countries of the global south. One example is the communist government in China, which accused pro-constitutionalists of attempts to Westernize the Chinese government.[52] Political interests are also the source of resistance to transnational constitutional influence. Tushnet observes that 'Elite preferences can counter pressures towards the globalisation of domestic constitutional law'.[53] In theory, for the political incentive of legitimacy or the material incentive of attracting foreign investment by a constitutional commitment to protection of property rights,[54] authoritarian governments like those in China and Vietnam may also adopt global constitutional norms. However, '[p]olitical elites are willing to forgo the economic benefits of inflows of investment or high level human capital, so as to ensure that their political power is not diminished by constitutionalizing civil rights and liberties',[55] and concomitantly, creating a judicial institution to enforce these rights and liberties.

The resistance model in constitutional design resonates with Scheppele's idea of 'aversive constitutionalism'. In her account, 'cross-constitutional

Li-ann Thio, 'Beyond the "Four Walls" in an age of transnational judicial conversations: Civil liberties, rights theories and constitutional adjudication in Malaysia and Singapore' (2006) 19 *Columbia Journal of Asian Law* 428–518.

[52] Rogier Creemers, 'China's constitutionalism debate: Content, context and implications' (2015) 74 *The China Journal* 91–109.

[53] Tushnet, 'The inevitable globalization of constitutional law', note 50, at 996.

[54] David Law, 'Globalization and the future of constitutional rights' (2008) 102 *Northwestern University Law Review* 11308–11313.

[55] Tushnet, 'The inevitable globalization of constitutional law', note 50, at 996.

influence' includes both positive and negative sides.[56] The manifestation of both sides are also varied. Positive responses to cross-constitutional influence include these ideas: 'taken entire, reverently accepted, reinvented through bricolage, mistranslated, misunderstood, and mangled'.[57] The negative responses also include various ideas, namely, 'refused, rejected, buried and maligned'.[58] Scheppele, however, focuses more on negative responses, which she believes are 'more crucial to the development of a constitutional sensibility' than positive constitutional adoption.[59] On that basis, she proposes the idea of 'aversive constitutionalism', a strong negative model in constitutional builders' response to cross-constitutional influence. Aversive constitutionalism

> is backward-looking, proceeding from a critique of where past (or other) institutions and principles went badly wrong and taking such critiques as the negative building blocks of a new constitutional order. Aversive constitutionalism does not just refer to those options considered second- or third-best and therefore not chosen because there was something better. Aversive constitutionalism identifies a deeper sense of knowing who you are by knowing what you are not; it incorporates a *nation-making sense of rejection of a particular constitutional possibility.*[60]

The idea of constitutional resistance can capture the strong negative sense denoted in Scheppele's aversive constitutionalism. Constitution designers decline to adopt a global norm or institution not simply because it is not suitable or because there are better options, but more negatively, because they resist it as a potential threat to local preferences.

Scheppele's explanation of aversive constitutionalism is emphatically temporary. Constitution builders are more informed by the constitutional past than the constitutional future, and hence, they have a clearer vision of what not to do than what they are going to do.[61] The negative consequence is a strong sense of constitutional refusal or resistance to past or foreign constitutional influences. But constitutional resistance can also be informed by contemporary practices. Constitutional resistance can be the consequence of the critical imagination of the bad practice of a contemporary institution. Moreover, Scheppele's version of aversive

[56] Scheppele, 'Aspirational and aversive constitutionalism', note 50, at 287.
[57] Ibid.
[58] Ibid.
[59] Ibid., 298.
[60] Ibid., 300 (original italics).
[61] Kim Lane Scheppele, 'A constitution between past and future' (2008) 49 *William & Mary Law Review* 1377–1407.

constitutionalism is connected to 'a more complicated process of defining a nation'.[62] Constitutional resistance may stem from nation-building or defining national identity. However, beyond that, public choice theories suggest that the constitutional choice to resist external influence is also driven by material calculus.[63] A foreign institution is resisted because its adoption may threaten a political elite's preferences. Constitutional resistance is the consequence of the mixture of different sources, which may be nationalist, institutional or individualistic.

The rejection of constitutional review can be explained as an example of constitutional resistance. Countries resist constitutional review not merely because it is unsuitable or because there are better alternative institutions for constitutional oversight. There is a more negative sense here: it is resisted as a consequence of political elites' construction of a negative understanding of constitutional review as a dangerous device that will threaten their preferences. This negative construction is informed by the past and contemporary practice of constitutional review. With that conceptual framework, the next part will analyse the working of this resistance model in Vietnam.

V Vietnam: The Resistance Model in Action

Constitutional review is rejected in Vietnam because some political elites consider it a threat to their preferences. One preference pertains to protecting the existing socialist regime. This explains why the opponents of constitutional review are mainly the leadership of state institutions responsible for protecting the socialist regime.[64] Of course, all state institutions in Vietnam are responsible for securing the existing regime. However, there are four institutions directly and specially responsible for this mission. The function of the public security force, defined by the Constitution, is 'to protect national security, to ensure social security and

[62] Scheppele, 'Aspirational and aversive constitutionalism', note 50, at 288.

[63] For a classical work on public choice theory, see James M. Buchanan and Gordon Tullock, *The Calculus of Consent: Logical Foundations of Constitutional Democracy* (Ann Arbor: University of Michigan Press, 1962).

[64] The case of the vice president of state is hard to understand. In the late stage of constitution-making, she seemed to be supportive, or at least less aversive, to constitutional review. She attended and co-chaired the aforementioned special workshop supportive of the constitutional council held by the Constitutional Amendment Committee. Other opponents of this institution did not attend this workshop although they were members of the committee.

order, and to fight against crimes'.[65] The Constitution also defines one of the key functions of the national defence force as 'to protect the socialist regime'.[66] The courts and the procuracies in the socialist system in Vietnam are not merely the place to pursue justice but are also instrumental to political power. The Constitution, therefore, requires these institutions 'to protect the socialist regime'.[67] The views of the leadership of the above institutions may not merely present their personal concern but the concern of their specific community defined by their specific functions regarding protecting the regime. Constitutional review is resisted as a menace to the socialist regime in Vietnam. Therefore, its opponents construct a negative image of constitutional review as associated with subversive actions. I will return to this negative construction later.

Apart from the general reason associated with the regime, the rejection of constitutional review is associated with specific institutional interests. To illustrate, constitutional review may impede the work of the public security authorities. The protection of national security, social order and security may involve employment of legal instruments that have the potential to conflict with constitutionally protected human rights, especially the rights to life, liberty, physical integrity, privacy and property. The creation of constitutional review may provide an institutional forum for the public to challenge the constitutionality of public security actions, so the public security authorities worry about the potential threat of constitutional review to their work. This worry actually has some empirical ground. For example, in 2005, in response to chaos in the transportation system, the Ministry of Public Security issued a legal instrument which provided that one person could only possess one motorbike. The legal instrument was challenged by the public in mass media as violating the constitutional right to property. The Ministry of Public Security was compelled to retreat from the policy before it was presented to the National Assembly's Legal Committee.[68] The 'motorbike case' was often cited by proponents of constitutional review, including the Assembly delegates, as the empirical ground for the need to create a constitutional review body to handle unconstitutional state actions.[69] Another case

[65] The Constitution of the Socialist Republic of Vietnam (2013), Article 67.
[66] Ibid., Article 67.
[67] Ibid., Articles 102 and 107.
[68] For more details on this case, see Mark Sidel, 'Motorbike constitutionalism: The emergence of constitutional claims in Vietnam', in *Law and Society in Vietnam* (Cambridge: Cambridge University Press, 2008) 74–91.
[69] Bui, 'The discourse of constitutional review in Vietnam', note 5, at 211.

concerning the household registration system (*hộ khẩu*) was also often cited by constitutional review supporters. Public security authorities are responsible for managing this system. Through popular media, the public challenged this system as inconsistent with the constitutional right to freedom of movement.[70] More recent cases also indicate that public security authorities are often challenged by lawyers, Assembly delegates and popular media on constitutional grounds. For example, in February 2015, Assembly delegates challenged several legal rules and practices concerning detention and custody, deposition and torture in criminal investigation, putting a suspect's feet in stocks, as restricting human rights protected by the constitution, especially the right to fair trial, including rights such as the presumption of innocence.[71] Another recent case concerns a circular by the Ministry of Public Security effective since January 2016 which allows transit police officers to requisition citizens' properties (such as motorbikes, cameras and mobile phones) in case of emergency. Through popular media, lawyers challenged this legal instrument as inconsistent with the constitutional right to personal property.[72] Despite the challenge, this policy has still been implemented. The creation of a constitutional review body would potentially impede the implementation of such policies by the public security forces. Therefore, the public security community has practical reasons to refuse constitutional review.

The People's Supreme Court also has institutional interests as reasons to resist constitutional review. The creation of constitutional review would cause problems for the court. At the abstract level, the conflict between constitutional courts and supreme courts is internal to the centralized judicial review system.[73] In the Vietnamese case, the People's

[70] For more details, see Huong Thi Nguyen, 'Constitutional rights and dialogic process in socialist Vietnam: Protecting rural-to-urban migrants' rights without a constitutional court', in Susan H. Williams (ed.), *Social Difference and Constitutionalism in Pan Asia*, (Cambridge: Cambridge University Press, 2014) 109–134.

[71] Thành Nam, 'Thảo luận Luật tạm giữ, tạm giam: Còn vấn đề vi phạm Hiến pháp? [Discussions on the law on detention and custody: Constitutional violations remained?]' (2015, 28 February) *Infonet*, http://infonet.vn/thao-luan-luat-tam-giu-tam-giam-con-van-de-vi-pham-hien-phap-post159021.info (accessed 6 October 2017, in Vietnamese).

[72] 'Trưng Dụng Phương Tiện Của Dân: 'Muốn Thực Thi Phải Sửa Cả Hiến pháp [Requisitioning citizen's properties: The practice that requires amending the Constitution]' (2016, 2 February) *Tintuc*, http://tintuc.vn/xa-hoi/trung-dung-phuong-tien-cua-dan-muon-thuc-thi-phai-sua-ca-hien-phap-100853 (accessed 6 October 2017, in Vietnamese).

[73] Lech Garlicki, 'Constitutional courts versus supreme courts' (2007) 5 *International Journal of Constitutional Law* 44–68.

Supreme Court has practical reasons to worry about the creation of an institution above its head. Public and other state institutions have raised serious concerns about the People's Supreme Court's unjust judgments. The Assembly delegates who supported constitutional review did raise the idea that a constitutional court could be a solution to cases for which legal proceedings in the ordinary courts system have been exhausted.[74] The president of the People's Supreme Court opposed this, arguing that the National Assembly can enact a statute to create a 'special mechanism' without formal constitutional change.[75] The creation of a constitutional review body would subject this court to higher judicial oversight. The People's Supreme Court is likely to find unpalatable the idea of creating a constitutional review body to review its unjust judgments on the grounds of constitutional rights. Constitutional review would be a potential threat to its power.

Similarly, the procuratorial community has an institutional interest in opposing constitutional review. The procuracy is a Leninist supervisory institution that Vietnam borrowed from the former Soviet Union. A constitutional amendment in 2001 significantly curtailed the power of the procuratorial system to supervise the legality of actions of ministerial bodies and local governments, which is called 'general supervision' in Vietnam.[76] This system now only has the power to supervise judicial activities and practise public prosecution. During the constitutional debate in early 2013, the procuratorial community attempted to get back this 'general supervision' power. Among 13,113 opinions in the procuratorial community on the draft constitution, 12,767 opinions called for restoration of the 'general supervision' power of the procuracies.[77] Meanwhile, the draft constitution provided for a constitutional council with the power to review the constitutionality of governmental actions. This anticipation conflicts with the procuratorial community's attempt to

[74] QH Tranh Cãi Về Sửa Sai 'Án Đụng Trần': Sẽ Có Một Cơ Chế Đặc Biệt ['The National Assembly debates on rectification of "exhausted cases": There will be a special mechanism]' (2010, 26 November) *Thư Viện Pháp Luật [Law Library]*, http://thuvienphapluat.vn/tintuc/vn/thoi-su-phap-luat/thoi-su/-36889/qh-tranh-cai-ve-sua-sai-%E2%80%9Can-dung-tran%E2%80%9D-se-co-mot-co-che-dac-biet (accessed 6 October 2017, in Vietnamese).

[75] Ibid.

[76] Mark Sidel, *The Constitution of Vietnam: A Contextual Analysis* (Oxford: Hart Publishing, 2009) 125.

[77] Supreme People's Procuracy, 'Report on the People's Procuracy's Opinions', note 26, at 69.

extend or regain its supervisory jurisdiction. Understandably, the president of the People's Supreme Procuracy strongly opposed constitutional review. Moreover, constitutional review also conflicts with the current function of the procuracies to supervise judicial activities. Currently, the People's Supreme Procuracy is vested with the power to supervise the work of the People's Supreme Court in individual cases. If a constitutional review body were created, it might have the power to review the constitutionality of the People's Supreme Court's decisions. Thus, the People's Supreme Procuracy has an incentive to avoid such a competing function.

Political elites who resisted constitutional review have to make sure that their voices are expressed and heard in the National Assembly, the main platform of constitution-making. The National Assembly is controlled by the communist elites, the key feature of Vietnamese authoritarianism. Therefore, it is not difficult for the dissenting elites to gain support from some National Assembly delegates. Unsurprisingly, National Assembly delegates' arguments rejecting constitutional review are relatively identical to those disseminated in the media controlled by the public security and military forces.

The question is why political elites do not attend to express their views, except for the president of the People's Supreme Procuracy. Three possible explanations can be offered. One is that, as the party-state is committed to open public constitutional discussions, influential political elites would be unlikely to want to expressly impose their negative views on the public. Compared to other dissenting elites, the president of the People's Supreme Procuracy is less influential as he is not a member of the Politburo. His view, therefore, is unlikely to appear to be an imposition. Second, as the public is highly enthusiastic for constitutional review, the influential political elites tried to avoid early disappointment for the public. The third reason is perhaps most likely: political elites do not want to publicly express their conflicting views. As there is a considerable division among political elites on the issue of constitutional review, both its proponents and its opponents avoided expressly articulating their competing views to preclude a negative public image of internal political struggle, which would undermine the sociological foundation of political legitimacy. Instead, contentious debates in the National Assembly and popular media are more indicative of 'democratic' discussions, which explains why controversial debates were tolerated.

Let us now turn to consideration of the arguments against constitutional review. These arguments are less indicative of rational reasoning than intentional construction of a negative image of constitutional review as a dangerous tool. The institutional and functional arguments do not simply suggest that constitutional review is unsuitable for Vietnam or that another alternative system of constitutional supervision is available in the country. The true story lies in the political arguments opposing constitutional review as associated with political struggles and subversive actions in divided capitalist polities as opposed to the Vietnamese socialist polity. The negative image that the opponents of constitutional review try to create is that the establishment of constitutional review in Vietnam is dangerous as it may be the forum for subversive forces employed to not only challenge the constitutionality of the state actions but more seriously, to change the socialist regime in Vietnam.

One of the sources for that negative image is constitutional pasts. The first to mention is the experience of constitutional review of the Republic of Vietnam in South Vietnam prior to national unification in 1975. Before the unification, the Republic of Vietnam in the South, supported by the United States, was the regime competing with the Democratic Republic of Vietnam, the communist regime in the North. In the view of the communist regime, which has prevailed as the official view of the communist government in contemporary Vietnam, the Southern government was an illegitimate government. One of the institutional distinctions between the two governments was the operation of judicial review power centrally vested in the Supreme Court. The nomenclature that Southern constitutional law scholars deployed to denote the idea of constitutional review is *bảo hiến* (literally, protecting the Constitution). Constitutional law scholars in contemporary Vietnam have rediscovered the *bảo hiến* legacy. Although they have not expressly referred to the *bảo hiến* practice of the allegedly illegitimate government, *bảo hiến* is the prevailing vocabulary for their supportive discussions of the prospect of constitutional review in Vietnam.[78] Moreover, the language of *bảo hiến* was also employed by other proponents of constitutional review, such as Assembly delegates and officials. The fact that constitutional review is associated with an allegedly illegitimate government is a source for its resistance in contemporary Vietnam. The *bảo hiến* history is the source for the contemporary negative image of constitutional review as associated with an alternative regime. Although the opponents do not expressly

[78] For more details, see Mark Sidel, 'Enforcing the constitution: The debate over "constitutional protection" and a constitutional court', in *The Constitution of Vietnam: A Contextual Analysis* (Oxford: Hart Publishing, 2009) 183–210.

refer to this source for reasons pertaining to national integration in the post-conflict era, when they opposed constitutional review as associated with an alternative regime, it is likely that they are informed by the *bảo hiến* experience of the Southern regime.

Another aspect of the constitutional past concerns the former members of the Soviet bloc. As mentioned above, the Vietnamese antagonists of constitutional review connect the creation of constitutional review in the socialist nations during the Soviet era to subversive actions. The intention is to create the image that constitutional review would be destructive to the socialist regime in Vietnam. Moreover, they are likely aware of the creation of constitutional courts in the post-Soviet era. The fact that most former communist regimes have created constitutional review during their transition from communism to democracy reasonably engenders the fear that constitutional review is associated with regime change. Therefore, constitutional courts are not positively conceived as constructive to democracy,[79] but they are negatively imagined as destructive to Vietnamese socialism.

In particular, the senior Vietnamese party members who opposed constitutional review would not be blind to the Communist Party case decided by the Russian Constitutional Court shortly after the collapse of the Soviet empire.[80] This court was created at a tumultuous turning point. The act regarding the court was passed on 12 July 1991, and by the end of that year, the Soviet Union was dissolved.[81] During its early years, in the seven-month long case, the court considered the constitutionality of the Communist Party of the Soviet Union (CPSU) and the Russian Communist Party (CP RSFSR). By late 1991, Boris Yeltsin, the first president of the Russian Federation, had issued several edicts banning activities of the communist parties and nationalizing their property.[82] On 16 November 1991, a group of people's deputies of the Russian Supreme Soviet filed a petition to the Constitutional Court challenging President Yeltsin's actions as unconstitutional, as the Constitution does not allow the president to ban political parties and seize their property.[83] But the pro-presidential camp, presented by Yuri Feofanov, lodged a

[79] For an Asian case, see Wen-Chen Chang, 'The role of judicial review in consolidating democracy: The case of Taiwan'(2005) 2 *Asia Law Review* 73–88.

[80] Jane Henderson, 'The Russian Constitutional Court and the Communist Party case: Watershed or whitewash?' (2007) 40 *Communist and Post-Communist Studies* 1–16.

[81] Ibid., 2.

[82] Ibid., 4.

[83] Ibid., 5.

counter-appeal with the Constitutional Court arguing that 'the CPSU was not a political party in the normal meaning of the term, but an anti-constitutional organisation which took over state functions'.[84] On 30 November 1992, navigating the complex terrain of law and politics, the court issued an ambiguous and unanticipated decision which simultaneously found the edicts legal and the party constitutional.[85] A long Russian book about this case was translated into Vietnamese and officially published in Vietnam.[86] It is likely that the Vietnamese opponents of constitutional review were aware of this case. The case reasonably induces the fear that if Vietnam established a constitutional review body, the dissidents who oppose the communist rule in Vietnam might one day use it to challenge the constitutionality of the Communist Party of Vietnam.

Scheppele argues that 'Constitution drafters invariably look even more toward a past than they do toward a future'.[87] That is because 'constitution drafters *know* about the past experiences of their country and its people ... What they do not know, and in fact *cannot know,* is the future'.[88] Consequently, 'constitutions in their moments of creation cannot be inspired solely by imagined futures. Perhaps even more crucially, they encode imagined pasts'.[89] Scheppele's argument can be extended. First, constitution builders are informed by national and comparative constitutional pasts. Additionally, constitution builders may look at foreign constitutional pasts, which may include imagined positive and negative experiences.[90] The second point is that the imagined futures are not necessarily aspirational. The imaged future informed by imagined past constitutional failure may be aversive. The imagined negative experiences may inspire a negative model in response to transnational

[84] Ibid., 6.
[85] For details, see ibid., 9.
[86] Ph. M. Ruđinxki, '*Vụ án Đảng cộng sản Liên Xô' tại Toà án Hiến pháp [The Case of The Communist Party of the Soviet Union' at the Constitutional Court]*', translated by The Academy of National Politics (Hà Nội: Publisher of National Politics, 2001). (The Russian name of the author is phonetically transcribed into Vietnamese by the translator.)
[87] Scheppele, 'A constitution between past and future', note 61, at 1379.
[88] Ibid. (original italics).
[89] Ibid., 1380.
[90] For example, India's constitution-makers rejected the phrase 'due process of law' for fear of repeating the American Lochner-era jurisprudence. Heinz Klug, 'Model and anti-model: The United States Constitution and the "Rise of world constitutionalism"' (2000) 3 *Wisconsin Law Review* 605–606.

constitutional influences. With that conceptual background, it can be said that Vietnamese political elites who resist constitutional review *know* more about the past national and comparative constitutional review than about its future in Vietnam. The past experience of constitutional review of the Southern regime and former members of the Soviet bloc creates a negative image of the danger of constitutional review for the socialist regime in a future Vietnam. The past experience that constitutional review was associated with the alternative regime, regime change and the trial of the communist parties induces negative images of constitutional review as destructive to the existing regime in Vietnam.

However, the resistance model is informed not only by constitutional pasts; it is also inspired by a negative image of contemporary comparative constitutional review. The Vietnamese opponents imagine judicial review power as well as what Tom Ginsburg and Zachary Elkins called 'ancillary powers of constitutional courts'[91] (such as the powers to determine the constitutionality of political parties and elections to impeach senior politicians) as a negative device for power struggle rather than for democracy, transition and consolidation. This negative image is informed by certain practices that get noticed in Vietnam. Particularly, the experiences of neighbouring jurisdictions are most relevant. One relevant practice in Thailand concerns the petition by twenty-eight senators submitted to the Constitutional Court calling for Prime Minister Thaksin Shinawatra's impeachment for constitutional violations.[92] This case was widely reported in the Vietnamese popular media,[93] and this reasonably creates a negative image of a constitutional court as a device for power struggle. There may even be a specific fear of the potential impeachment of senior governmental officers if a similar arrangement of constitutional review were available in Vietnam.

Another case concerns the neighbouring nation of Cambodia, happening at the moment when the issue of constitutional review in Vietnam was controversially being debated. In the general election in Cambodia on 28 July 2013, the ruling party, the Cambodian People's Party, won sixty-eight seats, leaving fifty-five seats to the opposition

[91] Tom Ginsburg and Zachary Elkins, 'Ancillary powers of constitutional courts' (2009) 87 *Texas Law Review* 1431–1461.

[92] See, further, Chapter 8 by Khemthong Tonsakulrungruang in this volume.

[93] For example, 'Thủ Tướng Thái Lan Sẽ Bị Luận Tội [Thailand's prime minister will be impeached]', (2006, 14 February) *Báo Người Lao Động Điện tử* [*Workers Online Newspaper*], http://nld.com.vn/thoi-su-quoc-te/thu-tuong-thai-lan-se-bi-luan-toi-142372.htm (accessed 6 October 2017).

party, the Cambodia National Rescue Party.[94] The opposition party rejected the election results on the basis of irregularities and called for an investigation.[95] The Cambodian Constitutional Council investigated the opposition party's claims and, on 31 August 2013, confirmed the validity of the election results,[96] a ruling that was also reported in Vietnamese popular media.[97] On the same day, Vietnam's Foreign Ministry spokesman said, 'Viet Nam congratulates Cambodia on the success of its 5th General Elections'.[98] It is likely that the opponents of constitutional review in Vietnam noticed this case due to the timing and popularization of the case in Vietnam. When they argued against constitutional review as a forum for election disputes between the ruling and opposition parties, they may have had the Cambodian case in mind, although for diplomatic reasons, they did not explicitly cite the case. They would be concerned with avoiding a repeat of the case in Vietnam. The negative image is that if Vietnam were to create a constitutional council like that of Cambodia, this would be a forum for dissidents to challenge the constitutionality of the national elections controlled by the single communist party.

Constitutional diffusion can precipitate negative effects. Unfortunately, theories of constitutional diffusion are dominated by the concern of positive effects. David Law and Mila Versteeg argue that successful lessons create the incentive for constitutional learning.[99] I contend that the imagined failed constitutional lessons engender an incentive for constitutional resistance. Along these lines, the resistance to

94 The committee for free and fair Elections in Cambodia, 'National Election 2013' *Comfre*, http://electionresults.cambodianvotervoice.org/index.php?vote-year=2013 (accessed 6 October 2017). See, further, Chapter 10.

95 Thomas Fuller, 'Cambodian opposition rejects election results' (2013, 29 July) *New York Times*, www.nytimes.com/2013/07/30/world/asia/cambodian-opposition-rejects-election-results.html (accessed 6 October 2017).

96 Walter Lohman and Olivia Enos, 'Promoting true democratic transition in Cambodia', The Heritage Foundation, www.heritage.org/research/reports/2014/03/promoting-true-democratic-transition-in-cambodia (accessed 6 October 2017).

97 See, for example, 'Hội đồng Hiến pháp Campuchia phán quyết kết quả bầu cử [Cambodia's Constitutional Council decides on elections results]', (2013, 31 August) *VOV*, http://vov.vn/thegioi/hoi-dong-hien-phap-campuchia-phan-quyet-ket-qua-bau-cu-278561.vov (accessed 6 October 2017).

98 'Remarks by foreign ministry spokesman Luong Thanh Nghi on Cambodia's general election', Ministry of Foreign Affairs, www.mofa.gov.vn/en/tt_baochi/pbnfn/ns130803160846 (accessed 6 October 2017).

99 Law and Versteeg, 'The evolution and ideology of global constitutionalism', note 48, at 1173–1175.

constitutional review in Vietnam is precipitated by a negative image of failed contemporary comparative constitutional review. Benedikt Goderis and Mila Versteeg highlight the positive relation of geographic proximity to constitutional diffusion: 'Geographically close countries may also be more likely to interact and exchange information'.[100] This argument is also valid in a negative sense. The diffusion of negative constitutional information from geographically close countries is more likely to create a negative effect. The diffusion of the negatively imaged constitutional stories from the two neighbouring countries (Thailand and Cambodia) into Vietnam reasonably induces a negative image of the usage of a constitutional review body for political struggle.

We have seen that beneath arguments rejecting constitutional review in Vietnam lies the fear of its threat to the elite's preferences pertaining to the regime and institutional interests. The opponents of constitutional review won not because their arguments dominated the public discourse on constitutional review. In the National Assembly, the supporting and rejecting arguments were equally presented. In the popular venues of constitutional consultation, the support for constitutional review was the dominant trend. In most influential popular media, including the national television broadcaster and many online official newspapers, the dominant trend was the dissemination of the arguments supporting constitutional review. The arguments against constitutional review were mostly circulated among media controlled by the institutions which opposed constitutional review. Only when the fate of constitutional review had been decided did other media spread the news of its rejection in a relatively neutral way. The fate of constitutional review was decided by top political leaders constituting the Politburo, which is comprised of sixteen members. The Constitutional Amendment Committee and the National Assembly would formally approve the Party's constitutional decision. As mentioned above, the formal statement released to the public by the Constitutional Amendment Committee explains that constitutional review was not adopted because there remained different opinions. The arguments presented by the opponents of constitutional review were not adopted as the official reasons for rejecting constitutional review. This leaves open the possibility for the return of the argument later, when the opportunity for discussion is available.[101]

[100] Goderis and Versteeg, 'The diffusion of constitutional rights', note 48, at 3.

[101] I thank Professor Andrew Harding for his suggestion of this addition.

These opponents were successful because their negative image of constitutional review created uncertainty about the future effects of constitutional review in Vietnam. Constitutional review can be facilitative to the construction of the rule of law state in Vietnam, as the proponents of constitutional review argue, but it can also be a threat to the regime and political elite's other preferences, as its opponents imagine. Not all political leaders resist constitutional review, but in reaching a definitive decision, they would not adopt something of which they do not yet have a clear vision.

Constitution-makers have different strategies when they are confronted with the uncertainty of constitutional futures. They may adopt ambiguous constitutional language or some form of constitutional deferral.[102] These strategies are more likely applicable to constitutional rights than structure provisions. Unlike constitutional rights, the adoption of constitutional structures tends to produce concrete consequences. When constitution-makers are not clear about the effects of structural design, rejection is more likely. This explains why Vietnam's 2013 Constitution lavishly adopts constitutional rights for the sake of legitimacy, but outright rejects constitutional review for the sake of future uncertain consequences.

VI Conclusion

Constitutional review has been spread globally, but it was also resisted locally in some corners of the globe. The Vietnamese case considered in this study illustrates the operation of the resistance model in constitutional review design. Some political elites intentionally construct a negative image about constitutional review as a threat to their preferences, for which they resist it. The resistance model is not dominant, but it is influential enough to induce an uncertainty about the future effects of constitutional review, which resulted in its rejection in Vietnam. I conclude with some reflections on further implications for inquiry into comparative constitutional review design.

Both constitutional review adoption and rejection are located in the complex interaction between constitutional law and constitutional politics. In the last two decades, political accounts have dominated the explanation of constitutional review adoption. The accounts of constitutional

[102] Rosalind Dixon and Tom Ginsburg, 'Deciding not to decide: Deferral in constitutional design' (2011) 9 *International Journal of Constitutional Law* 636–672.

review rejection may share similar political concerns. In particular, uncertainty in constitutional politics may be the common element of both constitutional review adoption and rejection, although it may have different meanings and roles in different contexts. The element of uncertainty can create both positive and negative effects on constitutional review design. When political elites are uncertain about their future power but are certain about the potential effect of constitutional review, constitutional review adoption is more likely. Conversely, when political elites are certain about their future power but are uncertain about the potential effect of constitutional review, constitutional review rejection is more likely. So, studies on constitutional review adoption and rejection may have different foci. The former is more concerned with the political elites' anticipation of the effects of the election market, while the latter may pay more attention to the political elite's anticipation of the effects of constitutional review. These deserve further qualitative empirical investigation.

INDEX